T0350730

Financial Markets Volatility and Performance in Emerging Markets

A National Bureau
of Economic Research
Conference Report

Financial Markets Volatility and Performance in Emerging Markets

Edited by **Sebastian Edwards and Márcio G. P. Garcia**

The University of Chicago Press

Chicago and London

SEBASTIAN EDWARDS is the Henry Ford II Professor of International Business Economics at the Anderson Graduate School of Management at the University of California, Los Angeles, and a research associate of the National Bureau of Economic Research. MÁRCIO G. P. GARCIA is an associate professor of economics at Pontifical Catholic University, Rio de Janeiro (PUC-Rio), and a researcher affiliated with the National Council of Scientific and Technological Development (CNPq) and the Research Support Foundation of Rio de Janeiro (FAPERJ).

The University of Chicago Press, Chicago 60637
The University of Chicago Press, Ltd., London
© 2008 by the National Bureau of Economic Research
All rights reserved. Published 2008
Printed in the United States of America

17 16 15 14 13 12 11 10 09 08   1 2 3 4 5
ISBN-13: 978-0-226-18495-1 (cloth)
ISBN-10: 0-226-18495-1 (cloth)

Library of Congress Cataloging-in-Publication Data

Financial markets volatility and performance in emerging markets /
    edited by Sebastian Edwards and Márcio G. P. Garcia.
        p. cm. — (A National Bureau of Economic Research conference
        report)
    Includes bibliographical references and index.
    ISBN-13: 978-0-226-18495-1 (cloth : alk. paper)
    ISBN-10: 0-226-18495-1 (cloth : alk. paper)
    1. Capital market—Developing countries. 2. Capital
movements—Developing countries. I. Edwards, Sebastian, 1953–
II. Garcia, Márcio Gomes Pinto.
HG5993.F558 2008
332'.0415091724—dc22

                                                            2007024129

Relation of the Directors to the Work and Publications of the National Bureau of Economic Research

1. The object of the NBER is to ascertain and present to the economics profession, and to the public more generally, important economic facts and their interpretation in a scientific manner without policy recommendations. The Board of Directors is charged with the responsibility of ensuring that the work of the NBER is carried on in strict conformity with this object.

2. The President shall establish an internal review process to ensure that book manuscripts proposed for publication DO NOT contain policy recommendations. This shall apply both to the proceedings of conferences and to manuscripts by a single author or by one or more co-authors but shall not apply to authors of comments at NBER conferences who are not NBER affiliates.

3. No book manuscript reporting research shall be published by the NBER until the President has sent to each member of the Board a notice that a manuscript is recommended for publication and that in the President's opinion it is suitable for publication in accordance with the above principles of the NBER. Such notification will include a table of contents and an abstract or summary of the manuscript's content, a list of contributors if applicable, and a response form for use by Directors who desire a copy of the manuscript for review. Each manuscript shall contain a summary drawing attention to the nature and treatment of the problem studied and the main conclusions reached.

4. No volume shall be published until forty-five days have elapsed from the above notification of intention to publish it. During this period a copy shall be sent to any Director requesting it, and if any Director objects to publication on the grounds that the manuscript contains policy recommendations, the objection will be presented to the author(s) or editor(s). In case of dispute, all members of the Board shall be notified, and the President shall appoint an ad hoc committee of the Board to decide the matter; thirty days additional shall be granted for this purpose.

5. The President shall present annually to the Board a report describing the internal manuscript review process, any objections made by Directors before publication or by anyone after publication, any disputes about such matters, and how they were handled.

6. Publications of the NBER issued for informational purposes concerning the work of the Bureau, or issued to inform the public of the activities at the Bureau, including but not limited to the NBER Digest and Reporter, shall be consistent with the object stated in paragraph 1. They shall contain a specific disclaimer noting that they have not passed through the review procedures required in this resolution. The Executive Committee of the Board is charged with the review of all such publications from time to time.

7. NBER working papers and manuscripts distributed on the Bureau's web site are not deemed to be publications for the purpose of this resolution, but they shall be consistent with the object stated in paragraph 1. Working papers shall contain a specific disclaimer noting that they have not passed through the review procedures required in this resolution. The NBER's web site shall contain a similar disclaimer. The President shall establish an internal review process to ensure that the working papers and the web site do not contain policy recommendations, and shall report annually to the Board on this process and any concerns raised in connection with it.

8. Unless otherwise determined by the Board or exempted by the terms of paragraphs 6 and 7, a copy of this resolution shall be printed in each NBER publication as described in paragraph 2 above.

Contents

Preface

Emerging markets share the characteristics of adolescence. They are in the transition from independence to interdependence. The latter has the higher expected return of the equivalent of adult life, increased economic growth, but also the much more pronounced risk of the (adult life) crises ignited or made worse by capital flight. Economists' opinions have varied on whether countries should complete their domestic financial markets integration with global capital markets or try to insulate themselves through capital controls on capital inflows.

This volume presents a number of contributions presented at the 2005 meeting of the Inter-American Seminar on Economics (IASE 2005) held on December 1–3, at the Pontifical Catholic University (PUC-Rio), Rio de Janeiro, Brazil. The articles tackle several aspects of the preceding dilemma: finance and trade, capital flows and crises, global financial integration, domestic credit, and economic policy in emerging markets. Most papers deal with the unifying theme of whether capital controls help reduce macroeconomic volatility by examining both cross-country evidence and country-specific episodes. Although more research is needed in the topics addressed in this volume, the general conclusion is that strong fundamentals are the most important element to survive the volatility inherent to global financial markets. Furthermore, where domestic financial markets are already sophisticated, including derivatives markets, as in the case of Brazil, controls on capital inflows simply do not work for periods longer than a few months.

Introduction

Sebastian Edwards and Márcio G. P. Garcia

During the last few years globalization has been under attack from different quarters. Many critics—including some prominent economists—have centered their analyses on the effects of free capital mobility. It has been argued, for example, that unrestricted capital mobility generates financial and macroeconomic instability in the emerging markets. In his critique of the U.S. Treasury and the International Monetary Fund (IMF), Nobel Laureate Joseph Stiglitz (2002) has argued that pressuring emerging and transition countries to relax controls on capital mobility during the 1990s was highly irresponsible. Stiglitz goes as far as arguing that the easing of controls on capital mobility were at the center of most (if not all) of the recent currency crises in the emerging markets—Mexico 1994, East Asia 1997, Russia 1998, Brazil 1999, Turkey 2000, Argentina 2001. Even the IMF has criticized free capital mobility and has provided (at least some) support to capital controls. Indeed, in a visit to Malaysia in September 2003, Horst Koehler, then the Fund's managing director, praised the policies of Prime Minister Mahatir, and in particular its use of capital controls in the aftermath of the 1997 currency crises (*Financial Times,* September 15, 2003, page 16). An important point made by critics of capital mobility is that most of the emerging markets lack the institutional strength to take full advantage of an open capital account (Rodrik and Kaplan 2003).

Sebastian Edwards is the Henry Ford II Professor of International Business Economics at the Anderson Graduate School of Management at the University of California, Los Angeles, and a research associate of the National Bureau of Economic Research. Márcio G. P. Garcia is an associate professor of economics at Pontifical Catholic University, Rio de Janeiro (PUC-Rio), and a researcher affiliated with the National Council of Scientific and Technological Development (CNPq) and the Research Support Foundation of Rio de Janeiro (FAPERJ).

According to this view, weak financial supervision and poorly developed domestic capital markets transform large changes in capital mobility in macroeconomic volatility. In many cases, sudden changes in capital inflows may result in significant and abrupt current account reversals, crises, and currency collapses. In some countries these problems are compounded by the existence of widespread dollarization (Calvo 2003). In this case, large (and not so large) nominal depreciations will affect balance sheets of domestic firms and tend to generate massive bankruptcies. To the extent that these sizable changes in the nominal exchange rate may be generated by abrupt declines in capital inflows, reducing the extent of capital mobility may be a desired policy action. Under these circumstances, strengthening financial markets is a key challenge for the emerging countries. These topics were discussed at the 2005 meeting of the Inter-American Seminar on Economics (IASE 2005) held on December 1 to 3, 2005, at the beautiful campus of the Pontifical Catholic University (PUC-Rio), Rio de Janeiro, Brazil. The IASE 2005 provided a setting for the interaction of NBER scholars with Latin American academics, policymakers and financial markets practitioners. This volume contains most of the papers and comments that were presented at that conference.

The IASE 2005 covered five broad issues related to financial markets and economic performance in an increasingly globalized world: finance and trade, capital flows and crises, global financial integration, domestic credit, and economic policy in emerging markets. In addition, there was also a very opportune panel, *Economic Policy in Latin American Countries: Revival of Populism?*

Many of the papers collected in this volume deal with different aspects of capital mobility and controls. A unifying theme among these contributions is whether capital controls help reduce macroeconomic volatility. The analyses presented deal both with cross-country evidence as well as with country-specific episodes. Some of the papers recognize that the extent of capital mobility is not an entirely exogenous variable and that it depends on economic developments. The papers presented at the IASE 2005 also deal with sudden stops of capital inflows, current account reversals, capital markets regulation, and dollarization. In this introduction we provide a brief summary and commentary of the papers in the volume.

A Brief Guide to the Volume

The first paper in the volume is by Joshua Aizenman and Ilan Noy and is titled "Links between Trade and Finance: A Disaggregated Analysis." In this contribution Aizenman and Noy examine the intertemporal feedbacks between disaggregated measures of trade and financial flows in developing countries. More specifically, they analyze the impact of (lagged) disaggregated measures of trade in goods, services, and incomes on disaggregated financial measures of foreign direct investment (FDI), portfolio loans, and trade credit flows. Lagged average trade is found to be correlated with FDI and loan flows, but not to equity and trade credit measures. The authors also find that the investment incomes accounts correlates positively with FDI, as FDI profits are repatriated. The most general empirical finding is that the increase in financial openness has been associated with an increase in FDI and equity flows but with a decline of the importance of loans.

An important implication of this work is that it suggests that, if embodied in the appropriate model, different measures of trade openness may be used to help construct indexes of capital mobility. The advantage of doing this resides on the fact that measures of trade openness (and restrictions) are more readily available than measures of financial integration.

The second contribution in the volume is "Ineffective Controls on Capital Inflows under Sophisticated Financial Markets: Brazil in the Nineties," coauthored by Bernardo Carvalho and Márcio G. P. Garcia. According to their econometric estimations, controls on capital inflows in Brazil were effective in deterring financial inflows for only a brief period, from two to six months. To uncover the causes of this ineffectiveness, Carvalho and Garcia decide to travel a novel methodological route; they asked financial traders what they did to get around and avoid the regulations. They collected several examples of the financial strategies engineered to avoid the effects of capital controls and, thus, to invest in the Brazilian fixed income market. The most popular methods consisted of disguising fixed income investments as other forms of investments that were not subject to the controls, including investments in the stock market or FDI. Because at the time Brazil had already quite a sophisticated derivatives market, those financial instruments were also widely used to bypass the controls. The main conclusion of this paper is that while controls on capital inflows may be desirable at a conceptual level, their effectiveness is very limited effectiveness under sophisticated financial markets as the Brazilian one. Their conclusion is of particular importance nowadays, when financial inflows cause the domestic currencies to appreciate in emerging markets. When sterilization policies became too expensive or ineffective to deter the appreciation of the real exchange rate, governments may flirt with the idea of controls on capital inflows. Carvalho and Garcia's paper suggests that the effects of this type of policy will be temporary at best.

The chapter by Sebastian Edwards is "Financial Openness, Currency Crises, and Output Losses." He uses a broad multicountry data set to analyze the relationship between restrictions to capital mobility and external crises. The question is whether, as critics of globalization such as Stiglitz have argued, the effects of a currency crisis on growth are lower in countries with stricter restrictions on capital mobility than in countries with freer mobility of capital. In order to address this issue, Edwards constructed a new data set on financial markets integration; he also uses two alternative definitions of exchange rate crises. Edwards's empirical results suggest that external currency crises have resulted in sharp decline in gross domestic product (GDP) per capita growth and that such effect is smaller in countries that use their international reserves to cushion the consequences of the crisis. These results are consistent with the idea, advanced almost fifty years ago by Albert O. Hirschman, that devaluations are contractionary. Edwards finds no evidence, however, suggesting that the effect of crises has been smaller in countries that restrict capital mobility than in countries with freer cross-border capital flows. Edwards points out that his results may depend on his measure of capital controls and capital mobility and argues that further progress in understanding the important issue of the consequences of liberalizing capital movements will require additional and better quality data.

The fourth chapter is by Augusto de la Torre, Juan Carlos Gozzi, and Sergio L. Schmukler and is titled "Capital Market Development: Whither Latin America?" In this useful contribution, the authors analyze the current status of the financial market reforms in the Latin American region. They argue that in spite of successive rounds of reform, capital markets in Latin America remain underdeveloped and that the positive effects of financial liberalization—including higher domestic savings and better conditions for financing smaller firms—have not materialized. This "underdevelopment" is particularly acute when compared with the expectations that policymakers and analysts had about the effects of reforms; it may be a case of "overly optimistic expectations," where reforms were oversold by their proponents. The authors argue that expectations about the outcome of the reform process may need to be revisited to take into consideration intrinsic characteristics of emerging economies that may limit the scope for developing deep domestic capital markets in a context of international financial integration.

The chapter by Ana Carla A. Costa and João M. P. De Mello is "Judicial Risk and Credit Market Performance: Microevidence from Brazilian Payroll Loans." The authors argue that the judicial ruling in Brazil that declared illegal the withholding of due credit installments directly from the payroll is an exogenous event that helps assess whether such legal decisions have an impact on market performance. Their original data set comes from the Brazilian Central Bank's Credit Information system and includes bank level information on interest rates and amount lent in several different risk categories, for both personal loans with and without payroll deduction. By comparing the dynamics of these two categories, the authors found that judicially imposed restrictions had an adverse impact on risk perception, interest rate, and amount lent. As a result of the legal ruling the equilibrium amount of credit decreased by almost 6 percent, and interest rates increased 7.5 percentage points (the average interest rate on payroll loans over the period was 45 percent annually). These results are important as they provide microeconomic evidence that institutional factors matter and can explain differences in capital markets' performance across countries. The results also provide support for findings at the macro level on the effects of regulation and institutions on capital markets behavior.

In his contribution to IASE 2005, Eduardo Levy Yeyati analyzed the functioning of capital markets in dollarized economies. "Liquidity Insurance in Financially Dollarized Economy" studies the implications for liquidity runs in an economy where domestic financial assets are denominated in foreign currency. This situation of dollarized balance sheets is quite common in a number of emerging countries and has been at the center of recent discussions on the dynamics of the 2001 to 2002 Argentine crisis. Levy Yeyati asks the following question: does dollarization impose limits on the central bank as the domestic lender of last resort? And, if so, what are the consequences of foreign currency denominated liabilities when there are dollar liquidity runs? The paper discusses the incidence of financial dollarization on banking crises propensity and shows that it has been a key determinant of efforts to self-insure through the accumulation of sizable international reserves. Levy Yeyati also highlights the moral hazard associated with centralized reserve accumulation. In an interesting discussion, the author addresses two recent episodes (Argentina 2001 and Uruguay 2002), where the authorities suspended convertibility of domestic financial assets into foreign currency. Levy Yeyati finishes his chapter by arguing that a combined scheme of decentralized liquid asset requirement and an ex ante suspension-of-convertibility clause or "circuit breaker" would reduce self-insurance costs while limiting bank losses in the event of a run.

The contribution by Barry Eichengreen, Poonam Gupta, and Ashoka Mody is titled "Sudden Stops and IMF-Supported Programs." This paper focuses on the impact of IMF programs on the incidence, severity, and effects of sudden stops of capital inflows. The authors point out that IMF programs are endogenous to countries' econometric circumstances and argue that empirical evaluations of IMF programs should take this into account. In their analysis Eichengreen, Gupta, and Mody correct for the nonrandom assignment of IMF programs across countries and find that sudden stops are fewer and generally less severe when an IMF arrangement exists. They then proceed to inquire when this type of "IMF-based" insurance works more effectively. They find that this form of "insurance" works best for countries with strong fundamentals. Their analysis also indicates that there is no evidence that a Fund-supported program attenuates the output effects of capital account reversals if these nonetheless occur. This analysis is important for discussions on the future role of the IMF. As the number of actual crises has declined, so has the number of IMF programs. This has led to a rethinking of what will be the role of the institution in the years to come.

We close the volume with the inaugural lecture given by Anne O. Krueger at the opening of the conference. Krueger's topic was "Mutual Reinforcement: Econometric Policy Reform and Financial Market Strength." In this paper, Krueger reviews the Korean high growth experience since the 1960s up to the Asian crisis (1997) and then analyzes the forces behind the 1997 collapse of the currency. Krueger argues that the existence of a large ratio of nonperforming loans (NPLs) in banks' portfolios was the main culprit for this crisis. The currency mismatch that triggered the crisis was created by the need to keep rolling the NPLs over and over. Krueger argues that the Korean case is a clear reminder of the importance of a well-regulated and transparent banking system and the damage that can be inflicted on the economy when the financial sector is not healthy. Krueger argues that weaknesses in the financial sector result in lower growth and make the economy more vulnerable to crises. Financial-sector health depends on a sound regulatory framework, relying on incentives, sound banking procedures that permit the proper assessment of risk, and the progressive widening and deepening of the financial sector to ensure that it continues to meet the needs of the economy. An important message of the Krueger paper is that just like economic policy reform in general, financial sector reform cannot be a one-off; it has to be a continuous process. She argues that reforms implemented in the context of an expanding national and global economy have lower adjustment costs and present fewer political difficulties than reforms that are undertaken during crises. This important point, which contradicts the position taken a few years back by scholars such as Robert Bates, suggests that financial reforms implemented in the midst of a boom are more likely to succeed.

Future Research

The East Asian currency crises of 1997 to 1998 changed economists' views with respect to macroeconomic policy. In the aftermath of these episodes—and of the crises that followed in Russia, Brazil, Turkey, Argentina, Uruguay, and the Dominican Republic—a more prudent approach toward macroeconomic management has emerged. The overall objective of this new approach is to reduce vulnerability to external shocks and to lower the likelihood of external crises, including sudden stops and major devaluations. This new view on macro policy has recognized the need of maintaining the public and external debts at prudent levels. An increasingly large number of countries has opted to have flexible exchange rates. In addition, the accumulation of international reserves has been used as a self-insurance mechanism, and current account deficits have generally been kept in check.

In spite of the emergence of a new view on macroeconomic policy, there are still some areas of disagreement. The most important one refers to the appropriate degree of capital mobility in emerging and transition countries. Some authors argue that limiting the extent of international financial integration reduces speculation and helps countries withstand external shocks without suffering massive crises. The papers presented in this volume deal with a number of issues related to the functioning of capital markets under different degrees of capital mobility. The results reported here suggest, by and large, that controls on capital mobility are not very effective. Market participants find ways of going around them, and there is little (if any) aggregate evidence that countries with controls do better than those that do not have them. At the same time, some of the papers in this volume provide evidence suggesting that the financial market liberalization reforms of the 1990s and early 2000s did not generate all the benefits that economists expected.

New research on this area should focus on a number of selected areas: first, there is still need to have better cross-country indicators of the degree of openness of the capital account. Although during the last few years there has been marked progress in this area, there is still need for indexes with a greater degree of granularity. Second, there is need to understand better the effects of capital controls on microeconomic efficiency, including on small firms' ability to raise capital. Third, issues related to endogeneity have to be addressed. In many contexts, capital controls are altered as a result of macroeconomic developments. Although a number of authors—including many collected in this volume—have corrected for endogeneity, we would benefit from further efforts along these lines. Finally, there is a need to investigate the effectiveness of monetary policy in open economies with flexible exchange rates and under alternative degrees of capital mobility. According to basic monetary policy theory, countries that adopt floating rates are able to have an independent monetary policy (in contrast, under fixed exchange rates, the nominal quantity of money is endogenous). However, in order for monetary policy to be truly independent, countries should be able to have, over prolonged periods of time, domestic interest rates that are different from international interest rates, across the yield curve. Some observers have recently argued, however, that this is a difficult condition to achieve in countries that do not restrict, at least partially, capital mobility. For example, analysts in New Zealand have argued that "monetary policy has lost traction." By this they mean that successive hikes in the policy interest rate have failed to generate an increase in longer rates; these stayed roughly in line with international interest rates. International comparative research in this area would help better understand issue related to the effectiveness of monetary policy.

References

Calvo, Guillermo A. 2003. Explaining sudden stops, growth collapse, and BOP crises: The case of distortionary output taxes. NBER Working Paper no. 9864. Cambridge, MA: National Bureau of Economic Research, July.

Rodrik, Dani, and Ethan Kaplan. 2003. Did the Malaysian capital controls work? In *Preventing currency crises in emerging markets,* ed. S. Edwards and J. Frankel, 393–431. Chicago: University of Chicago Press.

1

Links between Trade and Finance: A Disaggregated Analysis

Joshua Aizenman and Ilan Noy

1.1 Introduction and Overview

Traditional analysis of open developing countries viewed trade and financial integrations as two independent margins of openness. Accordingly, trade integration deals with "real issues" related to export orientation versus import substitution, whereas financial integration deals with "financial issues" related to the degree to which the domestic capital market is segmented from foreign ones. Yet recent research suggests that the two margins of openness are interrelated in various hidden channels. Examples of these links include market pressures through, for example, the need for trade financing and political economy considerations that may have an impact both on trade flows and through that on the degree of financial repression.

The market pressure channel follows the logic of arbitrage—segmentation implies gaps across borders in relative prices or returns, providing profitable opportunities. Goods smuggling may be viewed as endogenous outcome of costly enforcement of commercial policy. Similarly, trade misinvoicing may be viewed as an endogenous outcome of costly enforcement of financial segmentation, linking trade and financial integrations—in this case, greater trade openness will increase de facto financial openness (see Aizenman and Noy [2004] for further discussion).

A political economy channel is exemplified by Rajan and Zingales

Joshua Aizenman is a professor of economics at the University of California, Santa Cruz, and a research associate of the National Bureau of Economic Research. Ilan Noy is an assistant professor of economics at the University of Hawaii, Manoa.

We would like to thank Sebastian Edwards, Márcio G. P. Garcia, Maria Cristina Terra, Thierry Verdier, and the IASE-2005 Rio conference participants for their useful comments. Any errors are ours.

(2003), who propose an interest group theory of financial development whereby incumbents oppose financial development because it breeds competition. In these circumstances, the incumbents' opposition will be weaker when an economy allows both cross-border trade and capital flows. They predict that country's domestic financial development should be positively correlated with trade openness and identify the time varying nature of this association.

Other theoretical models that connect trade openness with financial factors also exist. Do and Levchenko (2004, 2006), for example, develop a two-sector trade model in which one sector is more financially intensive, and cross-border financial flows depend on the size of this sector. They conclude that in the country that uses this sector more intensively (the rich country), opening up to trade will result in more financial flows and a deeper financial system (the opposite is true for the other country). Rose and Spiegel (2004) develop a model of sovereign lending and suggest that if a credible threat to reductions in trade is what sustains sovereign lending, then one should observe more lending occurring between countries whose trade links are stronger. Petersen and Rajan (1997) focus on trade credits and investigate theoretically and empirically what firm characteristics will drive an increased usage of trade credits to finance trade transactions.

Most papers that do distinguish between different types of financial flows, however, do not investigate their impact on trade flows (e.g., Smith and Valderrama 2006). Several projects, though, focus on the theoretical links between foreign direct investment (FDI) and trade openness; Swenson (2004), for example, examines whether FDI and trade flows are complements or substitutes. She suggests a theory to support her findings of complementarities at a high level of data aggregation and substitution effects at the product level. Aizenman and Noy (2006), on the other hand, propose a theory of links that describe dynamic complementarities, both from FDI to trade and from trade to FDI.

A number of recent empirical papers have begun to examine the differences between the determinants of trade flows and financial flows. For example, Eaton and Tamura (1994) compare the determinants of Japanese and U.S. trade and foreign investment, while Guerin (2006) compares a gravity model for trade with similar gravity models for FDI and portfolio flows. Guerin (2006) builds on a growing literature that uses gravity models to empirically examine the determinants of financial flows focusing exclusively on FDI and portfolio flows (e.g., Portes, Rey, and Oh 2001; Razin, Rubinstein, and Sadka 2003; Wei 2000).[1] Interestingly, these papers typically do not examine the links between the financial flows and trade flows but rather compare their determinants and find similar specifications fit

1. For a survey of this literature, see Blonigen (2005).

both trade and financial flows. Another branch in this literature examines the joint effect of both financial and trade flows on a third variable as, for example, in Kose, Prasad, and Terrones (2006) investigation of their impact on output growth volatility. A different strand investigates and compares the determinants of different types of financial flows without investigating their relationship to trade flows (e.g., Daude and Fratzscher 2006). A recent survey of the literature on financial openness and its causes and effects is Kose et al. (2006).

In recent works we have looked at the degree to which the data is consistent with the presence of two-way feedbacks between trade and financial openness. We adopted a reduced form approach, where we tested the presence of two-way intertemporal linkages between trade and financial de facto openness. The results are reported in Aizenman and Noy (2004), where we confirm the presence of almost symmetric intertemporal feedbacks between trade and financial openness and in Aizenman and Noy (2006), where we report significant intertemporal feedbacks for FDI and goods trade. Following Bekaert, Harvey, and Lumsdaine's (2002) distinction between market liberalization (de jure) and market integration (de facto), we also found asymmetric importance of de jure measures of openness—trade policy has a robust effect on trade openness, but financial restrictions seem to have no significant impact on de facto financial openness.

This paper extends our previous analysis—having established the presence of strong two-way intertemporal feedbacks between trade and financial openness, we now examine the strength of the intertemporal feedbacks between disaggregated measures of trade and financial openness in developing countries. Specifically, we disaggregate the current account into trade in goods (split between manufacturing, metals/ores, fuel, and foodstuffs), services, and income. Similarly, we disaggregated the financial account into FDI, loans, equity, and trade credit. Such disaggregation provides us with more detailed information about the possible channels at work.

Among the interesting patterns we uncover, we observe systematic changes between the 1980s and the 1990s. Most financial flows in and out of developing countries have taken the form of loans. Yet these financial flows are the only type of flows that have decreased between the two decades. We thus see a growing importance to developing countries of portfolio flows and especially of FDI. The trade statistics do not present a clear temporal trend toward an increase from the 1980s to the 1990s. While services trade has increased, goods trade has seen a corresponding decrease. Once the information for trade in goods is disaggregated by type of good, we observe that manufacturing trade has increased dramatically, while trade in fuels has seen a dramatic decline as percent of domestic output. Investigating the patterns of the correlation coefficients between disaggregated financial openness measures and the trade openness measures reveals a significant correlation of FDI flow measures with goods and services trade and a very strong correlation between openness to trade in goods and trade in services.

Next, we looked at the impact of lagged disaggregated trade on disaggregated financial measures, allowing for macroeconomic controls. While past average trade in goods appears to be correlated with FDI and loan flows, this is not the case for the equity and trade credits measures. Trade in incomes is positively correlated with FDI, reflecting the repatriation of profits from foreign investments. Interestingly, and less expectedly, trade in services is negatively correlated with all the four measures of financial flows—while it is statistically significant only for the FDI and equity measures. For the subaccounts for goods trade, we observe that trade in foodstuffs is positive and statistically important for FDI flows, as is the measure for metals/ores trade. We conclude by tracing the reversed link—the impact of lagged disaggregated financial on disaggregated trade measures, allowing for the same macroeconomic controls. Interestingly, gross domestic product (GDP) per capita is negatively correlated with trade openness for goods and services (with the coefficient for goods trade three times as big as the one for services). We also observe a positive coefficient for the budget surplus, the inflation measure, the U.S. interest rate and the degree of democracy. In all those results, the control variables are more strongly associated with goods trade than with trade in services. Corruption is negatively and significantly associated with goods trade. Foreign direct investment openness is associated with trade openness, with the impact twice as large for goods trade than for trade in services. This impact is also much larger than the other various measures of financial openness (equity, loans, and trade credits). The coefficients on loan flows are negatively and typically statistically significant, while equity flows are positively associated only with goods trade. The measure of trade credits is never statistically significant.

Section 1.2 describes the data, section 1.3 discusses the methodology and results in more detail, and section 1.4 concludes.

1.2 Data

We include all nondeveloped countries and territories for which all data are available in the 2001 edition of the World Bank's *World Development Indicators.* Most of the data on the financial subaccounts are typically available only from the early 1980s, while the political data we require is available only up to 1998. Our data set, therefore, covers the years 1982 to 1998.

Blonigen and Wang (2004), among others, argue that pooling developed and developing countries in empirical studies of this type is inappropriate and likely to lead to misleading results. In previous work, we also found that industrialized/developed countries appear to be different from developing countries as the nature of financial flows for these groups is different (Aizenman and Noy 2006). For example, FDI inflows into developed countries might be mostly of horizontal FDI, while those into developing countries might be of vertical FDI. We thus focus our empirical investigation on developing countries only.

The developed economies deleted from the set are those economies that were members of the Organization for Economic Cooperation and Development (OECD) in 1990. We also exclude island economies from our estimations as these are often used as offshore banking centers, and their level of de facto openness to financial flows is often dramatically different from other countries with similar income levels. The sixty countries included in the data set are Algeria, Argentina, Bangladesh, Belize, Bolivia, Botswana, Brazil, Cambodia, Cameroon, Chile, China, Colombia, Costa Rica, Ivory Coast, Ecuador, Egypt, El Salvador, Gabon, Gambia, Ghana, Guatemala, Guyana, Honduras, India, Indonesia, Israel, Jamaica, Jordan, Kenya, Korea, Malaysia, Mauritius, Mexico, Morocco, Mozambique, Nepal, Nicaragua, Nigeria, Pakistan, Panama, Papua New Guinea, Paraguay, Peru, the Philippines, Senegal, Sierra Leone, South Africa, Sri Lanka, Swaziland, Syria, Tanzania, Thailand, Togo, Tunisia, Turkey, Uganda, Uruguay, Venezuela, Zambia, and Zimbabwe. Our sample is further restricted by the availability of data for some years.

We measure gross financial flows (de facto financial openness) as the sum of total capital inflows and outflows (in absolute values) measured as a percent of GDP. Capital flows are the sum of FDI, portfolio flows, trade credits, and loans. We construct an openness index for each one of these four components and briefly describe them in the following. The data on financial flows is taken from the International Monetary Fund's (IMF's) Balance of Payments Statistics data set and are exactly analogous to the standard measure of commercial openness (sum of exports and imports as percent of GDP).

We subdivide the standard measure of commercial openness into openness for trade in goods, trade in services, and trade in incomes following the classification adopted by the World Bank.[2] We further divide trade in goods into openness measures for trade in foodstuffs, in fuel, in manufacturing, and in metals/ores. This data is from the World Bank's *World Development Indicators*. We provide descriptive statistics in tables 1.1 to 1.3.

Table 1.1 presents averages for financial and trade openness for the 1980s and 1990s across geographical regions, while table 1.2 presents the financial and trade openness indexes disaggregated by type (FDI, loans,

---

2. Trade in income (net income) "refers to receipts and payments of employee compensation for nonresident workers, and investment income (receipts and payments on direct investment, portfolio investment, and other investments and receipts on reserve assets)." *World Bank Development Indicators 2005*. For a skeptical discussion of the measurement of trade in services, see Lipsey (2006).

Table 1.1   **Openness—Descriptive statistics by region**

	Financial openness		Trade openness	
	1980s	1990s	1980s	1990s
Developing countries	5.43	8.63	56.1	60.9
OECD countries	9.31	16.79	73.0	70.3
East Asia	8.47	16.53	55.9	72.0
Latin America	6.05	8.15	60.9	64.0
Other[a]	4.89	7.10	54.6	58.9
All	6.96	10.35	58.4	61.8

[a]Other includes Africa (north and sub-Saharan), the Middle East, and South Asia.

Table 1.2   **Openness—Descriptive statistics by type**

	1980s	1990s
Financial openness		
FDI	1.71	3.44
Trade credits	1.49	1.68
Portfolio flows	1.18	2.20
Loans	5.97	5.44
Trade openness		
Trade in incomes	9.14	9.07
Trade in services	20.79	22.76
Trade in goods	66.31	61.69
Manufacturing	28.84	37.78
Foodstuffs	13.42	11.19
Fuels	24.09	9.82
Metals/ores	2.98	2.46

Sources: Data for financial flows is from the *Balance-of-Payments Statistics*. Data for trade flows is from the *World Development Indicators*.
Note: The table presents averages of sum of inflows of outflows (by types) as percent of GDP.

trade credits, and equity flows for the financial measures and goods, services, and incomes for the trade measures). A number of noteworthy observations are obtained from these tables, summarized in figure 1.1. First,
the degree of financial and trade openness is universally larger during the
1990s than it was in the previous decade, although the degree of difference
differs substantially across geographical regions. The OECD countries and
the countries of East Asia were the most open to financial flows, and the
least financially open groups are sub-Saharan Africa, the Middle East and
North Africa (MENA) countries, and South Asia.

Secondly, when financial openness is disaggregated by type, we observe
that most financial flows in and out of developing countries have taken the
form of loans. Yet these financial flows are the only type of flows that have

Table 1.3   **Correlations for trade and financial flows by type**

	Equity flows	Trade credits	Loan flows	FDI flows	Trade goods	Trade in services	Trade in incomes
Equity flows	1	0.06	0.40	0.23	0.21	0.23	0.26
Trade credits		1	0.02	0.18	0.07	0.07	0.02
Loan flows			1	0.15	0.13	0.21	0.72
FDI flows				1	0.60	0.55	0.22
Trade in goods					1	0.87	0.30
Trade in services						1	0.38
Trade in incomes							1

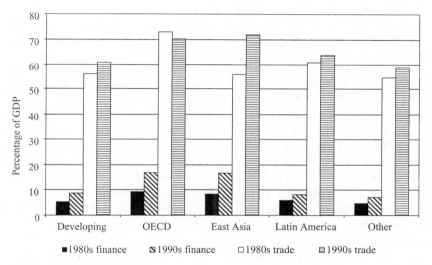

■1980s finance   ◨1990s finance   ▫1980s trade   ▤1990s trade

Fig. 1.1   Openness Indexes

decreased between the two decades. We thus see a growing importance to developing countries and portfolio flows and especially of FDI. The trade statistics do not present a clear temporal trend toward an increase from the 1980s to the 1990s. While services trade has increased (from about 21 percent to 23 percent of GDP), goods trade has seen a corresponding decrease (from about 66 percent to 62 percent). Once the information for trade in goods is disaggregated by type of good, we observe that manufacturing trade has increased dramatically (from 29 percent to 39 percent), while trade in fuels has seen a dramatic decline (from 24 percent to 10 percent of GDP).[3]

3. At the very least, part of the reason for this decline is average lower oil prices during the 1990s. The figures for trade in foodstuffs and in metals/ores were fairly constant between the two decades.

Table 1.3 presents correlation coefficients between the financial openness measures and the trade openness measures disaggregated by types of flows. The notable correlations are a significant correlation of FDI flow measures with goods and services trade (0.60 and 0.55, respectively) and a very strong correlation between openness to trade in goods and trade in services (0.87).

Because results from all the estimation procedures described in the following will be biased if any of the relevant series has a unit root, we are also required to establish stationarity. We conduct the common Phillips-Perron (1981) test for unit roots for the financial openness variables as well as the trade openness measures. Results are presented in table 1.4. We easily reject the existence of unit root in all cases.

In our multivariate estimations, we include several control variables that are described in the following. This list is based on our previous research on financial openness (Aizenman and Noy 2004). In order to ensure our results are not driven by a 'missing variables' bias, we include a host of macroeconomic control variables. In all regressions we use per capita GDP (measured in PPP dollars), a domestic interest rate spread (from a world rate of interest),[4] and a weighted average of G3 growth rates. In an initial specification, we also included the government's budget surplus (as percent of GDP), the inflation rate (CPI), a world interest rate (U.S. one-year T-bill rate), GDP (in $1995), and government consumption (as percent of GDP). None of these were significant, and all were dropped from the specifications we report. The macroeconomic data are taken from the World Bank's *World Development Indicators* and the International Monetary Fund's *International Finance Statistics.* Details are in the appendix.

For the political-economy determinants of financial openness, we include in our empirical investigation two political and institutional measures, an index of the political regime in place, and a measure of corruption. Our democracy index is taken from the Polity IV project and ranges from –10 (fully autocratic) to +10 (fully democratic).[5] In addition, following the work of Wei (2000) and Dreher and Siemers (2003), we examine whether corruption matters for the degree of openness. We use a measure of corruption that is taken from the *International Country Risk Guide.* The data are available in monthly observations. We obtain annual observations from 1982 onward by averaging the monthly data points for each year. This

---

4. We measure the spread between a domestic deposit rate and the IMF's special drawing rights (SDRs) interest.

5. The "Polity IV database includes annual measures for both institutionalized democracy (DEMOC) and autocracy (AUTOC). A third indicator, POLITY, is derived simply by subtracting the AUTOC value from the DEMOC value; this procedure provides a single regime score that ranges from +10 (full democracy) to –10 (full autocracy)" (Marshall and Jaggers 2000, 12). We use the POLITY variable in our regressions. For further discussion, see Aizenman and Noy (2004).

Table 1.4	Phillips-Perron test for unit root
Financial openness index	
FDI	−123.8***
Loans	−863.8***
Equity	−500.3***
Trade credits	−293.5***
Trade openness index for:	
Services	−123.7***
Incomes	−181.4***
Goods	−331.6***

Note: The table lists the z-statistic for ρ.
***Denotes statistical rejection of the unit-root hypothesis. All rejections are significant at the 1 percent level.

index ranges from −6 (low probability/risk of encountering corruption) to 0 (high risk of corruption).[6]

As the theoretical discussion in Aizenman and Noy (2004) suggests, one of the determinants of de facto financial openness should be the legal impediments to financial flows (de jure financial openness). Accordingly, we also include in our multivariate analysis a binary measure for restrictions on the capital account taken from the IMF's *Annual Report on Exchange Arrangements and Exchange Restrictions.*[7]

1.3   Methodology and Results

1.3.1   Causality from Trade to Capital Flows

In order to investigate whether past trade openness Granger-causes FDI gross flows, we start by positing a linear structure for the determination of the level of financial openness, whereby[8]

$$(1) \qquad FO_{it}^{Q} = \alpha_i + \beta_1 \mathbf{X}_{it} + \beta_2 \overline{\mathbf{CO}_{it-1}^{T}} + \varepsilon_{it}.$$

The dependent variable (FO_{it}^{Q}), financial openness for country i at time t and type Q (FDI, loans, trade credits or equity), is assumed to be dependent on separate country intercepts, a vector $\mathbf{X}_{it}$ of macroeconomic and

6. Two other political variables that were initially included but later dropped due to their insignificance were a measure of political risk (from the *International Country Risk Guide* data) and a measure of government unity (taken from the World Bank's *Database of Political Institutions 2000*).

7. This binary measure is the only internationally comparable measure of de jure financial openness available for a large sample of countries and over the entire sample period. Ideally, separate measures for the degree of de jure openness of the capital account to the various types of flows (FDI, loans, equity flows, etc.) should be used. These are unavailable for historical data.

8. See Granger (1969) and Sims (1972) for a definition of G-causality.

political and institutional control variables, a vector of average lagged trade openness measure $(\overline{CO^{T}_{it-1}})$ for country i, time t and type T (goods, services, etc.), and an error term. The null hypothesis that we investigate, in this case, is that past trade openness (in goods, services, and incomes) has no observed causal effect on the different types of financial flows.

Because we do not find any evidence of autocorrelation, lagged values of FO^{Q}_{it} are not included in the model's specification. In order to examine the suitability of fixed versus random assumption for the country-specific effects, we examine the standard Hausman chi-square statistic for the benchmark regressions. The statistic, at 28.5, 16.1, 39.6 and 40.3 for columns (1) to (4) of table 1.5, reject the null of uncorrelated errors necessary for an unbiased random-effects estimation. We therefore conduct all estimations with a fixed effects specification.

Table 1.5   Estimation of various financial openness indexes

	FDI (1)	Loans (2)	Equity (3)	Trade credits (4)
Per capita GDP	0.44***	0.58*	0.46***	0.15***
	(5.80)	(1.66)	(2.94)	(2.87)
Budget surplus (% of GDP)	−0.01	−0.09	−0.01	0.01
	(0.47)	(1.26)	(0.28)	(1.17)
Inflation (CPI)	0.04	−0.28**	−0.01	0.01
	(1.32)	(2.21)	(0.15)	(0.53)
U.S. Treasury bill rate	0.03	0.38	−0.10	0.12***
	(0.48)	(1.32)	(0.69)	(2.51)
Democratic regime	−0.02	−0.34**	−0.06	−0.01
	(0.47)	(2.37)	(0.79)	(0.30)
Corruption	0.12	0.45	0.06	0.09
	(0.81)	(0.64)	(0.17)	(0.85)
The 1990s	0.43	2.55**	0.85	−0.06
	(1.50)	(1.99)	(1.24)	(0.26)
Trade openness in:[a]				
Services	−0.11***	−0.09	−0.20**	−0.03
	(3.22)	(0.57)	(2.21)	(1.16)
Incomes	0.02**	−0.03	0.01	0.01
	(1.94)	(0.58)	(0.40)	(0.88)
Goods	0.02***	0.36***	0.00	0.00
	(3.60)	(11.95)	(0.17)	(0.96)
Estimated autocorrelation	0.23	0.05	0.10	0.02
No. of observations	652	723	472	378
Adjusted R^2	0.58	0.48	0.28	0.59

Notes: t-statistics for all variables are given in parentheses. The LHS variable is the sum of financial inflows and outflows by type (as percent of GDP). Estimation using least squares with country-fixed effects. For definitions of variables, see appendix.

[a]Average for $t-1, \ldots t-4$.

***Significant at the 1 percent level.

**Significant at the 5 percent level.

*Significant at the 10 percent level.

The adjusted R^2 in table 1.5 is between 0.28 and 0.59; these depend on the specific dependent financial openness indicator used with estimation having the highest explanatory power for the FDI and trade credits regressions (columns [1] and [4]). For our control variables in table 1.5, we find that the coefficient for per capita GDP is always positive and statistically significant—that is, an increase in domestic per capita GDP of PPP$1000 will facilitate 0.15 to 0.58 percentage points increase in the volume of gross financial flows (as percent of GDP) with the weakest impact for trade credits. The coefficient for the budget surplus is typically negative but never statistically significant. Inflation appears to play a statistically significant role only in its impact on openness to loans (a higher inflation implies less loan flows). The U.S. interest rate appears to have a significantly positive affect only on trade credit flows, while the political nature of the governing regime impacts loan flows. Corruption is always statistically insignificant (this is an interesting result as corruption was statistically correlated with aggregate financial openness as reported in Aizenman and Noy [2004]). A dummy variable for the 1990s is positive and significant for loans estimation (column [2]). Almost all of the results described in the preceding for the control variables in table 1.5 also hold for the estimations presented in table 1.6—the magnitudes of the coefficients are very similar and only occasionally do the significance levels change.

For our variables of interest, the trade openness measures for trade in services, incomes, and goods, the results for the different dependent variables (the financial openness measures) are quite different. While past average trade in goods appears to be correlated with FDI and loan flows, this is not the case for the equity and trade credits measures. Trade in incomes is positively correlated with FDI—this is not surprising as part of this measure included the repatriation of profits from foreign investments. Interestingly, and less expectedly, trade in services is negatively correlated with all the four measures of financial flows—while it is statistically significant only for the FDI and equity measures.

In table 1.6, we separate our measure of goods trade into openness measures for trade in foodstuffs, fuels, metals/ores, and manufacturing. As reported before, the other macroeconomic and political control variables are also included in these specifications, and the results are consistent with the previous table. The explanation of the model improves somewhat with the model best explaining FDI openness (an R^2 of 0.65).

In table 1.6, we observe that the result for trade in services remains negative, while the result for trade in incomes changes somewhat with statistical significance now only apparent for the loans measure. For the subaccounts for goods trade, we observe that trade in foodstuffs is positive and statistically important for FDI flows, as is the measure for metals/ores trade. The trade in fuels measure is statistically significant and negative for the FDI and loans measures. This is unsurprising considering fuel's role as an input in the production process and the high variability of its price.

Table 1.6   **Estimation of various financial openness indexes: Subaccounts for goods trade**

	FDI (1)	Loans (2)	Equity (3)	Trade credits (4)
Per capita GDP	0.30***	0.49	0.50**	0.06
	(2.72)	(0.85)	(1.99)	(0.91)
Budget surplus (% of GDP)	−0.03	−0.05	0.01	0.11
	(1.22)	(0.40)	(0.17)	(0.48)
Inflation (CPI)	−0.03	−0.36**	−0.02	−0.02
	(0.87)	(2.04)	(0.25)	(0.72)
U.S. Treasury bill rate	0.00	0.49	−0.06	0.17***
	(0.05)	(1.13)	(0.31)	(3.11)
Democratic regime	−0.05	−0.52***	−0.08	−0.03
	(1.23)	(2.70)	(0.91)	(0.74)
Corruption	0.21	1.29	0.12	0.11
	(1.07)	(1.25)	(0.27)	(0.86)
The 1990s	0.71**	2.55	1.00	−0.20
	(1.97)	(1.38)	(1.14)	(0.87)
Trade openness in:[a]				
Services	−0.17***	−0.21	−0.17	0.04
	(3.57)	(0.86)	(1.35)	(1.02)
Incomes	0.01	0.34***	0.01	−0.01**
	(0.81)	(9.07)	(0.51)	(2.50)
Goods				
Foodstuffs	0.25***	0.51	0.04	−0.02
	(3.49)	(1.50)	(0.18)	(0.40)
Fuel	−0.11***	−0.29**	−0.01	−0.04
	(4.07)	(2.15)	(0.18)	(1.36)
Metals/ores	0.30**	1.02	0.10	−0.25*
	(2.40)	(1.51)	(0.26)	(1.81)
Manufacturing	0.02	−0.01	−0.01	0.02
	(1.47)	(0.15)	(0.14)	(1.25)
Estimated autocorrelation	0.19	0.02	0.08	0.12
No. of observations	490	522	395	261
Adjusted R^2	0.65	0.48	0.26	0.49

Note: See table 1.5 notes.

[a]Average for $t-1, \ldots t-4$.

***Significant at the 1 percent level.

**Significant at the 5 percent level.

*Significant at the 10 percent level.

1.3.2   Causality from Capital Flows to Trade

We already suggested that causality might also run from past financial openness to present trade openness, and we therefore estimate the opposite specification:

$$(2) \qquad \mathbf{CO}_{it}^{T} = \gamma + \delta_1 \mathbf{X}_{it} + \delta_2 \overline{FO_{it-1}^{Q}} + \eta_{it},$$

where the dependent variable is now the trade openness index (for goods or services), while on the independent variables are the set of control and various measures of average past (last four years) of financial openness (FDI, loans, equity, and trade credits). The measures for trade credits and portfolio flows are not reported for many countries, so we subsequently drop them in the specifications reported in columns (2) and (4) and thus increase the sample size significantly. We use the same assumptions, methodology, definition of variables, and samples as before. Results are reported in table 1.7.

Interestingly, in all the specifications for table 1.7, GDP per capita is negatively correlated with trade openness for goods and services (with the coefficient for goods trade three times as big as the one for services). Besides that we observe a positive coefficient for the budget surplus, the inflation measure, the U.S. interest rate, and the degree of democracy. In all

Table 1.7   **Reverse specifications**

	Services (1)	Services (2)	Goods (3)	Goods (4)
Per capita GDP	−0.40***	−0.38***	−1.44***	−1.44***
	(2.31)	(3.00)	(2.90)	(4.23)
Budget surplus (% GDP)	0.01*	0.00	0.03*	0.00
	(1.72)	(0.25)	(1.63)	(0.45)
Inflation (CPI)	0.06	0.14***	0.35*	0.62***
	(0.85)	(2.92)	(1.62)	(4.87)
U.S. Treasury bill rate	0.06	0.04	0.92*	0.52*
	(0.34)	(0.39)	(1.72)	(1.79)
Democratic regime	0.13	0.08*	1.79***	0.81***
	(1.28)	(1.60)	(6.27)	(5.93)
Corruption	0.57	−0.11	−3.80***	−1.82***
	(1.52)	(0.43)	(3.50)	(2.68)
The 1990s	1.46*	1.55***	3.31	5.87***
	(1.59)	(3.34)	(1.26)	(4.70)
Financial openness in:[a]				
FDI	0.67***	0.05	1.36*	1.80***
	(2.54)	(0.39)	(1.80)	(4.94)
Loans	0.00	−0.04**	−0.50***	−0.38***
	(0.03)	(2.10)	(7.06)	(7.92)
Equity	−0.03		0.63**	
	(0.32)		(2.05)	
Trade credits	−0.49		0.18	
	(0.86)		(0.11)	
Estimated autocorrelation	0.84	0.58	0.55	0.56
No. of observations	192	620	192	620
Adjusted R^2	0.96	0.91	0.98	0.96

Note: See table 1.5 notes.

[a]Average $t − 1, \ldots t − 4$.

***Significant at the 1 percent level.
**Significant at the 5 percent level.
*Significant at the 10 percent level.

those results, the control variables are more strongly associated with goods trade than with trade in services. Corruption is negatively and significantly associated with goods trade, while trade openness is higher for the 1990s also in a multivariate framework.

For our variables of interest, perhaps unsurprisingly FDI openness is again associated with trade openness, with the impact twice as large for goods trade. This impact is also much larger than the other various measures of financial openness (equity, loans, and trade credits). The coefficients on loan flows are negatively and typically statistically significant, while equity flows is positively associated only with goods trade. The measure of trade credits is never statistically significant.

1.4   Concluding Remarks

In this paper, we studied the intertemporal feedbacks between disaggregated measures of trade and financial openness. Our results are consistent with the notion that, for many developing countries in recent years, there has been an increase in FDI flows and trade in manufacturing and services and that these are linked. Overall, the increase in financial openness we observe has also been associated with a decline of the importance of loans and an increase in the importance of equity and FDI flows. As the increase in financial openness is positively associated with GDP per capita, the positive association between greater financial openness and the increase in the importance of equity relatively to loans is consistent with Diamond (1984).[9] Somewhat surprisingly, we failed to detect the importance of trade credit, potentially because of underreporting—especially when trade credits are associated with imports that are financed by foreign producers.[10]

9. Diamond's (1984) approach explains the role of bank intermediation in financing capital formation in the presence of significant monitoring costs, showing the optimality of issuing unmonitored debt, which is subject to liquidation costs. The delegated monitor is a financial intermediary because it borrows from small investors (depositors), using unmonitored debt (deposits) to lend to borrowers (whose loans it monitors).

10. See Petersen and Rajan (1997) for further analysis of the possibility that trade credit are supplied by the party that has better access to the capital market.

Appendix

Table 1A.1   **Data sources**

Variable	Description	Source
KTOTAL	Sum of capital inflows and outflows (% of GDP)	IMF-BOP statistics
FDITOT	Sum of FDI inflows and outflows (% of GDP)	IMF-BOP statistics
TRADTOT	Sum of trade credit inflows and outflows (% of GDP)	IMF-BOP statistics
LOANTOT	Sum of loan inflows and outflows (% of GDP)	IMF-BOP statistics
EQTOT	Sum of portfolio inflows and outflows (% of GDP)	IMF-BOP statistics
TRADG	Sum of exports and imports (% of GDP)	WB-WDI
SERVG	Sum of service exports and imports (% of GDP)	WB-WDI
GOODG	Sum of goods exports and imports (% of GDP)	WB-WDI
INCOMG	Sum of trade in incomes (% of GDP)	WB-WDI
FUELG	Sum of trade in fuels (% of GDP)	WB-WDI
MANUG	Sum of trade in manufacturing (% of GDP)	WB-WDI
FOODG	Sum of trade in footstuffs (% of GDP)	WB-WDI
METALG	Sum of trade in metals and ores (% of GDP)	WB-WDI
GDPPCPP	GDP per capita, PPP (current international $)	WB-WDI
DLCPI	Inflation, consumer prices (annual %)	WB-WDI
BDGTG	Overall budget deficit (% of GDP)	WB-WDI
USTBILL	Interest rate on U.S. Treasury bill	IMF-IFS
CORRUPT	Level of corruption[a]	PRS: International Country Risk Guide
POLITY2	Political regime type[b]	POLITY IV project
KKCCAR	Binary measure for current or capital account restrictions	IMF-EAER

Notes: IMF-BOP statistics = IMF's *Balance-of-Payments Statistics.* WB-WDI = World Bank's *World Development Indicators.* IMF-IFS = IMF's *International Finance Statistics.* IMF-EAER = IMF's Annual Report on *Exchange Arrangements and Exchange Restrictions,* extended to 1998 by Glick and Hutchison (2005).

[a]This index runs from –6 (low probability/risk of encountering corruption) to 0 (highly corrupt).
[b]The index runs between –10 (fully autocratic) to +10 (fully democratic).

References

Aizenman, J., and I. Noy. 2004. Endogenous financial and trade openness: Efficiency and political economy considerations. NBER Working Paper no. 10496. Cambridge, MA: National Bureau of Economic Research, April.

———. 2006. FDI and trade. *Quarterly Review of Economics and Finance* 46 (3): 317–37.

Bekaert, G., C. R. Harvey, and R. L. Lumsdaine. 2002. Dating the integration of world equity markets. *Journal of Financial Economics* 65:203–47.

Blonigen, B. A. 2005. A review of the empirical literature on FDI determinants. NBER Working Paper no. 11299. Cambridge, MA: National Bureau of Economic Research, May.

Blonigen, B. A., and M. Wang. 2004. Inappropriate pooling of wealthy and poor countries in empirical FDI studies. NBER Working Paper no. 10378. Cambridge, MA: National Bureau of Economic Research, March.

Daude, C., and M. Fratzscher. 2006. The pecking order of cross-border investment. ECB Working Paper Series no. 590. Frankfurt, Germany: European Central Bank, February.

Diamond, D. W. 1984. Financial intermediation and delegated monitoring. *Review of Economic Studies* 51 (3): 393–414.

Do, Q. T., and A. A. Levchenko. 2004. Trade and financial development. Paper presented at LACEA 2004, San José, Costa Rica.

———. 2006. Comparative advantage, demand for external finance, and financial development. World Bank Policy Research Working Paper no. 3889. Washington, DC: World Bank, April.

Dreher, A., and L. Siemers. 2003. The intriguing nexus between corruption and capital account restrictions. University of Konstanz, Konstanz, Germany; and Ruprecht-Karls-University, Heidelberg, Germany. Unpublished Manuscript.

Eaton, J., and A. Tamura. 1994. Bilateralism and regionalism in Japanese and U.S. trade and direct foreign investment patterns. *Journal of Japanese and International Economies* 8:478–510.

Glick, R., and M. Hutchinson. 2005. Capital controls and exchange rate instability in developing economies. *Journal of International Money and Finance* 24:387–412.

Granger, C. W. J. 1969. Investigating causal relationships by econometric methods and cross-spectral methods. *Econometrica* 34:424–38.

Guerin, S. S. 2006. The role of geography in financial and economic integration: A comparative analysis of foreign direct investment, trade and portfolio investment flows. *World Economy* 29 (2): 189–209.

Kose, M. A., E. S. Prasad, K. Rogoff, and S.-J. Wei. 2006. Financial globalization: A reappraisal. IMF Working Paper no. WP/06/189. Washington, DC: International Monetary Fund, August.

Kose, M. A., E. S. Prasad, and M. E. Terrones. 2006. How do trade and financial integration affect the relationship between growth and volatility? *Journal of International Economics* 69:176–202.

Lipsey, R. E. 2006. Measuring international trade in services. NBER Working Paper no. 12271. Cambridge, MA: National Bureau of Economic Research, June.

Marshall, M., and K. Jaggers. 2000. Polity IV project—Political Regime Characteristics and Transitions, 1800–1999: Data Set and Users' Manual. University of Maryland. Manuscript.

Petersen, M. A., and R. G. Rajan. 1997. Trade credits: Theories and evidence. *Review of Financial Studies* 10 (3): 661–91.

Portes, R., H. Rey, and Y. Oh. 2001. Information and capital flows: The determinants of transaction in financial assets. *European Economic Review* 45:783–96.

Rajan, G. R., and L. Zingales. 2003. The great reversals: The politics of financial development in the 20th century. *Journal of Financial Economics* 69 (1): 5–50.

Razin, A., Y. Rubinstein, and E. Sadka. 2003. Which countries export FDI, and how much? NBER Working Paper no. 10145. Cambridge, MA: National Bureau of Economic Research, December.

Rose, A. K., and M. M. Spiegel. 2004. A gravity model of sovereign lending: Trade, default, and credit. *IMF Staff Papers* 51:50–63. Washington, DC: International Monetary Fund.

Sims, C. 1972. Money, income and causality. *American Economic Review* 62:540–52.

Smith, K. A., and D. Valderrama. 2006. The composition of capital flows when emerging market firms face financing constraints. U.S. Naval Academy and Federal Reserve Bank of San Francisco. Unpublished Manuscript.

Swenson, D. L. 2004. Foreign investment and the mediation of trade flows. *Review of International Economics* 12 (4): 609–29.

Wei, S.-J. 2000. How taxing is corruption on international investors? *The Review of Economics and Statistics* 82 (1): 1–11.

Comment   Maria Cristina Terra

This paper investigates empirically the interrelations between disaggregated measures of trade and financial openness. Trade flows are disaggregated into services, incomes, and goods, with a further disaggregation of goods flows into foodstuffs, fuel, metal/ores, and manufacturing. Financial openness, on its turn, is disaggregated into foreign direct investment (FDI), loans, equity, and trade credits. Each of these financial flow measures is regressed onto an average of four lagged periods of the trade measures and a set of macroeconomic and political variables used as controls. Analogously, trade in goods and in services are used alternatively as dependent variables in regressions using the same controls as the financial openness regressions, but including the lagged averages of the financial openness measures.

The paper uncovers some interesting feedback patterns between disaggregated trade and financial flows. It is very interesting the captured impact of past trade in goods on the FDI and loans flow and its lack of impact on the equity and trade credits measures. Also interesting is the fact that trade in income has a significant impact only on FDI.

The authors substantially revised their original work, for this is a very different paper from the one on which I commented in the conference. The original paper included two models to motivate the two-way feedbacks between financial and trade openness, and the empirical investigation was based only on aggregate measures of the trade and financial openness variables. Most of my comments on the original paper questioned whether the models chosen really captured the most relevant aspects of trade and financial openness issues concerning developing economies. They also discussed the link between the models presented and the empirical investigation carried out in the paper.

The authors chose to suppress the theoretical models from the paper and to focus on the empirical study. A theoretical framework, however, is crucial to guide the choice of control variables. Without it, the paper lacks a justification for the chosen empirical formulation, which also impairs the interpretation of the results. This seems especially important in this case, as most of the control variables coefficients turned out to be not significant.

Maria Cristina Terra is a professor in the Graduate School of Economics, Fundação Getúlio Vargas, Rio de Janeiro, and executive director of the Brazilian Society of Econometrics.

For example, per capita GDP has a positive and significant impact on trade credits and on loans in the regression with aggregated trade flows in goods, but the coefficient becomes zero when trade in goods is disaggregated. Were the regressions based on a theoretical framework, maybe we could have some hint on how to interpret this intriguing result.

All the regressions estimated, each one using a different disaggregated measure of trade and financial openness as dependent variables, use the same macro and political variables as controls. A theoretical model could indicate whether one should use different control variables for the different types of flows. As an example, the degree of financial deepening of an economy, a variable that was not included in the regressions, may have an impact on the magnitude of the financial flows, but no effect on the size of trade flows.

The original version of the paper had included variables of trade and financial restrictions in the regressions. This yielded the interesting result that the de jure restrictions on trade affected trade volumes, while those on financial transactions had no impact on financial flows. Unfortunately, these variables were not included in this new version.

Given that the objective of the paper is to explore the two-way feedbacks between trade and financial openness, it would be useful to have a framework that explored their channels. Here are some of the possible links that could be explored. On the one hand, FDI may foster trade in goods when it generates intrafirm trade between the subsidiaries of a multinational company or when a company chooses one country to concentrate production, trading final goods and inputs the others. On the other hand, trade in goods may provide the collateral for financial transactions, thereby encouraging more financial flows. Note that the very trade in goods does generate financial transactions, given that trade is not based on goods' exchanges. Finally, the fact that countries with higher international trade have higher stakes in international markets improves the expectations about a sound interaction between the government and the international financial market. This should also yield trade as an engine to promote more financial transactions.

Comment   Thierry Verdier

The purpose of this paper is to consider empirically the relationships between various disaggregated measures of trade and financial openness in developing countries and to show that there are important two-way causal-

Thierry Verdier is a scientific director of Paris-Jourdan Sciences Économiques (PSE), and director of studies at the School for Advanced Studies in Social Sciences (EHSS).

ity effects between these flows. On the one hand, trade flows are disaggregated into services, incomes, and goods (with a further disaggregation into foodstuffs, fuel, metal/ores, and manufacturing). On the other hand, financial openness is disaggregated into foreign direct investment (FDI), loans, equity, and trade credits. The authors provide first regressions of each of these financial flow measures on an average of four lagged periods of the trade measures, controlling for standard macroeconomic variables (per capita GDP, budget surplus, inflation, U.S. Treasury bill rate) and some political or governance variables (index of democratic regime, corruption). The authors then consider the reverse causality from financial flows to trade flows and, therefore, analogously regress trade flows in goods and services on the lagged averages of the financial openness measures, using the same macroeconomic and political controls as in the financial openness regressions.

Doing this, the authors discuss interesting causality patterns between trade and financial flows. Most notable is the fact that past trade in services has a negative effect on FDI flows, while trade in goods has a positive impact on FDI flows. As well (and quite surprisingly), there is no significant effect of past trade flows on equity and trade credits measures (see tables 1.5 and 1.6). On the other hand, past FDI flows have a positive effect on trade in services and goods, while past loans flows, on the contrary, seem to affect negatively current trade flows in goods and services (table 1.7).

This current piece of work is a very different paper from the one that was presented (and commented on!) in the conference. The original paper included an important theoretical section (with two models motivating the interactions between financial and trade openness) and an empirical section based on aggregate measures of the trade and financial openness variables for least-developed countries (LDC) and developed economies. Because of this, the comments I made on the original paper were focused on addressing the positive dimensions and the limits of the theoretical approach illustrating some channels of interactions between trade and financial openness. Then I was also discussing the links between the theoretical models and the empirical part of the paper.

In the current version, there is no theoretical framework and the paper is essentially about an empirical discussion of the relationships for developing countries between trade and financial flows at some disaggregated level. Let me say that I feel a bit disappointed by the new orientation of the paper. While I clearly recognize the effort to consider more disaggregated flow variables and uncover interesting results, I remain somewhat frustrated not to have an adequate theoretical framework to tell me a story providing an interpretation of these results.

As a matter of fact, many correlations provided by the regressions remain without much economic explanation. For instance, why is it that trade in services affects negatively FDI flows (table 1.6), while on the contrary, FDI flows seem to have a positive effect on trade in services (table 1.7)? As well, why is it that trade flows do not seem to have an effect on trade credits nor that trade credits have an effect on trade flows? Clearly, the paper would have gained much with a theoretical framework providing an interpretation of these puzzling results.

Similarly, a theoretical approach would have been useful to assess the significance and causality of some of the control variables used in some of the regressions. For instance, corruption seems to affect negatively trade flows in goods (table 1.7), but can't we explain this result by some reverse causality that less trade in goods implies less competition in the domestic markets and therefore more corruption (as emphasized, for example, by Ades and Di Tella in their work on the links between trade and corruption)?

Finally, a theoretical framework could have provided interesting avenues to discuss the policy implications of the two-way causality uncovered here between trade flows and financial flows. The usual presumption is that trade integration is good (because of the associated gains from trade inside the country), while financial integration may bring instability and volatility problems. Hence, one should have "free trade" and controls on capital accounts. Related to this, however, people have this whole discussion on the degree of effectiveness of controls on trade flows versus financial flows and the difference between de jure and de facto restrictions. The present paper suggests that it might indeed be difficult to separate trade integration from financial integration, generating therefore interesting trade-offs on the policy to adopt for international integration. A conceptual framework to assess normatively these dimensions is certainly something that needs to be done to fully appreciate the importance of the "nonseparability" between trade flows and financial flows.

Ineffective Controls on Capital Inflows under Sophisticated Financial Markets
Brazil in the Nineties

Bernardo S. de M. Carvalho and Márcio G. P. Garcia

2.1 Introduction

International economic literature has given substantial attention to the destabilizing effects of financial globalization, a process that became particularly strong since industrial countries liberalized their capital accounts in the 1970s and 1980s. Subsequently, in the 1990s, emerging markets (EMs) followed suit.

Among the diverse proposals for reforming the "international financial architecture" aimed at creating a more stable environment is taxation of international capital flows.[1] The idea, in fact, has been around since Keynes (1936) suggested that taxing financial transactions could strengthen the importance investors place on long-term fundamentals in pricing assets. Decades later, the idea gained popularity in the academic community through the Tobin Tax proposal (Tobin 1978).

Much of the recent literature has defended imposing controls on capital inflow, as Chile did during the 1990s. The objective would be to minimize the impact on EMs of capital flows instability and to reduce these countries' vulnerability to financial crises (Stiglitz 1999; Ito and Portes 1998; Eichengreen 1999; Fischer 2002). The proposals defend, in general, what we could call ex ante capital controls, that is, restrictions that are defined prior to funds entering the country, thereby respecting the contracts. This type of

Bernardo S. de M. Carvalho is a trader at Gávea Investments in Rio de Janeiro, Brazil. Márcio G. P. Garcia is an associate professor of economics at Pontifical Catholic University, Rio de Janeiro (PUC-Rio), and a researcher affiliated with the National Council of Scientific and Technological Development (CNPq) and the Research Support Foundation of Rio de Janeiro (FAPERJ).

1. Rogoff (1999), Eichengreen (1999), Stiglitz (1999), and Fischer (2002) are excellent references on the diverse proposals for reforming the international financial system.

control differs from those the literature has called controls on capital outflows, which are generally imposed during a financial crisis, typically after, or ex post, the entry of capital, and can thus be viewed as breaching contracts with foreign investors who have then already invested resources in the country. Ex ante capital controls usually try to deter capital inflows but could conceivably be also imposed to restrict capital outflows.

Here, we address the effects of ex ante capital controls. In contrast to ex post controls, ex ante controls should not jeopardize the emerging market country's reputation as they are included in contracts with foreign investors prior to their investing. We will analyze the effectiveness of inflow controls to limit short-term capital and modify the composition of financial inflows.

Several authors have suggested controls on capital inflows as an economic policy measure for managing excessive capital inflows into EMs. In periods of greater liquidity and low international risk aversion, it is common for substantial financial flows to move into Latin America and Asia. The years from 2004 to 2006 were classic examples: "dollar weakness," or expectations of greater depreciation of the U.S. dollar due to forecasts that the U.S. current account deficit had to be reversed,[2] together with low base interest rates in developed countries. Both factors led to substantial capital inflows into EMs. As a result, Colombia (2004), Argentina (2005), and Thailand (2006) adopted capital inflow controls to avoid accelerated appreciation of their currency,[3] and many countries, including Brazil, Russia, China, Japan, and other Asian countries, rapidly accumulated international reserves so as to manage the abundant inflow of foreign currency. In this context, discussion surrounding controls on capital inflow has gained considerable steam among economists.

The central goal of establishing capital controls is containing the inflow of short-term capital. Short-term capital flows are considered more volatile and fungible and thus more closely related to excessive exchange rate volatility and to sudden reversals of external financing that lead to harmful real results. Many articles actually argue that portfolio investments tend to be less stable than, for example, direct investment because financial assets can be sold more easily than real assets can be liquidated (Dixit and Pyndick 1994; Frankel and Rose 1996; Dornbusch 1998). Moreover, today's international financial scenario includes hedge funds, many of which are seeking immediate gains. As of August 2005, it was estimated

2. Obstfeld and Rogoff (2000, 2004), Kim and Roubini (2004), Blanchard, Giavazzi, and Sa (2005) are good references for discussion of the expected weakening of the U.S. Dollar as a result of the country's record current account deficits.

3. Colombia, Argentina, and Thailand have imposed Chilean-style capital inflow control, which obliges investors bringing capital into the country to withhold 30 percent of the total amount for one year at the Central Bank, without remuneration. But Colombian authorities banned the measures just few months afterwards, alleging they were ineffective in containing the capital inflows.

that there was around US$ 1.5 trillion in the hands of these financial institutions (Chan et al. 2006). This, together with more sophisticated information technology, has made capital flows extremely fungible. Capital controls would also avoid excessive exchange rate appreciation and allow the central bank to regain control of monetary policy.[4]

The economic literature is therefore brimming with debate about how to manage excessive capital inflow in an exceptionally volatile global financial environment. Volatile capital accounts and consequent volatile exchange rates (except in the case of fixed exchange rates) influence decisions on investing in physical capital as investors face greater uncertainty and higher costs on currency hedge operations, thereby affecting potential gross domestic product (GDP). In light of this, a few authors have suggested adopting capital inflow controls or accumulating international reserves as a way of handling heavy inflow of foreign currency and reducing the threat of sudden stops.

Forbes (2003) concludes that liberalization of capital accounts around the world did in fact intensify global financial instability, but the correlation between capital controls and limiting vulnerability to confidence crises is not particularly close or direct, as many writers have argued. Forbes (2004) also observes that the controls diminish microeconomic efficiency, for example, by increasing the cost of capital of small- and medium-sized companies, which have less access to financial markets. Large companies have access to the international financial market and to ways of circumventing restrictions on external financing so that they are less impacted by capital controls.

Glick and Hutchison (2004) explore the effectiveness of controls in avoiding or delaying financial crises. Based on an analysis of panel data from sixty-nine countries, they conclude that restricting capital did not bring the desired results. Eichengreen and Leblang (2003), analyzing a panel of forty-seven countries, examine whether capital controls were effective in reducing the impact of financial crises in the real economy. They conclude that the controls impaired economic growth in periods of stability but that they eased the effect on the country's product once the crisis unfolded. However, these papers do not separate the effects of capital controls on inflows from those on outflows.

This article narrows the analysis of the effectiveness of capital controls. We explore whether controls on capital inflows are effective in limiting and selecting capital flows. Thus, we analyze whether this type of control effectively meets its primary objective. The issue concerns positive economics and not normative economics. Naturally, if we were to show that the controls are not effective—as we will indeed claim it has been the case in

---

4. Cowan and De Gregorio (2005, 1) say that the goals of Chilean capital controls were to "stem net inflows, avoid a large appreciation and keep control of monetary policy."

Brazil—whether the controls are desirable or not would become irrelevant for policy purposes.

In general, the literature addresses short-term capital controls without considering the capacity of international investors to avoid the restrictions imposed. The general rule has been to implicitly assume that de jure imposition for capital controls is the same as their de facto application. However, developed and sophisticated financial markets present diverse substitute assets that may be used to engineer financial transactions that avoid part or all of the costs incurred by the capital controls. Garcia and Barcinski (1998) and Garcia and Valpassos (2000) focus on this issue for Brazil. They indicate the ineffectiveness of inflow controls in reducing the inflow of capital seeking the high returns of Brazilian public debt between 1994 and 1996. Papers addressing the case of Chile, such as those of Nadal-de-Simone and Sorsa (1999), Edwards, Valdés, and De Gregorio (2000), and Cowan and De Gregorio (2005), also stress that circumvention of capital controls may have limited its effectiveness in changing the composition of the financial inflows.

In this paper, we conduct econometric exercises—based on an analysis of impulse response functions inspired by the vector autoregression (VAR) analysis of Cardoso and Goldfajn (1997)—that show that the capital controls were only effective in restricting financial capital inflows in Brazil in the 1990s for two to six months. Our updated results corroborate those from previous papers.

The novelty of this paper is in the methodology aimed at explaining why capital controls lost de facto effectiveness. This paper's main contribution is its focus on the limiting effects that the avoidance of capital controls practiced by financial market players had on the effectiveness of controls on capital inflows. Based on interviews with financial market players active during the analyzed period, we exemplify methods (financial strategies) that could have been used to avoid capital control laws in Brazil during the 1990s.

The article is divided as follows: after this introduction, section 2.2 briefly discusses capital control legislation, section 2.3 presents a VAR analysis aimed at measuring the effectiveness of the capital controls in reducing short-term financial inflows sections 2.4 and 2.5 reports cases of avoidance of capital restrictions that explain how capital controls were rendered almost ineffective, and section 2.6 contains the conclusion.

2.2   Capital Controls in Brazil

Brazil's exchange rate and capital controls legislation is highly complex and confusing, mixing normative rulings from the period of the Vargas administration in the 1930s with modern resolutions. Exchange rate regulation is still considered an impediment to capital flows due to its complexity, and its reform is one of the most important issues for ensuring continued development of the Brazilian financial market.[5]

The following economic papers address Brazil's tangled exchange rate and foreign capital legislation: Franco (1990), Cardoso and Goldfajn (1997), Garcia and Barcinski (1998), Garcia and Valpassos (2000), Arida (2003), Franco and Pinho Neto (2004), and Goldfajn and Minella (2005). The annual bulletins of Brazil's Central Bank also address the issue, discussing exchange rate policy and summarizing the legal proceedings of the institution, the National Monetary Council (CMN), and the Ministry of Finance during the course of the year. In this section, we present an overview of this legislation to offer a context for discussing the effectiveness of controls on capital inflows.

The legal framework for exchange rate transactions and foreign capital establishes the following key points: foreign exchange must be converted into the national currency, the real (BRL), which is the only legal tender in the country; resources secured offshore or those addressed in Law 4131/62[6] must be brought back into the country; export revenues earned abroad must be brought back into the country (surrender requirements); and private exchange rate transactions are prohibited, meaning the Central Bank holds a monopoly on exchange rate transactions. In summary, the legal framework is aimed at keeping all possible foreign exchange in the country.

In March of 2005, the CMN simplified currency legislation in an effort to streamline and reduce the costs of capital flow with Brazil. It did not, however, change the legal framework or any laws, but rather published new CMN resolutions. These measures are part of a process of liberalization and correction of the asymmetries of legislation governing currency transactions with other countries, which the Central Bank undertook some years ago. Among the principal measures, we note merging of the free rate (MCTL) and floating rate (MCTF) exchange markets as Brazil still had a de jure (but not de facto) system with multiple exchange rates; authorization to make direct offshore remittances without use of the CC-5 accounts;[7] a longer period for bringing foreign currency revenues from exports back into the country; and authorization of foreign forward currency agreements (ACC) for exportation of services.

Much of prevailing exchange rate legislation was established over sixty

---

5. Reforms of exchange rate regulations are also needed to support the increased amount of international trade, but we will not touch on this important issue here.

6. Law 4131 of 1962 regulates foreign capital in the country.

7. CC-5 accounts were maintained by those not residing in Brazil and were created by the Central Bank's bulletin number 5 in 1969. These resources had free access to the MCTF to purchase foreign currency and send it offshore. It also authorized remittance from others through the account. CC-5 accounts were the main vehicle for both residents and nonresidents to access foreign markets.

years ago. Only exchange rate rules for foreign direct investments (FDIs) remained stable as Franco and Pinho Neto (2004) emphasize.

In 1931, Decree 20.451/31 conceded the monopoly of exchange rate transactions to the Banco do Brasil and established what was called the "centralization of foreign exchange transactions." Decree 25.258/33 consolidated the exchange rate policy and defined "illicit exchange rate transactions" as those conducted outside the official monopoly or subsequently by establishments the monopoly holder authorized for such. Today this holder is the Central Bank of Brazil. This Decree 25.258/33 is still in effect and stipulates that "understating the value of export cover or increasing prices of imported goods to obtain undue cover is punishable by law." Until today, this 1933 ruling requires exporters to convert their offshore revenues into domestic currency (surrender requirements) and penalizes overpricing of imports and underpricing of exports. The maximum term for bringing export revenues back to Brazil has changed numerous times. As noted in the preceding, in March of 2005 the term was extended to 210 days after shipping, as compared to the previous 180 days (Resolution 3266/05).

Rules for foreign capital in Brazil were consolidated under Law 4.131 of 1962, which remains in effect today. As Franco and Pinho Neto (2004) noted, "subsequent laws smoothed some of the more prominent edges of Law 4.131/62," but government authorities still have substantial discretionary power to impose or reverse restrictive measures for exchange rate flows.

In general, current legislation still clearly allows the CMN to set measures for controlling foreign capital flows. One example is the set of restrictive measures that may be enacted in the event of "urgent needs of foreign exchange," as defined in Article 28 of Law 4.131/62:[8] simple administrative

---

8. *Law 4.131/62 Art. 28*

"**Art. 28**—Any time there is extreme impurity in the balance of payments, or serious grounds for assessing there will be, the *National Monetary Council may impose restrictions, for a limited period of time, on the entry and exit of revenues in foreign currency,* and to this end, grant the Banco do Brasil a complete or partial monopoly on exchange rate transactions.

§ 1—In the case provided for in this article, *remittance of capital return are prohibited, and remittance of their profits limited to a maximum of 10% (ten percent) per year,* related to capital and reinvestments registered in the currency of the country of origin, in the terms set forth in Articles 3 and 4 of this Law.

§ 2—Revenues exceeding the percentage fixed by the National Monetary Council, as set forth in the preceding paragraph, must be listed with the Central Bank of Brazil, which, if the restriction provided for in this article is extended for over one fiscal year, may authorize the remittance, in the subsequent fiscal year, of the remaining amounts, if the profits made do not reach that limit.

§ 3—In the same cases of this article, the National Monetary Council may *limit remittance of funds for paying "royalties" and technical, administrative or similar support* up to the annual cumulative maximum of 5% (five percent) of the company's gross earnings.

§ 4—Also in the cases of this article, the National Monetary Council *is authorized to issue rulings limiting currency spending on "International Travel."*

§ 5—There are no restrictions, however, on remittances of interest of interest or amortization quotas contained in duly registered loan agreements."

decisions can establish controls on capital outflows and foreign exchange centralization. This attests to the uncertainties surrounding Brazil's legislation, signaled by Arida, Bacha, and Lara-Rezende (2005) as one of the major determinants of the country's very high sovereign risk.

Until the 1980s, exchange rate legislation focused primarily on foreign currency outflows in an environment of restricted capital account's transactions. It only authorized the sending of foreign capital whose ingress into the country was documented. The remittance of profits and dividends were taxed. With the 1980 debt crisis, international capital stopped flowing toward Latin America so that only the egress and not the ingress of foreign currency had to be contained.

Beginning in 1987, and especially after the 1994 institution of the Real Plan, the Brazilian government adopted a directive for liberalizing the current and capital accounts. In the early 1990s, inflows increased, and as the economy stabilized in the second half of the decade and Brazil returned to the foreign debt market, the pace of capital inflows accelerated considerably. Figure 2.1 demonstrates the evolution of the inflow of foreign portfolio investments.

Financial flows to Brazil gained momentum following renegotiation of the country's external debt in 1994, under the Brady Plan model applied in several Latin American countries, and with the success of the stabilization provided by the Real Plan.

The increase of capital inflows that began at the end of 1991 generated problems for managing the country's macro economy. Abundant inflows of foreign capital triggered appreciation and excessive exchange rate volatility or accumulation of international reserves and a consequent increase of the public debt due to sterilized intervention. Additionally, most of the capital that entered at that time was for short-term investments given the very high real interest rates prevailing in Brazil. This type of investment,

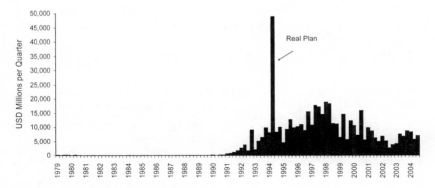

Fig. 2.1   Foreign portfolio capital inflows
Source: Banco Central do Brasil (all years).

termed "carry-trade," is usually reversed very quickly at the first sign of depreciation of the receiving country's currency. As such, it enhances the probability of a sudden stop and also sparks greater economic volatility.

In fact, the 1990s oscillated between periods of excessive inflow, such as between 1992 and 1995 and then between 1996 and the middle of 1997, and periods of shortage of foreign capital in times of international crises (crisis in Mexico that hit Brazil in 1995, Asian crisis in 1997, and crises in Russia and Brazil in 1998 and 1999, respectively). In periods of excessive inflows, controls were placed on capital inflows in an effort to limit short-term capital and alleviate the effects of too much foreign currency, causing appreciation or, to prevent it, forcing fiscally expensive sterilized interventions. In periods of shortage, controls were lifted in an attempt to attract capital to finance the Brazilian balance of payments as current account deficit grew from 3 percent of GDP in 1995 to 5 percent in 1999. Capital controls were, then, endogenous to external financing conditions and to monetary policy, as shown by Cardoso and Goldfajn (1997).

In 1987, incentives for foreign portfolio investments in the country were provided by the Central Bank of Brazil's Resolution 1289, which exempts foreign investors from income tax on capital gains in Brazil. The Resolution's Annex IV was the preferred channel by investors to make tax exempt investments in Brazil. However, in August 1993, to contain excess inflows of short-term capital aimed at profiting from the very high interest rates prevailing in Brazil, the CMN prohibited using the Annex IV mechanism to invest in government bonds. The purpose was actually to prohibit fixed income investing in general, authorizing only investing in the capital market. But numerous loopholes in the legislation opened the door for fixed income investments through this mechanism, as the following section shows. Fixed income investments then officially had to enter the country via specific funds that were subject to a tax on financial transactions (IOF) tax of 5 percent to 9 percent.[9] This was one of the main measures for controlling capital inflows in the 1990s, but the market managed to bypass it in numerous ways and reap gains from the high short-term interest rates without paying the IOF.

In 1999, Resolution 1289 was revoked by Resolution 2689, and the IOF

9. In November of 1993, the Foreign Capital Fixed Income Fund was established, charging a 5 percent IOF tax (IOF stands for Tax on Financial Transactions, which is a tax that can be easily and quickly imposed or changed by the Ministry of Finance, not having to wait to the following fiscal year to take effort). In October 1994, the IOF was raised to 9 percent. In March of 1995, due to the "Tequila Effect" (Mexican Crisis), the IOF was lowered to 5 percent, and then raised again in August of that year to 7 percent. In April of 1997, it was lowered from 7 percent to 2 percent, and in March of 1999 to 0.5 percent. In August of 1999 this IOF was eliminated, but the capital from the investment write-off had to be invested on the BOVESPA for at least one day or be held without remuneration for fifteen days. For investments of less than ninety days, a 5 percent IOF tax is levied even today (May 2006).

tax was removed for fixed income investments.[10] Currently, most capital flows are registered in the Central Bank's electronic registration system (RDE),[11] including most of those governed by Resolution 2689. The process allows for closer monitoring and greater transparency of financial flows. Only very short term (less than ninety days) fixed income investments are charged the 5 percent IOF tax. There are also rules in Annex V of Resolution 2689 for Depositary Receipts (DR), when shares of Brazilian companies are issued abroad with counterpart shares in Brazil. This movement is not registered in the RDE. Finally, until March of 2005, the account for nonresidents (CC-5) was still in place. It was not declared on the RDE and served as a vehicle for foreign capital to enter the country.

Controls on capital inflows, rather, ex ante controls on capital inflows, in the 1990s focused largely on limiting short-term inflows, restricting fixed income investments and short-term loans. Export revenues were also strictly regulated. As we have seen, since 1933 exporters have been subject to surrender requirements within a specified period, 360 days as of March 2007. Forward foreign currency agreements (ACC), a mechanism to provide credit for exports, are also restricted even today to a maximum 360 days prior to shipping.

Based on the methodology of Cardoso and Goldfajn (1997), we updated the indexes of controls on capital inflows and outflows through 2004. The original article had constructed the indexes through 1996, and we updated them. The methodology is simple: add +1 to the base index if the control restricts the analyzed type of flow (inflow or outflow) and –1 if it liberalizes it. The methodology applies to the indexes of the controls on both capital inflows and capital outflows.[12]

Figure 2.3 clearly shows that since the early 1990s a trend toward liberalizing outflows has prevailed, yet figure 2.2 shows that only beginning in 1997 was there an unequivocal trend toward liberalizing capital inflows. This is because between 1997 and 1999 there were several crises: in Asia, in Russia, and a currency crisis in Brazil. During those periods, because capital was fleeing the country, there was no need for adopting controls that restricted capital inflows. In 1999, Brazil floated its currency and defined a clear directive for liberalizing the capital account in order to reap the benefits of external savings. One example was in August of 1999, when the IOF

10. Traders in Brazil still refer to the investment mechanism of the prevailing Resolution 2689 as "Annex IV."

11. The RDE is divided into IED, ROF, and Portfolio registration. RDE-IED: foreign director investment; RDE-ROF: financial transaction registration (financing and importation, commercial leasing, rental and freight, services and technology, currency loans, advance payment of exports, and asset investments), RDE-Portfolio: portfolio investing.

12. However simple, this methodology has the drawback of considering that all measures had similar effects on capital flows, which is clearly a problem. Nevertheless, we believe that the indexes rightly capture the major trends.

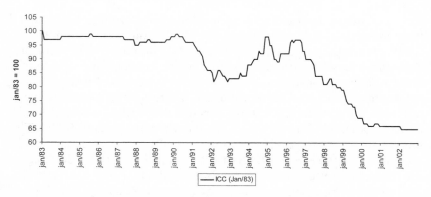

Fig. 2.2   Capital inflows controls index (Jan. 1983 = 100)

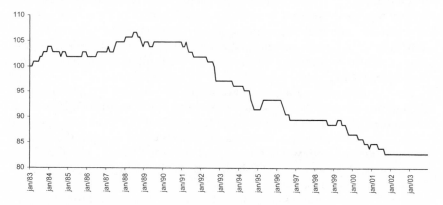

Fig. 2.3   Capital outflows controls index (Jan. 1983 = 100)

tax was lifted for fixed income foreign investments of over ninety days that were previously under Annex IV.

In the next section, we provide econometric evidence of the very limited effectiveness of the controls on capital inflows imposed by Brazilian authorities in the 1990s.

2.3   A VAR Analysis of the Effectiveness of Inflow Controls in Deterring Capital Inflows

In this section we conduct an econometric analysis using a vector autoregression model to examine whether controls on capital inflows in Brazil have been effective in reducing the inflow of financial capital.

The methodology is based on the articles of Cardoso and Goldfajn (1997) and Edwards, Valdés, and De Gregorio (2000), which used the VAR model to analyze the effectiveness of capital controls in Brazil and in Chile, respectively.

Cardoso and Goldfajn (1997) examined the effect of controls on capital inflows in the period from 1983 to 1995, concluding that the impact of inflow controls on the total net inflow was temporary (around six months). They used VAR estimation, because they showed that the controls are endogenous to the dynamic of the capital inflows. Here, we apply a similar procedure to the period between 1995 and 2001, using, however, different capital inflow measures and other endogenous variables. We chose not to extend the sample beyond 2001 given there were very few changes to legislation on capital inflows between then and 2004, so there is little to be inferred from the period about the effect of controls on capital flows.[13]

Edwards, Valdés, and De Gregorio (2000) estimated a VAR to analyze simultaneously the effectiveness of controls in containing capital inflows and in altering the term of foreign investments. They used as one of the endogenous variables a power index for monitoring the effect of control circumvention on the effectiveness of restrictions on short-term capital. We did not build a similar index from Brazil because we felt that, with the available data, its accuracy and reliability would not be sufficient.[14] Edwards, Valdés, and De Gregorio (2000) concluded that Chile's control on capital inflows did not effectively reduce the total capital inflow, but it did increase the percentage of long-term flows. In other words, the controls were effective in reducing short-term capital, but the total inflow remained stable as more long-term capital entered the country. However, they argued that the result may be distorted by short-term capital investments that were declared as long term. They could not guarantee that the control power index was able to isolate the effect of this type of avoidance.

In this section we estimate three VARs. They differ in the variable that measures capital inflows. Figures 2.4 and 2.5 show the different series we used on a monthly basis and accumulated in twelve months. The capital inflow measure of the first VAR is the Brazilian Central Bank series on the inflow of portfolio investments in Brazil. The inflow measure of the second VAR is the contracted exchange rate inflows for financial transactions. The measure for the third is net investments through the Annex IV channel. The use of three different measures of capital inflows is aimed at providing robustness to our analysis. All of the VARs have the same endogenous variables: the deviation of the effective real exchange rate to its equilibrium

13. See figure 2.2 and 2.3 with the capital inflow controls index in section 2.2.

14. The index is formed by attributing rates of 0 to 1 for each new restrictive measure. When the restriction was applied, the measure received a rating of 1. With the passing of time, if the restriction was circumvented, the rating moved closer to 0, where the measure was assessed as having lost all effectiveness. Establishing a similar index for Brazil was a complex task because it involved a large number of exchange rate of measures and because the Brazilian financial market was more developed than the Chilean.

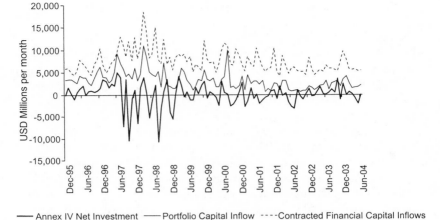

Fig. 2.4   Financial capital flows measures
Source: Banco Central do Brasil (all years) and Securities and Exchange Commission (CVM).

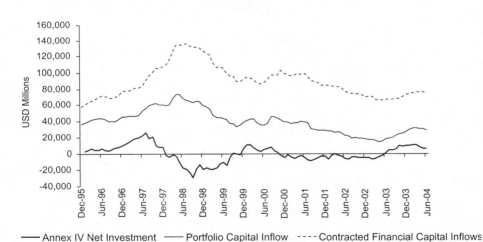

Fig. 2.5   Financial capital flows measures, accumulated in twelve months
Source: Banco Central do Brasil (all years) and Securities and Exchange Commission (CVM).

level, the covered interest parity differential, the measure of capital inflows, and the logarithmic difference of the index of capital inflow controls. The exogenous variables varied in the VAR specifications. The number of lags for each VAR was chosen based on the Akaike and the Schwartz information criteria. In order to obtain the impulse response functions, we applied the Cholesky decomposition for identifying a VAR's structural form. It is essential to note that the results were robust with the several orderings of contemporaneous causality among the endogenous variables, so this possible criticism does not affect our results.

The main objective of the estimation of these VARs is to analyze the impulse response function of the capital flows to a change in capital inflow controls. The variation from the index of capital inflow restrictions presented in section 2.3 was used as the measure of capital controls. It is important to clarify that the index's order of integration is equal to 1, so that we had to use the first differences to obtain a stationary series. In figure 2.6, we present the capital inflow controls variation series. From 1983 to 1995, the series was constructed, as we have already noted, on Cardoso and Goldfajn (1997) and updated for this article after 1995.

The results were as follows:

The first VAR has the following endogenous variables:

- Logarithmic variation of the equilibrium real effective interest rate (LOG(REER_DESV102)), which was calculated as the logarithm of the ratio between the index value of the real effective exchange rate and a series trend extracted by applying the Hodrick-Prescott filter beginning January of 1995.
- Covered interest parity differential (CIPD) in continuous capitalization, or LOG(1 + CIPD), where LOG is the logarithm in the Neperian base.
- Logarithm of the portfolio investment inflows as a percentage of the GDP (LOG(IEC_CRED/PIB)), which is our capital flow measure in this first VAR.
- Finally, the logarithmic variation of the index of capital inflow controls (D(LOG(ICC))).

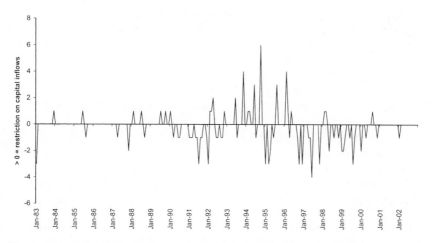

Fig. 2.6   Restrictions on capital inflows (first difference of capital inflows controls index)

The exogenous variables used were the American one-year futures rates (LOG(1 + US1Y)), which summarize the level of international liquidity; the variation of the index of capital outflow controls (D(LOG(ICC_S))), which was calculated as an exogenous variable because we considered that economic policy had lifted outflow controls independent of capital flows, as indicated by the downward trend of the ICC-O in figure 2.3 of section 2.2; and, last, some circumstantial dummies from the period of the Brazilian currency crisis. Dummies for other periods of financial crisis were not significant as the effects were probably captured by the endogenous variables, especially the real exchange rate and the CIPD. The exception was the wave of speculation in 1998, when there was a large inflow of capital even with the higher sovereign risk, followed by a mass exodus after depreciation, for which a binary dummy variable was applied.

Table 2.1 summarizes the output of the first VAR estimation, and figure 2.7 shows the impulse response function of the portfolio investment inflows to new restrictions on capital inflows. We see that a new control measure on capital inflows initially reduces the portfolio investment inflows and peaks in the second month. However, its effectiveness diminishes rapidly, and up to around six months following its implementation, the effect on capital flows disappears. Therefore, the exercise indicates that controls on capital inflows in Brazil are temporarily effective, lasting around two to six months. This period would be the time required for the market to discover investment alternatives for circumventing the restriction.[15]

Figure 2.8 shows the impulse response function of the capital inflow controls to an increase in capital inflows: we see that control tends to be tightened when capital inflows increase, which is consistent with the findings on endogeneity of controls indicated by Cardoso and Goldfajn (1997).

Table 2.2 has the same endogenous variables as the first with the exception of the capital inflow measure, which becomes the contracted exchange rate inflows for financial transactions as a percentage of the GDP (LOG(MOV_CAMBIO_FIN_COMPRA/PIB)). These are data from the Brazilian Central Bank that report the currency flows from all financial investments except for those going through the CC-5 account, that is to say, they do not include exchange rate flows from abroad and the CC-5 accounts. This series included all flows from protective capital, direct investments, and foreign loans. Because the capital controls exempted direct investment flows, we used these data as an exogenous variable. The other exogenous variables are the same as those in the first VAR.

Figure 2.9 shows the impulse response function of the contracted exchange rate inflows for financial transactions to the new restrictions on

15. The confidence intervals of the impulse response functions in our exercise are wide and limit the potential of our results. A similar problem occurred with the VARs of Cardoso and Goldfajn (1997) and Edwards, Valdés, and De Gregorio (2000). For future research, refining the capital controls index (CCI) may imply narrower confidence intervals.

Table 2.1   VAR 01—Portfolio investment capital flows (vector autoregression estimates)

	LOG(REER_DESVIO2)	LOG(1+CIPD)	LOG(IEC_CRED/PIB_USD)	D(LOG(CC))
LOG(REER_DESVIO2(-1))	0.848994	-0.063483	-0.065995	-0.04362
	-0.06995	-0.02975	-0.81052	-0.02845
	[12.1367]	[-2.13415]	[-0.08142]	[-1.53336]
LOG(1+CIPD(-1))	0.002434	0.993933	-0.057779	0.148311
	-0.15516	-0.06598	-1.7978	-0.0631
	[0.01569]	[15.0641]	[-0.0631]	[2.35048]
LOG(IEC_CRED(-1)/PIB_USD(-1))	-0.029375	-0.010079	0.465205	0.004209
	-0.00986	-0.00419	-0.11421	-0.00401
	[-2.98003]	[-2.40444]	[4.07310]	[1.04999]
D(LOG(ICC(-1)))	-0.055859	-0.235101	-5.725003	-0.001572
	-0.33932	-0.14429	-3.93165	-0.00401
	[-0.16462]	[-1.62932]	[-1.45613]	[-0.01739]
C	0.22708	-0.025619	-0.424531	-0.007136
	-0.07133	-0.03033	-0.82644	-0.02901
	[0.31836]	[-0.84466]	[-0.51368]	[-0.24601]
LOG(1+US1Y)	-2.027193	-0.088474	-19.21475	0.07025
	-1.25812	-0.535	-14.5774	-0.51163
	[-1.61129]	[-0.16537]	[-1.31812]	[0.13731]
D(LOG(ICC_S(-1)))	-1.346541	-0.294861	14.681138	-0.356286
	-0.89256	-0.37955	-10.3418	-0.36297
	[-1.50863]	[-0.77687]	[1.41961]	[-0.98158]
DUM98_06	-0.022205	-0.007393	-0.183745	0.000461
	-0.03602	-0.01532	-0.41732	-0.01465
	[-0.61651]	[-0.48273]	[-0.44030]	[0.03146]
DUM98_09	-0.017627	0.014355	-1.193587	-0.00198
	-0.03742	-0.01591	-0.43353	-0.01522
	[-0.47110]	[0.90224]	[-2.75317]	[-0.13015]

(continued)

Table 2.1   (continued)

	LOG(REER_DESVIO2)	LOG(1+CIPD)	LOG(IEC_CRED/PIB_USD)	D(LOG(CC))
DUM98_10	-0.072689	-0.031912	0.784007	-0.00372
	-0.04323	-0.01838	-0.50086	-0.01758
	[-1.68154]	[-1.73603]	[1.56532]	[-0.21161]
DUM98_11	-0.33384	-0.007341	-1.097422	-0.015072
	-0.03745	-0.01593	-0.43398	-0.01523
	[-0.89131]	[-0.46092]	[-2.52874]	[-0.98951]
DUM98_12	-0.055555	-0.016687	-0.69168	0.001728
	-0.03929	-0.01671	-0.45521	-0.01598
	[-1.49044]	[-0.99883]	[-1.51949]	[0.10816]
DUM99_01	0.141244	0.010355	-0.428468	-0.021543
	-0.03941	-0.01676	-0.45668	-0.01603
	[3.58358]	[0.61781]	[-0.93822]	[-1.34407]
R^2	0.863004	0.866213	0.404071	0.161514
Adj. R^2	0.834661	0.838533	0.280775	-0.011966
Sum sq. resids	0.06632	0.011993	8.903604	0.010968
SE equation	0.033815	0.014379	0.391804	0.013751
F-statistic	30.44762	31.29377	3.277248	0.931025
Log-likelihood	146.9012	207.6138	-27.03869	210.7849
AIC	-3.771866	-5.482079	1.12785	-5.571405
SC	-3.357572	-5.067785	1.542144	-5.157111
Mean dependent	-0.00975	0.068627	-2.797709	-0.004711
SD dependent	0.083161	0.035785	0.461994	0.01367
Determinant Residual Covariance		2.68E-12		
Log-likelihood (df adjusted)		542.9422		
AIC		-13.82936		
SC		-12.17218		

Notes: Sample period (adjusted): 1995:03 to 2001:01. No. of observations = 71, after adjusting endpoints. Standard errors are in parentheses and *t*-statistics are in brackets. SE = standard error. SD = standard deviation. AIC = Akaike Information Criteria. SC = Schwarz Criteria.

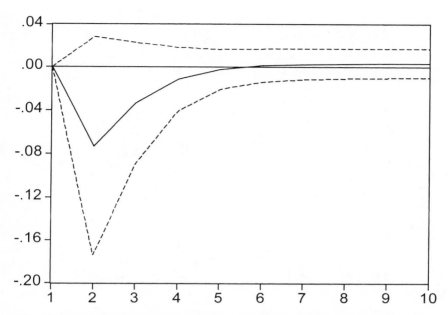

Fig. 2.7 Response of LOG(IEC–CRED/PIB_USD) to Cholesky, one S.D. D(LOG(ICC)) innovation

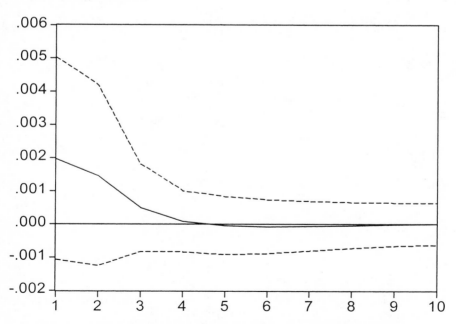

Fig. 2.8 Response of D(LOG(ICC)) to Cholesky, one S.D. LOG(IEC_CRED/ PIB_USD) innovation

Table 2.2   VAR 02—Contracted inflow of foreign exchange (vector autoregression estimates)

	LOG(REER_DESVIO2)	LOG(1+CIPD)	LOG(MOVCAMBIO_FIN_COMPRAS/PIB_USD)	D(LOG(CC))
LOG(REER_DESVIO2(-1))	1.596	0.2162	-1.297422	-0.100528
	-0.12063	-0.05501	-0.46469	-0.06268
	[13.2301]	[3.93000]	[-2.79201]	[-1.60372]
LOG(REER_DESVIO2(-2))	-0.76867	-0.268611	0.956407	0.0504
	-0.12135	-0.05534	-0.46743	-0.06305
	[-6.33453]	[-4.85404]	[2.04608]	[0.79931]
LOG(1+CIPD(-1))	-1.056099	0.679976	1.186595	0.169177
	-0.31673	-0.14444	-1.22005	-0.16458
	[-3.33442]	[4.70776]	[0.97258]	[1.02794]
LOG(1+CIPD(-2))	0.97209	0.198835	-0.827889	0.068802
	-0.36258	-0.16535	-1.3967	-0.18841
	[2.68102]	[1.20252]	[-0.59275]	[0.36518]
LOG(MOVCAMBIO_FIN_COMPRAS(-1)/PIB_USD(-1))	0.018765	0.002513	1.003293	0.00675
	-0.02638	-0.01203	-0.10163	-0.01371
	[0.71122]	[0.20883]	[9.87167]	[0.49163]
LOG(MOVCAMBIO_FIN_COMPRAS(-2)/PIB_USD(-2))	-0.035169	-0.009047	-0.359534	0.003547
	-0.02523	-0.01151	-0.09718	-0.01311
	[-1.39402]	[-0.78636]	[-3.69954]	[0.27054]
D(LOG(ICC(-1)))	0.059725	-0.1086	-2.215967	-0.070253
	-0.28181	-0.12851	-1.08555	-0.14643
	[0.21193]	[-0.84505]	[-2.04133]	[-0.47976]
D(LOG(ICC(-2)))	0.008505	0.124223	0.495162	-0.096286
	-0.27883	-0.12716	-1.07409	-0.14489
	[0.03050]	[0.97693]	[0.46101]	[-0.66456]
C	0.014042	-0.025425	0.111609	-0.045985
	-0.07082	-0.03229	-0.27279	-0.0368
	[0.19829]	[-0.78729]	[0.40914]	[-1.24965]
LOG(1+US1Y)	-0.868745	0.149802	-7.091789	0.770644
	-1.38204	-0.63025	-5.32373	-0.71814
	[-0.62860]	[0.23768]	[-1.33211]	[1.07311]
LOG(FDI/PIB_USD)	0.000618	-0.00281	0.12433	-0.001046
	-0.00637	-0.00291	-0.02456	-0.00331
	[0.09698]	[-0.96666]	[5.06297]	[-0.31565]

D(LOG(ICC_S))	-1.630759	3.996622	-0.129792
	-0.76518	-2.94752	-0.3976
	[-2.13122]	[1.35593]	[-0.32644]
DUM98_06	-0.006115	-0.248249	-0.002908
	-0.0287	-0.11056	-0.01491
	[-0.21305]	[-2.24530]	[-0.19501]
DUM98_09	-0.010423	-0.164069	0.000891
	-0.03136	-0.12078	-0.01629
	[-0.33243]	[-1.35836]	[0.05468]
DUM98_10	0.002162	-0.28825	0.003468
	-0.03334	-0.12844	-0.01733
	[0.06485]	[-2.24427]	[0.20015]
DUM98_11	-0.053352	-0.125101	-0.008403
	-0.02978	-0.11471	-0.01547
	[-1.79157]	[-1.09057]	[-0.54303]
DUM98_12	-0.021103	-0.114811	0.003305
	-0.03068	-0.11818	-0.01594
	[-0.68787]	[-0.97153]	[0.20729]
DUM99_01	0.172991	-0.032087	-0.020606
	-0.02993	-0.1153	-0.01555
	[5.77975]	[-0.27831]	[-1.32504]
R^2	0.925925	0.917272	0.227275
Adj. R^2	0.901708	0.890226	-0.025346
Sum sq. resids	0.035599	0.007403	0.009612
SE equation	0.026165	0.011932	0.013596
F-statistic	38.23482	33.91548	39.42249
Log-likelihood	166.1117	221.0752	211.9372
AIC	-4.231763	-5.802149	-5.541062
SC	-3.653578	-5.223964	-4.962878
Mean dependent	-0.010592	0.068454	-0.004352
SD dependent	0.083457	0.036013	0.013427

Determinant Residual Covariance	1.09E-13
Log-likelihood (df adjusted)	647.389
AIC	-16.43969
SC	-14.12695

Notes: Sample period (adjusted): 1995:04 to 2001:01. No. of observations = 70, after adjusting endpoints. Standard errors are in parentheses and *t*-statistics are in brackets. SE = standard errors. SD = standard deviation. AIC = Akaike Information Criteria. SC = Schwarz Criteria.

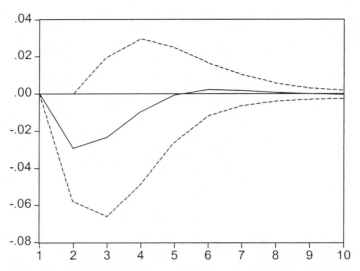

Fig. 2.9   Response of LOG(MOVCAMBIO_FIN_COMPRAS/PIB_USD) to Cholesky, one S.D. D(LOG(ICC)) innovation

capital inflows. Again, the exercise indicates that the effectiveness of inflow controls was temporary and lasted for around two to six months. Figure 2.10 shows the impulse response function of the capital inflow controls to an increase in capital inflows and it is also consistent with the findings on endogeneity of controls indicated by Cardoso and Goldfajn (1997). The third VAR will make even clearer the positive correlation between inflows and inflow controls.

Table 2.3 uses net investments through Annex IV as the capital flow measure. No series for capital inflows through this channel are available, but only data on the total portfolio value under Annex IV in the country. Therefore, in this VAR we used a logarithmic difference of the Annex IV portfolio as the measure of net capital inflow. As in our other estimations, we considered capital flows as a percentage of the GDP (D(LOG(CART_ANEXO4/PIB)). The other endogenous variables were the same as those of the previous estimations. As an exogenous variable, we used only one dummy for the Brazilian currency crisis because the other variables we adopted were not statistically significant in this exercise.

Once again, the impulse response function of the capital flow measure to a new capital inflow control measure (figure 2.11) indicated that restrictions on financial inflows were effective only temporarily. In the case of flows through Annex IV, the effect of the controls appears to be even more transitory, lasting only two to three months. Strikingly, most avoidance cases, as we saw in the previous section, continued using the Annex IV

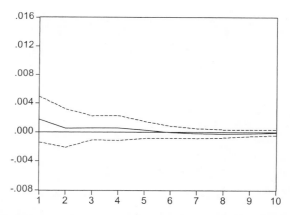

Fig.2.10   Response to Cholesky one S.D. innovations ± 2 S.E., response of D(LOG(ICC)) to LOG(MOVCAMBIO_FIN_COMPRAS/PIB_USD)

channel to invest so as to guarantee tax benefits. The impulse response function of figure 2.12 shows the authorities' reaction to the increase in Annex IV inflows. Greater capital inflows using this means led to tighter restrictions on capital inflows. This result shows the endogeneity of capital controls to capital inflows, consistent with the findings of Goldfajn and Cardoso (1997).

Therefore, the VAR exercises indicate that the controls on capital inflows were effective in reducing financial capital inflows only for short periods of time (two to six months). The probable cause of the limited duration of the restrictions' impact is avoidance of capital controls by the market, which continues to invest in the country without incurring in the capital controls' costs by renaming the type of investment made, or by conducting financial engineering operations.

In the next section, we document and analyze cases of avoidance of controls on capital inflows in Brazil. Outflow controls have also been frequently avoided since the 1980s through parallel (black) exchange rate markets, but our analysis focuses only on the effectiveness of controls on capital inflows.

The key point is that measures for controlling capital inflows are at best temporarily effective in containing and selecting capital inflows as financial agents have been able to dodge them in many different ways. The lesson to be learned is that in open and sophisticated capital markets, controls on capital inflows will probably be ineffective because the market has many alternative assets and transactions that can capture the desired return. In the following section, we discuss cases of circumvention and show a quantitative proof that this circumvention was at work. We do this by documenting the characteristic migration of capital inflows among Annex IV

Table 2.3 VAR 03—Capital flows through Annex IV Channel (vector autoregression estimates)

	LOG(REER_DESVIO2)	LOG(1+CIPD)	D(LOG(CART_ANEXO4/PIB_USD))	D(LOG(CC))
LOG(REER_DESVIO2(-1))	0.899085	-0.030183	0.423416	-0.040701
	-0.06799	-0.02438	-0.2035	-0.02269
	[13.2230]	[-1.23805]	[2.08071]	[-1.79397]
LOG(1+CIPD(-1))	-0.021034	0.987582	0.064443	0.139635
	-0.15871	-0.05691	-0.47501	-0.05296
	[-0.13252]	[17.3541]	[0.13567]	[2.63670]
D(LOG(CART_ANEXO4(-1)/PIB_USD(-1)))	-0.101546	-0.046076	-0.024486	0.027486
	-0.04225	-0.01515	-0.12646	-0.0141
	[-2.40343]	[-3.04149]	[-0.19364]	[1.94971]
D(LOG(ICC(-1)))	1.79E-05	-0.250229	-1.604453	0.00612
	-0.36086	-0.12939	-1.08001	-0.12041
	[5.0E-05]	[-1.93392]	[-1.48559]	[0.05083]
C	-0.004639	-0.001172	-0.003257	-0.013619
	-0.01232	-0.00442	-0.03686	-0.00411
DUM_BRASIL	0.036762	-0.001772	0.028608	-0.009482
	-0.01481	-0.00531	-0.04434	-0.00494
R^2	0.796892	0.858981	0.153832	0.163088
Adj. R^2	0.781269	0.848133	0.088742	0.09871
F-statistic	51.00551	79.1861	2.363378	2.53329
Determinant Residual Covariance		3.29E-13		
Log-likelihood (df adjusted)		617.3627		
AIC		-16.71444		
SC		-15.94959		

Notes: Sample period (adjusted): 1995:03 to 2001:01. No. of observations = 71, after adjusting endpoints. Standard errors are in parentheses and *t*-statistics are in brackets. AIC = Akaike Information Criteria. SC = Schwarz Criteria.

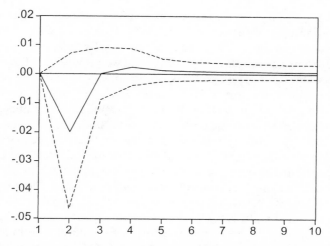

Fig. 2.11   Response to Cholesky one S.D. innovations ± 2 S.E., response of D(LOG(CART_ANEX04/PIB_USD) to D(LOG(ICC))

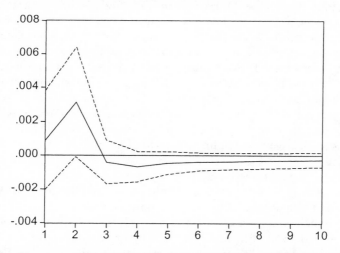

Fig. 2.12   Response of D(LOG(ICC)) to D(LOG(CART_ANEX04/PIB_USD)

items to avoid restrictions imposed on fixed income investments and the minimum terms for offshore funding.

2.4   Cases of Circumvention of Capital Inflow Controls in Brazil

Exchange rate and capital control legislation in Brazil, as previously noted, has a tradition of being highly complex and intricate. However, the Brazilian financial market is also quite sophisticated, particularly in derivatives trading.[16] The Futures and Commodities Exchange (BM&F) of São Paulo, for example, is one of the world's largest and most active derivatives exchange, comparable to the Chicago Mercantile Exchange. Furthermore, there are extensive derivatives trading abroad with underlying Brazilian instruments. One example is New York trading of Brazilian Real/U.S. Dollar NDFs (nondeliverable forwards). Derivatives allow traders to replicate financial strategies originally conceived with the underlying financial assets without the need to trade the underlying assets. For example, a box is a financial strategy involving only options that perfectly replicates a bond. The existence of derivatives makes the task of imposing capital controls much more burdensome. Because there was a well-established market for Brazilian financial instruments, including derivatives, there was, ipso facto, a variety of alternative instruments that made it possible to circumvent most capital controls.

Between 1993 and 1999, when investors were prohibited from investing in domestic Brazilian bonds through Annex IV of Resolution 1289 and charged a 5 percent to 9 percent IOF, there were many cases where this tax was avoided. The market found a range of methods for investing in fixed income and enjoying the tax benefits of Annex IV at very low cost. Even today, foreign investors have ways of avoiding the tax on fixed income returns, which is higher than the tax on returns in the equity market.[17]

In this section (and also in the appendix), we report numerous cases of capital controls avoidance in Brazil between 1993 and 2000, illustrating how difficult de facto application of capital controls actually is. We show that de jure imposition of restrictions in this period did not effectively contain capital inflows seeking short-term, tax exempt return on fixed income, nor was it effective in extending the term of foreign investments on fixed income.

Garber (1998) addressed the issue of how offshore derivatives trading may be used to bypass domestic controls. Garcia and Barcinski (1998) and Garcia and Valpassos (2000) analyzed how avoidance of capital controls impacted their effectiveness in restricting and selecting financial flows, and they reported a few of the methods used to circumvent controls in Brazil. Nadal-de-Simone and Sorsa (1999) concluded that the capital controls in Chile in the 1990s were only temporarily effective in restricting short-term capital due to capital control circumvention. Edwards, Valdés, and De Gregorio (2000) concluded that Chile's capital controls effectively changed the composition of capital inflows, increasing the inflows of long-term cap-

16. Years of crowding out and hyperinflation created both a hypertrophy of expertise in fixed income (short-term) and derivatives trading and a hypotrophy of credit granted by financial intermediaries.

17. Foreign investors do not necessarily reside outside Brazil. Brazilian financial institutions generally have offices abroad designed to obtain tax benefits given to foreign capital and also to shield against border risk, or restrictions of capital outflows.

ital, but they cast doubt on the reliability of this result, which could have been distorted given that short-term flows could have been labeled as long-term capital flows, that is to say, effectively bypassing the country's capital controls. Forbes (2004) noted that small- and medium-sized companies in Chile were more burdened by the higher cost of capital than were large ones because the latter had access to financial transactions on the international market that would enable them to avoid Chilean capital controls.

In this article we take a more in-depth look at capital controls avoidance practices in Brazil based on a field study involving members of the financial market, who offered extensive help in collecting information about what agents did in Brazil to avoid controls on capital inflows between 1993 and 2000.

The large majority of transactions reported was legal and merely took advantage of loopholes in the intricate exchange rate legislation. They included renaming as long-term flows that were ultimately directed at short-term rate investments. However, they were officially accounted on the balance of payments as flows destined for other purposes. For example, many flows were identified as "privatization money," which in theory would go to finance privatization programs; short-term capital was disguised as FDIs, which were not taxed; resources were declared as equity investments when in fact they were used to obtain fixed income return, and so on. In the following we will provide further details of these forms of circumvention.

The central idea is that financial agents were able to use a variety of means to bypass capital controls. The major restriction was prohibition of fixed income investments through Annex IV of Resolution 1289, which carried tax exemption rights, as we reported in the previous section. There were also numerous restrictions for minimum terms for amortizing overseas loans.

Prohibition of fixed income investments through Annex IV is the equivalent of charging an inflow tax τ that imposes a cost equal to the loss of tax benefits of investing in fixed income by other means. During the period, agents could invest in fixed income in Brazil through mutual funds specifically established for such, which were subject to an IOF tax of 5 percent to 9 percent. Hence, the official τ was the IOF.

However, the de facto cost for the short-term investor was the cost of circumventing the control, or τ^*, which was certainly less than he or she would lose by not investing in fixed income through Annex IV. It follows that the actual cost incurred by the investor due to the capital control is $\tau^* = \min \{\tau, \text{cost of circumventing inflow control}\}$.

Let us examine a few of the circumvention methods reported.[18]

---

18. The methods of passing capital controls were collected by the authors during interviews with Brazilian financial market players. The authors do not have information on who conducted them or even if they actually took place.

2.4.1   Disguising Short-Term Investments
        as Long-Term, Equity, or Trade Finance

Case 1: Disguise Short-Term Capital as Foreign Direct Investment

Foreign direct investment is considered to be the best form of capital flow to the receiving country because it is closely associated with investing in fixed capital and the transfer of technology and, consequently, with expansion of the potential GDP and employment. It is also thought to be the least fungible because compared to portfolio investments it is less reversible and has a longer investment horizon. Many articles do argue that portfolio investments tend to be less stable than direct investments because portfolio investments can be reversed more easily than real assets can be liquidated (Dixit and Pyndick 1994; Frankel and Rose 1996; Dornbusch 1998). Thus, direct investments would be less linked to capital flight. For these reasons, capital flow regulation commonly handles direct investments differently than portfolio investments.

Notwithstanding, in an environment of capital controls, when in general the flow of direct investments wanes, market agents tend to take advantage of this loophole in exchange rate legislation to disguise their short-term investments or loans as direct investments, thus bypassing the restrictions imposed. In Chile during 1996 through 1998, for example, what the Central Bank designated "Potentially Speculative Direct Investment" was also subject to *encaje,* that is to say, to Chile's prevailing capital controls. This was because between 1991 and 1996, when Chile required nonremunerated deposits of 10 percent to 30 percent for one year for short-term investments and foreign loans, many agents were found to circumvent the restriction by (inappropriately) identifying their flows as direct investments.

In Brazil, we reviewed a transaction, likely to be used even today, designed to disguise short-term capital as direct investment. The transaction has a simple structure.

At that time, investing in fixed income through Annex IV was restricted, but the channel was open for equity investments, and there were tax benefits for direct investments. Financial intermediaries could use the transaction to take advantage of these two loopholes.

The financial intermediary would create a public corporation (S.A.) and list its shares on the São Paulo Stock Exchange (BOVESPA). The company was strictly a legal entity and had no physical activity. Because the financial intermediary held all the company's shares, it could manipulate their price by arranging purchase and sell transactions with low liquidity. The price was completely artificial. The financial intermediary, having capital outside the country, would invest in the company as a foreign investor and declare this flow as direct investment. It acquired over 50 percent of the shares and subsequently conducted intercompany loans, considered FDIs. This money, then, as the company only existed on paper, would be invested in short-term fixed income. Returns would go to the company and be sent abroad as profit or dividends. Thus, Annex IV restrictions did not apply, even though the objective was short-term returns from the high interest rates of the day.

The cost of establishing this investment in short-term fixed income as a direct investment was quite low. Given the scale of capital invested, the cost of opening an S.A. corporation and listing its shares on the exchange was negligible. The agent's cost to come into the country, the aforementioned τ^*, was fixed and much lower than the official tax.[19] The financial intermediary's only expenses were for opening the corporation at the beginning of the operation. Subsequent investments had no inflow costs, meaning τ^* was equal to zero. The outflow costs were determined by legislation governing profit and dividend taxing of foreign companies, which have been much more advantageous for investors than taxing of portfolio investment gains. In fact, profit from foreign capital previously invested and declared in Brazil is exempt from taxes.

Case 2: Labeling Fixed Income Investments as Equity Investments

As noted in the preceding, the control on Annex IV capital inflows applied to fixed income investments. However, equity investments were not restricted because growth of the stock market was believed to lead to greater investment capacity for the companies and to contribute to the economy's expansion. Obviously, the market then sought to use the stock market to gain the coveted returns from the high Brazilian interest rates.

This Case 2 and the following Case 3 refer to avoidance of capital controls through the stock market. Case 2 involves a transaction that also takes advantage of the structure of the S.A. corporation in Case 1.

To bypass restrictions on fixed income investments via the securities market, the financial intermediary in Case 1 could use the corporation already created. The financial intermediary would then invest in the shares of that corporation. The means used would be the Annex IV channel for investments in the BOVESPA, which were permitted at that time and still today provide tax benefits for fixed income investments. Thus, the financial intermediary invested his offshore capital like a foreign investor in the BOVESPA by purchasing shares of the company he had opened. The amount paid for the shares was invested in fixed income and the returns remitted abroad as dividends or capital gains. Note that the financial in-

---

19. The cost of opening a joint-stock (S.A.) company and listing its shares on the exchange, without considering programs for attracting investors (contracting banks to manage the I.P.O., press, advertising, etc.) in 2005, is between US$20,000 and US$100,000. If the financial intermediary used this avoidance strategy to invest US$10 million in fixed income, it would already have saved, in the period when the IOF tax applied, at least US$500,000 in IOF (5 percent) expenses. The volume invested through this avoidance strategy can be much greater than US$10 million so that τ^* could become negligible.

termediary could also manipulate the company's share prices because it owned a 100 percent stake. Therefore, the investor declared equity investments while capturing the returns of fixed income.

Again the actual cost of the capital inflow in this case, the τ^*, was only the cost of opening the S.A. corporation and listing its shares on the exchange. The cost was low compared to the financial volume invested, and it was also diluted as the investor invested, free of taxes, for several years. We can thus consider that τ^* was fixed and much lower than the official τ.

The descriptions of Case 1 and Case 2 depict two similar methods of avoiding the restriction on gains from the short-term interest rate in Brazil between 1993 and 2000. The person interviewed did not, however, wish to go into great detail, but rather offered a general overview. For the third form of circumvention, which we will elaborate in the following, we were able to gather more details. It also involves disguising fixed income investment flows as equity investments in order to take advantage of the tax exemption provided for in Annex IV.

Case 3: ACC and Trading Companies

To control excessive capital inflows into Brazil, especially between 1993 and 1996, many restrictions on raising external resources were imposed. The prohibition of foreign investments in fixed income under Annex IV, for example, made it more difficult to raise funds, as loaning resources at fixed interest rates the investor had to pay the IOF tax because the Annex IV channel was prohibited. Moreover, minimum terms were required for beginning loan amortization, meaning there were restrictions on short-term loans. For example, in January 1993, a minimum period of ninety-six months was established for beginning amortization for principal and interest payments to be exempted from taxes.

At the same time, the use of ACCs for exports allowed for financing of less than 360 days. The exporter could close an ACC up to one year before shipping merchandise. Theoretically, the ACC was exclusively for financing exports, and financing by this means required a physical outflow of exports associated with the contract to demonstrate that the loan had in fact been used to finance foreign trade. The market soon saw in this legislation a way to get short-term loans, which additionally carried tax benefits.

The interest rate for ACC funds was normally less than the CDI, the short-term-benchmark interest rate in Brazil. This occurred because loans were less heavily taxed and because foreign investors seeking high return in Brazil offered capital at interest rates below the country's base rate due to restrictions on other investment means. Furthermore, financing foreign trade generally carries relatively low risk as most loans are released only after the export contract has been signed, and the exports serve as collateral.

Therefore, ACCs constituted a means of getting short-term loans with tax benefits and interest rates below the Interbank Certificate of Deposit (CDI). This was another opportunity that the Brazilian financial market players eagerly grabbed. The restriction a financial investor had to circumvent to raise funds via ACCs was demonstrating that the financing was associated with merchandise exports. An agent had a one-year period after signing an ACC to ship the financed export product.

The financial investor, of course, was not planning to use the resources to finance exports, so he had no product to ship. Exporters conducting foreign trade without ACCs, who did not use export financing, began selling their ACC rights to foreign investors. An ACC would then be signed to finance a specific export, but the capital would actually go to a financial investor who had purchased the exporter's right.

In this way, investors made short-term investments at rates below the CDI using the ACCs and were able to provide export documentation. Some exporters would pass this credit on to investors. In fact, until 2000 there was an underground market for export credits, that is to say, a parallel market developed for trading export documentation. An investor could simply make a loan to himself (disguised as an ACC, a loan to a Brazilian exporter) and buy this export documentation on the aforementioned market. A few banks even established trading companies, which specialized in financing foreign trade, to be able to better undertake this capital control avoidance strategy. These trading companies would contract ACC loans and then legalize the loan on the parallel market for trading ACC documentation. Because the financing cost was less than the CDI, a bank could close an ACC to finance its margin deposit on the BM&F (interest rate derivatives) or the overnight market and capture good returns with these standard operations. However, the money that theoretically was destined for financing foreign trade was actually invested in short-term fixed income investments. This is an important example of how difficult it is to apply, de facto, capital controls.

This means of avoidance only decreased with the liberalization of fixed income investments and of the loan terms for foreign borrowing. Still today, though, financial market players consider ACCs a way to negotiate better interest rates as the cost is less than the economy's base interest rate. Therefore, there are clear indications that this avoidance strategy would be widely adopted if new restrictions on short-term capital were imposed, such as applying an IOF tax on investments provided for in Resolution 2689. Because Brazilian exports increased remarkably in the recent years, this would pose an even larger hurdle to the effectiveness of capital controls nowadays.

The capital inflow cost, the τ^*, was the amount required to build a financial and legal structure for implementing this method of avoidance. The cost is minimal for a large, functioning bank, which additionally was compensated by using funds borrowed at less than CDI rates and invested on the overnight market. Thus, depending on the financial volume, τ^* could be negative.

2.4.2   Using Sophisticated Financial Engineering (Derivatives) to Avoid Controls

Case 4: Development of the International Derivatives Market: Avoiding Convertibility Risks

An increasingly common method used by international financial markets to avoid imperfect capital mobility in emerging countries (capital controls, risk of additional controls, and convertibility risks) involves foreign derivatives over-the-counter operations, most notably in New York. Foreign investors trade local assets but without exposing themselves to the risks and costs of actually moving resources into the country.

A classic example is the trading of Real against the U.S. Dollar futures in New York, the currency NDFs. By trading this asset in New York rather than on the BM&F in São Paulo, the foreign investor avoided all capital controls and convertibility risks.

Garber (1998) analyzes the development of the international derivatives market and its impacts on capital flows and reports diverse ways that financial intermediaries circumvented regulations on credit risk using derivatives overseas. He also points out the possible role of these offshore operations in avoiding capital controls.

In recent years, the international derivatives market has substantially developed. One of the main engines of this transnational market is capital controls and currency convertibility risk in emerging market countries. They offer assets with greater volatility, which therefore have greater potential return, but the associated border risks hamper investing in the countries. Because the market wants to trade with them, it has developed international markets designed to avoid restrictions on capital mobility. The idea is to break down the risks involved so that one can pick and choose which risks one wants, with the corresponding returns.

Case 5: Investing through Box Operations: Strategies with Options for Earning Fixed Income Returns

Initially, the Annex IV restriction only applied to fixed income investments. Other types of investments, such as in securities and derivatives, could still use this channel. The market was able to use these types of investments to profit from Brazil's short-term interest rates. Cases 2 and 3 were methods of circumventing the control via the stock market. Another commonly used method was to use the derivatives market adopting options strategies that guaranteed fixed return, as we are about to see.

An operation was conducted that was known as a box consisting of four options, two calls and two puts, with the price on the established strike date fixed. By a nonarbitrage argument, it is shown that box return must be equal to the benchmark interest rate in Brazil's case, the CDI.[20] A box is, therefore, a financial strategy involving options that is akin to a loan.[21]

Because derivatives investments were not restricted, the market began conducting Box operations on the BM&F and the BOVESPA to capture the return of Brazil's high base interest rates. This lasted until the Central Bank detected this market movement and subjected box operations to the same regulations that applied to fixed income investments.

The box strategy actually went further than avoiding foreign capital controls: it also aimed at saving on taxes levied on domestic fixed income investments. Instead of using traditional means, like investing in government bonds, many agents began conducting box operations on the BM&F and BOVESPA to earn fixed returns and bypass Brazil's internal revenue service's (Secretaria da Receita Federal [SRF]) regulations. This form of tax avoidance ended when the SRF detected the loophole in the legislation and imposed the IOF tax on box transactions as well. However, many agents were still able to disguise their box operations.

The cost of avoiding capital controls using the box strategy, the τ^*, is only the cost of conducting the option transactions on an exchange. The operation itself has no more cost than traditional fixed income investments because the difference between earnings from the buying and selling of the puts and calls is the amount invested. The cost difference may be only the brokerage fee charged by the financial agents, which is minimal in light of the volume invested. We can consider, then, that τ^* in this case is equal to zero. Therefore, this legislation loophole rendered the capital control completely ineffective.

Case 6: Increased Eurobond Issues with Embedded
Options for Bypassing the Minimum Loan Term

In August of 1995, the government set a 5 percent IOF tax on foreign loans in order to avoid excessive capital inflows. In September of the same year, the government changed the legislation in an effort to encourage long-term loans, establishing a sliding IOF according to the loan term. For up to two years, the tax was 5 percent, up to three years, 4 percent; four years, 2 percent; five years, 1 percent; and six years or more, 0 percent.

The market soon perceived in this legislation a chance for circumventing the restriction: it began raising funds through issues of long term bonds (over six years), but with embedded put option clauses. This meant the foreign creditor could shorten the loan term by exercising the option. In practice, therefore, the loan was short term.

---

20. The CDI is the base overnight interest rate for transactions between financial institutions.
21. See Hull (2005) for further explanations about box option strategy.

The government then began to levy a retroactive IOF if the option was exercised, and the borrower had to reverse the capital brought into the country within six years. Those interviewed in our field research stated that it was still advantageous to issue a six-year bond with a put option exercisable within one year, even with the retroactive IOF, because this did not eliminate the transaction's gains.

This case illustrates the difficulty of implementing, in practice, controls on capital inflows. It is an example of a contract subject to capital control taxes that encourages the short-term investor to disguise his investments as long term while planning to recover the investment before it matures.

Because the intent of capital controls was to deter excess volatility of capital flows, the renaming of actual short-term flows as long term would seriously jeopardize it. After all, if the status quo that prevailed when the investment was first made continued to hold, the short-term capital would, ex post, become a long-term investment. This appears to have been the case of Chile (Edwards, Valdés, and De Gregorio 2000). However, if conditions changed, and the carry-trade strategy no longer seemed to be a good deal, funds would be sent back home. The IOF tax would not be sufficient to keep the funds in the country if devaluation or default became very likely. For example, a 5 percent IOF tax would be sufficient to counterbalance a devaluation of only 10 percent within a year with a 50 percent probability. After the Asian crisis, the odds for devaluation were certainly much higher than those, which explained why it was worth it to issue a six-year bond and exercise the option, paying the IOF tax retroactively, if the scenario changed. Carvalho (2005) develops a simple dynamic model that shows that the tax rates necessary to deter capital outflows if a confidence or currency crisis became likely would be too high to be implemented.

Case 7: Back-to-Back Operations: Blue Chip Swaps and CC-5 Transactions for Avoiding the IOF on Exchange Rate Transactions

In August of 1995, the government tightened capital controls in an attempt to contain excessive financial capital inflows, especially short term. It raised the IOF tax on foreign capital fixed income funds from 5 percent to 7 percent, raised the IOF on overseas loans from 0 percent to 5 percent, prohibited foreign investments in the domestic derivatives market,[22] and established a 7 percent IOF on operations between institutions in the country and overseas through the floating rate exchange market.

The market avoided the IOF on fixed income investments by engineer-

22. The complete prohibition of foreign investors to access domestic derivative markets was the logical culmination of the process that started with the tax on box operations, described in the preceding. After all, there is a theorem in finance that states that any return may be reproduced by option trading if enough options are available. Therefore, taxing one strategy, as the box, would only make the market move to another, still untaxed, one with quite similar results.

ing financial operations like those previously described. But the IOF on operations between domestic and international institutions drove the market to find other loopholes in the exchange rate legislation: they found what they were looking for in the famous CC-5 accounts.

The accounts of nonresidents created by the Central Bank under circular number 5 in 1969 were a resource for facilitating the flow of foreign capital. The CC-5 allowed a nonresident institution to hold an account in Brazil in national currency with greater ease to send funds outside the country. In 1992, the CC-5 was overhauled, giving this channel greater freedom implying higher capital account convertibility. With this new structure, the CC-5 deposit could be freely remitted through the MCTF. Moreover, third-party deposits could be made to the account, which meant third parties then began to make international transfers through the CC-5 account. This type of transfer became known later as the "International Transfer of Reais" (TIR).

Until March of 2005, to send money abroad unilaterally, a resident had to deposit it in the CC-5 of a financial institution residing outside Brazil, then this institution would transfer it to his bank in Brazil, convert it into foreign currency, and send it overseas. The nonresident financial institution was usually an overseas branch of the domestic institution. With changes effected in March of 2005, the resident can now deposit the money directly in his bank. This simplification meant lower transaction costs and greater transparency on transfers.

Figure 2.13 shows the movement of transfers through the CC-5 from January 1993 until 2004. It also contains the covered interest parity differential, which is a measure of country risk. During periods of higher capital inflows to Brazil, even net inflows of capital through the CC-5 occurred, as in 1995 through 1996.[23] In the exchange rate band period (1995 to 1999), the CC-5 channel was more heavily used to send resources abroad. This is associated with the greater restrictions on capital during this period and with the economic turbulence that shook the Brazilian economy, namely the crisis in Asia and the crisis in Brazil itself.

The IOF established in August of 1995 on international transactions between financial institutions was assessed at the time of the exchange rate transaction (like a Tobin tax). So to bypass this tax, the market sought ways to avoid converting currency. One of these was what was called at the time a "Blue Chip Swap." This involved a foreign asset that the investor would transfer to the offshore branch of a Brazilian financial institution against a CC-5 credit of the investor in Brazil. The foreign investor delivered the foreign asset, and the domestic counterpart made the deposit in Brazil in the foreign agent's CC-5 account. Through the CC-5, the foreign investor had

23. As figure 2.4 clearly shows, the CC-5 net balance was clearly one of net transfers abroad. Of course, gross flows occurred both ways.

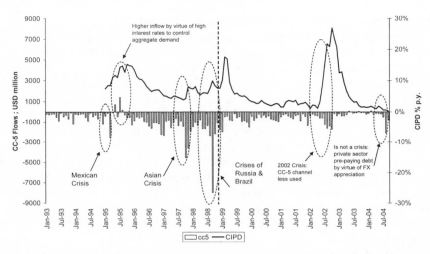

Fig. 2.13   Capital flows through CC-5 and covered interest parity differential (CIPD)
Source: Banco Central do Brasil (all years), Brazilian Mercantile and Futures Exchange (BM&&F), and authors' calculations.

free access to the MCTF and sent the money abroad without restrictions when the operation was finalized. With this, international transactions between financial institutions bypassed the IOF tax by not officially converting currency.

These operations involving unofficial currency exchange, in defiance of the Central Bank's monopoly, were known as back-to-back operations. The Blue Chip Swap is one example of this type of operation.[24]

2.4.3   Disguising Short-Term Investments as Equity and Using Sophisticated Financial Engineering (Derivatives) to Avoid Controls

Case 8: Labeling Fixed Income Investments as Equity Investments II: Share Loans in Brazil and Swaps Abroad

The operation described in Case 3 is designed for a domestic financial intermediary that also seeks to offer offshore mutual funds to foreign investors. In truth, these foreign investors could include Brazilians with non-declared resources abroad or those seeking to capture the advantages extended to nonresidents of investing in fixed income in Brazil.

The Brazilian financial intermediary would offer its offshore clients a

---

24. Back-to-back operations are also mentioned as a capital control's circumvention method in other countries. For example, an Argentinean journal (*Ambito Financiero*) published on December 22, 2006 states that the tax charged by the money changers for a simple back-to-back operation was at an unusual rate: 1.25 percent to those willing to have dollars in Argentina and 1.5 percent to those seeking to take them out.

mutual fund in a tax haven that profited from Brazil's short-term interest rates. In theory, using Annex IV to this end was prohibited due to the capital controls. So the financial intermediary engineered a financial transaction that enabled it to invest in fixed income via Annex IV, avoiding the restriction. With this operation, the financial intermediary was also able to save on taxes on the institution's profit in Brazil.

The strategy basically involved the financial intermediary borrowing a company's shares that had low liquidity on the BOVESPA, selling them in a buyback agreement with a foreign investor who entered under Annex IV, then conducting a swap outside the country with this investor to exchange returns. If it so desired, rather than borrowing illiquid shares, the financial intermediary could create a publicly held corporation, as in Cases 1 and 2.

Let us examine the case more thoroughly with the help of figures 2.14, 2.15 and 2.16. In figure 2.14 we present the operation's agents: Bank X, which was Brazilian, had a branch in the Cayman Islands and wanted to offer an offshore mutual fund that earned the returns of Brazil's short-term interest rate and whose quota holders were investors with foreign capital. The branch of Bank X in the tax haven managed this offshore fund, which invested in Brazilian fixed income.

To move the fund's capital into Brazil, an Annex IV Portfolio for equity investments was opened, and it was managed by the securities dealer (DTVM) of Bank X with headquarters in Brazil. With this, the agent of the Annex IV Portfolio was the domestic securities dealer, as required by legislation at that time. Investments regulated by Annex IV of Resolution 1289 had to be made according to this procedure, where a qualified do-

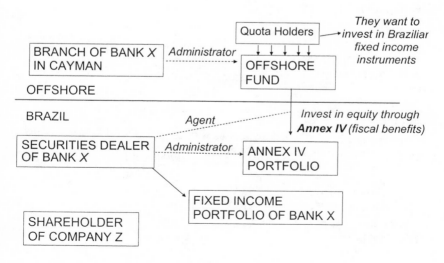

Fig. 2.14   Circumvention Case 3: Actors

mestic financial institution was the agent of the foreign investor's investment portfolio.

The securities dealer of Bank X also retained its own portfolio for investments in fixed income, legally independent of this Annex IV Portfolio. The national resources of Bank X were allocated to this fixed income portfolio to capture the returns of the high domestic interest rate.

The bank also borrowed the shares of a company whose shares were listed on the BOVESPA and had very little liquidity. It's worth highlighting that this was a company that did exist physically, not one created solely for financial transactions. Illiquidity was key to prevent sudden price moves.

In figure 2.15 we present the beginning of the transactions, which we divide into two steps. The second part of the transaction is illustrated in figure 2.16.

(1) The offshore fund invested in its Annex IV Portfolio declaring its objective was obtaining returns on equity investments, which was permitted and had tax benefits. (2) The securities dealer of Bank X borrowed the company's shares, which we will call Z, and (3) sold them through a buyback agreement after a specified period of time to the Annex IV Portfolio of the offshore fund. The buyback agreement established the deadline for recovering the sale of the shares and stipulated that the buyback would be based on the share price on the day the contract expired. (4) The money from the sale of the shares loaned to foreign investors was invested by the securities dealer in its own fixed income portfolio.

The foreign investor, then, brought his resources into the country via Annex IV and transferred them to the securities dealer by purchasing the shares of Company Z. The securities dealer then invested this money in the overnight interest rate.

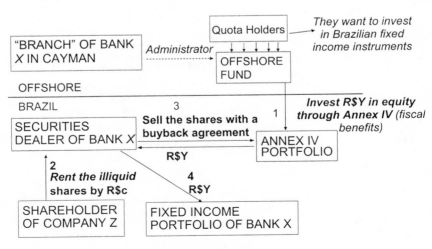

Fig. 2.15   Circumvention Case 3: Operations ($t = 1$)

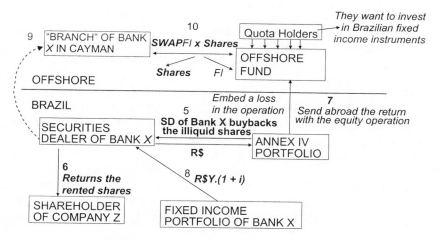

Fig. 2.16   Circumvention Case 3: Operations ($t = 2$)

Figure 2.16 illustrates the operation's unwinding.

(5) The buyback agreement was then settled. The Annex IV Portfolio resold the shares to the bank's securities dealer, but because the shares had very low liquidity, their prices were easily manipulated. The bank drove the share price up and repurchased them at a price higher than that at which he had sold them to the foreign investors. All players on the financial market know that the main rule is "buy low and sell high," but in this case, the bank preferred to sell low and buy high. There was a reason for this: it enabled him to embed a loss for the securities dealer in this operation, reducing his profits. Bank X would then save on Brazilian taxes due to the dealer's profit, and as we shall see, recover the loss in Cayman through the derivatives market.

(6) After buying back the loaned shares, the securities dealer returned them to the Company Z shareholder who had entered into the loan agreement. (7) The return made by the Annex IV Portfolio of the foreign investors on the share purchase operation was sent abroad legally through Annex IV as it was gained on the stock market.

(8) The securities dealer obtained the returns of its fixed income portfolio. (9) The dealer then nationalized the money in its Cayman branch, which was perfectly legal. The amount sent to the tax haven was equal to the principal plus interest earned by the fixed income portfolio, that is, the amount desired by the offshore fund offered by the Bank X branch in Cayman.

So the return the offshore fund desires was still with the Bank X branch in Cayman, and the loss incurred by Bank X in the share transaction was passed as the profit of the offshore fund. (10) To finalize the operation and meet its objectives, the bank conducted a swap in Cayman between its branch and the offshore fund, where they exchanged the gains from the share transaction with the fixed income returns. The swap's underlying instruments were the difference between the price of Company Z shares on the BOVESPA and the return on the Brazilian fixed rates, so the fixed income return went to the fund and the profit from the share transaction went to the branch of Bank X.

When concluded, the foreign investors had the fixed income returns and Bank X had saved on Brazilian taxes. The capital inflow cost incurred by this circumvention method, the τ^*, was only the price of borrowing the shares and conducting the swap abroad, plus that of the bank to nationalize the money in its Cayman branch. The latter two items have virtually no cost, so that τ^* is only the cost of the share loan. But because the bank saved on taxes, τ^* could actually be negative as the tax savings offset the cost of the share loan. This strategy provides a clever example of how regular corporate income taxes could also be avoided through a financial operation originally designed to avoid capital controls.

2.5   Conclusion of Cases of Capital Controls Circumvention

In the preceding section, we have presented diverse strategies for circumventing controls on capital inflows in Brazil in the 1990s. Most strategies were designed to avoid the IOF tax on fixed income investments that was imposed with the prohibition of investments in government bonds using the Annex IV channel although we also reviewed cases with strategies for bypassing the IOF on foreign exchange transactions and the minimum terms for foreign loans.

Controls on capital inflows in Brazil varied based on two factors: the amount of capital inflows and the means the market found to bypass restrictions.

The first point was addressed by Cardoso and Goldfajn (1997), who pointed out the endogeneity of capital controls in Brazil. In periods of heavy capital inflows, restrictions were placed on the capital inflows, and in periods of scarce foreign financing, the controls were lifted so as to attract foreign capital.

The second point was addressed in Garcia and Barcinski (1998) and in Garcia and Valpassos (2000), who pointed out the consecutive changes in legislation aimed at closing the loopholes the market found for circumventing restrictions. In fact, analyzing the composition of the total portfolio of Annex IV investments, one readily perceives the game of "cat and mouse" underway between the Central Bank/CMN and the financial market.

Table 2.4 shows the composition of the total portfolio of Annex IV investments from January 1993 until mid 2004 (since 1999, these investments have actually been governed by Resolution 2689).

Between January 1993 and August 1993, the "Others" item in the table accounted for around 15 percent to 25 percent of total investment. This item contained investments in government bonds that were destined for

Table 2.4　　　　　**Composition of Annex IV Channel for financial inflow**

	Annex IV Composition (% total)						
	Portfolio value (in US$ billions)	Equity (%)	Derivatives (%)	Debentures (%)	Privatization currency (%)	Others (%)	Fixed income (%)
Jan. 1993	2.37	82.50	0.00	2.30	0.00	15.20	
Feb. 1993	2.35	73.90	0.00	4.80	0.80	20.50	
Mar. 1993	2.49	85.00	0.00	0.30	1.50	13.20	
Apr. 1993	3.42	79.00	0.00	3.80	0.10	17.10	
May 1993	4.05	80.00	0.00	2.20	0.10	17.70	
June 1993	4.83	82.60	0.00	2.70	0.10	14.60	
July 1993	5.15	73.50	0.00	4.80	0.10	21.60	
Aug. 1993	6.88	70.30	0.00	4.00	0.50	25.20	
Sept. 1993	6.76	77.20	0.00	19.00	2.60	1.20	
Oct. 1993	7.45	68.20	0.00	29.30	1.60	0.90	
Nov. 1993	8.96	65.20	0.00	33.60	0.90	0.30	
Dec. 1993	10.38	80.10	0.00	18.50	1.10	0.30	
Jan. 1994	12.12	82.50	0.00	15.90	1.40	0.20	
Feb. 1994	13.23	83.32	0.00	14.14	2.33	0.21	
Mar. 1994	14.51	78.26	4.93	13.31	3.40	0.10	
Apr. 1994	12.83	75.32	4.19	15.97	4.44	0.08	
May 1994	12.97	67.90	7.60	16.10	8.33	0.07	
June 1994	13.57	66.68	8.60	15.16	9.49	0.07	
July 1994	16.15	70.99	5.66	15.12	7.84	0.39	
Aug. 1994	21.31	73.40	5.40	11.20	5.20	4.80	
Sept. 1994	21.61	78.10	3.20	12.30	5.00	1.40	
Oct. 1994	20.77	77.35	4.06	12.72	5.13	0.74	
Nov. 1994	21.83	78.62	4.02	11.15	5.56	0.65	
Dec. 1994	20.97	77.54	3.85	12.41	5.41	0.79	
Jan. 1995	17.84	76.69	1.95	13.93	5.86	1.57	
Feb. 1995	15.76	77.44	3.20	12.20	6.20	0.96	
Mar. 1995	13.30	82.77	1.43	8.43	4.26	3.11	
Apr. 1995	15.08	84.87	2.32	6.80	5.24	0.77	
May 1995	16.99	85.84	1.24	7.89	4.39	0.64	
June 1995	16.92	85.19	2.13	7.61	4.42	0.65	
July 1995	18.58	84.78	2.96	7.57	4.12	0.57	
Aug. 1995	20.63	86.46	3.19	5.94	3.75	0.66	
Sept. 1995	19.75	86.35	3.01	6.02	4.12	0.50	
Oct. 1995	18.97	86.51	1.89	7.22	3.79	0.58	
Nov. 1995	18.81	88.95	0.66	4.95	3.72	1.72	
Dec. 1995	18.65	89.46	1.09	5.54	3.68	0.23	
Jan. 1996	20.29	90.84	0.04	4.72	3.52	0.88	
Feb. 1996	20.33	90.33	0.04	4.46	4.14	1.03	
Mar. 1996	19.27	89.79	0.09	4.75	4.32	1.05	
Apr. 1996	19.77	89.16	0.09	5.64	3.92	1.19	
May 1996	21.21	90.09	0.05	5.66	3.48	0.72	
June 1996	23.33	91.11	0.03	4.48	3.21	1.17	
July 1996	23.28	90.22	0.00	5.65	3.59	0.54	
Aug. 1996	24.07	90.51	0.00	5.52	3.45	0.52	
Sept. 1996	25.03	91.06	0.00	5.63	3.19	0.12	
Oct. 1996	25.71	91.22	0.00	5.58	3.27	−0.07	

(continued)

Table 2.4   (continued)

	Annex IV Composition (% total)					
	Portfolio value (in US$ billions)	Equity (%)	Derivatives (%)	Debentures (%)	Privatization currency (%)	Others (%)	Fixed income (%)
Nov. 1996	26.63	91.53	0.00	5.50	3.20	−0.23	
Dec. 1996	28.16	91.96	0.00	5.72	2.79	−0.47	
Jan. 1997	31.71	92.58	0.00	4.85	2.11	0.46	
Feb. 1997	34.75	93.06	0.00	4.45	1.94	0.55	
Mar. 1997	36.35	93.30	0.00	4.32	1.88	0.50	
Apr. 1997	38.89	94.21	0.00	3.65	1.74	0.40	
May 1997	40.94	94.85	0.00	3.29	0.19	1.67	
June 1997	46.03	95.16	0.93	2.99	0.92	0.00	
July 1997	49.89	95.47	0.69	3.00	0.84	0.00	
Aug. 1997	42.64	94.79	0.63	3.71	0.87	0.00	
Sept. 1997	46.11	95.24	0.56	3.37	0.83	0.00	
Oct. 1997	35.56	94.43	0.88	4.00	0.69	0.00	
Nov. 1997	34.73	95.67	0.52	3.08	0.72	0.01	
Dec. 1997	35.78	96.46	1.39	2.12	0.00	0.03	
Jan. 1998	29.19	95.75	1.93	2.28	0.03	0.01	
Feb. 1998	30.90	96.38	1.48	2.11	0.03	0.00	
Mar. 1998	34.87	97.30	1.27	1.40	0.02	0.00	
Apr. 1998	35.31	96.49	2.04	1.45	0.02	0.00	
May 1998	30.06	96.67	1.57	1.73	0.03	0.00	
June 1998	28.72	96.50	1.57	1.73	0.03	0.17	
July 1998	30.97	96.69	1.66	1.62	0.03	0.00	
Aug. 1998	20.21	94.57	2.53	2.86	0.04	0.01	
Sept. 1998	17.21	95.25	3.48	1.22	0.05	0.00	
Oct. 1998	18.00	95.49	3.37	1.11	0.04	0.00	
Nov. 1998	21.42	96.84	2.30	0.83	0.03	0.00	
Dec. 1998	17.37	94.80	4.16	1.00	0.04	0.00	
Jan. 1999	11.85	94.90	3.85	0.81	0.00	0.43	
Feb. 1999	11.83	95.50	3.59	0.71	0.07	0.13	
Mar. 1999	16.02	97.60	1.61	0.50	0.10	0.10	
Apr. 1999	18.04	97.90	1.42	0.46	0.20	0.03	
May 1999	17.54	98.40	0.90	0.52	0.20	−0.02	
June 1999	18.23	98.76	0.23	0.72	0.29	0.00	
July 1999	17.09	98.95	0.19	0.69	0.15	0.02	
Aug. 1999	15.90	98.72	0.02	0.92	0.10	0.24	
Sept. 1999	17.51	98.72	0.02	0.87	0.30	0.10	
Oct. 1999	17.79	98.70	0.08	0.83	0.28	0.11	
Nov. 1999	20.00	98.77	0.09	0.81	0.20	0.13	
Dec. 1999	23.11	98.98	0.04	0.82	0.02	0.14	
Jan. 2000	22.32	98.48	0.09	1.17	0.01	0.25	
Feb. 2000	22.95	98.49	0.07	1.26	0.01	0.17	
Mar. 2000	23.10	98.44	0.06	1.29	0.01	0.20	
Apr. 2000	22.45	96.83	0.05	1.36	0.01	−0.01	1.76
May 2000	20.05	96.42	0.11	1.19	0.01	−0.01	2.28
June 2000	23.07	94.13	0.10	1.15	0.01	0.01	4.61
July 2000	23.58	91.63	0.05	1.24	0.01	0.45	6.62
Aug. 2000	23.61	92.67	0.13	1.23	0.01	0.19	5.77

Table 2.4   (continued)

	Annex IV Composition (% total)					
	Portfolio value (in US$ billions)	Equity (%)	Derivatives (%)	Debentures (%)	Privatization currency (%)	Others (%)	Fixed income (%)
Sept. 2000	21.09	92.52	0.16	1.27	0.01	0.12	5.92
Oct. 2000	18.93	91.48	0.15	1.31	0.01	0.12	6.93
Nov. 2000	17.78	90.89	0.24	1.26	0.01	0.10	7.50
Dec. 2000	18.53	91.92	0.05	0.91	0.01	0.07	7.04
Jan. 2001	21.25	92.58	0.10	0.89	0.01	0.05	6.37
Feb. 2001	18.55	92.35	0.05	0.67	0.01	0.08	6.84
Mar. 2001	17.09	89.71	0.16	0.78	0.01	0.07	9.27
Apr. 2001	18.65	89.20	0.26	0.84	0.01	0.03	9.66
May 2001	17.75	88.32	0.23	0.80	0.01	0.04	10.59
June 2001	17.82	89.47	0.14	0.72	0.01	0.04	9.61
July 2001	15.81	87.17	0.15	0.70	0.01	0.04	11.93
Aug. 2001	14.62	86.47	0.55	0.72	0.01	0.05	12.20
Sept. 2001	13.99	75.99	0.70	2.33	0.01	0.03	20.94
Oct. 2001	13.67	78.67	0.16	2.79	0.01	0.85	17.52
Nov. 2001	14.42	85.02	0.50	1.54	0.01	1.07	11.86
Dec. 2001	15.50	88.45	0.29	0.73	0.01	1.20	9.32
Jan. 2002	14.59	87.44	0.75	0.67	0.01	1.41	9.73
Feb. 2002	16.57	89.08	1.97	0.34	0.01	0.22	8.37
Mar. 2002	16.34	90.24	0.41	0.60	0.01	0.22	8.52
Apr. 2002	16.78	89.55	1.48	0.59	0.01	0.11	8.27
May 2002	15.02	89.72	1.38	0.59	0.01	0.11	8.19
June 2002	12.31	87.50	2.03	0.67	0.01	0.11	9.68
July 2002	9.18	83.20	4.21	0.57	0.01	0.11	11.90
Aug. 2002	10.22	85.56	3.64	0.43	0.01	0.20	10.16
Sept. 2002	9.96	77.29	5.19	0.43	0.01	0.16	16.92
Oct. 2002	8.95	79.97	3.14	1.01	0.01	0.20	15.67
Nov. 2002	9.06	78.75	3.02	1.11	0.01	0.17	16.94
Dec. 2002	10.40	74.70	2.35	1.15	0.01	0.27	21.51
Jan. 2003	10.04	73.84	1.88	1.24	0.01	0.30	22.72
Feb. 2003	9.85	72.13	3.26	1.29	0.01	0.32	22.99
Mar. 2003	10.68	76.43	2.85	1.47	0.01	0.31	18.93
Apr. 2003	12.48	78.05	2.69	1.43	0.01	0.40	17.41
May 2003	12.64	80.01	1.71	1.39	0.01	0.38	16.50
June 2003	12.80	80.30	1.20	1.40	0.01	7.19	9.90
July 2003	13.31	80.94	1.44	1.50	0.01	0.51	15.60
Aug. 2003	14.60	82.81	1.19	1.38	0.01	0.48	14.13
Sept. 2003	15.05	83.94	1.07	1.24	0.01	0.48	13.26
Oct. 2003	18.68	76.76	4.61	0.95	0.01	0.43	17.23
Nov. 2003	17.64	86.10	0.82	0.94	0.01	0.50	11.63
Dec. 2003	20.12	86.79	0.62	0.68	0.01	0.30	11.60
Jan. 2004	20.02	86.84	0.61	0.57	0.01	0.28	11.69
Feb. 2004	20.72	86.30	0.50	0.60	0.01	0.29	12.30
Mar. 2004	20.96	86.02	0.55	0.57	0.00	0.35	12.51
Apr. 2004	20.40	85.21	2.29	0.57	0.00	0.26	11.67
May 2004	18.41	87.40	1.10	0.65	0.00	0.23	10.62
June 2004	18.50	87.67	1.31	0.84	0.00	0.24	9.94

fixed income gains. Investments in government bonds directed toward privatization were discriminated in the item "Privatization Funds." The other portfolio components were investments in securities, derivatives, and debentures. Since 2000 and the publication of Resolution 2689, the fixed income investments item has been distinguished from the "Others" item.

With the August 1993 prohibition of Annex IV fixed income investments, the 25 percent of "Others" in the portfolio has fallen to approximately just 1 percent as investments in government bonds with this objective could no longer be declared under Annex IV. The investments then had to be made via special fixed income funds for foreign capital, which incurred an IOF tax of 5 percent to 9 percent.

However, in the month following this prohibition, September of 1993, the percentage of debenture investments jumped from 4 percent to 19 percent, reaching 34 percent in November, indicating the market had begun circumventing by investing in debentures that earned fixed income, such as those of the Siderbrás Company. At the end of November of 1993, the government placed a restriction on some debenture investments, but only in February of 1996 prohibited investing in those of Siderbrás.

After debenture investments were restricted in November of 1993, the market began bypassing the IOF tax on fixed income investments using the loophole for using privatization funds and the derivatives market (using box operations as explained in the preceding). The table shows that the percentage of privatization funds rose in September of 2003 and peaked at almost 10 percent of the Annex IV Portfolio in June of 1994. The government then prohibited NTN investments (Treasury bonds) with privatization resources,[25] precluding fixed income gains through this loophole. The percentages for derivatives were only made available beginning in March of 1994, and we are unable to trace the development of these flows.

Finally, only equity investing was left unrestricted, and the other items were subject to diverse rules before permitted to invest through Annex IV. The market then began to use circumvention strategies involving the stock market, as seen in Cases 2 and 3 in the previous section. Another method that has been adopted since August of 1993 was disguising short-term capital as direct investments as described in Case 1. These two methods for circumventing the controls were not prohibited by any legal measure. Strategies such as the one in Case 2 may still be used by financial institutions seeking to avoid the income tax on fixed income gains, which is higher than that on capital market gains, or to invest in fixed income for less than ninety days without paying the 5 percent IOF tax.

The market, then, appears to always find a means of circumventing re-

---

25. Funds in privatization funds were allowed to be invested in domestic bonds until the privatization took place. However, investors parked their funds in the bonds indefinitely to avoid the tax, without true intention to participate in privatizations.

strictions placed on foreign capital, rendering capital controls ineffective in the medium term. However, the price to be paid in terms of how the market is viewed when controls are imposed could endure for some time. Some argue that ex ante controls on capital inflows do not compromise the country's reputation and are prudent measures for avoiding destabilization caused by excessive capital inflows. However, to quote one of the financial market agents that we interviewed in our field research: "An ex-alcoholic can't touch a bottle of whiskey." Also, the operations of controls on capital inflows are not very well understood and may create misunderstandings harmful to the country's reputation. For example, in the aftermath of the Mexican 1994 crisis, Brazil reduced the IOF on capital inflows. The (albeit temporary) reduction of a tax should be considered a liberalization; however, it was taken by two highly trained scholars as just the opposite.[26]

As expressed in Forbes (2004), economic literature has still not been able to prove conclusively that imposing controls on capital inflows effectively reduces the vulnerability of the countries that employ them. Forbes states, "although capital account liberalization may increase country vulnerability to crises in some cases, the relationship between capital controls and financial crises is not so straightforward" (2004, 18). However, the literature extensively defends increased liberalization of the capital account: financing via foreign savings allows for more investment, increased potential GDP, and intertemporal consumption smoothing.

Our main conclusion is that although from a welfare point of view ex ante capital controls may be desirable in certain cases, their implementation when sophisticated financial markets are present is very difficult. This ineffectiveness comes from three facts:

1. Developed financial markets are very good in performing arbitrage.
2. Capital is fungible.
3. Usually, a country wants to control only a few forms of capital inflows (e.g., short-term portfolio investments) while providing total freedom to other forms (e.g., long-term fixed investment).

With these three characteristics, financial markets can lower the cost of effectively investing in the country, as we have documented for Brazil.[27]

---

26. "Capital flows to developing countries fell by one-fifth from 1993 to 1994, with the February rise in U.S. interest rates often viewed as the turning point. At the same time, while some countries stayed the course to liberalization, others which had earlier liberalized (for example, Venezuela, **Brazil,** Ecuador, and Nigeria) resorted to re-imposing capital controls or to tightening existing regulations and delaying announced liberalization plans"; Drazen and Bartolini (1997).

27. One market player remarked that things may have changed somewhat in regard to the ability of the financial market to avoid controls. This would be because current legislation carries penal liabilities to the partners of institutions that are found guilty of breaching the legislation. Therefore, financial market players may have become more risk averse in devising financial engineering strategies to avoid capital controls, but that remains to be seen.

2.6   Conclusion

We have analyzed the effectiveness of controls on capital inflows in restricting and selecting financial inflows. We saw that in Brazil in the 1990s, controls on capital inflows only effectively limited financial inflows for short periods: two to six months. The hypothesis we submitted was that operations aimed at avoiding capital controls during this period rendered ineffective the measures and restrictions. We gave numerous examples of the operations that were reportedly used in this period and that allowed external investors to invest in Brazil while bypassing government restrictions.

The ability to circumvent controls on capital inflows implies that the cost of short-term capital inflows is not necessarily the official tax rate imposed by the capital controls, but rather the lesser of the two between the official tax rate and the cost of avoiding the controls. We reported numerous cases in Brazil during the 1990s that showed that the cost of circumventing capital controls in that period was less than that of complying with regulation. As such, the effectiveness of measures restricting capital inflows was very limited. We conducted an analysis using impulse response functions to measure the effectiveness of inflow controls in restricting financial inflows in Brazil in the 1990s, and we found that the measures were able to reduce capital inflows for up to six months. Financial inflows through the Annex IV channel—which were often seen as the short-term villains at the time—were even less affected and reversed the impact of the restriction in only two to three months.

The impact of capital controls avoidance on their effectiveness has not yet been thoroughly addressed in economic literature. It is common to assume that the implementation of the controls is a given and to disregard the effect of circumvention. However, the imposition of capital controls will be influenced by the following factors: the development of the domestic financial market and alternatives in overseas derivatives markets (which enlarge avoidance alternatives); the ability of authorities to monitor inflows; the penalties for avoidance; and, the most difficult to prevent, regulation loopholes.

In summary, the effectiveness of controls on capital inflows will depend on the market's ability to circumvent restrictions and the government's ability to establish a covered interest parity differential that will balance capital flows. As long as the country's risk-adjusted earnings are attractive for the carry-trade strategy, controls on capital inflows will be at best only temporarily effective in a developed, sophisticated financial market. And policymakers should take this restriction into account when designing economic policies. Capital controls may very well be desirable, a topic we do not discuss here. But if they are ineffective, there is no point in spending the scarce resources of bank supervision trying to implement them. Instead, improving economic policy should be the main focus.

Appendix
Other Circumvention Methods

Case 9: Privatization Currency

Another loophole in Brazil's capital control legislation between 1993 and 1995 was that it granted permission for funds investing in the country's privatization to use Annex IV for investing in national treasury notes (NTNs). Initial legislation sought to encourage inflows of foreign capital directed at investments in privatization, but the market began establishing short-term fixed income investments as privatization investments, thereby capturing the tax benefits of investing in Brazil's domestic debt through Annex IV. This method of capital control avoidance seemed to be widely employed. One indication is that the flow for privatization via Annex IV between April and July of 1993 averaged US$4.36 million. In August of 1993, a capital control was applied that prohibited fixed income investments via Annex IV and permitted only investing through specific fixed income funds that were subject to a 5 percent IOF tax. In September of 1993, the flow declared as privatization resources rose to US$176 million. This means that when fixed income investments were restricted, the flow declared as destined for privatization increased more than 3000 percent in less than two months.

Case 10: Resolution 63 "CAIPIRA" ("Country 63")

Another strategy for raising foreign funds with tax benefits was provided for by Central Bank of Brazil Resolution number 63 for agriculture financing. The operation was similar to those involving ACCs. Rural producers were permitted to borrow abroad, with tax benefits, and began selling them to financial investors so that short-term loans declaring agricultural destinations were a common market practice. The loan, however, was redirected to financial market transactions.

In general, the cost of these loans was also less than the CDI. This meant that the same strategy undertook with ACCs could be replicated with the "63 Caipira," that is, raising funds at a cost well below the CDI and investing the money in the overnight market or in margin deposits required by the BM&F interest derivatives. The capital that in theory was for agriculture investments was actually redirected to short-term fixed income investments. The transaction was strictly within legal boundaries because rural producers officially took out the loans.

Through this 63 Caipira strategy, investors raised funds at short-term rates to perform the carry-trade. At the same time, investors with foreign capital could use this channel to invest in fixed income given the ease with which it was redirected to the financial market. This legislation loophole meant gains for both the borrower and the lender.

Only in 1996 did the Central Bank limit transactions using Resolution 63. The institution's 1996 Report clarified: "In order to *avoid the application of resources from long term loans in speculative investments.* Circular No. 2.660, of 2.8.96, limited the alternatives for investing funds raised under Resolution 63 when not used by their final borrower" (107).

The next case of circumvention involves a loophole in legislation that permitted investments in debentures under Annex IV. Prices of some of the debentures were linked to Brazil's benchmark interest rate, opening a door for bypassing restrictions on fixed income investments.

Case 11: Siderbrás Debentures and Others

One method for avoiding the restriction on fixed income investments with tax benefits provided for by Annex IV was to take advantage of the loophole in legislation that permitted investing in debentures through this channel. Between August 1993 and November 1993, this loophole allowed investors to earn the returns of fixed income by investing in debentures that were linked to the base interest rate. One example involved the debentures of the company Siderbrás.

In August of 1993, the volume of debenture investments under Annex IV was US$275 million, or 4 percent of the total Annex IV Portfolio in the country. In September, after the capital control was introduced, this amount jumped to US$1.3 billion, and in November of 1993 reached its highest to date at US$3 billion, or 34 percent of the portfolio. In November of 1993, the government prohibited debenture investments using Annex IV, closing the door on this form of circumvention.

In this section's conclusion, we exhibit a table with the composition of the total Annex IV Portfolio in the country, and we analyzed, as in Garcia and Barcinski (1998), the dynamic of flow shifts among items in Annex IV prompted by capital controls.

The cost of bypassing controls by investing in debentures, the τ^*, was zero, because the yield of these debt instruments was tied to the interest rates sought by investors and, moreover, offered the tax benefits of Annex IV investments.

References

Arida, P. 2003. Aspectos macroeconômicos da conversibilidade: O caso Brasileiro [Macroeconomics aspects of convertibility: The Brazilian case]. Economic Policy Studies Institute (IEPE) Casa das Garças, http://www.casadasgarcas.com.
Arida, P., E. Bacha, and A. Lara-Resende. 2005. Credit, interest, and jurisdictional uncertainty: Conjectures on the case of Brazil. In *Inflation targeting, debt, and the Brazilian experience, 1999 to 2003,* ed. F. Giavazzi, I. Goldfajn, and S. Herrera, 266–93. Cambridge, MA: MIT Press.

Banco Central do Brasil. 1997. *Relatório do Banco Central do Brasil: 1996* [*Brazilian Central Bank Report: 1996*]. Brasilia, Brazil: BCB.
————. 1998. *Relatório do Banco Central do Brasil: 1997* [*Brazilian Central Bank Report: 1997*]. Brasilia, Brazil: BCB.
————. 1999. *Relatório do Banco Central do Brasil: 1998* [*Brazilian Central Bank Report: 1998*]. Brasilia, Brazil: BCB.
————. 2000. *Relatório do Banco Central do Brasil: 1999* [*Brazilian Central Bank Report: 1999*]. Brasilia, Brazil: BCB.
————. 2001. *Relatório do Banco Central do Brasil: 2000* [*Brazilian Central Bank Report: 2000*]. Brasilia, Brazil: BCB.
————. 2002. *Relatório do Banco Central do Brasil: 2001* [*Brazilian Central Bank Report: 2001*]. Brasilia, Brazil: BCB.
————. 2003. *Relatório do Banco Central do Brasil: 2002* [*Brazilian Central Bank Report: 2002*]. Brasilia, Brazil: BCB.
————. 2004. *Relatório do Banco Central do Brasil: 2003* [*Brazilian Central Bank Report: 2003*]. Brasilia, Brazil: BCB.
Blanchard, O., F. Giavazzi, and F. Sa. 2005. The U.S. current account and the dollar. NBER Working Paper no. 11137. Cambridge, MA: National Bureau of Economic Research. February.
Cardoso, E., and I. Goldfajn. 1997. Capital flows to Brazil: The endogeneity of capital controls. IMF Working Paper no. WP/97/115. Washington, DC: International Monetary Fund, September.
Carvalho, Bernardo S. de M. 2005. *A eficácia dos controls de entrada de capitais no Brasil* [*The efficiency of capital controls in Brazil*]. Master's thesis. Pontifical Catholic University-Rio.
Chan, N., M. Getmansky, S. Haas, and A. Lo. 2006. Systemic risk and hedge funds. Paper presented at Federal Reserve Bank of Atlanta Financial Markets Conference 2006, Sea Island, GA.
Cowan, K., and J. De Gregorio. 2005. International borrowing, capital controls and the exchange rate lessons from Chile. NBER Working Paper no. 11382. Cambridge, MA: National Bureau of Economic Research, May.
Dixit, A., and R. Pindyck. 1994. *Investment under uncertainty.* Princeton, NJ: Princeton University Press.
Dornbusch, R. 1998. Capital controls: An idea whose time is past. In Should the IMF pursue capital account convertibility? Princeton Essays in International Finance no. 207. Princeton University, Department of Economics, International Economics Section.
Drazen, A., and L. Bartolini. 1997. When liberal policies reflect external shocks, what do we learn? *Journal of International Economics* 42 (3–4): 249–73.
Edwards, S., R. Valdés, and J. De Gregorio. 2000. Controls on capital inflows: Do they work? NBER Working Paper no. 7645. Cambridge, MA: National Bureau of Economic Research, October.
Eichengreen, B. 1999. *Toward a new international financial architecture: A practical post-Asia agenda.* Washington, DC: Institute for International Economics.
Eichengreen, B., and D. Leblang. 2003. Capital account liberalization and growth: Was Mr. Mahathir right? *International Journal of Finance and Economics* 8 (3): 205–24.
Fischer, S. 2002. Financial crises and reform of the international financial system. NBER Working Paper no. 9297. Cambridge, MA: National Bureau of Economic Research.
Forbes, K. 2003. One cost of the Chilean capital controls: Increased financial constraints for smaller trade firms. NBER Working Paper no. 9777. Cambridge, MA: National Bureau of Economic Research, June.

———. 2004. Capital controls: Mud in the wheels of market discipline. NBER Working Paper no. 10284. Cambridge, MA: National Bureau of Economic Research, February.

Franco, G. H. B. 1990. A regulação do capital estrangeiro no Brasil: Análise da legislação e propostas de reforma. PUC-Rio Discussion Paper no. 246. Rio de Janeiro, Brazil: Pontifical Catholic University-Rio de Janeiro.

———. 2000. The real plan and the exchange rate. Princeton Essays in International Finance no. 217. Princeton University, Department of Economics, International Economics Section.

Franco, G. H. B., and D. Pinho Neto. 2004. A desregulação da conta de capitais: Limitações macroeconômicas e regulatórias [The deregulation of the capital account: Regulatory and macroeconomics limitations]. PUC-Rio Working Paper no. 479. Rio de Janeiro, Brazil: Pontifical Catholic University.

Frankel, J. A., and A. Rose. 1996. Currency crashes in emerging markets: An empirical treatment. *Journal of International Economics* 41 (November): 351–66.

Garber, P. 1998. Derivatives in international capital flow. NBER Working Paper no. 6623. Cambridge, MA: National Bureau of Economic Research, June.

Garcia, M., and A. Barcinski. 1998. Capital flows to Brazil in the nineties: Macroeconomic aspects and the effectiveness of capital controls. *The Quarterly Review of Economics and Finance* 38 (3): 319–57.

Garcia, M., and M. Valpassos. 2000. Capital flows, capital controls and currency crisis: The case of Brazil in the nineties. In *Capital flows, capital controls and currency crises: Latin America in the 1990s,* ed. F. Larraín, 143–91. Ann Arbor, MI: University of Michigan Press.

Glick, R., and M. Hutchinson. 2004. Capital controls and exchange rate instability in developing economies. *Journal of International Money and Finance* 24 (3): 387–412.

Goldfajn, I., and A. Minella. 2005. Capital flows and controls in Brazil: What have we learned? NBER Working Paper no. 11640. Cambridge, MA: National Bureau of Economic Research, September.

Hull, J. 2005. *Options, futures and other derivatives.* 6th ed. Upper Saddle River, NJ: Prentice Hall.

Ito, T., and R. Portes. 1998. Dealing with Asian financial crises. *European Economic Perspectives* 17:3–4.

Keynes, J. M. 1936. *The general theory of employment, interest and money.* London, UK: Macmillan for the Royal Economic Society.

Kim, S., and N. Roubini. 2004. Twin deficit or twin divergence? Fiscal policy, current account, and real exchange rate in the U.S. Paper presented at the Econometric Society 2004 North American Winter Meeting, San Diego, CA.

Nadal-de-Simone, F., and P. Sorsa. 1999. A review of capital account restrictions in Chile in the 1990s. IMF Working Paper no. WP/99/52. Washington, DC: International Monetary Fund, April.

Obstfeld, M. 1994. The logic of currency crises. NBER Working Paper no. 4640. Cambridge, MA: National Bureau of Economic Research, September.

Obstfeld, M., and K. Rogoff. 2000. Perspectives on OECD economic integration: Implications for U.S. current account adjustment. CIDER Working Paper no. C00-116. Berkeley: Center for International and Development Economics Research, University of California at Berkeley.

———. 2004. The unsustainable U.S. current account position revised. NBER Working Paper no. 10869. Cambridge, MA: National Bureau of Economic Research.

Rogoff, K. 1999. International institutions for reducing global financial instability. *Journal of Economic Perspectives* 13 (4): 21–42.

Stiglitz, J. 1999. Bleak growth prospects for the developing world. *International Herald Tribune,* April 10–11, 1999, 6.
Tobin, J. 1978. A proposal for international monetary reform. *Eastern Economic Journal* 4 (July–October): 153–59.

Comment   Gustavo H. B. Franco

The issue of the effectiveness of capital and foreign exchange controls in general, and their relevance for emerging markets in particular, has always been a high temperature one, though in recent years, given advanced globalization, banking and financial crises, and the worldwide adoption of the Basel Accord, new ramifications in the basic issue of effectiveness are yet to be properly addressed. While old-style foreign exchange controls are being phased out around the world, adversaries of globalization increasingly align capital controls as one crucial mechanism to sand the wheels of international finance. The notion of an international Tobin Tax has been especially appealing to these audiences and popular to some politicians though no practical application has yet been truly discussed. Mainstream economists and central bankers do not generally take proposals along these lines very seriously, most usually dismissing capital controls across the board with the same arguments normally thrown at price freezes and other forms of artificial intervention in the working of markets. It is true, however, that the velocity with which antiglobalization proposals to limit capital mobility are sidelined is not the same at which public policy has advanced in the topic of capital account convertibility as a general proposition. In fact, the 1997 defeat of the proposal to advance in this realm in the context of the Articles of Agreement of the International Monetary Fund (IMF) can be taken as an eloquent demonstration that there was less certainty in this field than many people thought. Indeed, an indication toward this ambiguity is the development of two distinct branches of empirical literature: one positive, on the association of measures of capital mobility, or convertibility, and economic growth, and another negative, on the association between capital mobility and currency crises; neither, actually, is especially conclusive. Indeed, the successive episodes of instability, sudden stops, banking and currency crises, not to mention the growing concern with money laundering and terrorism's money, have made deregulation in the financial industry, especially when it involves international transac-

Gustavo H. B. Franco is a founding partner of Rio Bravo Investments, and a professor of economics at the Pontifical Catholic University, Rio de Janeiro.

The author wishes to thank José Maria Carvalho, Márcio G. P. Garcia, and Bernardo S. de M. Carvalho, as well as the other participants of the IASE Meeting in Rio de Janeiro for many suggestions to this comment. Views herein are mine, under the usual caveats.

tions, a very cautious process. Yet in one way or the other, the debate on the regulation of foreign exchange transactions, and within which the scrutiny on capital flows, has been kidnapped into the grand world controversy around globalization where it was torn by ideological misconception and prejudice. While antiglobalization groups intend to save the world with capital controls, mainstream economics seems unprepared to concede *any* role for capital controls or regulation even in times of unambiguous exuberance.

The question to address, however, in connection with Carvalho and Garcia's paper, is very much circumscribed to a specific context, namely, whether there is some middle ground between these extremes, when one considers a brief but relevant episode of targeted restrictions to short-term capital *inflows* into 1993 to 1998 Brazil, *combined* with a liberalization of *outflows,* and during years in which there was little doubt that a "capital surge" was taking place. My personal position at the Central Bank, starting in October, 1993 as deputy governor in charge of International Affairs and directly responsible for the creation and implementation of the regulatory changes in the field of foreign exchange regulation through 1997, when I was elected governor, where I stayed until early 1999, places me at a privileged position to look back at the episode from a firsthand practitioners' point of view, though in a somewhat uncomfortable position to judge "ineffectiveness," as argued by Carvalho and Garcia. The reader should be warned of the presence of bias in the views expressed in what follows, which, I guess, might be a redundant advice in this profession.

Some context is also very much required. In the early 1990s, Brazil was still enforcing old-style foreign exchange controls, though with great strides toward liberalization. Foreign exchange shortage seemed to be the rule since the 1950s, and the notion of *excessive inflows,* bound to deserve *restrictions* rather than incentives, was by all means novel. Indeed, in the early to mid-1990s, these were times in which the concern with "capital surges" and its consequences to exchange rates (and the concrete threat of the "Dutch Disease" phenomenon) led to academic production and also practical experiences with various sorts of impediments to capital inflows deemed of a "lesser quality," as in Calvo, Leiderman, and Reinhart (1993), Corbo and Hernández (1996), Dooley (1995), Gavin, Hausmann, and Leiderman (1995) and Schadler et al. (1993).[1] More specifically, the experi-

---

1. The conclusion of Calvo, Leiderman, and Reinhart (1993, 149) may offer a fair summary of the wisdom of these years.

> To summarize, there are grounds to support a mix of policy intervention based on the imposition of a tax on short term capital imports, on enhancing the flexibility of exchange rates, and on raising marginal reserve requirements on short term bank deposits. Given the likely fiscal cost, it is hard to make a strong case in favor of sterilized intervention, unless countries exhibit a strong fiscal stance and capital inflows are expected to be short lived. In any case, we believe that none of the above policies will

ence of Chile, and also of some Asian countries, received some attention in the late 1980s and early 1990s while excess liquidity had been there, in some cases, for more than a decade, and there are mixed reviews as to the effectiveness of controls. Yet as the pendulum of world liquidity retreated from abundance to scarcity a few years later after the Asian, Russian and other crisis that followed, it was curious to see that capital account convertibility fell into disregard, and the idea of restriction to inflows, as a way to reduce the impact of sudden stops, regained some popularity even where it was criticized. As put by Fischer (2002, 12–13):[2]

> The IMF has cautiously supported the use of [*market-based capital inflow controls,*] Chilean style. These could be helpful for a country seeking to avoid the difficulties posed for domestic policy by capital inflows. The typical instance occurs when a country is trying to reduce inflation using an exchange rate anchor, and for anti-inflationary purposes needs interest rates higher than those implied by the sum of the foreign interest rate and the expected rate of currency depreciation. A tax on capital inflows can help maintain a wedge between the two interest rates. In addition, by taxing short-term capital inflows more than longer-term inflows, capital inflow controls can also in principle influence the composition of inflows. . . . In a nutshell: capital controls may be useful provided they are exercised with care; they are likely to be transitional— albeit possibly in use for a long time—and caution is likely to be necessary in removing them.

Restrictions are never popular in this profession, nevertheless, and looking back at the specific Brazilian 1993 to 1998 experience with *controls imposed on inflows,* even considering that this was *combined with deregulation on the outflow side,* it is not too uncommon to see economists attempting to fit these measures into the stereotype of bureaucrats trying to fight market fundamentals with pointless controls. Capital and foreign exchange controls are easy targets, and mainstream profession would always be willing to welcome the claim of ineffectiveness of controls in general, and the one provided by Carvalho and Garcia for the Brazilian experience in particular, especially if we miss the details, and these details can be very confusing to academic researchers with incidental contact with the practitioners' world. Carvalho and Garcia's paper has the undisputed merit of penetrating the obscure realm of the trading desks to see what *actually* takes place

---

drastically change the behavior of the real exchange rate or interest rate. The choice of appropriate policies, however, could decidedly attenuate the detrimental effects of sudden and substantial future capital outflows.

2. Italics are mine. Perhaps it would be more appropriate to say that, as to the restrictions to capital inflows in Brazil, the Fund had mixed views and loudly ignored what was going on for quite some time. By 1997, in view of the commitment to the attempt to amend the Articles of Agreement toward capital account convertibility, there was some indication that the Fund did not like the restrictions Brazilian style.

in response to specific policy or regulatory measures. Whether they suc-
ceeded in forming a comprehensive picture and a fair judgment is an entirely different matter. In fact, in what follows, it is argued that the eleven
alleged examples of circumvention of controls and restriction to inflows
are not as nearly relevant as argued. If not outright unimportant, then
some of the examples are such as to deserve so many qualifications that
Carvalho and Garcia's conclusion is mostly invalidated. Yet in arguing
along these lines, one does *not* intend to make a case for exchange controls
or capital controls *in general,* neither a case for the effectiveness of restrictions to inflows as a general proposition, in times of capital surges. The
point here is that under the particularly exuberant circumstances lived by
Brazil in the mid 1990s, and having in mind a number of institutional features of the relevant market environment and associated regulation and institutions, the regulatory innovations for both inflows and outflows were
relevant and effective *given their terms of reference.* The relevant metric to
assess effectiveness as we move into the third- or fourth-best realm where
the practitioners are found are difficult to obtain. Yet a look at the data on
the amounts of taxes (on capital inflows) collected and on the nature of inflows (average tenor, spreads, volumes) also help to raise serious doubts on
Carvalho and Garcia's conclusions.

The rest of this comment is divided into three sections: the first section
draws attention to the new regulatory realities and particularly to the role
of controls to banking operations in a world ruled by the Basel Accord
within which it is quite important to have in mind the size of the penalties,
and even criminal implications, of evading or circumventing the regulator's
directives. The second section provides specific clarifications on each of the
circumvention possibilities and indications on how the Central Bank acted
on each situation. The last section presents numbers for the collection of
taxes on capital inflows of several types, which are significant, thus weakening the circumvention claim. In addition, the data on the nature of the
mainstream capital inflows into Brazil 1992 to 1999 reveal a clear trend toward extended maturities in external loans, even with significantly decreasing spreads. The aim of restrictions, the improvement in the quality of
inflows, was accomplished; the precise magnitude of their contribution of
restriction certainly deserves more work.

Controls and Compliance after the Basel Accord

As a background to more specific observations as to the alleged eleven
ways to circumvent controls to inflows, one should bear in mind that,
notwithstanding undisputed sophisticated financial markets creativity and
the fact that capital can move around under countless types of disguises,
foreign exchange transactions are basically *banking transactions* and, as
such, subject to the scrutiny of regulators on several grounds. As one asks

whether capital controls on inflows are *possible at all* and, further, whether *selective* controls on capital inflows are feasible or even when one argues that such controls are effective *only in the short run,* what is at stake is whether the Central Bank is capable of looking into specific operations of banks and imposing limitations to certain families of transactions. In fact, there is no reason to assume that forex transactions are any less an object of the regulators' surveillance than any other banking transaction. In fact, these days past the Basel Accord, most controls directed to banking activities have been internalized through compliance rules that aim at aligning interests of the regulator and its subjects. Internal compliance rules have been created and developed by all banks around the globe with the more specific objective of minimizing problems with the regulator in all its areas of concern, from risk-weighted capital, credit scoring, and derivatives exposure to the precise identification of clients and the nature of foreign exchange operations. Indeed, the control of capital inflows can be seen as an activity conducted by banking supervision departments, which are perfectly capable of monitoring individual transactions and exercising the discretionary power to veto specific trades or deals as they are seen as possible violations in existing regulations, whether targeting risk, crime, or other endeavors.

It is a fact that banks comply with directives of central banks as a general proposition, even when they restrain their activities and profit possibilities. In many cases, banks go beyond the Central Bank's directives. If, for instance, the Central Bank issues guidelines regarding foreign exchange transactions aiming at preventing money laundering, it is common to see banks *expanding* the directive into their compliance departments in order to prevent any questioning that might be transformed into very costly liabilities or damages to the bank's reputation. It is rare to see anyone questioning the overall compliance, for instance, to Basel rules regarding risk weighted capital, even though the bypassing may be as profitable as the bypassing of capital controls. Why then should one assume that banks would be willing to jump at any possibility to bypass regulatory directives in the subject of limitations to capital inflows of certain kinds when banks tend to be "well behaved" in other areas?

Indeed, there is no literature or bias in the issue of alleged ineffectiveness of Basel rules or banking regulation at large as there is in the case of capital controls. However, as it is common to see in the regulation and in the "crime and punishment" literature, one may say compliance is a game involving a payoff highly dependent on not being caught breaking the law. Yet in the repeated game between banks and their regulators, and in view of the importance of reputation in this business, and also for the normal flow of banking, one hardly see banks challenging aggressively and repeatedly regulatory directives, especially when the negative payoff of a controversy with the regulator may be very costly penalties possibly endangering the continuity of the bank. It is common to see controversies and discrepancies in views during the course of the banking supervision activity and a wide range of activities, from credit scoring and associated provisioning to foreign exchange transactions, but the instruction of the regulator is always the final word in practically all matters related to banking supervision. Why does this propensity to discipline not exist when directives are concerning controls to capital inflows? Why is this particular subset of regulations less effective than the rest?

It is true that there were times past, long ago, in which foreign exchange regulation was so unrealistically restrictive that one would see the development of black markets and curb markets, yet not usually within the banking system and mostly involving cash transactions. It is hard to imagine that controls to capital inflows would be such as to provoke any major dislocation toward the black market or that the restricted portions of the capital account of the balance of payments could be channeled into transaction technologies and platforms mostly used by criminals. As a practical matter, it is not possible in Brazil for the parallel market to develop outside the financial systems in a dimension large enough to disturb macroeconomic policies. It is well known that a black market remains in existence in Brazil, as in any other country in the world, in which transactions are almost exclusively in cash and related to crime.[3]

In addition to the argument made in the preceding that banks strive to preserve a good working relationship with the regulator when it comes to compliance, it is also important to clarify the exact nature of penalties and problems related to the violations that may be involved in the eleven alleged circumvention operations described by Carvalho and Garcia. Seven of these eleven Cases (1, 2, 4, 6, 7, and 9) involve penalties defined in Article 23 of Law 4.131/62, according to which, the furnishing of "false information" (paragraph 2) in foreign exchange operations contracts and "fraud" (or "false identity," paragraph 3) in such contracts would trigger penalties of up to 100 percent and up to 300 percent of the value of the contract respectively. In both cases, penalties are applicable not only to the seller of foreign exchange but *also to the bank, sometimes to their directors,* and to the broker if acting on the operation. This is an incredibly powerful directive as it makes the bank a partner to the sponsor of any wrongdoings associated with the foreign exchange transaction. This is reason enough for banks to be very selective when it comes to creative operations or more compliance prone in this area than they normally are.

These seven operations also involve violations in tax laws as they result in evading the tax due at the time of the foreign exchange sale (often the tax on financial operations [IOF] but also, sometimes, on the withholding tax

3. For a review of empirical findings on the size and scope of black markets around the world with much consideration given to developed countries, see Galbis (1996).

on income earned) and the attempt to disguise the liability. Penalties are a multiple of the tax values due and unpaid and are comparable to the ones applicable by the Central Bank for the violation of foreign exchange regulations (which are proportional to the principal amount involved), but their consequences are far worse as tax evasion is also a crime. Furthermore, in these seven transactions, in addition to tax evasion, there are also other crimes involved such as financial fraud and conspiracy. In fact, both the foreign exchange authority and the tax authority are obliged to inform the Public Prosecutor (*Ministério Público*) of the *possible* presence of crime (if they do not inform, these authorities may face criminal charges themselves). Based in such reports, prosecutors usually do not hesitate in starting criminal investigations, often followed by wide press coverage, on the parts involved. It is not hard to imagine the amount of the damage that could do to banks and the effort of compliance units to prevent any occurrence that might possibly entail such course of events.

In view of the preceding, it seems hardly likely that any significant number of banks would enter in any significant amounts of transactions of these types considering the risks of getting caught and the consequences of such conducts. Compliance units exist with the precise aim at avoiding conducts that might lead to confrontations with the regulator. Of course, lots of anecdotal evidence may be collected on ideas or attempts of by-passing regulations on capital inflows, especially amongst traders, as one considers the agency problem that evolves as traders try to force quasi or even fully illegal transactions onto their employers as they would earn the bonuses before the regulatory, tax, and criminal charges and liabilities are presented later on, when traders have already moved into different banks. These were the years in which Nick Leason was active in Singapore; something along these lines may have taken place in Brazil, though with little macroeconomic relevance. The collective memory of trading desks from times of regulatory change must be treated with considerable caution as it moves into the realm of the academic debate on the effectiveness, however defined, of the regulatory policy mix implemented in 1993 to 1998 Brazil.

The "Circumventions"

After these general comments, we turn to specific observations on the eleven models of transactions depicted as ways to circumvent controls or taxes on inflows of capital. It is useful to group the transaction according to their nature and examine what took place separately.

Disguised FDI

From the onset, one should squarely disregard Cases 1 and 2 that, in the point of view of the undersigned, belong in the realm of fantasy. Given the documentary needs of companies with foreign ownership in Brazil, the "disguise" is very simply impossible and also way too risky in view of the sanctions mentioned in the preceding. It is true that the Central Bank saw a more intensive usage of inter company loans, and very specifically in 1993, but the increase in foreign direct investment was much larger, dissolving the impression that multinationals could have been using loans to undertake financial arbitrage and in excess of what would be normal to expect in light of their equity investments into Brazil.

Portfolio Investment under Annex IV

It should be said from the start that the misrepresentation, on the part of the investor and the bank undertaking the forex transaction, of a given investment through the regulatory window for inflows of foreign portfolio investment (Cases 4, 7, and 9), known by an acronym related to the regulatory directive, "Annex IV,"[4] would involve the violations and penalties as described in the preceding. The problem here was not circumvention but *grandfathering fixed income investments made before the restrictions,* thus avoiding complaints along the lines of disrespect of contracts and preserving the ex ante character of the restrictions. In fact, in order to be worthy of what Stanley Fischer described as "market-based" restrictions, a key aspect of the restrictions would be that their nature and cost should be fully known *before* the foreign investor decides to invest. In this connection, Brazil preferred to work with a tax paid at the moment of entry, with no other obligations in the future, than the Chilean system of a quarantine, necessarily involving the Central Bank receiving, managing and remunerating deposits from investors for prolonged periods of time.

Yet the problem with Cases 4, 5, and 7 was that foreign investment into some specific fixed income instruments in Brazil before December 1993 could take place through the portfolio investment foreign exchange window—Annex IV—without any misrepresentation. Commodities mutual funds, debentures, privatization currency (securitized Treasury bonds), and derivatives (entailing constructions such as the box with options deals, producing a synthetic of a fixed income instrument) were all permitted up to mid-1993. From then on, each such instruments was withdrawn from Annex IV in a sequence and moneys invested thereof had to be reallocated. In each case, as time was given to investors to reallocate their investments into different instruments, one saw a sequence of shifts of resources in a succession as resources into commodities mutual funds flew partly into debentures then partly to box with options, until all varieties of fixed income instruments were formally forbidden. The fact that these restrictions were not done all at once, but in sequence, produced these shifts, which

---

4. Resolution 1,289 of the National Monetary Council (the regulatory body with the legal competence to issue foreign exchange regulation) regulated portfolio investment in its varied forms. The annexes of the Resolution had regulations for each family of investments. The most popular was Annex-IV, regulating investments into the Brazilian stock exchange.

gave the impression of a cat and mouse game. More essentially, however, there was little or no circumvention as resources were *already invested within the country* in Real denominated instruments. At the end of 1994, all new flows into the portfolio investment window fell to US$5.0 billion, from US$6.5 billion in 1993, while the inflows into the special class of fixed income funds created for the specific purpose of removing all fixed instruments, even synthetics from the portfolio investment rules, received US$1.3 billion, with all taxes duly paid, as seen in table 2C.1 in the following. Another vehicle, "Privatization funds," was created to capture investors' interest in privatization, received US$1.9 billion in 1994. The fact was that after the grandfathering was completed through 1994 and after, there was practically no claim or indication of any fixed income investments into Annex IV, except for rumors of operations known as Blue Chip Swaps examined later.

The CC-5 Accounts

Case number 10 involves nonresident banking accounts within Brazil (known as "CC-5 accounts") that enjoy full convertibility. Indeed, because the nonresident that can open such an account must be a bank, and this bank can transact on behalf of third parties, one is right in pointing out that this vehicle, in theory, represents a full fledged opening of the capital account. The interesting question to raise here is why this platform is not used more widely as there is no restriction whatsoever in the amounts and on the nature of the transactions made *at the outflow end.*[5] Interestingly, the problem here is disclosure. Any such transactions would necessarily involve the full identification of the parties involved and all explanations as to the nature of the transaction made. And, of course, at the inflow end, if the transaction is identical or even similar to the ones that involve a special tax payment or any other restriction, the Central Bank will make sure that restrictions are obeyed and taxes paid or simply instruct the bank not to do or to undo the transaction. The public and the regulator scrutiny on the movements in the CC-5 accounts is very severe, given cases of fraud, misuse, and money laundering, and for this very reason banks and individuals tend to be extra careful with transactions of this kind; it does not seem plausible that operations to circumvent restrictions to inflows were made in this channel in any significant way; it suffices to look at the flows that are chronically negative. In any event, explicit taxes on inflows through CC-5 accounts were enacted by mid-1995 in line with the taxation of fixed income mutual funds.

5. For a review on the status of the capital account liberalization in Brazil, see Franco and Pinho Neto (2005).

Leads and Lags

Case 5 in Carvalho and Garcia treats as circumvention what may be described as an exception. In Brazil, exporters are allowed to enjoy leads, that is, to anticipate export revenues through bank lines offered by local banks against the collateral of the export receivables. These advances were made and continue to be made at international costs and indexed to the dollar. They are perfect to allow exporters to arbitrate interest rate differentials, and surely a very relevant part of the profitability of exporting from Brazil is related to this possibility. Many see this as a financial subsidy, as exporters are thus capable of undertaking interest rate arbitrage in ways that were forbidden to financial players more generally by this time. Yet the fact that restrictions and taxes to short-term inflows could not reach leads and lags undertaken by exporters and importers meant that these groups were exempted from the restrictions, which, however, did not seem to bother regulators at all as any help into exporters profitability and into the increase in import penetration ratios was warmly welcome in times the foreign exchange anchor was deemed crucial to end hyperinflation. There was some concern, however, with the case of a nonexporter who could go into a Brazilian bank, draw funds from a line backed by export receivables he did not actually possess, and use the resources to invest in fixed income instruments. The only condition this fellow had to obey was to actually prove the shipment of such exports after a maximum of 180 days. There were some such cases, and what happened, though in a small scale, was that this fellow would have to purchase export performance from an exporter that did not advance receivables. The exporter would sell his rights at a premium, capturing most of the gain of the arbitrageur. Again, the exporter would stand to gain, even if some of the gain is reaped by the financial middlemen. Again, there was no circumvention, or loss of effectiveness, as described.

Derivatives, BTBs, and BCSs

Case 11 is not really a transaction; it is more like a statement of fact, or faith, that in a world so rich in derivatives, including specifically nondeliverable forwards (NDFs) traded over the counter in New York or futures in the Chicago Mercantile Exchange (CME), anything is possible, namely a "synthetic" of a fixed income investment can be made in New York or in the Caribbean without anybody bothering with foreign exchange and banking regulations in Brazil. Yet this is only true if *some connection* is established with the fixed income market in Brazil; if not, how can the interest rate arbitrage be done?

With derivatives, loans, or stocks, one can indeed build what has been called a "back-to-back" (BTB) operation. Case 7 is one such operation, not quite the typical one. The most common was what was called the "blue chip swap" (BCS) mentioned a bit out of context by Carvalho and Garcia in connection with CC-5 accounts, and also mentioned in the preceding as related to Annex IV. It consists of two theoretically unconnected transactions done in Brazil and offshore. A bank buys, for instance, Petrobras American depository receipts (ADRs) with a repo in New York, and the Brazilian branch of the same bank sells the same stock with a reverse repo agreement. The foreign leg of the deal was exactly the opposite of the Brazilian leg, the short and long positions in the same asset cancel out, but the different financing cost at both repo and reverse repo operations is where the interest rate differential could be captured, if and only if the same entity could bank the two legs at the same balance sheet and other market risks are controlled for.

As these deals started to appear, many regulators, in Brazil and abroad, jumped in to understand the transaction and fit it into their rules. Tax authorities in Brazil grasped the spirit of the transaction, as it involved very visible fingerprints in the stock exchange, and attacked very directly all parties suspect of such dealings. The Central Bank, in turn, leveraged the attack as the foreign exchange regulation forbids what is called "private compensation," or schemes through which parties evade a foreign exchange transaction offsetting credits and debits on shore and offshore. Penalties here may go up to 100 percent of the values transacted.

The BCS deals existed much more as legend than fact, and known deals were subject to very high penalties whose values were made public to further discourage banks from undertaking such risks.[6] The BTB deals became a primary model of laundering moneys offshore that could not enter the country either in view of tax consideration or worse. During the course of 2005, in a high profile Congressional Commission of Inquiry, it was found that the Workers Party appeared to have entered into several BTB transactions to use illegal campaign money held abroad to pay for things and bribe people within the country. This deal certainly belongs to the circumvention family described by Carvalho and Garcia: moneys held offshore by Partido dos Trabalhadores (PT) could have been deposited in an offshore branch (or parallel bank) of a Brazilian bank, which, quid pro quo, lent money to PT in Brazil through an intermediary, entirely out of market conditions, especially regarding collateral.

Indeed, as a conclusion, one may admit that there are many theoretical ways to circumvent banking and foreign exchange regulations and undertake fraud. It is an entirely different matter to presume that this could be done on large scale to the point of turning regulations into a pointless exercise, given compliance discipline and penalties involved.

---

6. Often the Central Bank implemented its penalties and informed the tax authorities, which, however, queue the process so as to apply the penalty only at the year before the expiration of the five-year prescription period.

IOF Collection and the Nature of Inflows

Last, some interesting pieces of evidence could be offered to provide some comfort to taxpayers, understandably concerned about Carvalho and Garcia's allegations. One of the most important restrictions to inflows subject to the accusation of ineffectiveness, given alleged circumvention possibilities, is the IOF, the financial transactions tax due after the liquidation of certain foreign exchange transactions. I searched my archives to find the documents used at the time by the Central Bank to indicate the amounts to be collected by the tax authorities. Table 2C.1 offers the estimates of the Central Bank of the amounts collected in the several varieties of incidence of the IOF tax through time. Even though these amounts are *not* the ones reported by tax authorities based on actual collection,[7] there is no reason to doubt that these amounts were actually paid as the Central Bank works technically as a substitute to the tax authority requesting the proof of tax payment in order to confirm the registration of foreign capital along the lines of existing legislation and to authorize any remittances such as interest and repatriation.

Table 2C.1 provides a history of the IOF usage for that purpose as it covers all changes occurring between November of 1993—when the first presidential decree was issued creating the possibility of taxing certain foreign exchange transactions at certain rates and delegating to the Finance Minister limited powers to change the tax rate—until June of 1996. This specific cutoff date is arbitrary; the active use of the IOF continued more or less unchanged at a restrictive stance until the Asian crisis, when most restrictions were removed and tax rates changed to zero. Early in 1998, however, after what was seen as a very successful response to the Asian crisis—a combination of a fiscal package with monetary tightening—capital inflows regained momentum very rapidly, international reserves reached their all time high, and, as a consequence administrative restrictions to inflows were reinstated, and the IOF tax on certain types of inflows was reestablished very quickly. A few months later, with the Russian and long-term capital management (LTCM) crisis, such restrictions were removed and were not to be seen again.[8] Table 2C.1 does not cover the whole period in which the IOF and other restrictions to inflows were deployed—November 1993 to mid-1998—but its coverage and numbers provide important indications as to the impacts of the IOF on capital inflows.

During the period covered by table 2C.1, the total amount collected was

---

7. These, by the way, are not published with this level of detail.

8. The procyclical character of restrictions to capital inflows should be seen as an obvious thing, at least in the minds of those, amongst whom I am included, who created and managed these instruments through time: for what *other* possible reason would the authorities possibly introduce such restrictions? Yet for those interested in econometric technique to set proof of firsthand accounts of declared intentions, please refer to Cardoso and Goldfajn (1997).

Table 2C.1 Some forms of capital inflows into Brazil, IOF tax rates,[a] and estimates of amounts collected,[b] December 1993 to June 1996 (monthly flows, in US$ millions)

Time period	Fixed income funds			Privatization funds			Borrowing abroad (all formats)[c,d,e]				
	Inflows	Rate (%)	$	Inflows	Rate (%)	$	Inflows	Agriculture	Taxable	Rate (%)	$
Dec. 1993	80	5.0	4	0	0.0	0	1,714	0	1,714	3.0	51
Jan. 1994	82	5.0	4	0	0.0	0	745	0	719	3.0	22
Feb. 1994	82	5.0	4	0	0.0	0	770	0	563	3.0	23
March 1994	102	5.0	5	6	0.0	0	714	0	710	3.0	21
April 1994	119	5.0	6	137	0.0	0	932	0	498	3.0	28
May 1994	68	5.0	3	232	0.0	0	283	0	256	3.0	8
June 1994	450	5.0	23	266	0.0	0	304	0	241	3.0	9
July 1994	6	5.0	0	54	0.0	0	351	0	348	3.0	11
Aug. 1994	81	5.0	4	87	0.0	0	349	0	348	3.0	10
Sept. 1994	216	9.0	19	60	0.0	0	540	0	529	3.0	16
Oct. 1994	226	9.0	20	846	0.0	0	925	0	824	3.0	28
Nov. 1994	0	9.0	0	174	0.0	0	1,404	0	1,370	7.0	96
Dec. 1994	2	9.0	0	77	0.0	0	1,459	0	1,300	7.0	102
1994 total	1,434		89	1,939		0	8,776	0	7,706		374
Jan. 1995	0	9.0	0	16	0.0	0	401	0	200	7.0	28
Feb. 1995	0	9.0	0	79	0.0	0	193	0	193	7.0	14
March 1995	0	5.0	0	128	0.0	0	103	0	79	7.0	7
April 1995	1	5.0	0	67	0.0	0	650	0	635	0.0	0
May 1995	64	5.0	3	95	0.0	0	858	0	850	0.0	0
June 1995	1	5.0	0	120	0.0	0	2,839	5	1,804	0.0	0
July 1995	91	5.0	5	164	0.0	0	2,383	85	1,497	0.0	0
Aug. 1995	41	5.0	2	484	0.0	0	2,318	98	1,832	0.0	0
Sept. 1995	0	7.0	0	62	0.0	0	1,121	383	688	2.7	31
Oct. 1995	0	7.0	0	170	0.0	0	1,786	112	1,549	2.2	39

Table 2C.1 (continued)

Time period	Fixed income funds			Privatization funds			Borrowing abroad (all formats)[c,d,e]				
	Inflows	Rate (%)	$	Inflows	Rate (%)	$	Inflows	Agriculture	Taxable	Rate (%)	$
Nov. 1995	12	7.0	1	219	0.0	0	1,275	187	996	2.9	37
Dec. 1995	1	7.0	0	351	0.0	0	1,768	189	1,481	2.5	45
1995 total	211		11	1,955		0	15,695	1,059	11,804		201
Jan. 1996	2	7.0	0	2	0.0	0	1,359	112	949	2.7	37
Feb. 1996	4	7.0	0	4	5.0	0	1,677	203	1,392	3.3	56
March 1996	2	7.0	0	2	5.0	0	1,467	258	876	2.1	30
April 1996	3	7.0	0	3	5.0	0	1,670	499	1,107	2.1	35
May 1996	0	7.0	0	0	5.0	0	2,717	397	2,228	1.2	33
June 1996	0	7.0	0	0	5.0	0	3,343	585	2,090	1.7	58
1996 total	11		1	11		0	12,233	2,054	8,642		249
Grant total	1,736		105	3,905		0	38,418	3,113	29,866		875

Source: Banco Central do Brasil, Personal Archive.

[a]Legal instruments: Decree 995, Nov. 25, 1993—3 percent IOF on fixed income funds and 3 percent on foreign borrowing generally defined. Finance Minister Directive (*Portaria*) n. 534, Oct. 19, 1994—9 percent IOF on fixed income funds, 7 percent on foreign borrowing, and 1 percent on inflows of portfolio investments (stock exchange); *Portaria* n. 95, March 9, 1995—5 percent IOF on fixed income funds, zero for all other inflows; *Portaria* n. 202, Aug. 10, 1995—7 percent IOF on fixed income funds, 5 percent on foreign borrowing, 7 percent on CC-5 accounts inflows, and zero for portfolio investments (stock exchange); *Portaria* n. 205, Aug. 15, 1995—zero for loans directed to agriculture; *Portaria* n. 228, Sept. 15, 1995—5 percent on foreign borrowing with tenors up to two years, 4 percent for those up to three years, 2 percent for those up to four years, 1 percent for loans up to five years, and zero if longer; *Portaria* n. 28, Feb. 8, 1996—adds a 5 percent IOF on inflows to privatization funds; *Portaria* n. 149, June 11, 1996—exempts BNDES.

[b]Values for taxes due listed according to the date of the inflow, not the date of payment.

[c]There are other nontaxable forms of borrowing not included in the table, such as import financing, leasing contracts, and flows from multilateral agencies.

[d]After September 1995, rates are averages, as they depended on the maturity of each loan.

[e]Taxes due might be larger than taxable inflow multiplied by the rate given taxation, not reported in the table, of similar transaction made through CC-5 accounts.

slightly over a billion dollars, including what is reported in the table, in addition, (a) the revenues produced by the IOF on inflows directed to the stock exchange, which were taxed with a rate of 1 percent between November of 1994 and March 1995, with estimated revenues of US$88 million; and (b) the revenues produced by the 7 percent IOF on CC-5 based inflows in force from September 1995 to the last month covered by the table, with total revenues of US$24 million.

Table 2C.1 shows that the fixed income funds lost their popularity after the 9 percent IOF tax, the same happening to privatization funds after the 5 percent IOF tax early in 1996. In any event, the largest part of the *taxable inflows* was in the foreign borrowing column; it was on this region that most of the Central Bank's action—through the IOF and through minimum tenors—was conducted. Table 2C.2 helps complete the picture of the impact of restrictions to capital inflows into Brazil during these years.

The numbers in table 2C.2 cover the most part of the capital account so that if there is any field of play as regards the impact of restrictions, whether taxes of minimum tenors, it is here. The period covered starts when the concern with excessive capital flows started and goes up to the first quarter of 1999. It is very clearly visible that the number of issues and volumes grew constantly, with some seasonal variation and also with declines entirely within what would be expected in mid-1994 (critical months of the Real Plan), early 1995 (Tequila Crisis, very short lived) and 1997-IV (the Asian crisis). The impact of the Russian and LTCM crisis is way much larger than all the other crises, as we all know.

The one interesting aspect of this table in connection to the topic of this note refers to the average maturity and the spreads. The trend toward lower spreads only highlights the importance of the fact that tenors are extended more or less constantly through time.[9] One should note that IOF taxes pictured in table 2C.1 combines with direct impositions as to minimum tenors, for instance, in order to affect the outcomes reported in table 2C.2. There seems to be no doubt that as one looks into the evolution of these flows that the quality (tenors and spreads) improved through time, just as aimed by the regulatory restrictions, whether tax or administrative. In order to argue the ineffectiveness of regulatory policies toward improving the quality of capital inflows, one has to seek alternative explanations for the developments shown in table 2C.2. The course of economic reforms and the success of the Real Plan are surely very relevant explanations to the improved access to international capital markets, but most likely with a little help from regulatory restrictions to short-term inflows.

---

9. Carvalho and Garcia rightly remark that since withholding tax on interest on foreign loans depended on the maturity and that there were restrictions as to minimum maturities, there were several cases of "puts" and "calls" designed to shorten the maturity, if necessary. These options were reported to the Central Bank and were denied if their exercise would conflict with minimum tenors required, but accepted otherwise. In these cases, the withholding tax was charged as if the loan was shorter.

Table 2C.2   **Foreign borrowing from Brazilian residents in the form of registered loans: number of issues, volume, average maturity, spreads, and costs, from 1992-I to 1999-I (quarterly flows, in US$ millions)**

Year/quarter	No. of issues	Value (in US$ millions)	Average tenor	Average spread	Total cost (%)
1992					
I	49	1.551	2.6		12.02
II	84	1.763	3.0	568	11.32
III	38	1.130	3.7	532	10.27
IV	31	1.127	3.7	614	11.38
1993					
I	47	1.879	3.5	704	11.68
II	81	3.977	3.6	713	11.67
III	65	2.749	4.8	609	10.7
IV	74	3.544	4.4	534	9.92
1994					
I	79	5.019	4.0	497	10.17
II	57	1.587	6.0	453	10.9
III	39	1.813	5.1	526	12.05
IV	55	3.153	4.8	490	11.87
1995					
I	42	1.496	5.1	436	11.82
II	57	3.325	4.4	527	11.27
III	91	5.866	4.1	529	11.26
IV	68	3.630	6.2	517	10.92
1996					
I	66	4.688	6.6	462	10.52
II	113	6.488	7.0	465	11.11
III	77	3.735	7.2	465	11.28
IV	110	6.657	7.7	407	10.22
1997					
I	71	3.712	8.1	352	9.77
II	79	9.433	12.4	436	11.02
III	95	6.865	8.5	386	10.09
IV	82	5.852	7.4	407	9.94
1998					
I	120	12.076	7.1	464	10.12
II	104	11.121	9.0	571	11.24
III	96	16.939	8.1	532	10.53
IV	77	3.094	6.2	779	12.45
1999					
I	98	4.165	4.2	604	10.87

Source: Bulletin of Banco Central do Brasil, Personal Archive.

References

Calvo, Guillermo, Leonardo Leiderman, and Carmen M. Reinhart. 1993. Capital inflows, and real exchange rate appreciation in Latin America. *IMF Staff Papers* 40 (1): 108–51. Washington, DC: International Monetary Fund.

Cardoso, Eliana, and Ilan Goldfajn. 1997. Capital flows to Brazil: The endogene-

ity of controls. IMF Working Paper no. WP/97/115. Washington, DC: International Monetary Fund, September.
Corbo, Victorio, and Leonardo Hernández. 1996. Macroeconomic adjustment to capital inflows: Lessons from recent Latin American and East Asian experience. *The World Bank Research Observer* 11 (1): 61–85.
Dooley, Michael P. 1995. A survey of academic literature on controls over international capital transactions. *IMF Staff Papers* 43 (4): 639–87. Washington, DC: International Monetary Fund.
Fischer, Stanley. 2002. Financial crises and the reform of the international monetary system. NBER Working Paper no. 9297. Cambridge, MA: National Bureau of Economic Research, October.
Franco, Gustavo, and Demonstenes M. Pinho Neto. 2005. A desregulamentação da conta de capitais: Limitações macroeconômicas e regulatories [Capital account deregulation: Macroeconomic and regulatory limitations]. In *Aprimorando o mercado de câmbio brasileiro,* ed. Daniel L. Gleizer, 211–40. São Paulo. Bolsa Mercantil e de Futures.
Galbis, Vincent. 1996. Currency convertibility and the Fund: Review and prognosis. IMF Working Paper no. WP/96/39. Washington, DC: International Monetary Fund, April.
Gavin, Michael, Ricardo Hausmann, and Leonardo Leiderman. 1995. The macroeconomics of capital flows to Latin America: Experience and policy issues. Inter-American Development Bank Working Paper no. 310. Washington, DC: Inter-American Development Bank.
Schadler, Susan, Maria Carkovic, Adam Bennet and Robert Kahn. 1993. Recent experiences with surges in capital inflows. IMF Occasional Paper no. 108. Washington, DC: International Monetary Fund.

Comment   Marcelo Abreu

It is perhaps important to insist on the persistent relevance of the issue in Latin America as populist strains of economic policy prove to be extremely resistant in several economies, and a backlash does not seem out of the question in the more extreme cases. Only last Monday (November 28, 2005), Brazilian newspapers carried an article by a former Finance Minister who feigned surprise to find out that there were still economists who proposed a deepening of the liberalization of capital controls in Brazil.

Carvalho and Garcia's paper is structured in three parts. There is a perhaps too short history of capital controls in Brazil, followed by a detailed discussion of cases of circumvention of capital controls between 1993 and 2000, and a vector autoregression analysis testing whether controls on capital inflows in Brazil have been effective in reducing the inflow of financial capital.

Marcelo Abreu is a professor of economics at Pontifical Catholic University, Rio de Janeiro.

It would be interesting to have a bit more material and also more precision on the historical aspects on capital flows. It does not ring true that exchange rate controls did not apply to foreign direct investment in the past. Recurrent wrangles about how reinvestment should be treated both in the early 1950s and in the early 1960s had to do with registration of reinvestment as foreign direct investment and so with capital controls even if in a roundabout way. Still clearer is the relevance of circumvention of desincentives of foreign direct investment inflows implied in the incredibly complex multiple exchange regimes adopted in the 1950s. The possibility of importing capital goods without going through the foreign exchange market was a vital discretionary element in the attraction of foreign direct investment coupled with all sort of subsidies, absolute protection, and carefully controlled right of establishment.

The treatment of a long list of techniques used to circumvent capital inflow control is extremely interesting. But perhaps too many circumvention cases are examined in detail in the paper, with a resulting loss of focus. It would be useful to have such cases classified under some taxonomy. Focus could then be centered on those circumvention techniques that are less country specific or relatively more sophisticated. Good candidates would be short-term capital flows disguised as foreign direct investment (Case 1), labeling fixed investments as equity investments (Cases 2 and 3) and investing through box operations with options for earning fixed income returns (Case 4). And also swaps of blue chips and CC-5 (nonresident accounts) positions (Case 10) and trade in international derivatives markets (Case 11). The other cases—privatization currency (Case 5); ACC (foreign forward currency arrangements; Case 6); Central Bank of Brazil (BACEN) Resolution 63, so-called Caipira operations (Case 7); Siderbrás debentures (Case 8); bond issues with options to exceed the minimum loan terms (Case 9)—seem all to be of relatively secondary interest and too specifically focused on Brazilian recent experience. It would have been good to get a clearer picture of the relative actual and potential importance of such circumvention techniques even if based on rough estimates of market size.

The econometric analysis depends crucially on measures of the importance of capital controls. The indexes for capital inflow and capital outflow controls are derived from the accumulation of specific measures introduced by the Brazilian authorities updated to 2004 (Cardoso and Goldfajn 1998). These indexes are a rather crude proxy to measure restrictions imposed by capital controls as recognized in a specific note. But the acknowledgment is perhaps not enough to reassure us. Very significant measures are deemed to have had the same impact as rather minor ones, for instance, for the period before 1995, minor changes in travel foreign exchange allowances and major changes in the taxation of foreign borrowing. It would perhaps pay to go beyond counting and look more closely into specific measures and assess their relative importance so as to capture their different intensity.

It is slightly disturbing that indexes purporting to measure the impact of capital controls inflow do not somehow reflect the paper's essential idea, which is that capital controls lose power over time. The paper's conclusion would seem to imply a criticism of the index used to measure capital controls.

In any case a list of measures that were considered relevant in 1995 to 2004 would be welcome and complete extant lists for the former period (Cardoso and Goldfajn 1998).

The vector autoregression analysis testing whether controls on capital inflows in Brazil have been effective in reducing the inflow of financial capital covers only the 1995 to 2001 period. Does the number of observations warrant too strong conclusions based on the vector autoregression analysis? Zero impulses are included within intervals of confidence in all four exercises based on different capital inflow measures. These problems should have been explicitly discussed.

Reference

Cardoso, E., and I. Goldfajn. 1998. Capital flows to Brazil: The endogeneity of capital controls. *IMF Staff Papers* 45 (March): 161–202. Washington, DC: International Monetary Fund.

Financial Openness, Currency Crises, and Output Losses

Sebastian Edwards

3.1 Introduction

In early March, 2006, India's Prime Minister Manmohan Singh, announced that his country would take measures toward making the rupee a convertible currency. Capital controls would be dismantled, and freer international mobility of capital would be allowed.[1] This step was unthinkable only a few years back; for decades analysts associated India with a strict policy of capital controls and restrictions. Indeed, in his criticism of the International Monetary Fund (IMF), Stiglitz (2002) argued that the fundamental reason why India and China had been spared from massive currency crises was that they did not allow free capital mobility. Stiglitz went even further and argued that the easing of controls on capital mobility was at the center of most (if not all) of currency crises in the emerging markets during the last decade—Mexico 1994, East Asia 1997, Russia 1998, Brazil 1999, Turkey 2001, and Argentina 2002.

Whether capital controls are beneficial for emerging countries continues to be a controversial issue among experts. Those authors that support capital controls have argued two important benefits: (a) capital controls reduce a country's vulnerability to external shocks and currency crises, and (b) they allow countries that have suffered a currency crisis implement progrowth policies and emerge out of the crisis sooner than what they would have done if otherwise. According to supporters of restricting the

Sebastian Edwards is the Henry Ford II Professor of International Business Economics at the Anderson Graduate School of Management at the University of California, Los Angeles, and a research associate of the National Bureau of Economic Research.

I thank Roberto Alvarez for his comments and excellent assistance. Discussions with Igal Magendzo have been very helpful.

1. See "India Plans to Remove Controls on the Rupee," *Financial Times,* March 20, 2006.

capital account, controlling capital outflows would give crises countries additional time to restructure their financial sectors in an orderly fashion.[2] The overall argument of controls supporters may be summarized as follows: "stricter controls on capital mobility reduce the costs of external crises in emerging countries."

Interestingly, most of the evidence in support of this claim has been country specific. There have been no attempts at analyzing large data sets that would include the experience in many countries. In part, this paucity of empirical analyses is the consequence of the difficulty in measuring the degree of capital mobility accurately (Eichengreen 2001). In this paper I use a broad multicountry data set to analyze the relationship between restrictions to capital mobility and currency crises. The analysis focuses on two definitions of currency crises: (a) a substantial change in an index of macroeconomic stability, calculated as a weighted average of nominal exchange rate changes and changes (declines) in the stock of international reserves[3] and (b), a significant change in the nominal exchange rate that is not accompanied by a (very) large change in international reserves. I am particularly interested in addressing the following two specific questions:

- What are the effects of these two different types of crises on real economic growth?
- Does this effect depend on the degree of capital mobility in the country in question?

Both of these questions are related to the "contractionary devaluation" issue, first addressed by Hirschmann (1949) and Diaz-Alejandro (1963, 1965) and recently discussed by a number of authors including Calvo (1999) and Cespedes, Chang, and Velasco (2004). In traditional open economy models in the Mundell-Fleming tradition, a currency depreciation is expansionary and results in an increase in aggregate demand. This is because the depreciation encourages net exports, without affecting other economic aggregates such as investment or consumption.[4] However, as Hirschmann and Diaz-Alejandro point out, in more complete models there are a number of reasons why a depreciation may be contractionary, at least in the short run. This could be the case, for instance, if exports use imports as intermediate inputs, or if there are distortions in the credit market, or if the depreciation generates a substantial negative wealth effect that affects negatively consumption or investment (Edwards 1989). Recently, a number of

2. Most well-trained economists would agree that there are trade-offs associated with the imposition of capital controls. Whether the costs offset the benefits is a complex empirical question, whose answer will depend on the specificities of each particular country. Doing a full-blown cost-benefit analysis is well beyond the scope of this paper, however.

3. This is the traditional definition of "external crisis" proposed by Eichengreen, Rose, and Wyplosz (1996).

4. This assumes that the Marshall-Lerner condition holds.

authors have revisited the question of whether currency depreciations are contractionary in the context of the "fear of floating" debate (Calvo and Reinhart 2002). These authors, among others, have argued that because in emerging countries many firms issue dollar-denominated debt, a large depreciation generates significant "balance sheet effects." These may be so large that they may more than offset the positive effects of a weaker currency on net exports. If this is indeed the case, an exchange rate depreciation will result in output contraction. From an empirical perspective, an important question refers to the magnitude of these effects and whether they are different for different types of currency crises. In addition, from a policy standpoint, it is important to investigate if these contractionary effects are different in countries with different degrees of capital mobility. I address these two questions in this paper.

The rest of the paper is organized as follows: In section 3.2 I discuss the evolution of capital account restrictions during the last thirty years. The section opens with an analysis on the evolution of capital account openness based on a new index, which I have constructed by combining three data sources: (a) the index developed by Quinn (2003); (b) the index by Mody and Murshid (2002); and (c) country-specific information obtained from various sources, including country-specific sources (see Edwards [2005] for further details). Section 3.3 deals with the anatomy of the two types of currency crises described in the preceding. This analysis is performed for three groups of countries classified according to the degree of capital mobility: "low capital mobility," "intermediate capital mobility," and "high capital mobility" countries. My main interest in this analysis is to compare the two extreme groups: low and high capital mobility. In section 3.4 I report new results on the costs of external crises. I am particularly interested in determining if the cost of these three types of crises—measured in terms of lower growth—is different for countries with different degrees of capital mobility. Finally, in section 3.5 I provide some concluding remarks. The paper also has a data appendix.

3.2   Thirty Years of Capital Mobility in the World Economy

In this section I discuss a new index on capital mobility, which was introduced in Edwards (2005). I then analyze the evolution of restrictions to capital mobility in the last three decades. The section ends with a brief analysis of recent (last decade) episodes of capital account liberalization.

During the decade and a half, there has been an increase in the degree of international capital mobility. There is not complete agreement, however, on the exact magnitude of this phenomenon. The reason for this is that it is very difficult to measure in a precise way a country's degree of capital mobility. Indeed, with the exception of the two extremes—absolute freedom or complete closeness of the capital account—it is not easy to provide effective measures that capture the extent of capital market integration. What has been particularly challenging has been constructing indexes that allow for useful comparisons across countries and across time.[5]

In order to analyze the evolution of capital account restrictions, I constructed a new index on capital mobility that combines information from Quinn (2003) and Mody and Murshid (2002), with information from country-specific sources.[6] In creating this new index, a three-steps procedure was followed: first, the scales of the Quinn and Mody and Murshid indexes were made compatible (see Edwards [2005] for further details). The new index has a scale from 0 to 100, *where higher numbers denote a higher degree of capital mobility;* a score of 100 denotes absolutely free capital mobility. Second, I use *STATA's "impute"* procedure to deal with missing observations in the new index. In order to impute *preliminary* values to the missing observations, I use data on the two original indexes (Quinn and Mody and Murshid), their lagged values, openness as measured by import tariffs collections over imports, the extent of trade openness measured as imports plus exports over gross domestic product (GDP), a measure of openness obtained from the fitted values of a gravity model of trade and GDP per capita.[7] In the third step, I use country-specific data to revise and refine the preliminary data created using the impute procedure discussed in the preceding. The new index covers the period 1970 to 2000 and has data for 163 countries (although not every country has data for every year). It is important to note that although this new index represents an improvement over alternative indexes, it still has some shortcomings, including the fact that it does not distinguish very sharply between restrictions on capital inflows and restrictions on capital outflows.[8]

Figure 3.1 depicts the evolution of the index for six groups of countries: (1) Industrial; (2) Latin America and the Caribbean; (3) Asia; (4) Africa; (5) Middle East and North Africa; and (6) Eastern Europe. This figure shows that the degree of capital mobility has increased in every one of these six regions during the last three decades. A comparison of the 1970 to 1989 and the 1990 to 2000 period suggests that, on average, the industrial countries made the most progress in moving toward greater capital mobility. The Middle East and North African (MENA) region, on the other hand, experienced only moderate capital account liberalization. Figure 3.1 also shows that this process of financial openness has followed different patterns in the

5. Some studies that have attempted to measure the degree of capital mobility include Edwards (1989), Klein and Olivei (1999), Leblang (1997), Razin and Rose (1994), Chinn and Ito (2002), Montiel and Reinhart (1999), Quinn (1997), Edison et al. (2004), Quinn and Toyoda (2003), Mody and Murshid (2002), Miniane (2004), and Quinn (2003).

6. For greater details, see Edwards (2005).

7. See Aizenman and Noy (2004) on the relationship between trade account openness and capital account openness.

8. See the discussion in the preceding section for an analysis of the shortcomings of different indexes. See also Eichengreen (2001) and Edwards (1999).

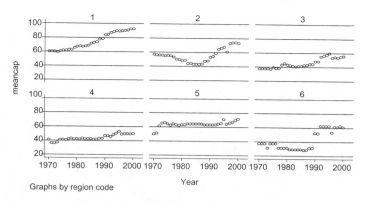

Fig. 3.1   Capital mobility index, 1970–2000

Notes: 1 = Industrial countries, 2 = Latin American and Caribbean, 3 = Asia, 4 = Africa, 5 = Middle East, and 6 = Eastern Europe.

different regions. For instance, in the industrial countries, it has been a relatively smooth process. In the Latin American countries, the story is quite different. As may be seen, the region had stricter capital account restrictions during the 1970s and 1980s; during the 1990s, on the other hand, the region experienced an increase in capital mobility. In Asia, there was an increase in capital mobility during the early 1990s, followed by a somewhat abrupt imposition of controls after the 1997 crises. Since then, capital mobility has increased somewhat. Eastern Europe is the region that has experienced the greatest discrete jump in the degree of capital mobility.

I divide the sample into three equal-size groups depending on the extent of mobility. These groups have been labeled *High, Intermediate* and *Low* mobility.[9] This three-way division of the sample clearly captures the fact that the degree of capital mobility has increased significantly during the last thirty years. In 1970, 44 percent of the observations corresponded to Low mobility, 26 percent to Intermediate, and 30 percent to High mobility. In the year 2000, in contrast, 24 percent of the observations corresponded to Low mobility, 25 percent to Intermediate, and 52 percent to High mobility. Table 3.1 contains summary data on the index of capital mobility for the Low and High mobility groups.[10] As may be seen, the mean and median values of the index are very different across groups. Indeed a

9. Because the unit of analysis is a country/year observation and there has been a trend toward higher capital mobility (see figure 3.1), most observations in the High mobility group correspond to recent country/year observations. Likewise, by construction most (but by no means all) observations in the Low mobility group correspond to early (1970s and 1980s) country/year observations.

10. In much (but not all) of the analysis that follows I will deal only with the Low and High mobility groups. That is, in many of the results that follow the group of countries with Intermediate mobility has been dropped.

Table 3.1   **Capital mobility index by groups**

Group	Mean	Median	Standard deviation
Low capital mobility	30.0	37.5	9.9
High capital mobility	82.5	87.5	12.3

test with the equality of means indicates that the null hypothesis is rejected at a high degree of confidence (t-statistic = 136.9).

In table 3.2, I present a list of nations with what I call "Very High" and "Very Low" capital mobility. These two groups focus on the "extremes" of the distributions and capture countries with an index value equal or higher than 87.5 (for Very High) and an index value lower or equal to 12.5 (Very Low).[11] As may be seen, while the number of countries with Very High capital mobility increased from decade to decade, the number with Very Low mobility declined, until the 1990 to 2000 decade there were no nations with an index value below 12.5.

3.3   The Anatomy of Currency Crises: Is There a Difference between High and Low Capital Mobility Countries?

3.3.1   Currency Crises: Definition

In this section, I investigate the nature of currency crises in the world economy during the last thirty years. I am particularly interested in finding out whether currency crises have had a higher incidence in countries with a high degree of capital mobility.

The first step in this analysis is the construction of two indexes of currency crises. The starting point is the definition of an index of "external pressures" along the lines suggested by Eichengreen et al. (1996):

$$(1) \qquad I_t = \frac{\Delta e}{e} - \left(\frac{\sigma_e}{\sigma_{it}} \right) \cdot \left(\frac{\Delta R}{R} \right),$$

where ($\Delta e/e$) is the rate of change of the nominal exchange rate, and ($\Delta R/R$) is the rate of change of international reserves. A positive value of ($\Delta e/e$) represents a depreciation. σ_e is a standard deviation of changes in exchange rates, and σ_R is the standard deviation of changes in international reserves. Traditional analyses define a crisis (C_t) to have taken place when the index in equation (1) exceeds the mean of the index plus k standard deviations.

11. These break-points were selected in an arbitrary fashion.

Table 3.2   Countries with very high or very low capital mobility

Very high capital mobility					
1970–1979		**1980–1989**		**1990–2000**	
Bahrain	87.5	Antigua and Barbuda	87.5	Austria	87.5
Gambia, The	87.5	Bahrain	87.5	Belgium	96.6
Germany	96.3	Germany	98.8	Canada	100.0
Hong Kong, China	95.0	Hong Kong, China	100.0	Denmark	100.0
Lebanon	87.5	Kuwait	87.5	Estonia	87.5
Panama	100.0	Lebanon	87.5	Finland	95.4
Switzerland	93.8	Netherlands, The	92.5	France	90.9
United Arab Emirates	87.5	Panama	95.0	Germany	100.0
United States	95.0	Singapore	100.0	Guatemala	100.0
		Switzerland	100.0	Guatemala	100.0
		United Arab Emirates	87.5	Ireland	93.1
		United Kingdom	100.0	Italy	96.6
		United States	100.0	Kuwait	87.5
		Uruguay	95.0	Kyrgyz Republic	87.5
		Vanuatu	87.5	Latvia	87.5
				Lebanon	87.5
				Lithuania	87.5
				Netherlands, The	100.0
				New Zealand	93.1
				Norway	100.0
				Singapore	97.7
				Sweden	87.5
				Switzerland	100.0
				United Arab Emirates	87.5
				United Kingdom	100.0
				United States	100.0
				Uruguay	93.1
				Vanuatu	87.5

Very low capital mobility					
1970–1979		**1980–1989**		**1990–2000**	
China	0.0	Bangladesh	12.5		
Ethiopia	12.5	Iceland	12.5		
Iceland	12.5	Morocco	10.0		
Morocco	3.8	Sri Lanka	12.5		
South Africa	7.3				
Sri Lanka	12.5				

Notes: Very high capital mobility countries are those with average mobility index higher or equal than 87.5. Very low capital mobility countries are those with average mobility index lower or equal than 12.5.

The crisis indicator C_t takes a value of one (crisis) or zero (no crisis) according to the following rule:[12]

(2)
$$C_t = \begin{cases} 1 \text{ if } I_t > = \text{mean } (I_t) + \kappa\sigma_I, \\ 0 \text{ otherwise} \end{cases}$$

In this paper I use a value of $k = 2$ to define the basic Crisis Index. An important characteristic of this index is that it is possible to have a crisis even if the exchange rate does not change in a significant way. That is, it is possible that the depletion in reserves is so significant, that on its own, it will move index I by more than 2 standard deviations. In addition to the traditional index defined in equations (1) and (2), I construct an alternative crisis indicator that helps understand more fully the nature of the external crises. This indicator is exchange rate driven and detects crises where the currency depreciates very significantly, while international reserves do not decline in a substantial way. More specifically this alternative indicator—which I call "Exchange Rate Crisis" (Crisis_Er)—is defined as follows: The index takes a value of one if the change in the nominal exchange rate, *by itself,* triggers the C_t crisis indicator in equation (2). Here the country lets the exchange rate depreciate significantly, *before* it has experienced a major loss in international reserves. That is, the country gives up defending the peg *before* international reserves suffer a major depletion.

3.3.2   Currency Crises: Incidence

Table 3.3 presents a summary of the occurrence of the two types of crises for the complete sample as well as for each one of the six groups of countries defined in figure 3.1. Table 3.3 also includes the Pearson tests for independence across groups. Three conclusions emerge from this table: (a) surprisingly perhaps, the more general type of crisis captured by the index Crisis Index has been a rather frequent event.[13] For the sample as a whole, the incidence is 15.3 percent. The highest incidence is in Asia and the lowest in MENA; (b) the incidence of Crisis_Er is much lower than that of the combined crisis; 7.0 percent versus 15.3 percent (this is not surprising, given that the definition of Crisis_Er is stricter); and (c) the occurrence of Crisis_Er is statistically different across regions (see the chi-square statistic).[14]

12. The pioneer work here is Eichengreen, Rose, and Wyplosz (1996), who suggested that the index (2) also included changes in domestic interest rates. Most emerging and transition economies, however, don't have long time series on interest rates. For this reason, most empirical analyses are based on a restricted version of the index, such as 2.

13. This is, in a way, by construction, since k was chosen to be equal to 2.

14. As it has been usually done in empirical work on crises, I also built alternative indicators that considered a three-year window after each crisis. The results, however, are very similar to those obtained when the basic definitions are used. For this reason, and due to space considerations, I don't report them in this paper.

Table 3.3   **Incidence of crises**

Region	Crisis index	Exchange rate crisis
Industrial countries	12.5	4.5
Latin American and Caribbean	14.1	6.8
Asia	17.5	6.4
Africa	15.5	8.3
Middle East	12.0	4.3
Eastern Europe	31.3	17.2
Total	15.3	7.0
No. of observations	3,710	3,695
Pearson		
Uncorrected χ^2 (5)	33.0	34.1
Design-based F(5, 14710)	6.6	6.8
P-value	0.00	0.00

3.3.3 External Crises and Capital Mobility

The analysis presented in the preceding, on two different types of crises (table 3.3), did not group countries according to their degree of capital mobility. In tables 3.4 and 3.5, I report their incidence for the two categories of capital mobility defined in the preceding: High, Intermediate, and Low capital mobility. The tables also present the p-values for Pearson tests on the equality of incidence under High mobility and Low mobility on the one hand, and equality of incidence under High mobility and Intermediate mobility, on the other hand (these tests are presented both at the country-group as well as aggregate levels). The results obtained may be summarized as follows:

- As may be seen from table 3.4, for the complete sample, the incidence of the broad definition of crisis (Crisis Index) is lowest in the high capital mobility countries. This is the case in every subgroup, with the exception of the Eastern European countries.
- Table 3.5 shows that for the Crisis_Er definition of crisis there is no significant diVerence in incidence across capital mobility categories, when the complete sample is analyzed. In three of the subgroups, however, the incidence of crisis is lowest in the High capital mobility countries: Industrial, Latin America, and Middle East.

The results presented in tables 3.4 and 3.5 were obtained when the contemporaneous value of the index was used to classify countries as having High, Intermediate, or Low degree of capital mobility. It is possible to argue, however, that what matters is not the degree of capital mobility in a particular year, but the policy stance on capital mobility in the medium term. In order to investigate whether an alternative classification makes a difference, I reclassified countries as High, Intermediate, and Low capital

Table 3.4   **Incidence of crisis index by categories of capital mobility**

				t-test	
Region	High	Intermediate	Low	H = I	H = L
Industrial	11.2	14.1	31.2	0.87	4.39**
Latin America and Caribbean	10.9	13.6	17.4	0.97	2.40**
Asia	13.9	23.5	17.5	1.88	0.97
Africa	17.7	15.6	15.0	0.61	0.80
Middle East	10.1	14.8	13.6	0.93	0.83
Eastern Europe	43.8	29.7	25.8	1.20	1.78
Total	12.8	16.2	17.0		
P-value	0.00	0.07	0.01	0.02	0.00

Note: t-test is in absolute values.
**Significant at the 5 percent level.

Table 3.5   **Incidence of exchange rate crisis by categories of capital mobility**

				t-test	
Region	High	Intermediate	Low	H = I	H = L
Industrial	3.3	6.6	9.8	1.65	2.44**
Latin America and Caribbean	4.9	6.3	8.8	0.71	1.94
Asia	7.9	11.8	3.7	0.96	1.86
Africa	10.6	7.0	8.7	1.40	0.71
Middle East	1.9	9.3	5.7	2.47**	1.61
Eastern Europe	25.0	20.0	11.5	0.48	1.69
Total	5.4	7.8	7.8		
P-value	0.00	0.06	0.09	0.02	0.00

Note: t-test in absolute values.
**Significant at the 5 percent level.

mobility using the average value in the index in the previous five years. The results obtained—not reported due to space considerations, but available on request—are very similar to those reported in tables 3.4 to 3.5.

3.4   Capital Controls and the Costs of External Crises

In this section, I investigate whether external crises—as defined by the two indicators proposed above—have historically had significant costs in terms of a lower GDP growth. More important, in terms of the current paper, I analyze whether the (potential) costs of external crises have been different in countries with different degrees of capital mobility. As pointed out earlier, this analysis deals with two important policy issues: the "contractionary devaluation" controversy and the discussion on the effectiveness of capital controls. The section is organized as follows: I first present a preliminary analysis, where I compare growth before and after the two types of crises, for countries with different degrees of capital mobility. I then present results obtained from an econometric analysis that uses random effect panel techniques to estimate the effects of external crises on deviation of growth from their long-run trend. As pointed out, the main interest in this analysis is to determine whether the extent of capital mobility plays a role in explaining the costs associated with crises.

3.4.1 External Crises and Growth: A Preliminary Analysis

In table 3.6, I present a before and after analysis on GDP per capita growth for the two definitions of crisis: Crisis Index and Crisis_Er. This analysis has been done for all countries, as well as for countries grouped according to their degree of capital mobility. The "before" data corresponds to average GDP per capita growth during the *three years* before the crisis. I have computed two "after" rates of growth: (a) the year of the crisis, and (b) the average during three years after the crisis. Panel A in table 3.6 contains the results for one year after the crisis; panel B contains results for three year after the crisis. The first four columns in both panels in table 3.6 contain the average difference in the rate of per capita growth for after and before the crisis (that is, it is defined as the rate of growth after the crisis, minus the rate of growth before the crisis). Column (1) is for all countries; columns (2) through (4) are for countries with High, Intermediate, and Low capital mobility. The numbers in parentheses are t-statistics for

Table 3.6	Before and after GDP per capita growth					
Event	All (A)	High (B)	Intermediate (C)	Low (D)	High-Intermediate (E)	High-Low (F)
A. Year of crisis						
Crisis_Index	−0.68	−1.10	−0.29	−0.66	−0.81	−0.83
	(2.56)**	(1.71)*	(0.69)	(1.86)*	(1.06)	(0.64)
Cri_Er	−0.75	−2.13	−0.19	−0.33	−1.95	−1.81
	(1.80)*	(2.00)**	(0.32)	(0.56)	(1.65)*	(1.63)
B. During three years after crisis						
Crisis_Index	−0.12	−0.22	0.21	−0.27	−0.44	−0.25
	(0.65)	(0.55)	(0.66)	(1.04)	(0.84)	(0.11)
Cri_Er	0.00	−0.98	0.54	0.22	−1.53	−1.20
	(0.02)	(1.44)	(1.10)	(0.57)	(1.84)*	(1.66)*

Notes: Crisis_Index is a broadly defined crisis; Cri_Er is exchange rate crisis. The "before" data corresponds to average GDP per capita growth during the three years before the crisis. In Panel A, "after" rates of growth is for year of the crisis. In Panel B, "after" is average growth rate during three years after the crisis. Absolute value of t-test in parentheses.
**Significant at the 5 percent level.
*Significant at the 10 percent level.

the null hypothesis that the before and after rates of growth are equal. The final two columns are diffs-in-diffs columns, which report the difference in the before and after growth rates for High and Intermediate and High and Low capital mobility; that is the number in column (E) is equal to column (B) minus (C). The number in parentheses is for the null hypothesis that this diffs-in-diffs is equal to zero.

As may be seen from table 3.6, these (preliminary) results suggest that there are significant differences in the before and after rates of per capita growth when the shorter horizon is considered (panel A). These differences appear to be somewhat larger in the High capital mobility countries (column [2]). For the three-years horizon, the diffs-in-diffs result for Cri_Er in panel B suggest that there is a significant difference in the differences in per capita growth in countries with different degrees of capital mobility. Notice that only seven out of the twenty-four t-statistics in table 3.6 are significant at conventional levels. As emphasized in the preceding, however, these results are only preliminary as no attempt has been made to control for other factors or to incorporate the determinants of the probability of a crisis.[15] In the subsection that follows I deal with these issues by using a random effect panel regression methodology.

3.4.2   An Econometric Analysis

In this subsection, I present results from an econometric analysis that deals with two questions: (a) do currency crises—as defined by the two indicators discussed in the preceding—have a negative effect on growth? and (b) does the degree of capital mobility affect the nature of this effect?

Growth Effects of Currency Crises: Preliminary Econometric Results

The point of departure of the empirical analysis is a two-equation empirical model for the *dynamics* of real GDP per capita growth of country j in period t. Equation (3) is the long-run GDP growth equation, while equation (4) captures the growth dynamics process.

$$(3) \qquad \tilde{g}_j = \alpha + \mathbf{x}_j \beta + \mathbf{r}_j \theta + \omega_j$$

$$(4) \qquad \Delta g_{jt} = \lambda \, (\tilde{g}_j - g_{jt-1}) + \varphi v_{jt} + \gamma u_{jt} + \varepsilon_{jt}$$

$\tilde{g}_j$ is the long-run rate of real per capita GDP growth in country j; $\mathbf{x}_j$ is a vector of structural, institutional and policy variables that determine long-run growth; $\mathbf{r}_j$ is a vector of regional dummies; α, β and θ are parameters, and ω_j is an error term assumed to be heteroscedastic. In equation (4), g_{jt} is the rate of growth of per capita GDP in country j in period t. The terms v_{jt} and u_{jt} are shocks, assumed to have zero mean, finite variance, and to be uncorrelated among them. More specifically, v_{jt} is assumed to be an *exter-*

---

15. Hong and Tornell (2005), however, have used a similar methodology and found that there are growth effects of crises. Their definition of crisis, however, is different from the two definitions I have used here.

nal terms of trade shock, while u_{jt} captures other shocks, including *currency crises.* ε_{jt} is an error term, which is assumed to have a variance component form, and λ, φ, and γ are parameters that determine the particular characteristics of the growth process. Equation (4) has the form of an equilibrium correction model and states that the actual rate of growth in period t will deviate from the long-run rate of growth due to the existence of three types of shocks: v_{jt}, u_{jt} and ξ_{jt}. Over time, however, the actual rate of growth will tend to converge toward its long-run value, with the rate of convergence given by λ. Parameter φ, in equation (4), is expected to be positive, indicating that an improvement in the terms of trade will result in a (temporary) acceleration in the rate of growth and that negative terms of trade shock are expected to have a negative effect on g_{jt}.[16]

If, as posited by the contractionary devaluation hypothesis, large depreciations have a negative effect on growth, we would expect the coefficient γ to be significantly negative. In the actual estimation of equation (4), I used dummy variables for the crisis indicators. An important question—and one that is addressed in detail in the subsection that follows—is whether the effects of different shocks on growth are different for countries with different degrees of capital mobility. I address this issue by adding to the estimation of equation (4) a term that interacts the crisis indicator with the index of capital mobility developed in the preceding.

Equations (3) to (4) were estimated using a two-step procedure. In the first step I estimate the long-run growth equation (3) using a cross-country data set. These data are averages for 1970 to 2001, and the estimation makes a correction for heteroscedasticity. These first stage estimates are then used to generate long-run predicted growth rates to replace $\tilde{g}_j$ in the equilibrium error correction model (4). In the second step, I estimated equation (4) using generalized least squares (GLS) for unbalanced panels; I used both random effects and fixed effects estimation procedures.[17] I calculate robust standard errors, clustered at the country level. The data set used covers 157 countries for the 1970 to 2001 period; not every country has data for every year, however. See the data appendix for exact data definition and data sources. In subsection 3.4.3, I present some extensions. The results from the first-step estimation of equation (3) are not reported due to space considerations.[18]

Table 3.7 presents the results from the second-step estimation of the

16. See Edwards and Yeyati (2005) for details.

17. Due to space considerations, only the random effect results are reported.

18. In estimating equation (1) for long-run per capita growth, I follow the by now standard literature on growth, as summarized by Barro and Sala-i-Martin (1995) and use average data for 1974 to 2000. In terms of the equation specification, I include the following covariates: the log of initial GDP per capita; the investment ratio; the coverage of secondary education; an index of the degree of openness of the economy; the ratio of government consumption relative to GDP; and regional dummies for Latin American, sub-Saharan African and Transition economies. The results are quite standard and support what by now has become the received wisdom on the empirical determinants of long-term growth.

Table 3.7   **Currency crises and growth (random effects GLS estimates)**

	(1)	(2)	(3)	(4)
Growth gap	0.80	0.80	0.80	0.80
	(19.89)***	(19.68)***	(19.63)***	(19.53)***
Change in terms of trade	0.08	0.08	0.08	0.08
	(9.18)***	(9.21)***	(9.22)***	(9.25)***
Crisis index	−0.91	−0.82		
	(3.72)***	(3.39)***		
Lagged crisis index		−0.40		
		(1.56)		
Cri_Er			−1.27	−1.17
			(3.55)***	(3.36)***
Lagged Cri_Er				−0.63
				(1.75)*
Constant	−0.23	−0.18	−0.31	−0.26
	(2.02)**	(1.51)	(2.84)*	(2.41)**
No. of observations	1,971	1,971	1,971	1,971
No. of countries	91	91	91	91
R^2	0.52	0.53	0.53	0.53

Notes: Crisis index is a broadly defined crisis; Cri_Er is exchange rate crisis. Absolute value of t-statistics are reported in parentheses.

***Significantly at the 1 percent level.
**Significant at the 5 percent level.
*Significant at the 10 percent level.

growth dynamics equation (3). The first two equations refer to the broad crisis indicator Crisis Index, while the next two equations focus on Crisis_Er. As may be seen, the results are quite interesting. The estimated coefficient of the growth gap is, as expected, positive, significant, and smaller than one. The point estimates are on the high side—in the neighborhood of 0.80—suggesting that, on average, deviations between long-run and actual growth get eliminated rather quickly. Also, as expected, the estimated coefficients of the terms of trade shock are always positive and statistically significant, indicating that an improvement (deterioration) in the terms of trade results in an acceleration (deceleration) in the rate of growth of real per capita GDP relative to its long-term trend. As may be seen, the coefficients of both external crises indicators are *significantly negative,* providing support to the contractionary devaluation hypothesis. The point estimates for the Crisis_Er indicator is higher (in absolute values) than that for the broader index Crisis Index. This suggests that using international reserves to absorb part of the effects of a crisis helps reduce its impact on GDP growth. Finally, the results in table 3.7 indicate that lagged values of the crisis indicators are not significant at conventional levels and that the contractionary effect of an external crisis is concentrated on its first year. Notice, however, that given the dynamics nature of equation (3), GDP growth remains below potential growth for quite some time.

External Crises and Capital Mobility

An important issue in policy debates is whether, as suggested by some authors such as Stiglitz (2002), countries that restrict capital mobility are able to reduce the costs of external crises. In order to investigate whether the degree of capital mobility affects the cost of an external crisis characterized by the two indicators defined in the preceding, in the estimation of the growth equation (4), I also included a variable that interacts each of the crisis indicators with the capital mobility index. The results obtained are reported in table 3.8. In the first two columns, I used the broader Crisis

Table 3.8	Currency crises, capital mobility, and growth (random effects GLS estimates)			
	(1)	(2)	(3)	(4)
Growth gap	0.81	0.80	0.81	0.82
	(17.59)***	(16.95)***	(17.49)***	(17.91)***
Change in terms of trade	0.07	0.07	0.07	0.07
	(7.97)***	(8.08)***	(8.07)***	(8.09)***
Crisis index	−1.18	−0.88		
	(3.41)**	(1.81)*		
Crisis index · Cap	0.005	0.001		
	(0.65)	(0.15)		
Lagged crisis index		−1.00		
		(1.91)**		
Lagged crisis index · Cap		0.011		
		(1.31)		
Cri_Er			−0.80	−0.55
			(1.26)	(0.89)
Cri_Er · Cap			−1.01	−0.01
			(0.80)	(1.32)
Lagged Cri_Er				−1.32
				(1.84)
Lagged Cri_Er · Cap				0.01
				(0.97)
Constant	−0.24	−0.18	−0.32	−0.26
	(1.58)	(1.51)	(2.33)**	(1.84)*
No. of observations	1,942	1,937	1,942	1,937
No. of countries	90	90	90	90
R^2	0.52	0.53	0.52	0.53

Notes: Crisis index is a broadly defined crisis; Cri_Er is exchange rate crisis; Cap is an index of capital mobility. Absolute value of *t*-statistics are reported in parentheses.
***Significant at the 1 percent level.
**Significant at the 5 percent level.
*Significant at the 10 percent level.

Index indicator of crisis; the two last columns are for the Crisis_Er indicator. As may be seen, the coefficient of the interacted variable is not significant in any of the regressions. In table 3.9, I investigate whether these results are affected by the sample used. In table 3.9, I present results obtained from emerging and transition countries only. The results, however, are very similar to those presented in the preceding: once again, the variable that interacts crisis and capital mobility is insignificant. This is the case in every regression.

The results reported here suggest that countries that restrict capital mobility have not expressed milder crisis than countries that allow for a freer mobility of capital. These results, then, are at variance with the position taken by a number of globalization critics that have argued that the presence of capital controls reduce the costs of crisis. These results, however, should be considered as preliminary. The issue deserves more attention, and additional research may result in different results. Three aspects of this analysis deserve particular attention. First, and as discussed in section 3.2 of this paper, measuring capital mobility is a difficult and challenging enterprise. Efforts should be made to improve the quality of these indexes. Second, alternative definitions of crises should be considered. It is possible that the degree of capital mobility has some effects on the way some types

Table 3.9	Currency crises, capital mobility, and growth (random effects IV estimates)		
		(1)	(2)
Growth gap		0.81	0.84
		(29.51)***	(23.78)***
Change in terms of trade		0.07	0.07
		(8.26)***	(7.94)***
Crisis index		−5.11	
		(2.35)**	
Crisis index · Cap		0.03	
		(0.68)	
Cri_Er			−8.93
			(2.80)***
Cri_Er · Cap			0.03
			(0.53)
Constant		0.40	0.25
		(1.47)	(0.93)
No. of observations		1,239	1,239
No. of countries		66	66
R^2		0.45	0.41

Note: See table 3.8 notes.
***Significant at the 1 percent level.
**Significant at the 5 percent level.

of crisis manifest themselves. Future research should concentrate on the consequences of sudden stops as well as on current account reversals.[19] And third, there may be issues of endogeneity. It is possible—although in my opinion not very likely—that countries with decelerating growth are the ones that experience currency crises. In the subsection that follows, I address this specific issue, and I report results obtained when instrumental variables versions of equation (4) were estimated.

3.4.3   Endogeneity and Robustness

The results presented in tables 3.7 and 3.8 assume that both crisis and capital mobility are exogenous variables. However, as pointed out in the preceding, this needs not be the case. In this subsection I report the results obtained when equation (4) was estimated using an instrumental variables random effect procedure. I also discuss the results obtained when alternative time periods were used in the estimation and when different samples were considered. Finally, I investigate the role of (potential) outliers. As will be seen, the results are robust to these alternative estimation procedure and data sets and suggest that the effects of external crises on economic activity are not affected by the degree of capital mobility.

Endogeneity

As pointed out in the preceding, it is possible that capital controls are endogenous and that their level is affected—through political economy channels—by the level of economic activity. For instance, it is possible that the economic authorities restrict capital mobility when the economy enters into a slowdown and allow capital to move more freely when the economy is expanding. The external crises variables may also be endogenous and, thus, were also instrumented. The following instruments were used in the instrumental variables (IV) estimation of equation (4): a trade openness index computed by the fitted value of the imports plus exports to GDP ratio obtained from a gravity model of bilateral trade;[20] a measure of unanticipated capital inflows;[21] an index that measures the (lagged) incidence of sudden stops in the country's region;[22] the lagged value of the current account balance; the lagged fiscal deficit to GDP ratio; lagged and current

19. In a recent paper on the growth consequences of current account reversals I found some weak and preliminary evidence suggesting that countries with a more open capital account experienced a higher growth reduction than countries with more restricted capital mobility.

20. Frankel and Cavallo (2004) have convincingly argued that this gravity-based index of openness is exogenous. Aizenman and Noy (2004) have shown that there is a close relationship between trade and capital account openness.

21. This was computed from the residuals of a random effect panel equation on capital flows to GDP for the countries in the sample.

22. I consider the same six regions as the ones used in the analysis reported in sections 3.2 and 3.3: Advanced countries, Latin America, Asia, Africa, Middle East and North Africa, and Eastern Europe.

changes in the terms of trade; the log of per capita GDP in 1970; and regional dummies. The results obtained are reported in table 3.9. As may be seen, the estimated coefficients of the external crises indexes continue to be negative and statistically significant at conventional levels. The coefficients of the growth gap and of the terms of trade are significantly positive. Also, as in the results reported in table 3.8, the coefficient of the interactive variable is insignificant.

Alternative Data Sets

In order to investigate the robustness of the results I reestimated equation (4) for alternative time periods and samples. In particular, I considered data sets that covered the shorter 1982 to 2002 and 1987 to 2002 periods. I also reestimated equation (4) for emerging countries only. The results for these alternative data sets (not reported here due to space considerations, and available on request) confirmed the most important results from tables 3.7 and 3.8: (a) both types of external currency crises considered in this paper had negative effects on growth, and (b) there is no evidence indicating that these effects have been different in countries that restrict capital mobility than in countries with freer capital mobility.

Outliers

As a way to further investigate the robustness of the results I analyzed whether the estimates reported in the preceding had been influenced by outliers. I performed an influence analysis using Cook's distance estimators. The results indicate that the result obtained have not been affected by extreme or outlier observations.

Concluding Remarks

In this paper, I have used a broad multicountry data set to analyze the relationship between restrictions to capital mobility and external crises. The analysis focuses on two manifestations of external crises. The analysis has focused on the following important policy question: does the extent of capital mobility determine the depth of external crises—as measured by the decline in growth—once a crisis occurs? In analyzing these issues I relied on two complementary approaches: first, I used a methodology based on nonparametric tests. And second, I used a regression-based analysis that estimates the effects of external crises on the dynamics of economic growth. Overall, my results cast some doubts on the assertion that countries that restrict capital mobility fare better during a crisis than countries with freer mobility. These results cast doubts on the claims, made by a number of critics of globalization, that freer capital mobility amplifies external crises (Stiglitz 2002).

The issues discussed in this paper deserve more attention in the future.

In particular, there are three aspects of this analysis that warrant additional research. First and foremost, measuring capital mobility is a difficult and challenging enterprise. Efforts should be made to improve the quality of these indexes. Although the measures of capital mobility used in this paper represent a clear improvement over previous indexes, they still classify countries in rather coarse groupings. Second, alternative definitions of crises should be considered. It is possible that the degree of capital mobility has some effects on the way some types of crisis manifest themselves. Future research should concentrate on the consequences of sudden stops as well as on current account reversals. And third, the analysis should be expanded to the determinants of the probability of countries experiencing a crisis. The question here is whether the extent of capital mobility affects the likelihood that a country will face a major external crisis.

Appendix

Table 3A.1   **Description of the data**

Variable	Definition	Source
Index of capital mobility	Index: (low mobility) to 100 (high mobility)	Author's elaboration based on indexes of capital restrictions computed by Quinn (2003), Mody and Murshid (2002), and on country-specific data.
Growth gap	Deviation from long-run economic growth rate	Author's elaboration. See text.
Change terms of trade	Change in terms of trade-exports as capacity to import (constant LCU)	World Development Indicators.
Crisis Index	Dummy for broad definition of crisis	Author's elaboration. See text.
Crisis Er	Dummy for exchange rate crisis	Author's elaboration. See text.

References

Aizenman, Joshua, and Ilan Noy. 2004. On the two way feedback between financial and trade openness. NBER Working Paper no. 10496. Cambridge, MA: National Bureau of Economic Research, May.

Barro, Robert J., and Xavier Sala-i-Martin. 1995. *Economic growth.* Cambridge, MA: MIT Press.

Calvo, Guillermo A. 1999. Fixed vs. flexible exchange rates: Preliminaries of a turn-of-millennium rematch. University of Maryland. Mimeograph.

Calvo, Guillermo A., and Carmen M. Reinhart. 2002. Fear of floating. *Quarterly Journal of Economics* 117 (2): 379–408.

Cespedes, Luis F., Roberto Chang, and Andrés Velasco. 2004. Balance sheets and exchange rate policy. *American Economic Review* 94:1183–93.

Chinn, Menzie, and Hiro Ito. 2002. Capital account liberalization, institutional and financial development. NBER Working Paper no. 8967. Cambridge, MA: National Bureau of Economic Research.

Díaz-Alejandro, Carlos F. 1963. A note on the impact of devaluation and the redistributive effect. *Journal of Political Economy* 71:577–80.

———. 1965. *Exchange rate devaluation in a semi-industrialized country: The experience of Argentina 1955–1961.* Cambridge, MA: MIT Press.

Edison, Hali, Michael W. Klein, Luca Ricci, and Torsten Sloek. 2004. Capital account liberalization and economic performance: Survey and synthesis. *IMF Staff Papers* 52 (1): 220–56. Washington, DC: International Monetary Fund.

Edwards, Sebastian. 1989. *Real exchange rates, devaluation and adjustment.* Cambridge, MA: MIT Press.

———. 1999. How effective are capital controls? *Journal of Economic Perspectives* 13 (4): 65–84.

———. 2005. Capital controls, sudden stops and current account reversals. NBER Working Paper no. 11170. Cambridge, MA: National Bureau of Economic Research, March.

Edwards, Sebastian, and Eduardo Levy Yeyati. 2005. Flexible exchange rates as shock absorbers. *European Economic Review* 49 (8): 2079–2105.

Eichengreen, Barry J. 2001. Capital account liberalization: What do cross-country studies tell us? *The World Bank Economic Review* 15:341–65.

Eichengreen, Barry J., Andrew K. Rose, and Charles Wyplosz. 1996. Contagious currency crises. NBER Working Paper no. 5681. Cambridge, MA: National Bureau of Economic Research, July.

Frankel, Jeffrey A., and Eduardo Cavallo. 2004. Does openness to trade make countries more vulnerable to sudden stops, or less? Using gravity to establish causality. NBER Working Paper no. 10957. Cambridge, MA: National Bureau of Economic Research, December.

Hirschmann, Albert. 1949. Devaluation and the trade balance: A note. *Review of Economics and Statistics* 31:50–53.

Hong, Kiseok, and Aaron Tornell. 2005. Recovery from a currency crisis: Some stylized facts. *Journal of Development Economics* 76 (1): 71–96.

Klein, Michael W., and Giovanni Olivei. 1999. Capital account liberalization, financial depth and economic growth. NBER Working Paper no. 7384. Cambridge, MA: National Bureau of Economic Research, October.

Leblang, David A. 1997. Domestic and systemic determinants of capital controls in the developed and developing world. *International Studies Quarterly* 41 (3): 435–54.

Miniane, Jacques. 2004. A new set of measures on capital account restrictions. *IMF Staff Papers* 51 (2): 276–308. Washington, DC: International Monetary Fund.

Mody, Ahoka, and Antu P. Murshid. 2002. Growing up with capital flows. IMF Working Paper no. WP/02/75. Washington, DC: International Monetary Fund, April.

Montiel, Peter, and Carmen Reinhart. 1999. Do capital controls and macroeconomics policies influence the volume and composition of capital flows? Evidence from the 1990s. *Journal of International Money and Finance* 18 (4): 619–35.

Quinn, Dennis P. 1997. The correlates of changes in international financial regulation. *American Political Science Review* 91:531–51.

———. 2003. Capital account liberalization and financial globalization, 1890–1999: A synoptic view. *International Journal of Finance and Economics* 8 (3): 189–204.

Quinn, Dennis P., and Ana Maria Toyoda. 2003. Does capital account liberalization lead to economic growth? An empirical investigation. Georgetown University. Mimeograph.

Razin, Asaaf, and Andrew K. Rose. 1994. Business cycle volatility and openness: An exploratory cross-section analysis. In *Capital mobility: The impact on consumption, investment and growth,* ed. L. Leiderman and A. Razin, Cambridge, UK: Cambridge University Press.

Stiglitz, Joseph. 2002. *Globalization and its discontents.* New York: W. W. Norton.

Comment   Edmar L. Bacha

Edwards's paper is an important contribution to the debate on the impact of financial openness on output volatility. Reading this paper was for me a most rewarding educational experience. But in my role as discussant I focus on doubts and divergences.

First, I find it difficult to understand Edwards's postulated direction of causality between current account reversals and gross domestic product (GDP) slowdowns, for it is easy to understand that GDP contractions lead to current account reversals, through fewer imports and more exports. The reverse mechanism is less clear. Causality thus seems to be the opposite of that assumed in the paper. The use of dummies to focus only on major current account reversals does not seem to resolve this causality issue.

Second, sudden capital stops should lead first to international reserve losses and only then to GDP contractions. There is thus a time lag in the causation chain that is not considered in the paper. Moreover, Edwards's net capital inflow variable seems to suffer from measurement problems. The first problem is that Edwards includes the "errors and omissions" item of the balance of payments as part of the capital flows, when in fact it also includes unimputed current account items. One wonders if his econometric tests would be robust to a shift to the current account of the "errors and omissions" item. More importantly, compensatory/official financing is included in the net capital inflow variable, thus making it less procyclical, as output falls may be expected to be accompanied by more compensatory/official financing. The relevant exogenous variable for Edwards's tests should be lagged net private capital inflow rather than current total capital inflow. The use of an inadequate variable for capital inflows and the impact of output changes on the trade balance may explain why Edwards finds GDP contractions to have a weaker correlation with sudden stops than with current account reversals.

A third problem is the use of a "country" independently of size as the unit of observation. This tends to bias Edwards's results toward the experience of the more fragile Africa's and island economies. A weighted re-

Edmar L. Bacha is director of the Casa das Garças Institute for Economic Policy Study in Rio de Janeiro, Brazil.

gression, with countries being weighted either by population or GDP, would solve this problem.

My fourth point requires a digression on Brazil's experience since 1970. In table 3C.1, one can observe five episodes of GDP slowdowns, defined as growth rates lower than 1 percent: 1981 to 1983, 1988, 1990 to 1991, 1998 to 1999, 2003. The first observation is that none is associated to a "hard" current account reversal or a sudden stop, defined as variation of 4 percent of GDP—as these never occurred. Only 2003 is associated to a soft sudden stop (2 percent of GDP), whereas 1983, 1989, and 2003 are associated to soft (2 percent of GDP) current account reversals. This evidence would seem to justify Edwards's assertion that sudden stops by themselves are not as important as current account reversals to explain GDP contractions. Note, however, in the table that substantial reserves losses occurred either previously to or simultaneously with the GDP slowdowns. More often than not, such reserves losses were associated to domestic factors rather than international shocks—the blow-up of the "Brazilian miracle" in the early 1980s, the failed Cruzado plan of 1986, the after-effect of the 1994 exchange rate based stabilization, and the "fear of Lula" in 2002. Thus,

Table 3C.1   Brazil's GDP slowdowns and external shocks, 1970–2004

Year	CA	Y$	Y%	NKI	deltaR	deltaR/Y$	dCA/Y$	dNKI/Y$
1979	−10,708	222,285		7,624	−3,214	−1.45		
1980	−12,739	236,841	9.2	9,610	−3,472	−1.47	0.91	0.89
1981	−11,706	257,269	−4.25	12,746	625	0.24	−0.44	1.32
1982	−16,273	269,900	0.83	12,101	−4,542	−1.68	1.78	−0.25
1983	−6,773	188,532	−2.93	7,419	−24	−0.01	−3.52	−1.73
1986	−5,323	256,509	7.49	1,432	−3,836	−1.50		
1987	−1,438	280,949	3.53	3,259	1,015	0.36	−1.51	0.71
1988	4,180	304,185	−0.06	−2,098	1,249	0.41	−2.00	−1.91
1989	1,032	413,564	3.16	629	886	0.21	1.03	0.90
1990	−3,784	466,635	−4.35	4,592	481	0.10	1.16	0.96
1991	−1,407	405,097	−2.93	163	−369	−0.09	−0.51	−0.95
1992	6,109	387,277	5.4	9,947	14,670	3.79	−1.86	2.42
1997	−30,452	807,215	3.27	25,800	−7,907	−0.98		
1998	−33,416	787,346	0.13	29,702	−7,970	−0.01	0.37	0.48
1999	−25,335	536,318	0.79	17,319	−7,822	−1.16	−1.03	−1.57
2000	−24,225	601,942	4.36	19,326	−2,262	−0.38	−0.21	0.37
2001	−23,215	509,623	1.31	27,052	3,307	0.65	−0.17	1.28
2002	−7,637	460,732	1.93	8,004	302	0.07	−3.06	−3.74
2003	4,177	505,533	0.54	5,111	8,496	1.68	−2.56	−0.63
2004	11,669	626,346	5.20	−7,310	2,244	0.36	−1.18	−2.46

Source: Institute of Applied Economic Research (IPEA) data.

Notes: CA = Current account in US$ millions; Y$ = GDP in US$ millions; Y$ = GDP growth rate; NKI = net capital inflows in US$ millions; deltaR = change in international reserves in US$ millions; dCA = change in the current account in US$ millions; dNKI = change in net capital inflows in US$ millions.

Brazil's experience suggests that the relevant variable for growth slow-downs should be the cumulative reserve loss (i.e., current account deficits systematically higher than net capital inflows), rather than current account reversals or sudden stops by themselves. Perhaps this could be a good start-ing point for a new Edwards's paper on the subject.

Finally, in the original paper a critical variable was missing—the ex-change rate regime. Supposedly floating rates help mitigate sudden capital splurges/stops as well as current account reversals, thus leading to less GDP volatility. The paper now allows for this variable, and it does have the expected impact. However, Edwards still does not provide an adequate test for the impact of exchange rate regime change on the statistical significance of the dummies standing for the current account reversals and the sudden stops.

Comment   Marcelo Kfoury Muinhos

This is a very interesting paper that tries to shed light on an important issue related to the real effects of cross-border capital movements. The pa-per is an empirical one, and, as such, the required tests present several diffi-culties, especially regarding a study that works with economic data for a wide range of countries.

The paper presents the argument's procapital controls: (a) It reduces a country's vulnerability to external shocks and financial crisis, and (b) it al-lows countries that suffered a currency crisis to lower interest rate, imple-ment progrowth policies, and emerge out of the crisis sooner.

The objective of the paper is to go against capital control and so dis-qualify those claims. There is some evidence that high capital mobility is not correlated with current account reversal or sudden stops. At least for high capital mobility, the incidence of current account reversal is lower (table 3.4, H ≠ L).

For sudden stops, the paper does show little statistical evidence that they occur more or less frequently in more open or closed capital accounts (table 3.5).

In section 3.4, when he presents the second estimation of growth dy-namics, the coefficients that interact with the crisis indicator and capital are found not significant (table 3.8), so it is not possible to insure that the more open the capital account is, the less severe is the crisis after, so he could not have evidence against claim b.

Marcelo Kfoury Muinhos was head of the research department of the Central Bank of Brazil. He is currently chief economist for Citibank-Brazil.

In section 3.3.1, Edwards explained how his index of capital mobility was calculated.

- It fills the gap of missing variables using a STATA's impute procedure.
- He used a two-order index, their lagged values, and two definitions of openness.

One important aspect that is not present in the index is the amount of inflow and outflow of capital. Large current account deficits may therefore imply large capital inflows. Capital mobility is also related to the liquidity condition in the international capital markets; that is, supply and demand conditions in the home and host countries of capital have to be taken into consideration. It seems inconvenient to dissociate current account reversal from sudden stops as these two effects are part of just one event.

Developments in the external current account are directly related to the inflows of capital to finance deficits—directly through trade financing or indirectly through other capital inflows. If the country suffers a sudden stop crisis, it is healthy if it is able to promote a current account reversal. This reversal in general has an expenditure-switching component promoted by the exchange rate devaluation and a reduction of expenditure that causes recession.

My question is related to whether the standard errors in the growth equations are corrected for the fact that the "reversal variable" is estimated in a previous step. He uses a treatment with an instrument variable to avoid endogeneity problems. So I think it is fine.

Capital Market Development
Whither Latin America?

Augusto de la Torre, Juan Carlos Gozzi,
and Sergio L. Schmukler

4.1 Introduction

Back in the early 1990s, economists and policymakers had high expectations about the prospects for capital market development in emerging economies.[1] This led to significant reforms, including financial liberalization, the establishment of stock exchanges and bond markets, and the development of regulatory and supervisory frameworks. These reforms, together with improved macroeconomic fundamentals and capital market-related reforms, such as the privatization of state-owned enterprises and the shift to privately managed defined contribution pension systems, were expected to foster financial development.[2]

Despite the intense reform efforts, the performance of domestic capital

Augusto de la Torre is chief economist for Latin America and the Caribbean, The World Bank. Juan Carlos Gozzi is a researcher at The World Bank and a Ph.D. student in economics at Brown University. Sergio L. Schmukler is lead economist in the Development Research Group of The World Bank.

This paper is part of a broader study on capital markets, conducted at the Chief Economist Office, Latin America and the Caribbean Region, The World Bank, available at http://www.worldbank.org/laccapitalmarkets. We thank participants at the PUC-Rio de Janeiro (Brazil) conference for very useful discussions. We are particularly grateful to Sebastian Edwards, Márcio G. P. Garcia, Eduardo Loyo, Ugo Panizza, and two anonymous referees for very helpful comments. The findings, interpretations, and conclusions expressed in this paper are entirely those of the authors and do not necessarily represent the views of The World Bank.

1. Capital market development has been deemed an important goal, as growing evidence supports the view that a sound financial system is not just correlated with a healthy economy, but actually causes economic growth. See Levine (2005) for a comprehensive review of the literature on the finance-growth nexus.

2. These expectations were supported by the cross-sectional empirical evidence on the determinants of financial development, which shows that countries with sounder macroeconomic policies, better institutional environments, and more efficient legal systems, especially regarding the protection of creditors and minority shareholders, have more developed do-

markets in many emerging economies has been disappointing. Although some countries experienced growth of their domestic markets, this growth in most cases has not been as significant as the one witnessed by industrialized nations. Other countries experienced an actual deterioration of their capital markets. Stock markets in many developing countries have seen listings and liquidity decrease, as a growing number of firms have cross-listed and raised capital in international financial centers, such as New York and London.[3] In many emerging economies, stock markets remain highly illiquid and segmented, with trading and capitalization concentrated on few stocks. Also, bonds tend to be concentrated at the short end of the maturity spectrum and denominated in foreign currency, exposing governments and firms to maturity and currency risks.[4] The large number of policy initiatives and the disappointing performance of capital markets have left policymakers without clear guidance on how to revise the reform agenda going forward, and many do not envision a bright future for domestic capital markets in developing countries.

In this paper, we analyze the state of capital market in Latin America and discuss how to rethink the reform agenda going forward in light of this evidence. Our focus on Latin American countries is motivated by the fact that these countries were at the forefront of the capital market reform process over the last decades.[5] Despite the intense reform effort, capital markets in the region seem to have lagged behind, not only relative to developed countries, but also compared to emerging economies in other regions, such as East Asia (de la Torre and Schmukler 2006). Analyzing the experience of Latin American countries may provide significant lessons for the capital market reform agenda going forward, which may also apply to emerging economies in other regions.

We start by documenting the extent of capital market development in Latin America and comparing it to other regions. We then use formal analyses to further understand how the state of stock markets in the region

mestic financial markets (see, for example, Boyd, Levine, and Smith 2001; La Porta, Lopez de Silanes, and Shleifer 2006; and La Porta et al., 1997, 1998).

3. Karolyi (2004) and Moel (2001) offer evidence on how the use of American Depositary Receipts (ADRs) is related to stock market development in emerging economies. Levine and Schmukler (2006a,b) analyze the impact of migration to international markets on domestic market trading and liquidity.

4. See Mihaljek, Scatigna, and Villar (2002) for an overview of the characteristics of bond markets in emerging economies.

5. Starting in the late 1980s and early 1990s, most Latin American countries implemented macro stabilization programs and liberalized their financial systems, ending a long period of financial repression. Apart from macro stabilization and liberalization, governments throughout the region approved new legislation aimed at creating the proper market infrastructure and institutions for capital markets to flourish. These capital market reforms were complemented in a number of cases by privatization efforts and by comprehensive pension system reforms. See de la Torre and Schmukler (2006) for an overview of the capital market reform process in Latin America.

differs from that in other regions. In particular, we are interested in assessing whether there is a gap between fundamentals and policies, on the one hand, and actual stock market development, on the other. This issue is highly relevant for the policy debate. The observed lack of capital market development in Latin America may be a consequence of the region's poor fundamentals, suggesting the need to push further ahead in the reform effort to achieve a higher level of economic and institutional development, which in turn should result in more developed capital markets. On the other hand, the finding of a shortfall between actual capital market development in the region and the level of development predicted by its economic and institutional fundamentals could indicate that reforms and improvements in these fundamentals have not had the expected results so far. This suggests that it might be necessary to revise the reform agenda and related expectations to take into account certain characteristics of these countries that may limit the scope for developing deep domestic securities markets. Finally, we discuss alternative ways of interpreting the evidence, with the goal of drawing lessons for the reform agenda going forward.

The evidence shows that despite the intense reform effort, capital markets in Latin America remain underdeveloped compared to markets in East Asia and developed countries. Furthermore, we find that stock markets in the region are below what can be expected, given economic and institutional fundamentals. In particular, we find that there is a shortfall in domestic stock market activity (market capitalization, trading, and capital raising) in Latin America after controlling for many factors, including per capita income, macroeconomic policies, and measures of the legal and institutional environment.

We discuss how different lines of thought would assess this gap between predicted and observed outcomes. This exercise helps to gain a better understanding of the possible reasons for this divergence and sharpen the criteria to guide an appropriate reformulation of policy recommendations. We argue that two stylized views dominate the current reform debate in this regard. The first view, encapsulated in the message "be patient and redouble the effort," contends that the gap between expectations and observed outcomes is due to the combination of impatience with imperfect and incomplete reform efforts. This view argues that past reforms were basically right, that reforms needed in the future are essentially known, and that reforms have long gestation periods before producing visible results.[6] The second view, encapsulated in the message "get the sequence right," claims that the gap is due to faulty reform sequencing. This view draws attention to the problems that arise when some reforms are implemented

---

6. Renditions of this view, in the more general context of assessing the impact of reforms on economic development, can be found, for instance, in Fernandez Arias and Montiel (2001), Krueger (2004), Singh et al. (2005), and World Bank (1997).

ahead of others and argues that key preconditions should be met before fully liberalizing domestic financial markets and allowing free international capital mobility.[7]

Though differing in diagnoses and policy prescriptions, these views are not necessarily incompatible, and both capture important aspects of the problem at hand, yielding considerable insights. Our main argument, however, is that neither of the two views may adequately address a number of salient questions posed by the evidence. We therefore propose a third, complementary view that is much less prescriptive. This view can be encapsulated in the message "revisit basic issues and reshape expectations."[8] It contends that, although more research is needed, it is difficult to pinpoint which factors may explain the relative underdevelopment of domestic capital markets in Latin America. Future research might find that the gap between predicted and observed outcomes is explained by some factor not included in the long list of controls used in this paper. Nevertheless, we claim that there might as well be important deficiencies with the expectations and design of past reforms. This view argues that policy initiatives need to take into account the intrinsic characteristics of developing countries (such as small size, lack of risk diversification opportunities, presence of weak currencies, and prevalence of systemic risk) and how these features limit the scope for developing deep domestic capital markets in a context of international financial integration. These limitations are difficult to overcome by the reform process. In other words, even if emerging economies carry out all the necessary reforms, they might not obtain a domestic capital market development comparable to that of industrialized countries.

The rest of the paper is structured as follows. Section 4.2 presents descriptive statistics on capital market development in Latin America and compares them to other regions. Section 4.3 describes the econometric estimations of whether stock market development in Latin America is close to the level predicted by fundamentals. Section 4.4 discusses the typological views on why the state of capital markets is different than expected. Section 4.5 concludes.

4.2   Capital Markets in Latin America

This section analyzes the state of capital markets in Latin American countries and compares them to those in other countries. Figure 4.1 shows different indicators of financial development for selected Latin American, East Asian, and developed countries. In particular, this figure presents data on credit to the private sector by financial institutions, stock market capitalization, and the amount outstanding of private sector domestic

7. This view is articulated, for example, in Bhagwati (1998) and Stiglitz (2002).
8. This view is described in more detail in de la Torre and Schmukler (2006).

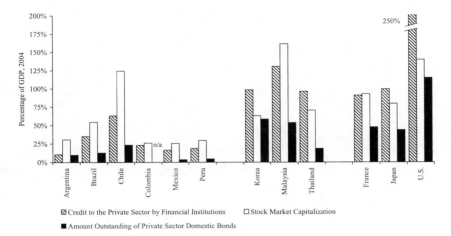

⊠ Credit to the Private Sector by Financial Institutions   □ Stock Market Capitalization

■ Amount Outstanding of Private Sector Domestic Bonds

Fig. 4.1   Domestic financial sector development across countries

Note: This figure shows credit to the private sector by financial institutions over GDP, domestic stock market capitalization over GDP, and the amount outstanding of private sector domestic bonds over GDP at year-end 2004 for selected countries.

Sources: BIS, IMF International Financial Statistics, S&P Emerging Markets Database, World Bank.

bonds, all as a percentage of gross domestic product (GDP), at year-end 2004. As this figure shows, although there are differences among Latin American countries, most countries in the region have significantly smaller financial markets than G7 and East Asian countries. Chile is the only exception, as the size of its financial markets, especially its stock market, vastly exceeds that of other Latin American countries and also compares favorably with financial markets in developed and East Asian countries. However, analyzing measures of actual stock market activity, such as value traded, shows that Chile's stock market remains underdeveloped compared to markets in East Asia and developed countries.[9]

Figures 4.2 and 4.3 display average values of different measures of stock market development for Latin American, G7, and East Asian countries for the years 1990 and 2004. As figure 4.2 shows, stock markets in Latin America have grown considerably over the last decades. The average domestic stock market capitalization in terms of GDP in the seven largest markets in the region (Argentina, Brazil, Chile, Colombia, Mexico, Peru, and Venezuela) more than tripled between 1990 and 2004. Value traded in domestic stock markets also increased significantly during this period, from an

9. Value traded over GDP reached 12.4 percent in Chile in 2004, compared to 65.5 percent in France, 74.2 percent in Japan, and 165.9 percent in the United States. The East Asian countries presented in the graph also had significantly higher levels of trading activity than Chile, with value traded over GDP reaching 94 percent in Korea, 50.8 percent in Malaysia, and 66.7 percent in Thailand.

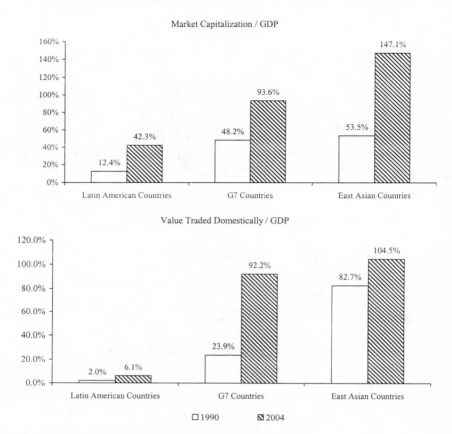

Fig. 4.2   Domestic stock market development

Notes This figure shows market capitalization over GDP and value traded domestically over GDP. The series are averages across countries. The data for G7 countries are averages for Canada, France, Germany, Italy, Japan, the United Kingdom, and the United States. The data for East Asian countries are averages for Hong Kong, Indonesia, Korea, Malaysia, the Philippines, Taiwan, and Thailand. The data for Latin American countries are averages for Argentina, Brazil, Chile, Colombia, Mexico, Peru, and Venezuela.

Sources: S&P Emerging Markets Database, World Bank.

average of 2.0 percent of GDP in 1990 to 6.1 percent in 2004. Despite this strong growth, stock markets in Latin America are still small when compared to those in other regions. At the end of 2004, stock market capitalization in this region reached 42.3 percent of GDP, compared to 93.6 and 147.1 percent in G7 and East Asian countries, respectively. Regional differences are more striking when analyzing trading activity, with Latin American countries appearing to be caught in a low liquidity trap. While value traded in domestic stock markets stood at 6.1 percent of GDP in Latin

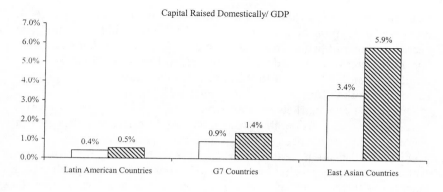

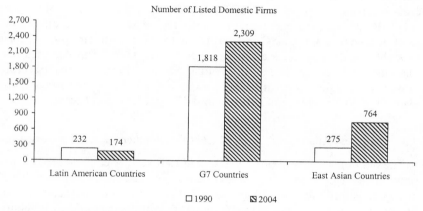

□ 1990   ◪ 2004

Fig. 4.3   Domestic stock market development

Notes: This figure shows capital raised over GDP and the number of listed domestic firms. The series are averages across countries. The data for G7 countries are averages for Canada, France, Germany, Italy, Japan, the United Kingdom, and the United States. The data for East Asian countries are averages for Hong Kong, Indonesia, Korea, Malaysia, the Philippines, Taiwan, and Thailand. The data for Latin American countries are averages for Argentina, Brazil, Chile, Colombia, Mexico, Peru, and Venezuela.

Sources: S&P Emerging Markets Database, World Federation of Exchanges, World Bank.

America in 2004, it reached 92.2 percent in G7 countries and 104.5 percent in East Asia.[10]

Similar regional differences are visible when analyzing capital raising activity (figure 4.3). Capital raised as a percentage of GDP in Latin American

10. We also estimated the figures for East Asia excluding Hong Kong, as it may serve as a regional financial center for corporations from mainland China and other Asian countries. Although this reduces the average values for East Asian countries, these countries still show significantly higher stock market capitalization and trading than Latin American countries. When excluding Hong Kong, the average capitalization for the remaining East Asian countries included in the figures stood at 83.6 percent of GDP in 2004, whereas their value traded in that year reached 77 percent of GDP.

stock markets is lower than in other regions, reaching 0.5 percent in 2004, compared to 1.5 percent in G7 countries and 5.9 percent in East Asia.[11] The average number of firms listed in domestic stock markets in Latin America has decreased over the last decades, from 232 in 1990 to 174 in 2004.[12] This reduction stands in contrast to the increase in the number of listings experienced by both G7 and East Asian countries during this period.[13]

Domestic bond markets in both developed and developing countries have experienced considerable growth over the last decades. This growth was especially pronounced in East Asia following the 1997 crisis, as governments and firms increasingly switched to bond financing.[14] In Latin America, most progress has been made in the development of public bond markets, with the stock of domestic government bonds outstanding increasing from 12.3 percent of GDP in 1993 to 20.7 percent in 2004 (figure 4.4).[15] Public sector bond markets in the region present a development level close to that of East Asian markets. On the other hand, in spite of their growth over the last decades, private bond markets in Latin America remain underdeveloped. The amount outstanding of domestic private sector bonds in the region stood at 10.7 percent of GDP in 2004, compared to an average of 36.3 percent in East Asia and 47.7 percent in G7 countries.

4.3   Empirical Analysis of Stock Market Development in Latin America

The data on stock and bond markets in Latin America presented in the previous section show that, although securities markets in the region have grown substantially since 1990, Latin American capital markets remain underdeveloped when compared to markets in industrial and East Asian

11. Capital raising activity tends to be very volatile, varying widely from year to year. This could generate some concerns about whether the years presented in figure 4.3 are representative of the general patterns. However, similar regional differences are visible if one considers average values from 1990 to 2004. The average annual amount of capital raised in domestic stock markets in Latin American countries for this period reached 0.8 percent of GDP, compared to 1.3 percent in G7 countries and 4.6 percent in East Asia.

12. The reduction in the number of listed firms has been associated with the increasing migration of Latin American firms to international markets. Merger and acquisition activity, as well as majority shareholders trying to increase their controlling stakes, have also been brought forward as possible explanations for the growing stock market delistings in Latin America (see de la Torre and Schmukler 2006).

13. Different explanations have been proposed for the diverging trend in stock market listings between Latin America and East Asia. For one, unlike the European and U.S. stock markets, which performed well during the 1990s, stock markets in Hong Kong and Tokyo, the natural candidates for migration in Asia, have not done well in recent years (World Bank 2004).

14. Following the financial crisis, it was argued that capital markets in East Asia had not been diversified enough and that well-developed bond markets would have made several Asian economies less vulnerable to the crisis (see, for example, Batten and Kim 2001; Herring and Chatusripitak 2001).

15. The sample of East Asian and Latin American countries and the period presented in this figure differ from those used in figures 4.2 and 4.3 due to data availability.

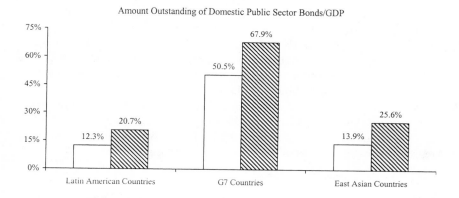

Amount Outstanding of Domestic Public Sector Bonds/GDP

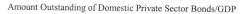

Amount Outstanding of Domestic Private Sector Bonds/GDP

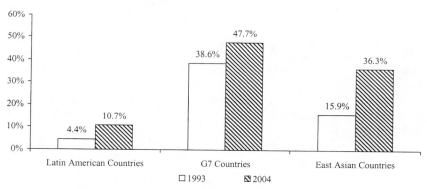

□ 1993   ◪ 2004

Fig. 4.4   Domestic bond market development

Notes: This figure shows the amounts outstanding of public and private sector bonds in domestic markets over GDP. The series are averages across countries. The data for G7 countries
are averages for Canada, France, Germany, Italy, Japan, the United Kingdom, and the United
States. The data for East Asian countries are averages for Hong Kong, Korea, Malaysia, Taiwan, and Thailand. The data for Latin American countries are averages for Argentina, Brazil,
Chile, Mexico, and Peru.

Sources: BIS, World Bank.

countries. This evidence suggests that the high expectations of the early
1990s about capital market development in the region have not been met.
An open question is whether this lack of development is a consequence of
the failure to build an environment conducive to capital market development, despite the intense reform effort, or if even when Latin American
countries have built such an environment, markets have failed to develop
as predicted. In this section we focus on answering this question. Doing so
requires a formal analysis of the determinants of capital market develop-

ment and then testing whether, once we control for those determinants, Latin American countries have less-developed capital markets. We focus our analysis on stock markets, as data on different measures of stock market development are available for a large cross-section of countries and a relatively long time series. In contrast, comprehensive data on domestic bond market development are available for a shorter period and a smaller sample of economies, making it more difficult to capture differences between Latin America and other regions. We first describe the dependent and explanatory variables and the methodology we use, then present the regression results, and finally discuss some robustness tests.

4.3.1 Data and Methodology

For the empirical analysis of stock markets, we follow Claessens, Klingebiel, and Schmukler (2006), who analyze the factors driving domestic stock market development and internationalization. We use three measures of domestic stock market development: market capitalization, value traded, and capital raised, all as a percentage of GDP.[16]

The data on market capitalization and value traded on the major local stock exchanges come from the Standard & Poor's Global Stock Markets Factbook and cover the period 1975 to 2004 for 117 countries. The amount of equity capital raised by domestic firms in the local stock market comes from the World Federation of Exchanges and covers the period 1982 to 2004 for 46 countries.

In terms of explanatory variables, we include several factors found to be important in the literature on stock market development. First, because more-developed countries tend to have deeper domestic stock markets (see, for example, La Porta, Lopez de Silanes, and Shleifer 2006; La Porta et al. 1997; and Rajan and Zingales 2003), we use GDP per capita as a measure of countries' overall economic development. Higher income countries also tend to have better institutional and legal environments, which have been found to matter for financial development (see Beck and Levine 2005).[17] To further address this issue, we include an index of the strength of minority shareholder rights from Djankov et al. (2008).[18]

The regressions include two alternative indicators of macroeconomic

16. We also estimated regressions using turnover (defined as value traded over market capitalization) and obtained results similar to those reported below.

17. Gross domestic product per capita is highly correlated with different measures of the institutional environment. For our sample, the correlation between GDP per capita and indexes of bureaucratic quality, corruption, and law and order reported by the International Country Risk Guide (ICRG) service is 0.73, 0.67 and 0.71, respectively, and in all cases it is significant at the 1 percent level. All the results reported in the paper are robust to replacing GDP per capita with any of these measures of the institutional environment.

18. Djankov et al. (2008) present revised estimates of the antidirector rights index from La Porta et al. (1998) and expand the sample of countries covered. All the results reported in the paper are robust to replacing this updated index with the original measure from La Porta et al. (1998).

soundness, the annual inflation rate and the government deficit over GDP, given that a better macroeconomic environment promotes financial development (see Bencivenga and Smith 1992; Boyd, Levine, and Smith 2001; and Huybens and Smith 1999).

We include three alternative variables to control for the extent of financial openness and liberalization, as that has been found to affect stock market development (see Bekaert and Harvey 2000, 2003; Edison and Warnock 2003; Henry 2000; and Levine and Zervos 1998). First, we include a de jure measure of capital account liberalization constructed by Chinn and Ito (2006). Second, as we are analyzing stock markets, we also use a de jure indicator of stock market liberalization. Our data for dating the liberalization of stock markets come from three sources: Bekaert, Harvey, and Lundblad (2005), who present official liberalization dates, mostly for developing countries; Kaminsky and Schmukler (2003), who construct an index of the extent of stock market liberalization which also includes developed economies; and Vinhas de Souza (2005), who extends this index to Eastern European countries.[19] We combine these three sources to get the widest possible coverage.[20] Finally, as a measure of de facto openness, we use equity flows, including both portfolio equity flows and foreign direct investment (FDI) flows, relative to GDP. This variable captures the effective integration with international capital markets and the de facto openness of the stock market; it can also be viewed as a measure of foreign demand for domestic equity.[21]

We also control for the possibility that local stock market development is affected by the growth opportunities that firms face. Growth opportunities may be particularly relevant for explaining capital raising behavior, as the literature on initial public offerings (IPOs) has highlighted (see Ritter and Welch [2002] for a review). Countries with better growth opportunities may need larger stock markets to satisfy a higher demand for external funds. Therefore, we include the global growth opportunities index from Bekaert et al. (2006), which measures how each country's industry mix is

19. For the data from Kaminsky and Schmukler (2003) and Vinhas de Souza (2005), we consider the first year when a country's stock market is fully liberalized as the liberalization date. Alternatively, we also used the date of the first partial liberalization and obtained similar results.

20. We also ran regressions using only the Bekaert, Harvey, and Lundblad (2005) dates and their "first sign" stock market liberalization measure, which is based on the earliest of three possibilities: the launching of a country fund, an ADR announcement, and the official liberalization date. We obtained similar results using these measures.

21. We include FDI flows because those flows, apart from new investment, also represent purchases of existing equity. In fact, equity flows are classified as FDI flows when they represent a purchase of at least 10 percent of a company's equity. Note that this variable could be affected by endogeneity, as foreign investment tends to go to countries with more developed financial markets. To reduce this potential problem and because good instruments are hard to obtain, we use this variable lagged one period. To check that our results are not affected by the inclusion of this variable, we also report estimations without it and find that the coefficients on the rest of the variables are unaffected.

priced in global capital markets, using the price earnings ratios of global industry portfolios.[22]

We additionally include GDP as a control variable in our regressions. Securities markets can gain efficiency by expanding their volume and number of participants because of economies of scale and scope and network externalities.[23] Consistent with these arguments, the literature has found the size of the economy to be an important factor for the development of liquid, well-functioning securities markets. See, for example, McCauley and Remolona (2000) and Shah and Thomas (200).

Finally, to test whether the level of stock market development in Latin America differs from that predicted from fundamentals, we include a Latin American dummy variable, which takes the value one if the country is located in Latin America and the Caribbean and zero otherwise.[24] If stock market development in Latin America is close to the level predicted by the region's fundamentals, this dummy should not be significant.

After removing outliers, countries with missing data on the independent variables, and countries with less than five annual observations, we are left with a sample of ninety-five countries covering the period 1975 to 2004.[25] The sample includes eighteen Latin American countries, which account on average for seventeen percent of the observations used in the regressions.[26] In all cases, we pool the data over time and across countries. Regarding the estimation technique, we use least squares estimators adjusting the standard errors for clustering at the country level.[27]

4.3.2   Regression Results

The results for stock market capitalization over GDP, value traded over GDP, and capital raised over GDP are presented in tables 4.1, 4.2, and 4.3,

---

22. Bekaert et al. (2006) use two country-specific industry weightings to calculate each country's growth opportunities index. One is based on the relative market capitalization of each industry in the local stock market. The other one is based on the relative value added of each industry in the respective country. We report the results using the latter weighting scheme but also estimated the regressions using the former and obtained similar results.

23. Network effects are an intrinsic feature of securities trading: the benefits of participating in a given market increase with the number of participants (Economides 1993, 1996; Di Noia 1999). This generates positive feedback, as a liquid market attracts more participants and each new participant brings additional trading opportunities and liquidity, benefiting all market participants and making the market more attractive to others. There is also evidence of economies of scale in stock exchange activities, especially regarding order execution (Malkamaki 1999).

24. For defining this dummy we consider the World Bank regional classification, which includes Latin American and Caribbean countries. We also estimated all the regressions excluding the Caribbean countries and obtained similar results.

25. We also estimated the regressions constraining the sample to countries with at least three annual observations and without imposing any restrictions on the number of observations and obtained results similar to those reported in the paper in both cases.

26. See table 4A.1 for the list of countries covered.

27. We also estimated all the regressions using panel feasible generalized least squared (FGLS), allowing for heteroscedastic error structures and different autocorrelation coefficients within countries, and obtained similar results.

respectively. The tables provide in the first column the results for a regression with GDP per capita, inflation, and capital account liberalization as the only explanatory variables. The tables then report a regression with government deficit over GDP instead of inflation as these two constitute alternative indicators of macroeconomic soundness and stability. To keep the size of the tables manageable, we just continue to use one of the macro variables, government deficit over GDP.[28] In the third and fourth column, the tables report regressions with the stock market liberalization index and equity flows as a percentage of GDP, respectively, replacing the capital account liberalization dummy. In the fifth and sixth columns, the shareholder rights index is introduced. In the sixth column, we include the growth opportunities measure. In the seventh and eighth columns, we control for GDP instead of GDP per capita. We do not include GDP and GDP per capita in the same specification as these variables are highly correlated.[29] Note, however, that all our results are robust to controlling for both variables and to replacing GDP per capita with GDP. We discuss the results in turn.

The regression results for market capitalization as a ratio of GDP (table 4.1) indicate that stock market development in our sample is related to the variables in ways already identified in the literature. In particular, GDP per capita, financial openness (measured by stock market liberalization and equity flows over GDP), shareholder rights, and the size of the economy are positively and significantly associated with market capitalization, while government deficits are negatively related to stock market development. The growth opportunities variable enters positively and significantly in the regressions.

More relevant for our analysis, the dummy variable for Latin America enters negatively and significantly in all the specifications. The effect is also economically relevant: the average coefficient for the dummy in these regressions is –0.17, which means that market capitalization over GDP in Latin American countries is on average 17 percentage points below the level predicted by their fundamentals and policies. This is a large difference, given that the average market capitalization over GDP for Latin American countries in these regressions is 18 percent.

Similar conclusions are obtained when analyzing value traded domestically over GDP (table 4.2). Most of the control variables have the expected sign: more developed countries, with sounder macroeconomic policies and more financial openness, tend to have higher trading activity. Also, countries with better growth opportunities have more domestic trading. The dummy for Latin American countries enters negatively and significantly at the 1 percent level in all the specifications, indicating that countries in the

28. We choose this variable because inflation is not statistically significant in most regressions. We obtained results similar to those reported in the paper when controlling for both inflation and fiscal deficit.

29. The correlation between the logarithm of GDP per capita and the logarithm of GDP is 0.54 for our sample of countries and is significant at the 1 percent level.

Table 4.1   Domestic stock market development—Market capitalization

	Market capitalization/GDP							
	(1)	(2)	(3)	(4)	(5)	(6)	(7)	(8)
Log of GDP per capita	0.104***	0.094***	0.119***	0.104***	0.101***	0.077***		
	(4.321)	(3.344)	(4.060)	(4.665)	(4.254)	(3.190)		
Log of GDP							0.076***	0.054***
							(3.432)	(2.176)
Shareholder rights					0.091**	0.078*	0.075*	0.059
					(2.229)	(1.736)	(1.719)	(1.260)
Log (1 + inflation)	−0.057							
	(1.234)							
Government deficit/GDP		−2.403***	−2.215***	−1.336***	−1.314***	−1.224***	−1.636***	−1.396***
		(3.515)	(3.117)	(3.325)	(3.554)	(3.044)	(3.795)	(3.151)
Capital account liberalization	0.056**	0.036						
	(2.088)	(1.196)						
Stock market liberalization			0.111**					
			(2.439)					
Total equity flows/GDP (one year lagged)				4.266***	5.378***	8.693***	6.482***	9.891***
				(2.778)	(3.304)	(4.609)	(3.742)	(5.107)
Global measure of country growth opportunities						0.245***	0.218***	0.218***
						(4.595)	(4.447)	(4.447)
Latin American dummy	−0.126*	−0.194***	−0.177***	−0.168***	−0.132**	−0.167***	−0.163**	−0.208***
	(1.880)	(3.082)	(2.812)	(2.995)	(2.455)	(2.971)	(2.448)	(3.236)
No. of observations	1,661	1,364	1,419	1,291	1,133	836	1,133	836
No. of countries	87	79	82	83	63	45	63	45
No. of Latin American countries	18	18	16	15	12	7	12	7
R^2	0.243	0.259	0.235	0.268	0.348	0.445	0.331	0.426

Notes: This table shows ordinary least square regressions with standard errors adjusted for clustering at the country level for a panel of ninety-five countries between 1975 and 2004. A constant is estimated but not reported. Absolute values of t-statistics are in parentheses.

***Significant at the 1 percent level.

**Significant at the 5 percent level.

*Significant at the 10 percent level.

Table 4.2 Domestic stock market development—Value traded domestically

	Value traded domestically/GDP							
	(1)	(2)	(3)	(4)	(5)	(6)	(7)	(8)
Log of GDP per capita	0.081*** (4.356)	0.062*** (3.087)	0.099*** (3.182)	0.074*** (3.105)	0.074*** (3.065)	0.063*** (2.993)		
Log of GDP							0.081*** (4.019)	0.076*** (3.419)
Shareholder rights							0.007 (0.464)	-0.007 (0.320)
Log (1 + Inflation)	0.015 (0.771)				0.020 (1.446)	0.012 (0.728)		
Government deficit/GDP		-1.321*** (3.654)	-1.020** (2.145)	-0.778*** (2.668)	-0.810** (2.493)	-0.728** (2.045)	-0.976** (2.634)	-0.735* (1.985)
Capital account liberalization	0.030** (2.433)	0.024** (2.409)						
Stock market liberalization			0.058* (1.768)					
Total equity flows/GDP (one year lagged)				2.579*** (3.006)	3.007*** (2.923)	4.625*** (3.002)	3.928*** (3.502)	5.732*** (3.627)
Global measure of country growth opportunities						0.252*** (3.944)		0.188*** (4.030)
Latin American dummy	-0.143*** (5.513)	-0.125*** (4.488)	-0.145*** (3.538)	-0.128*** (4.466)	-0.120*** (3.710)	-0.137*** (3.283)	-0.134*** (3.559)	-0.169*** (3.689)
No. of observations	1,627	1,342	1,394	1,268	1,138	830	1,138	830
No. of countries	83	75	78	80	64	46	64	46
No. of Latin American countries	16	16	14	14	12	7	12	7
R^2	0.206	0.207	0.141	0.210	0.226	0.294	0.285	0.340

Notes: This table shows ordinary least square regressions with standard errors adjusted for clustering at the country level for a panel of ninety-five countries between 1975 and 2004. A constant is estimated but not reported. Absolute values of *t*-statistics are in parentheses.

***Significant at the 1 percent level.

**Significant at the 5 percent level.

*Significant at the 10 percent level.

region have lower value traded domestically than warranted by their fundamentals.

When analyzing capital raised domestically over GDP (table 4.3), we find similar results as for the other two measures of stock market development, although fewer variables are statistically significant, in part due to the lumpy and volatile nature of capital raising activity. Countries with sounder macro policies tend to see more capital raising, although government deficit over GDP is not always statistically significant. More open countries (as measured by equity flows over GDP), as well as countries with a better legal protection of shareholder rights and more growth opportunities, also have higher capital raising activity. The Latin American dummy enters negatively and significantly at the 1 percent level in all specifications.

Overall, the results in tables 4.1, 4.2, and 4.3 yield similar conclusions: countries with higher income, sounder macroeconomic policies, better protection of shareholder rights, greater financial openness, larger economies, and higher growth opportunities, have more developed local stock markets. Regarding Latin America, the results indicate that there is a shortfall in the actual development of stock markets in the region, relative to its fundamentals. In other words, Latin American countries have lower stock market development than countries with similar fundamentals and policies in other regions.

4.3.3 Robustness Tests

The results presented in this section show that stock markets in Latin American are below what can be expected, given the region's economic and institutional fundamentals and policies. Given the relevance of these results, we subjected them to a number of robustness tests by including several additional control variables suggested by the literature on capital market development.

First, we controlled for macroeconomic volatility as the empirical evidence suggests that the depth of domestic financial systems is inversely related to volatility (see, for example, IDB 1995). To the extent that macroeconomic volatility might have been higher in Latin America than in other regions and was not fully captured by the control variables included in the regressions, this could explain the negative sign and statistical significance of the Latin American dummy.[30] To address this issue, we reestimated the regressions including measures of inflation and interest rate volatility at different time horizons.[31] We find that these variables tend to have a negative

---

30. Note that the regressions include two indicators of macroeconomic soundness, the annual inflation rate and the government deficit over GDP.

31. We controlled for the volatility of inflation and real interest rates over the previous three, five, and ten years. Also, as Boyd, Levine, and Smith (2001) highlight the nonlinear relation between inflation and financial-sector performance, we explored nonlinear effects of inflation on stock market development. Although the results suggest that nonlinear effects might be important, they do not affect the basic conclusions reported in the tables.

Table 4.3   Domestic stock market development—Capital raised domestically

	(1)	(2)	(3)	(4)	(5)	(6)	(7)	(8)
					Capital raised domestically/GDP			
Log of GDP per capita	-0.001 (0.891)	-0.002 (1.223)	-0.001 (0.272)	-0.003 (1.553)	-0.002 (1.527)	-0.003** (2.119)		
Log of GDP							0.001 (1.125)	0.000 (0.631)
Shareholder rights					0.004*** (2.741)	0.003** (2.453)	0.005** (2.663)	0.004** (2.348)
Log (1 + Inflation)	-0.003 (1.494)							
Government deficit/GDP		-0.098*** (2.878)	-0.092** (2.550)	-0.015 (0.931)	-0.013 (0.759)	-0.018 (1.094)	-0.004 (0.246)	-0.007 (0.422)
Capital account liberalization	0.001 (0.777)	0.000 (0.321)						
Stock market liberalization			0.005* (1.874)					
Total equity flows/GDP (one year lagged)				0.256*** (4.159)	0.217*** (3.355)	0.229*** (3.370)	0.220*** (3.620)	0.226*** (3.514)
Global measure of country growth opportunities						0.012*** (3.525)		0.011*** (3.116)
Latin American dummy	-0.010*** (2.754)	-0.013*** (3.077)	-0.013*** (3.497)	-0.014*** (4.200)	-0.013*** (5.302)	-0.014*** (6.023)	-0.010*** (5.193)	-0.011*** (5.580)
No. of observations	688	564	617	520	505	468	505	468
No. of countries	40	37	40	35	33	31	33	31
No. of Latin American countries	5	5	5	5	5	4	5	4
R^2	0.036	0.085	0.045	0.184	0.231	0.254	0.224	0.237

Notes: This table shows ordinary least square regressions with standard errors adjusted for clustering at the country level for a panel of forty-six countries between 1982 and 2004. A constant is estimated but not reported. Absolute values of *t*-statistics are in parentheses.

***Significant at the 1 percent level.

**Significant at the 5 percent level.

*Significant at the 10 percent level.

(although usually not statistically significant) relation with stock market development, but their inclusion does not affect the sign and significance of the Latin American dummy. Also, the size of the coefficients on this dummy is mostly unaffected by the inclusion of these controls.

Second, the lower level of stock market development in Latin American countries may be due to a worse institutional environment in these countries, which was not adequately captured by the control variables used in the regressions. To address this issue, we included a number of additional measures of the quality of the institutional framework. In particular, we controlled for indicators of corruption, bureaucratic quality, law and order, political risk, government stability, and investment profile developed by International Country Risk Guide; an index of the quality of accounting standards constructed by Bushman, Piotroski, and Smith (2004); and different proxies for the functioning of the judicial system, including the time it takes to resolve disputes (Djankov et al. 2003) and an index of the overall efficiency of the judicial system, as reported by Business International Corporation. We also controlled for a country's legal tradition, as this has been found to be associated with the protection of shareholder rights (La Porta et al. 1997, 1998), the efficiency of the judicial system (Djankov et al. 2003), and the protection of property rights (Beck, Demirgüç-Kunt, and Levine 2003). While many of these variables are statistically significant and have the sign suggested by the literature, the Latin American dummy remains statistically significant and negative and the size of its coefficients is mostly unchanged.

Finally, we controlled for the level of savings in each country. A higher savings level means that more local resources are available to be invested in the domestic financial system and therefore may be associated with a higher stock market development (see, for example, Garcia and Liu 1999).[32] The relative underdevelopment of stock markets in Latin America may be explained by the low savings rate in the region.[33] To address this issue, we reestimated the regressions controlling for savings as a percentage of GDP. This variable tends to be positive (although usually not statistically significant); however, its inclusion does not affect the sign, significance, or size of the Latin American dummy.

Although more research is needed, the robustness of the results indicates

32. Causality may also run in the other direction, from more developed financial markets to higher savings. For instance, deeper domestic financial markets may offer investors more investment opportunities and higher returns, potentially resulting in more savings. To address this concern, we use savings lagged one period.

33. Savings rates in Latin America have stagnated over the last two decades, standing at about 17 percent of GDP. In contrast, savings in East Asia averaged more than 30 percent of GDP over this period. Several studies have pointed to low savings rates in Latin America as a significant constraint to the region's growth (see, for example, Edwards [1995] and Schmidt-Hebbel and Serven [1997]). See Plies and Reinhart (1999) for an overview of the behavior of savings in Latin America.

that it is difficult to identify the factors behind the underdevelopment of Latin American capital markets. This suggests that certain characteristics of Latin American countries, beyond those usually highlighted in the literature on capital market development, limit the scope for developing deep domestic securities markets in the region.

4.4 What Went Wrong and What to Do Next?

The evidence reported in sections 4.2 and 4.3 shows that capital markets in Latin America are underdeveloped, not only compared to markets in East Asia and industrialized nations, but also relative to the level predicted by the region's fundamentals and policies. We now turn to the analysis of these two findings to draw lessons for the capital market reform agenda going forward. Assessing the evidence is a process that, by nature, involves significant resort to judgment calls. There is thus ample scope for differing yet reasonable explanations for the gap between expectations and outcomes. This section aims at providing a flavor of the range of perspectives on this question by identifying three typological views. This typology is used mainly for presentational purposes, to help depict the nature of the debate and highlight the policy issues under discussion. A more detailed discussion of these issues is presented in de la Torre and Schmukler (2006).

The first view, encapsulated in the message "be patient and redouble the effort," ascribes the observed gap between outcomes and expectations to a combination of insufficient reform implementation with impatience. In effect, despite what many claim, key reforms were in some cases not even initiated, while other reforms were often implemented in an incomplete or inconsistent fashion. In many cases, laws and regulations were approved, but they were not duly implemented, nor were they adequately enforced.[34] Moreover, policymakers have been too impatient, often expecting results to materialize sooner than warranted. However, complex reforms tend to have long gestation periods. According to proponents of this view, the emphasis going forward should be on forging ahead persistently with the hard work of improving the enabling environment for capital markets; enhancing market discipline through greater competition; upgrading the regulatory and supervisory framework for securities markets; and improving key areas such as accounting and disclosure standards, corporate governance practices, and securities trading, custody, clearing, and settlement systems.[35]

34. To the extent that the quality of reforms was lower in Latin America and the control variables used in our regressions did not capture this difference, this could explain the significance and negative sign of the Latin American dummy.

35. This is broadly consistent with our empirical findings, as our results show that economies with sounder macro policies, better protection of shareholder rights, and greater openness tend to have more developed stock markets. Also consistent with this view, de la Torre, Gozzi, and Schmukler (2006) find that capital market-related reforms tend to be followed by significant increases in domestic stock market capitalization, trading, and capital raising.

The second view, encapsulated in the message "get the sequence right," claims that the gap between outcomes and expectations is due to faulty reform sequencing. This view contends that capital market reforms were—to one degree or another—part of the problem rather than the solution and draws attention to the problems that arise from the adoption of certain reforms before others are in place.[36] The most familiar rendition of this view focuses on the pitfalls of premature financial market liberalization, arguing that liberalizing the financial system before achieving a minimum threshold of institutional strength—in terms of the legal and regulatory framework, supervisory capacity, accounting and disclosure standards, and so forth—is likely to exacerbate distortions in financial markets.[37] According to proponents of this view, the task of recasting the reform agenda going forward hinges on the success of efforts devoted to systematically clarifying sequencing issues.

The third view, encapsulated in the message "revisit basic issues and reshape expectations," arises from the identification of shortcomings in the previous two views. This view focuses on the gaps in our knowledge and is, as a result, much less prescriptive. It contends that policy initiatives need to take into account the intrinsic characteristics of developing countries (such as small size, lack of risk diversification opportunities, presence of weak currencies, and prevalence of systemic risk), and how these features limit the scope for developing deep domestic capital markets. These limitations are difficult to overcome by the reform process. This view therefore calls for a more varied reform agenda, as a one-size-fits-all approach is destined to fail. It emphasizes that a key step in designing country-specific reforms going forward should be a determination of whether the emerging economy in question can sustain an active domestic market for private sector securities. It also argues that ultimately, any reform agenda for capital markets needs to be couched within a broader vision of financial development for emerging markets in the context of international financial integration.

Confronting the first two views with relevant aspects of the evidence leads to the conclusion that important things are inadequately addressed by them. Perhaps the most questionable aspect of both views, in light of the

36. To the extent that reform sequencing in Latin America was imperfect and worse than in other regions and that the control variables used in our regressions failed to capture this difference, this may account for the sign and significance of the Latin American dummy in the regressions.

37. A standard policy recommendation therefore is to upgrade the financial regulation and supervision and improve the health of the financial system before deregulating financial markets and opening up the capital account (see, for example, Johnston and Sundararajan [1999] and McKinnon [1993]). Not all sequencing arguments are related to financial liberalization. Some emphasize the building block nature of financial development, whereby interlinkages across different markets make certain reforms necessary for the success of others (see, for example, Karacadag, Sundararajan, and Elliott 2003).

evidence presented in this paper, is their implicit assumption that domestic capital market development in emerging economies should be measured against the benchmark of capital markets in industrialized countries. For the first two views, the reform path may be long and difficult, and it may require an adequate sequencing of reforms, but the expected outcome is, in most cases, only one. The expectation is that, as reforms advance, domestic capital markets in emerging markets will increasingly resemble those in developed countries. But it is difficult to accept this premise given the evidence presented so far. Despite the intense reform efforts, capital markets in Latin America remain underdeveloped, not only compared to other regions, but also relative to the level predicted by the region's fundamentals and policies. These results suggest that certain characteristics of Latin American countries, beyond those usually highlighted in the capital market reform literature, limit the scope for developing deep domestic markets. Therefore, it is very difficult to pinpoint which policies Latin American countries should pursue to overcome the lack of development of their capital markets.

A salient characteristic of many emerging economies that the reform debate has failed to adequately take into account is their small size. Secondary market liquidity is a positive function of market size and the related network and agglomeration effects. Consistent with this idea, our results show that the size of the economy is positively related to domestic stock market development. The small size of many emerging economies may therefore present a significant structural barrier for developing deep and liquid domestic markets. However, this factor alone does not account for the observed lack of capital market development in Latin America, as our estimations show that the regional dummy remains negative and significant when controlling for size. In the case of Latin America, the adverse effect of smallness may be exacerbated by the higher concentration exhibited by markets in the region (de la Torre and Schmukler 2006). In effect, a general pattern in Latin American markets is that only few firms are capable of issuing securities in amounts that meet the minimum thresholds for liquidity, and these securities are mostly purchased by few institutional investors that tend to follow buy and hold strategies, further contributing to low trading activity. In the case of equity markets, lack of trading is also the result of low float ratios (a low percentage of listed shares available for trading), reflecting concentrated ownership patterns and the reluctance to give up control. To the extent that these characteristics are more prevalent in Latin America than in other regions, this may account for the significance of the Latin American dummy in our regressions.

The policy discussion on capital market reform has tended to focus on the development of domestic financial systems. This fails to reflect the fact that, in a globalized context, financial development has much to do with the extent and type of integration with international financial markets. Financial globalization calls for a more general approach to understanding financial development—one that looks at the domestic and international sides of the process simultaneously. In this perspective, successful financial development is best characterized as the sustainable deepening and broadening of access to financial services, regardless of whether such services are provided at home or abroad, by securities markets or other markets. A greater attention to financial globalization does not imply, however, that the much wider scope for cross-border financial contracting resulting from globalization renders domestic markets useless. It is difficult to imagine that international financial markets would become a perfect substitute of local markets in every respect.[38] Thus, the point is not to deny the relevance of local financial markets but to stress that such relevance acquires meaning under globalization to the extent that domestic markets are a complement, rather than a substitute, to the international market integration.

One significant policy concern about the financial globalization process is that the increasing migration of firms to international financial centers may affect domestic stock markets adversely as too little activity remains at home.[39] This might help to explain our empirical results, as the evidence shows that the level of internationalization of Latin American stock markets far exceeds that of other regions (de la Torre and Schmukler 2006). To the extent that this higher level of internationalization was not captured by the controls included in our regressions and that internationalization adversely affects domestic markets, this may explain the sign and significance of the Latin American dummy.

4.5   Conclusions

In this paper, we analyzed the state of capital markets in Latin America. We found that despite the intense reform effort, capital markets in the region remain underdeveloped compared to markets in East Asia and developed countries. Furthermore, we found that stock markets in Latin America are below what can be expected, given the region's economic and institutional fundamentals. In particular, our results indicate that there is a shortfall in domestic stock market activity (market capitalization, trading, and capital raising) in the region after controlling for many factors, including per capita income, macroeconomic policies, the size of the economy, and measures of the legal and institutional environment.

We described alternative ways of interpreting this evidence and dis-

38. Guiso, Sapienza, and Zingales (2004) find that local financial development is an important determinant of the economic success of firms (especially smaller ones) even in an environment where there are no frictions to capital movements.

39. A number of publications have expressed concerns that local markets are becoming illiquid due to internationalization (see, for example, Bovespa 1996; Federation des Bourses de Valeurs 2000; *Financial Times* 1998; *Latin Finance* 1999; and *The Economist* 2001).

cussed the lessons for the reform agenda. We argued that two stylized views dominate the current debate. The first contends that the gap between expectations and outcomes is due to the combination of impatience with imperfect and incomplete reform efforts. The second claims that the gap is due to faulty reform sequencing. Though differing in diagnoses and policy prescriptions, these views are not necessarily incompatible, and both capture important aspects of the problem at hand. Our main argument, however, is that neither of the two views may adequately address a number of salient questions posed by the evidence. The third, complementary view is much less prescriptive. It highlights the need to step back, revisit certain basic issues, and reshape expectations, as a prior step to ensure more solid grounds for a reformulation of the reform agenda.

Our study comes with several caveats. Although we used as explanatory variables what we believe are the main drivers of stock market development, some variables were not included. For example, the quality of the banking system and securities market infrastructure (like the efficiency and reliability of clearing and settlement systems) may be important determinants of domestic market development. Furthermore, it is possible that the variables we used as controls are too general and fail to capture specific aspects of the institutional and regulatory framework that are particularly relevant for domestic stock market development. To the extent that Latin American countries score worse than other countries in those respects, this may help to explain the significance and negative sign of the Latin American dummy in our regressions. However, one potential difficulty in performing empirical analysis is that some factors that are relevant for capital market development may show little or no variation over time, making it difficult to separate their effects from those of a simple regional dummy. Finally, while we discussed different factors that may explain our results, we kept the discussion at a general level and have not evaluated our hypotheses empirically. Thus, we believe that our conclusions should remain tentative and that further research is needed to identify the factors behind the lower level of capital market development in Latin America unearthed by our analyses.

Appendix

Table 4A.1	List of countries	
Argentina[a]	Hong Kong	Panama[a]
Armenia	Hungary	Paraguay[a]
Australia	Iceland	Peru[a]
Austria	India	Philippines, The
Bangladesh	Indonesia	Poland
Barbados[a]	Iran	Portugal
Belgium	Ireland	Romania
Bolivia[a]	Israel	Russia
Botswana	Italy	Saudi Arabia
Brazil[a]	Jamaica[a]	Singapore
Bulgaria	Japan	Slovak Republic
Canada	Jordan	Slovenia
Chile[a]	Kenya	South Africa
China	Kuwait	South Korea
Colombia[a]	Latvia	Spain
Costa Rica[a]	Lithuania	Sri Lanka
Côte d'Ivoire	Malawi	Swaziland
Croatia	Malaysia	Sweden
Cyprus	Malta	Switzerland
Czech Republic	Mauritius	Taiwan
Denmark	Mexico[a]	Tanzania
Ecuador[a]	Moldova	Thailand
Egypt	Mongolia	Trinidad and Tobago[a]
El Salvador[a]	Morocco	Tunisia
Estonia	Namibia	Turkey
Fiji	Nepal	United Kingdom
Finland	Netherlands, The	United States
France	New Zealand	Uruguay[a]
Germany	Nigeria	Venezuela[a]
Ghana	Norway	Zambia
Greece	Oman	Zimbabwe
Guatemala[a]	Pakistan	

Note: This table shows the list of countries used in the regressions.
[a]The country is in the Latin American and Caribbean region.

References

Batten, J., and Y. H. Kim. 2001. Expanding long-term financing through bond market development: A post-crisis policy task. In *Government bond market development in Asia,* ed. Y. H. Kim, 5–48. Manila, The Philippines: Asian Development Bank.

Beck, T., A. Demirgüç-Kunt, and R. Levine. 2003. Law, endowments, and finance. *Journal of Financial Economics* 70:137–81.

Beck, T., and R. Levine. 2005. Legal institutions and financial development. In

Handbook of new institutional economics, ed. C. Menard and M. Shirley, 251–80. Norwell, MA: Kluwer Academic Publishers.

Bekaert, G., and C. R. Harvey. 2000. Foreign speculators and emerging equity markets. *Journal of Finance* 55:565–614.

———. 2003. Emerging market finance. *Journal of Empirical Finance* 10:3–55.

Bekaert, G., C. R. Harvey, and C. Lundblad. 2005. Does financial market liberalization spur growth? *Journal of Financial Economics* 77:3–55.

Bekaert, G., C. R. Harvey, C. Lundblad, and S. Siegel. 2006. Global growth opportunities and market integration. *Journal of Finance,* forthcoming.

Bencivenga, V. R., and B. D. Smith. 1992. Deficits, inflation and the banking system in developing countries: The optimal degree of financial repression. *Oxford Economic Papers* 44:767–90.

Bhagwati, J. 1998. The capital myth. *Foreign Affairs* 77:7–12.

Bovespa. 1996. Nova York ataca e os mercados reagem [New York attacks and the markets react]. *Revista Bovespa,* May.

Boyd, J. H., R. Levine, and B. D. Smith. 2001. The impact of inflation on financial sector performance. *Journal of Monetary Economics* 47:221–48.

Bushman, R. M., J. D. Piotroski, and A. J. Smith. 2004. What determines corporate transparency? *Journal of Accounting Research* 42:207–52.

Chinn, M. D., and H. Ito. 2006. What matters for financial development? Capital controls, institutions, and interactions. *Journal of Development Economics* 81:163–92.

Claessens, S., D. Klingebiel, and S. Schmukler. 2006. Stock market development and internationalization: Do economic fundamentals spur both similarly? *Journal of Empirical Finance* 13:316–50.

De la Torre, A., J. C. Gozzi, and S. Schmukler. 2006. Stock market development under globalization: Whither the gains from reforms? *Journal of Banking and Finance,* forthcoming.

De la Torre, A., and S. Schmukler. 2006. Emerging Capital Markets and Globalization: The Latin American Experience. Palo Alto, CA: Stanford University Press.

Di Noia, C. 1999. The stock exchange industry: Network effects, implicit mergers, and corporate governance. Notebook of Finance no. 33. Rome, Italy: Commissione Nazionale per le Societa e la Borsa.

Djankov, S., R. La Porta, F. Lopez de Silanes, and A. Shleifer. 2003. Courts. *Quarterly Journal of Economics* 118:453–517.

———. 2008. The law and economics of self-dealing. *Journal of Financial Economics,* forthcoming.

Economides, N. 1993. Network economics with application to finance. *Financial Markets, Institutions and Instruments* 2:89–97.

———. 1996. The economics of networks. *International Journal of Industrial organization* 14:673–99.

Edison, H., and F. Warnock. 2003. A simple measure of the intensity of capital controls. *Journal of Empirical Finance* 10:83–105.

Edwards, S. 1995. Why are saving rates so different across countries? An international comparative analysis. NBER Working Paper no. 5097. Cambridge, MA: National Bureau of Economic Research, April.

Federation des Bourses de Valeurs. 2000. Price discovery and the competitiveness of trading systems. Report presented at FIBV annual meeting. Brisbane, Australia.

Fernandez Arias, E., and P. Montiel. 2001. Reform and growth in Latin America: All pain, no gain? *IMF Staff Papers* 48:522–46. Washington, DC: International Monetary Fund.

Financial Times. 1998. ADRs prove a double-edged sword, April 6.

Garcia, V. F., and L. Liu. 1999. Macroeconomic determinants of stock market development. *Journal of Applied Economics* 2:29–59.

Guiso, L., P. Sapienza, and I. Zingales. 2004. Does local financial development matter? *Quarterly Journal of Economics* 119:929–69.

Henry, P. B. 2000. Stock market liberalization, economic reform, and emerging market equity prices. *Journal of Finance* 55:529–64.

Herring, R., and N. Chatusripitak. 2001. The case of the missing market: The bond market and why it matters for financial development. Wharton Financial Institutions Center Working Paper. Philadelphia: University of Pennsylvania.

Huybens, E., and B. Smith. 1999. Inflation, financial markets, and long-run real activity. *Journal of Monetary Economics* 43:283–315.

Inter-American Development Bank. 1995. *Overcoming Volatility.* Report on Economic and Social Progress in Latin America, Washington, DC: IADB.

Johnston, B. R., and V. Sundararajan. 1999. *Sequencing financial sector reforms: Country experiences and issues.* Washington, DC: International Monetary Fund.

Kaminsky, G., and S. Schmukler. 2003. Short-run pain, long-run gain: The effects of financial liberalization. NBER Working Paper no. 9787. Cambridge, MA: National Bureau of Economic Research, June.

Karacadag, C., V. Sundararajan, and J. Elliott. 2003. Managing risks in financial market development: The role of sequencing. IMF Working Paper no.WP/03/117. Washington, DC: International Monetary Fund, June.

Karolyi, G. A. 2004. The role of American depositary receipts in the development of emerging equity markets. *Review of Economics and Statistics* 86:670–90.

Krueger, A. 2004. Meant well, tried little, failed much: Policy reforms in emerging market economies. Remarks at the Roundtable Lecture at the Economic Honors Society, New York University, New York.

La Porta, R., F. Lopez de Silanes, and A. Shleifer. 2006. What works in securities laws? *Journal of Finance* 61:1–32.

La Porta, R., F. Lopez de Silanes, A. Shleifer, and R. W. Vishny. 1997. Legal determinants of external finance. *Journal of Finance* 52:1131–50.

———. 1998. Law and finance. *Journal of Political Economy* 106:1113–55.

Latin Finance. 1999. The incredible shrinking markets, September.

Levine, R. 2005. Finance and growth: Theory and evidence. In *Handbook of economic growth,* ed. P. Aghion and S. Durlauf, 865–934. Amsterdam, The Netherlands: Elsevier.

Levine, R., and S. Schmukler. 2006a. Migration, spillovers, and trade diversion: The impact of internationalization on domestic stock market liquidity. *Journal of Banking and Finance,* forthcoming.

———. 2006b. Internationalization and stock market liquidity. *Review of Finance* 10:153–87.

Levine, R., and S. Zervos. 1998. Capital control liberalization and stock market development. *World Development* 26:1169–83.

Malkamaki, M. 1999. Are there economies of scale in stock exchange activities? Bank of Finland discussion paper no. 4/99. Helsinki, Finland: Bank of Finland.

McCauley, R., and E. Remolona. 2000. Size and liquidity of government bond markets. *BIS Quarterly Review* (November): 52–58.

McKinnon, R. 1993. *The order of economic liberalization, financial control in the transition to a market economy.* Baltimore, MD: Johns Hopkins University Press.

Mihaljek, D., M. Scatigna, and A. Villar. 2002. Recent trends in bond markets. BIS Papers no. 11. Basel, Switzerland: Bank for International Settlements.

Moel, A. 2001. The role of American depositary receipts in the development of emerging markets. *Economia* 2:209–73.

Plies, W., and C. M. Reinhart. 1999. Saving in Latin America: An overview. In *Accounting for saving: Financial liberalization, capital flows and growth in Latin America and Europe,* ed. C. M. Reinhart, 3–47. Washington, DC: Inter-American Development Bank.

Rajan, R. G., and L. Zingales. 2003. The great reversals: The politics of financial development in the twentieth century. *Journal of Financial Economics* 69:5–50.

Ritter, J., and I. Welch. 2002. A review of IPO activity, pricing, and allocations. *Journal of Finance* 57:1795–1828.

Schmidt-Hebbel, K., and L. Serven. 1997. Saving across the world: Puzzles and policies. World Bank Discussion Paper no. 354. Washington, DC: World Bank.

Shah, A., and S. Thomas. 2001. Securities markets infrastructure for small countries. World Bank. Mimeograph.

Singh, A., A. Belaisch, C. Collyns, P. De Masi, R. Krieger, G. Meredith, and R. Rennhack. 2005. Stabilization and reform in Latin America: A macroeconomic perspective on the experience since the early 1990s. IMF Occasional Paper no. 238. Washington, DC: International Monetary Fund.

Stiglitz, J. 2002. *Globalization and its discontents.* New York: W. W. Norton.

The Economist. 2001. A survey of globalisation, September 27.

Vinhas de Souza, L. 2005. Financial liberalization and business cycles: The experience of the new EU member states. In *Emerging European financial markets: Independence and integration post-enlargement,* ed. J. Batten and C. Kearney. Amsterdam, The Netherlands: Elsevier.

World Bank. 1997. *The long march: A reform agenda for Latin America and the Caribbean in the next decade.* Washington, DC: World Bank.

———. 2004. *Global development finance 2004—Harnessing cyclical gains for development.* Washington, DC: World Bank.

Comment   Ugo Panizza

In this paper Augusto de la Torre, Juan Carlos Gozzi, and Sergio Schmukler analyze the impact of financial reforms on the development of the Latin American capital market and provide possible explanations of why the reform process did not yield the expected results.

The paper contrasts two possible views of the dismal outcome of the reform process. The first view is the one maintained by the Talibans of the Washington consensus and is summarized by de la Torre, Gozzi, and Schmukler as "be patient and redouble the effort." The second view still maintains that reforms could have a beneficial effect but claims that there was a problem with the sequencing of the reforms process. De la Torre,

Ugo Panizza is chief of the Debt and Finance Analysis Unit in the Division on Globalization and Development Strategies at the United Nations Conference on Trade and Development (UNCTAD).

Gozzi, and Schmukler label this position as the "get the sequence right" view.[1] De la Torre, Gozzi, and Schmukler argue that both views capture important aspects of the problem but neither of them is fully satisfactory and propose a third view that they label "revisit basic issues and reshape expectations." In particular, de la Torre, Gozzi, and Schmukler make the point that it is not easy to identify which policies should be pursued to foster the development of the Latin American capital market and that expectations about the outcome of the reform process should be adjusted. Furthermore, they recognize that there are intrinsic characteristics of emerging market countries that may limit the development of their capital markets.

I tend to agree with this conclusion. In fact, in a recent paper on the development of the Latin American bond market written with Eduardo Borensztein and Barry Eichengreen, we conclude that "While this clearly does not mean that policies and institutions do not matter [for the development of the Latin American bond market], it means that there is no convenient short-cut . . . the same policies that are necessary for economic development in general are also necessary for the development of domestic bond markets" (Borensztein, Eichengreen, and Panizza 2006, 21).

As I agree with the big picture, I will focus my discussion on some of the details of de la Torre, Gozzi, and Schmukler's work. A way of doing so is to frame my discussion as if it were the outline of a "shadow paper," that is, the paper I would like to write if I were asked to rewrite de la Torre, Gozzi, and Schmukler's paper.[2]

The Shadow Paper

As there seem to be a disconnect between the title and the content of de la Torre, Gozzi, and Schmukler's paper (the title talks about capital market, but the paper is really about the development of the stock market), I would title my shadow paper: "*Stock* Market Development: Whither Latin America."

As in de la Torre, Gozzi, and Schmukler, I would start by comparing the development of Latin America's stock market with those of East Asia and the industrial countries. However, I would put more attention on the metric used to compare these markets. This is not an irrelevant detail. Look, for instance, at figure 4C.1 and 4C.2 (both taken from Borensztein, Eichengreen, and Panizza 2006). These figures compare the development of the government, corporate, and financial bond markets in Latin America, East Asia, and industrial countries. Figure 4C.1 scales the size of the bond mar-

---

1. Interestingly, de la Torre, Gozzi, and Schmukler do not mention a third view. This is the view of the antiglobalizers who are extremely critical of any type of market friendly reform.

2. Clearly, my shadow paper is a rhetorical device that has the benefit of hindsight because it internalizes what I learned by reading de la Torre, Gozzi, and Schmukler's work. Furthermore, it allows me to say what I would like to do without the need of actually doing it.

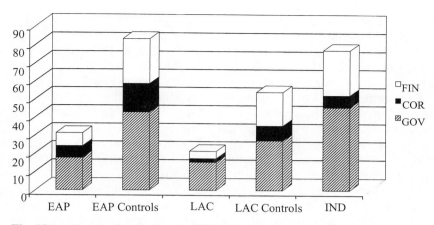

Fig. 4C.1   Outstanding bonds over GDP, with controls and without controls (simple average, 1991–2004)

Source: Borensztein, Eichengreen, and Panizza (2006).

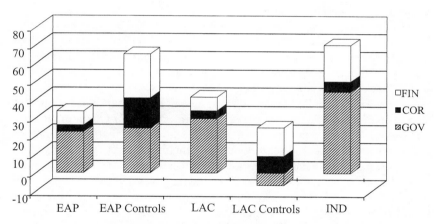

Fig. 4C.2   Outstanding bonds over domestic credit, with controls and without controls (simple average, 1991–2004)

Source: Borensztein, Eichengreen, and Panizza (2006).

ket by gross domestic product (GDP) and figure 4C.2 scales the size of the bond market by domestic credit. Focus for the moment on the columns with no controls. In figure 4C.1, we find that the industrial countries have the largest bond market, followed by East Asia (with a bond market which is 60 percent smaller than that of industrial countries), and Latin America (with a bond market which is 30 percent smaller than that of East Asia). In figure 4C.2, we still find that the industrial countries have the largest bond market, but we now find that Latin America has a bond market that is 20 percent larger than that of East Asia (furthermore, the difference with respect to industrial countries goes from 73 to 41 percent). This suggests that while Latin American bond markets are small relative to GDP, they are not so small relative to the size of the domestic financial sector. Hence, it is the Latin American financial sector and not merely the bond market that is underdeveloped. It would be interesting to conduct a similar experiment focusing on the Latin American stock market and check if there is something specific about this particular segment of the region's financial system or if, as in the case of the bond market, the underdevelopment of the Latin American stock market is just another aspect of the level of financial underdevelopment that characterizes Latin America.

After having compared simple averages (and possibly weighted averages), I would also follow de la Torre, Gozzi, and Schmukler and conduct a formal statistical analysis of the main drivers of cross-country differences in stock market development. Here, I have two issues with de la Torre, Gozzi, and Schmukler's approach. The first has to do with the set of explanatory variables included in the model and the second with the set of countries included in the sample.

Although de la Torre, Gozzi, and Schmukler do not lack degrees of freedom (their smaller sample has more than 400 observations, and in most cases they have more than 1,000 observations), they decided to adopt an extremely parsimonious specification with at most five explanatory variables plus a dummy for Latin America. As a consequence, they manage to explain a rather small share of the variance of stock market development (up to 45 percent of it in one regression but less than 25 percent in most regressions). I would definitely try to include a larger number of explanatory variables and report the regressions that include these explanatory variables.[3] Besides the variables mentioned by de la Torre, Gozzi, and Schmukler in their "Robustness Test" section, I would also include the squares of log GDP and log GDP per capita (to better control for nonlinearities), the effect of measures of the efficiency of the banking system (like banking spreads and bank concentration), the overall size of the financial system, and the effect of having large institutional investors (for instance, the effect of having privatized pension systems). Controlling for the overall size of the financial system is particularly important because it would allow me to check whether there is something specific about the stock market or whether having a small stock market is just another manifestation of financial underdevelopment. In the concluding section of their paper, de la Torre, Gozzi, and Schmukler recognize that there are a host of variables that they do not include in their analysis, and some of these variables are exactly the ones mentioned in the preceding. They argue that these vari-

---

3. De la Torre, Gozzi, and Schmukler include some extra explanatory variables in a robustness section but do not report the regressions that include these variables.

ables are not included because they do not vary much over time; hence, it is difficult to separate their effect from that of the Latin America and Caribbean (LAC) dummy. This argument is not fully convincing. First of all, the authors do include shareholder rights, which is a variable that does not vary over time (not because it cannot change but because there are no panel data on this variable). Second, I will argue later that it would be interesting to decompose the factors that explain the difference between Latin America and industrial countries into three groups, and having information on such time-invariant variables would help us in such a decomposition (especially because some of these variables like shareholder rights, bank concentration, and bank efficiency could be object of policy and hence change over time).[4]

I would also augment the model with a full set of regional fixed effects. For instance, I would add three dummy variables, one for East Asia, one for East Europe and Central Asia, and for other developing countries (industrial countries would be the excluded dummy). By doing so, I would be able to test whether the Latin America dummy is mostly capturing the difference between Latin America and the industrial countries or whether there are also significant differences between Latin America and other developing regions (my tables would provide F-tests on the difference between the LAC dummy and each of the other regional dummies included in the various regressions).

Finally, I would relax the assumption that the relationship between the explanatory variables and the dependent variables is homogenous across countries and reestimate the model by restricting the sample to emerging market countries. This is important because Borensztein, Eichengreen, and Panizza's (2006) study of the determinants of bond market development and show that certain results (the effect of capital controls, for instance) reverse when industrial countries are excluded from the sample.[5]

After having estimated the model, I would use its results to perform two sets of comparisons.

First, I would use the regional dummies to evaluate which share of the difference with respect to industrial countries can be explained by the factors included in the various regressions. This is not very different from what de la Torre, Gozzi, and Schmukler do when they look at the LAC dummy.

4. I would also include year fixed effects to control for common trends.
5. Another issue has to do with sample size. Consider, for instance, table 4.1 in de la Torre, Gozzi, and Schmukler. The first column includes eighty-seven countries (and over 1,600 observations), and the last column includes forty-five countries (and 836 observations). It would be interesting to know what would happen if I were to estimate the model of columns (1) to (5) using the sample of column (6). Also, note that table 4A.1 lists ninety-five countries, but the regressions of tables 4.1 to 4.3 use at most eighty-seven countries and in most cases less than eighty countries. It would be good to know which countries are included in the various regressions or at least how many countries for each region (LAC, East Asia, East Europe, industrial countries, other emerging market countries).

However, by having included other regional dummies in the model and a much larger set of explanatory variables, I would be able to have a clearer picture. Consider again figures 4C.1 and 4C.2, and now focus on the columns with controls. These columns show what would happen to the bond markets of Latin America and East Asia if these regions had the same country characteristics as the industrial countries. The figures show that when we scale the size of the bond market by GDP, the difference between Latin America and industrial countries drops drastically but remains large (without controls the Latin American bond market is less than one-third that of industrial countries, but after we control for country characteristics, the relative size of the Latin American bond market more than doubles and reaches 70 percent of the size of the industrial countries' bond market). In the case of East Asia, instead, we find that country characteristics fully explain the difference with respect to industrial countries. Interestingly, if we scale bond market by domestic credit, we find that if we were to assign to Latin America the same country characteristics of the industrial countries we would find a substantial *drop* in the size of the Latin American bond market.[6] It would be very interesting to conduct a similar analysis for the stock market.

Second, I would use the point estimates to separate the impact of three types of variables: (a) historical and geographical variables (like latitude, origin of the legal code, colonial history, etc.); (b) variables that measure country size or the level of development (GDP, GDP per capita, rule of law, financial development, etc.); (c) policy variables (shareholder rights, government deficit, stock market liberalization, privatization, etc.). Such a decomposition is interesting because it would tell me how policies could help me to close the gap with industrial countries. Suppose, for instance, that we were to find that 30 percent of the difference between average stock market capitalization in Latin America and industrial countries is not explained by our model (this is the LAC dummy); another 30 percent is explained by geographical and historical variables; another 30 percent by country size, the level of development, and financial development; and the remaining 10 percent by policy variables. Then we would know that changes in policies would have a limited direct effect on the size of the stock market (they could have a larger indirect effect if they affect GDP growth and the size of the financial system). This is important because it would help policymakers in forming the right expectations on the impact of the reform process and also in conducting cost benefit analyses of the process of financial reforms. Note that this decomposition is very close to what is implicitly done by de la Torre, Gozzi, and Schmukler, and the potential results from such

---

6. This is due to the negative relationship between the size of the financial market and the ratio between government bonds and domestic credit. As average domestic credit in industrial countries is about three times that of Latin America if we substitute the value of domestic credit of industrial countries into Latin America we obtain a much smaller bond market.

a decomposition are likely to be consistent with their view "revisit basic issues and reshape expectations." In fact, presenting the results of such a decomposition is likely to strengthen, by quantifying it, the authors' main message.

Reference

Borensztein, E., B. Eichengreen, and U. Panizza. 2006. Building bond markets in Latin America. Inter-American Development Bank and The University of California, Berkeley. Mimeograph.

Judicial Risk and Credit Market Performance
Micro Evidence from Brazilian Payroll Loans

Ana Carla A. Costa and João M. P. De Mello

5.1 Introduction

In recent years, the literature has built a near consensus that "sound" institutions are congenial to good economic performance (North 1994). Institutions, insofar as they determine the economic environment agents operate in, should be important for explaining economic outcomes. Quite often, the specific mechanism through which institutions influence economic performance is protection from expropriation. In environments in which expropriation is likely, agents underinvest (from a social perspective) relative to more secure ones. In the end, a plethora of suboptimal microeconomic decisions amount to a poorer aggregate economic performance.

Indeed, most of the empirical effort in associating institutional "soundness," however defined, and economic performance has been on the aggregate level. An observation on a typical study is a country (La Porta et al. [1998b] is a seminal example). Institutional measures are then linked to economic performance on various dimensions. La Porta et al. (1998b), for example, document that the origin of the legal system is associated with the

Ana Carla A. Costa is a researcher at Tendências, a consulting firm in São Paulo, Brazil. João M. P. De Mello is an assistant professor of economics at Pontifical Catholic University in Rio de Janeiro, Brazil.

Mrs. Costa would like to stress that opinions expressed here are solely hers and do not reflect any official position of the Brazilian Central Bank. We are especially thankful to Cornélio Pimentel, Daniel Sanchez, and Plinio Romanini from the Department of Off-Site Supervision and Information Management at the Brazilian Central Bank (DESIG/BCB) for sharing the data, and to Johan Sabino for the information about judicial disputes over payroll lending. We would also like to thank Tony Takeda, Marcelo de Paiva Abreu, Renato Flôres, Benny Parnes, Johan Ribeiro, Sebastian Edwards, Márcio G. P. Garcia, two anonymous referees, and participants at the IASE-NBER conference for comments and suggestions. The usual disclaimer applies.

degree of creditor protection. La Porta et al. (1997) find that a lower degree of creditor protection implies smaller debt and equity markets (Djankov et al. 2003).[1] Another set of articles study the financial deepening-economic growth link (King and Levine 1993; Levine and Zervos 1998), finding a positive relationship. Taken all together, these papers seem to imply the following chain of causality. At the basic level, legal origin (institution) causes creditor protection (protection from expropriation). At the second stage, better creditor protection causes financial deepening. Finally, financial deepening causes economic growth.

This chain of causality would be more convincing were microeconomic evidence available. The missing link is due to the level of analysis, much broader than the relevant *locus* of economic decisions. There is, for example, an implicit assumption that agents do invest less if creditor protection is lower. For several reasons, it is hard to be completely convincing with such an aggregate level of analysis. One such reason is reverse causality. The following example, however farfetched, is illustrative. Assume investment is completely inelastic, and creditor protection is a superior good. Creditor protection, in this setting, has only distributive, not allocative, effects. For demand reasons, there is, however, a reverse causality running from income to creditor protection. Evidently, investment is not completely inelastic, but the demand driven story is still conceivable. Most of the studies do recognize this possibility, and try to find sufficiently exogenous variation to relate institutions and economic performance. Acemoglu, Johnson, and Robinson (2001) and Levine (1998) are good examples of careful searches for such variation.

Another problem stems from the fact that legal procedures are "chosen" by society and, hence, may be endogenously designed to tackle the issues often put as the dependent variables in the regressions. La Porta et al. (2004) face this difficulty. They argue that legal formalism reduces the quality of the judicial system. But formalism, as they recognize it, could also be a response to "weaker law and order environment." Their strategy is to use the fact that most countries inherit their legal tradition (and that French civil law is more "formalistic"), which makes the legal tradition a source of exogenous variation. Again, the story is compelling insofar as it is prohibitively costly for countries to "change" their legal tradition because otherwise "maintenance" of tradition would itself be endogenous.

However well argued (as it is the case in all papers cited), identification

---

1. Pinheiro and Cabral (1998) follow this tradition for the Brazilian credit market. Using state-level data on outstanding volumes of credit and an index of judicial efficiency (based on the results of a survey conducted with businessmen on each state where they rate the quality of the local judiciary), they relate variation in judicial inefficiency to differences in outstanding volumes of credit across the states. The authors conclude, corroborating the institution-development hypothesis, that improving the efficiency of judicial enforcement is important for credit markets development.

is mostly a rhetorical issue as one can only test for *over*identification. With micro level evidence, these issues can be bypassed, and one can directly assess how market participants respond to varying institutional environments. Creditor protection and financial deepening is an example. If there is evidence that creditors price judicial risk or restrain quantities in the face of weak protection, then it becomes much more compelling that legal protection induces financial deepening. In this case, one could be much more confident that the causality from creditor protection to income is of first-order, as opposed to demand driven explanations, such as protection being a superior good.

A third reason is omitted factors. Several other countries' characteristics might determine both institutional setting (such as legal origin and level of credit protection, the usual explanatory variables) and economic performance (the usual regressand). Consider again the Acemoglu-Johnson-Robinson strategy (2001) for finding exogenous variation in institutional soundness to estimate the institution-economic performance link.[2] For former colonies, one conceivable alternative story is the type of colonization. Suppose that, for sheer coincidence, while countries with a French civil law tradition (usually interpreted as "unsound" institutions) occupied lands that had valuable goods for the European market (silver in Peru and sugar in Brazil, for instance), countries with common law tradition ("sound" institutions) arrived at places that had few "tradable" goods with Europe (early English colonization of the United States). Suppose as well that this trade feature determined how exploitative colonization was and that exploitation had long-lasting effects. In this case, the (omitted) driving force is whether there were comparative advantages to be explored. However, sound institutions and (later) economic performance would still relate empirically although causal interpretation would not be warranted. We do not claim the institutional settings do not matter and that the legal tradition only enters the picture through trade "causing" both institutional settings and economic performance. The crucial point is that, with micro-level evidence, it is unnecessary to be concerned about such alternative explanations.

Finally, measurement is intrinsically more problematic with aggregate data. In La Porta et al. (1998), (country-level) creditor protection is measured by characteristics of the countries' corporate laws and by several indexes.[3] Besides the inherent arbitrariness in constructing such indexes, theory not always provides clear guidance in interpreting the results. For

---

2. Acemoglu, Johnson, and Robinson (2001) document that "better institutions" arose in countries where mortality rates due to native diseases were low when colonizers originally arrived. This, according to the authors, shifts the equation that determines institutions but not the equation that determines current economic performance.

3. They have indexes for, among others, efficiency of the judicial system, risk of expropriation, and risk of repudiation of contracts by government.

example, is it theoretically clear that restricting the behavior of managers always increases the amount of finance *in equilibrium?* It is conceivable that, if you sufficiently restrict managers' behavior, the size of debt and equity market will be small, for reasons pertaining to the supply of securities? Without a clear theoretical support, an empirical finding that restricting managers' behavior is associated with "larger" equity, and debt markets are subject to criticisms that micro evidence is not. One such criticism is the presence of nonlinearities in the creditor protection-market performance relation.[4]

It might seem puzzling the *relative* lack of micro evidence on the institution-development *nexus.* We conjecture that this is due to the scarcity of a fortunate coincidence: data on both the relevant economic decision locus (firms, consumers) linked to variation on institutional settings. La Porta et al.'s (2004) study on the formality of legal procedures and the quality of the legal system is something of an exception.[5] They do not, however, directly associate market-level performance with different institutional settings.

In this work, we take advantage of a particular set of events that provide variation on a relevant institutional setting, and we are able to associate this variation with data on the relevant economic decision locus. The empirical setting is the market for Payroll Debit Loans in Brazil, which are personal loans with principal and interest payments directly deducted from the borrowers' payroll check. Automatic deduction from payroll, in practice, makes a collateral out of future income. In June 2004, a high-level federal court upheld a regional court ruling that had declared payroll deduction illegal.[6] The decision by the federal court has a case-specific nature, that is, only applies to this particular dispute. There is, however, evidence from market practitioners that there was an increase in the perceived probability that the decision could establish precedent and turn useless the future income collateral. Using personal loans without payroll deduction as a control group, a difference-in-differences procedure assesses whether the judicial decision had an impact on market performance. Our results suggest that the decision had an adverse impact on banks' risk perception, on interest rates, and on the amount lent. In this sense, this is direct evidence of market participants' reaction to institutional risk.

Our theory is simple to the point of trivial: an increase in the chance of expropriating the collateral should shift the supply of loans inward, worsening market performance. Whether the empirical consequences are first

4. Dubey, Geanakoplos, and Shubik (2005) show that with incomplete markets that intermediate levels of debtor punishment can induce a larger quantity of credit that extreme levels of debtor punishment.

5. In this paper, the authors study the link between formality of the legal system and the time elapsed to evict nonpaying tenants and to recover a bounced check. Furthermore, they associate formality with other measures of judicial system performance, such as corruption and access to justice.

6. The court ruled at the very end of June (28th). However, the press release was on July 1.

order is far from self-evident. This is, indeed, the goal of the paper: investigate whether a clear-cut shift in the institutional setting has microeconomic consequences. Evidence from market practitioners is ambiguous. While some important players had the perception that the decision could have strong adverse effects, equally important ones thought the effect would be second order.

The market-level evidence is a complement, not a substitute, to the aggregate-level evidence. Indeed, our results in no way contradict the literature. On the contrary, they corroborate it. While aggregate evidence indicates that institutional differences are of first-order importance in explaining variation in countries' performances, micro- and market-level evidence evaluates directly the implicit assumption necessary to interpret the aggregate evidence as indeed causal.

The result has an additional interest given the empirical application. Payroll lending is one of the workhorses of the recent Brazilian credit market expansion. Brazil, in the La Porta-Lopez-Silanes-Shleifer-Vishny tradition, is a French civil law country, with low creditor protection. Credit markets are relatively underdeveloped. Recently, however, it has made several efforts toward a more creditor friendly institutional environment. Courts may be particularly important in an environment with weak creditor protection, where other protective institutions, such as laws, are weak or inexistent.

The paper is organized as follows. Section 5.2 outlines the recent evolution of credit market in Brazil and the chronology of payroll lending, emphasizing the relevant events, such as the approval in congress of the law regulating payroll lending for retirees and the judicial decision on the legality of payroll deductions. Section 5.3 presents the data, and section 5.4 presents the empirical strategy. We argue that the presence of an identical product, except for deduction in payroll, provides a good control for associating changes in the institutional environment to market changes in payroll lending. Results are presented and discussed in section 5.5. Section 5.6 concludes.

5.2 Credit Market in Brazil: Recent Evolution and Payroll Lending

In recent years, bank lending experienced a pronounced increase in Brazil, especially in lending out of banks' "free lending funds" (those not earmarked by mandatory programs). Between July 1999 and September 2005, the free loans/gross domestic product (GDP) ratio went from 8.3 percent to 17.1 percent (figure 5.1). This free loan segment now represents 67 percent of total banking credit, changing positions with directed credit operations, that now stands at 33 percent.[7]

---

7. Numbers for December, 2005. Banking credit portfolios in Brazil have two types of loans: free market operations, where banks can set quantity and prices according to their profit maximizing behavior; and compulsory directed credit operations, mostly channeled to housing and rural sectors at subsidized interest rates.

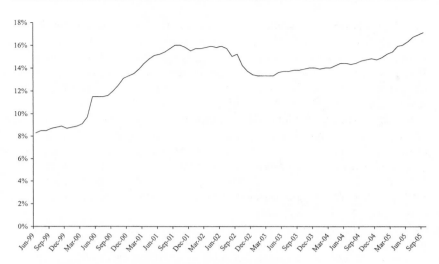

Fig. 5.1   Private bank credit/GDP ratio, 1999 to 2005

Interestingly, this tendency of financial deepening took place during a period of tight monetary policy.[8] Despite this fact, free market lending expanded remarkably. Several factors help explain this trend.

These specific factors are all linked to institutional reforms that took place in Brazil since the end of 1999. Measures included efforts to reduce information asymmetries in credit markets (such as the new credit ranking and provisioning regulation, through Resolution 2.682/99, and the Central Bank Credit Information System (SCR), implemented in 1999 and improved in 2000 and 2004); more efficient instruments of collateral recognition and contract enforcement (as the so-called *Cédula de Crédito Bancário,* a claim with faster execution procedures, in 2001 and 2004;[9] a better insolvency resolution system (through a new bankruptcy law, approved by Congress in the end of 2004); and regulation of creative credit instruments, such as payroll lending. They provided an improved institutional environment and possibly led to the observed higher volumes of credit concessions by the Brazilian banking sector. As suggested in the previously cited literature, the evolution toward a more creditor friendly environment might have engendered this initial movement of financial deepening in Brazil.

---

8. Brazil adopted inflation target and floating exchange rate regimes in 1999 during a liquidity crisis, exchange rate devaluation, and inflation pressure. Interest rates were the main instrument used to stabilize the economy. Inflation targets are set by Nacional Monetary Council, and basic interest rates are defined monthly by Central Bank in Monetary Policy Committee (COPOM) meetings.

9. The SCR brings detailed information on borrowers' credit contracts of over R$5,000.00 (roughly US$2,200.00).

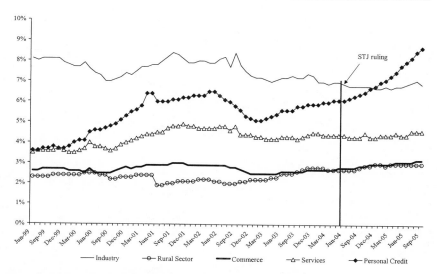

Fig. 5.2   Evolution of private bank credit as a percentage of GDP, by economic sector

Nevertheless, this rapid expansion path—more pronounced during the last two years—is not observed in all credit market segments. On the contrary, this acceleration is mainly explained by growing volumes of consumer lending. Credit to this segment, which in 1999 represented 3.6 percent of GDP (or 9 percent of total private bank credit portfolio), reached outstanding volumes that amount to 8.7 percent of GDP in 2005 (or 31 percent of total private bank credit portfolio). Consequently, since December 2004, personal loans became the biggest part of total bank loans, with an even higher participation than industrial credit, that has been stable around 6.9 percent of GDP (figure 5.2).

Consumer credit loans in Brazil can be divided into three main types of loans: the personal loan, for consumption purposes; loans for vehicle acquisition; and *Cheque Especial,* a consumer overdraft facility. It is, however, in the personal loan category—the largest category, that a major growth is observed (52 percent during the last twelve months), as shown in figure 5.3.

This paper is concerned with personal loans, which are further divided into two subcategories: the standard loan contract (hereafter standard loan), and a special type of personal loan contract that has an automatic monthly payment deducted from the borrower's salary. This is the payroll lending operation (*Crédito Consignado em Folha de Pagamento,* hereafter payroll loan), which represents over 35 percent of all consumer credit in Brazil and whose growth path has shown a particularly noticeable increase. Figure 5.4 shows the evolution of payroll lending operations and its in-

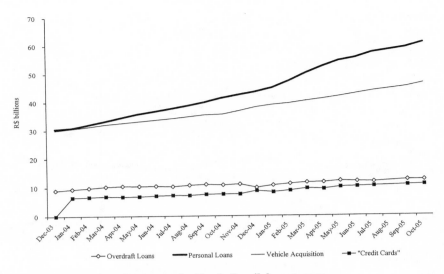

Fig. 5.3   Evolution of consumer lending in Brazil, by category

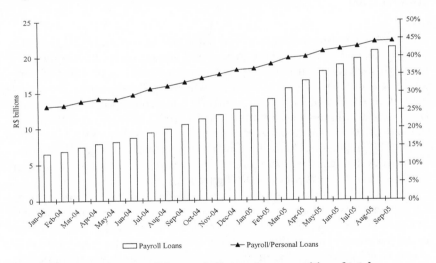

Fig. 5.4   Evolution of payroll loans, absolute and as proposition of total personal loans

creasing participation on total personal loans for the thirteen largest active banks in this segment.[10]

Payroll lending has existed in Brazil since the beginning of the 1990s. It

10. Brazilian Central Bank collects this data for this small—but representative—sample of banks since January 2004. It now aims to expand it to all banks operating with this specific type of credit.

was restricted to government personnel and was originally operated by peculium institutions, which had the possibility to act as trusts before public administration agencies.[11] But since the second half of the 1990s, some financial institutions identified in this type of loan a good business opportunity, with low credit risk and high return. Those banks entered this credit market through the acquisition of peculium institutions already registered as trustees.

5.2.1 Payroll Loans: Description of the Product, Chronology of Events, and Practitioners' Opinions

The decisive expansion of payroll lending operations occurred in September 2003, when the government sent to Congress a provisory law (*Medida Provisória* [MP] 130), subsequently turned into Law 10.820/03.[12] The law regulated the possibility of salary consignment for private-sector formal workers and for retired workers from private sector and pensionaries covered by the National Institution of Social Security (INSS).[13]

In practice, payroll deduction turns future income into a collateral. Evidently, future income is valuable as a collateral insofar as it is not too volatile. This is precisely why payroll lending is mainly used by the following three types of borrowers. Before the 2003 law extended regulation to private-sector retirees, banks lent to public servants, which have employment stability. Banks then started operating with private-sector workers, but in association with the labor unions and employers. Contracts are collective, which mitigates idiosyncratic income risk. Finally, after the December 2003 law, banks started operations with retirees from the private sector, which also have a constant income flow. The main risk lenders face is death, which is diversifiable and insurable.

Lenders, however, face another peril: judicial risk. Collateral has value only if courts recognize it as such. Payroll lending in Brazil provides an excellent empirical setting to assess judicial risk. In 2002, a public servant of the city of Porto Alegre (the capital of the state of Rio Grande do Sul) sued Banco Sudameris claiming the payroll deduction on his salary was illegal.[14] A state-level court (Tribunal de Justiça do Rio Grande do Sul) ruled for the plaintiff. The decision did not draw much attention for two reasons. First,

11. Law 8.112/90 admits the possibility of payroll consignment for government personnel.
12. *Medida provisória* is a legislative device in which the executive sends a bill to congress that is effective immediately, pending approval. It has an urgency status that forces the legislator to appreciate its merit. For practical purposes, it is almost equivalent to a full-blown law.
13. The Brazilian pension system, a pay-as-you-go scheme, is publicly managed by the INSS.
14. The deduction was R$58.66 (roughly US$22 by then) to cover amortization and interest expenses on a R$1.015 loan. The precise claim was that wages are essential for subsistence and therefore cannot be pawned. Furthermore, the monthly nominal interest rate of 3.8 percent was ruled "abusive." See *Valor Econômico* 07/02//2004. For the actual decision, see the STJ Web site at http://www.stj.gov.br.

by that time, payroll lending was not such an important credit instrument. Second, the decision did not set a precedent, once it was related to a claim that started before the 2003 law, and had been ruled by a state-level court. Sudameris appealed to the second highest ranking federal court in the country, the Superior Tribunal de Justiça (STJ).[15] In late June 2004, the STJ upheld the regional court ruling. Although technically this decision also did not set precedent on the issue, it could signal the direction of future rulings.[16] In this case, the future income collateral could become useless. At the time, Minister Edson Vidigal, from the STJ, declared that "[when] analyzed through the salary perspective, the consignation can be suspended," and "[banks] might have to search for alternative forms of guarantees."[17]

Statements by some key practitioners suggest that banks perceived this as a hazard to their payroll loans operations. Right after the decision, the Chief of Judicial Operations of Federação Brasileira de Bancos (FEBRABAN, the main bankers' association), Johan Albino Ribeiro, declared to the press that "undoubtedly there will be a repercussion in terms of higher interest rates" since "[one] of the elements that sustain the low interest rates is the low risk on these loans. If the legality of the contract is contested, the risk increases."[18] Luis Marinho, then the head of Central Única dos Trabalhadores (UT), the main workers' union, reported that he had received phone calls from several bankers informing "[that] banks would hit the break on new loans, at least temporarily, until they have a better understanding of the extension of the STJ decision."[19]

However, whether banks indeed reacted to the decision in an economically meaningful way is not obvious. Indeed, it was not even clear whether, legally, the court ruling would have a lasting effect. As it was noted, the decision only applied to one specific claim, related to a public servant and which took place before the December 2003 formal regulation. Therefore the STJ decision could not, technically set precedent for future lawsuits. Several banking lawyers thought the law regulating payroll loans (Law 10.820/03) was crystal clear.[20] In this sense, all the decision could signal was the courts' mood toward payroll loans. Furthermore, banks could have simply ignored it. Indeed, Gabriel Jorge Ferreira (a former head of FEBRABAN), from UNIBANCO (the third largest private bank in Brazil), declared that "[the program] is still intact, and I do not think there

15. Hierarchically, the STJ stands between the STF (Supremo Tribuinal Federal), the equivalent of the American Supreme Court, and the TFJs (Tribunais Federais de Justiça), the equivalent to the American Federal Circuit Courts.

16. The STJ rulings are case specific and do not set precedent.

17. See *Gazeta Mercantil,* July 16, 2004.

18. See *Valor Econômico,* July 2, 2004.

19. Mr. Marinho would later be appointed Minister of Labor. See *Universo Online,* July 4, 2004, http://an.uol.com.br/2004/jul/04/0eco.htm.

20. See *Valor Econômico,* July 2, 2004, August 13, 2004.

will be an upward pressure in interest rates."[21] Indeed, this is precisely our object of study: whether there is evidence that this judicial hazard had a first-order impact on market performance. In our application, an affirmative answer would be even more meaningful given the ambiguity of both the (practical) legal consequences of the ruling and the bankers' reactions. As figure 5.4 shows, it is clear that the court ruling has not prevented the recent growth of payroll loans. There is, nonetheless, a couple of interesting contrafactual questions left to ask. Absent the decision, would this growth have been more pronounced? Would terms be better (i.e., lower interest rates)?

5.3   Data

Using original data from the SCR, we constructed a data set on payroll and standard loans. For both types of credit contracts, we have bank-level monthly data over a period starting in January 2003 and ending in May 2005. There is, initially, data for 109 active banks on outstanding volumes of payroll and standard personal lending operations. We have bank-level information on the total amount of loans, average risk rating, average interest rate, number of credit contracts, and average size of the credit contract.[22]

The data has information on loan contracts above R$5,000 (US$2,270). An average sized contract is R$84,719 (US$38,508). This strongly indicates that contracts in the data are mainly indirect, that is, with entities such as labor unions and governmental agencies, which intermediate the negotiation, and afterwards refer the bank to their employees or members. Contracting directly with individuals began mostly after the December 2003 law, which regulated payroll lending to private-sector retirees. Because it took at least another five months for a significant group of banks to be chartered by the INSS, the fact that these loans do not show in our data is relatively immaterial.[23]

In order to keep consistency among observations, banks had to satisfy several criteria to be part of the final sample used. First, only banks that consistently operated in both credit products were included. This avoids picking up unrelated (to the court ruling) entry and exit decisions, which are but noise for our purposes. Only banks that supplied both standard and payroll loans for the whole January 2004 to December 2004 period were included. Second, banks that had inconsistent pricing behavior were excluded. For example, several banks had annual nominal interest rates at 12

21. See *Universo Online,* July 4, 2004, http://an.uol.com.br/2004/jul/04/0eco.htm.

22. Interest rate is weighted by the volume of new concessions at each risk category. Credit risk rating goes from 1 (or AA operations: less risk) to 10 (or HH operations: maximum risk), following provisioning and classification criteria set by Nacional Monetary Council regulation.

23. The December 2003 law required the bank to be chartered by the INSS in order to supply payroll lending to private-sector employees. The first bank to be charted was the Caixa Econômica Federal (a federal government bank), in May 2004.

percent, which are clearly out of line with the rest of the market. Twelve percent operations are either reporting errors or special loans such as those to own employees, which we conjecture to have a different risk assessment nature. Other banks had inconsistent structural breaks on the interest rate series.[24] Finally, it is not clear whether government-owned banks (both state and federal) have the same objective function as their private counterparts. The literature is ambiguous with this respect. Although some works suggest that there is no evidence that public owned banks are less efficient than the private counterparts (Altubas, Evans, and Molyneux 2001), there is little controversy over their different lending behavior (Sapienza 2002). And, for Brazil, even if government-owned banks had the same objective function as private banks, payroll loans is an important piece of policy for the current federal government, and federally owned banks might be responding to public policy rather than maximizing profits regarding payroll loans.[25] For these reasons, government-owned banks were excluded.

After these adjustments, the sample consists of forty banks, representing 67.8 percent of total payroll lending volumes as of May 2005. The sample includes four out of the five major private Brazilian banks.

5.4 Empirical Strategy

The opinions voiced by market participants in the press suggest the three economic variables that might have been affected by the June 2004 STJ ruling: risk assessment, the pricing of loans, and the amount lent. The empirical strategy consists in comparing the evolution, over a period of time that contains the ruling, of two products: payroll and standard loans. The difference in their evolution over the period is interpreted as the causal effect of the STJ decision, as in any difference-in-differences model.

5.4.1 The Control Group

As mentioned in section 5.2, although payroll lending has existed since 1990, only in December 2003 was legislation regulating its application to private-sector formal workers and retirees and pensionaries of social security passed. Moreover, only since January 2003 have we had available—and good quality—split data on payroll and standard personal loans.

24. It is important to emphasize that we identified some problems with the interest rate variable in SCR data set. For this reason, we are less confident about the interest rate results than the other results presented in section 5.5. The SCR regulation states that interest rates must be reported on a yearly basis. Nevertheless, not only do inconsistent numbers such as zero or very low rates abound but also rates that seem to be monthly or contract period based systematically appear. Those observations were discarded.

25. Nonprofit maximizing behavior should not come as a surprise in Brazil when analyzing public banks' portfolios. Banco do Brasil (BB) and Caixa Econômica Federal (CEF), the two largest government-owned banks are, respectively, the major players in rural and housing subsidized credit. Banco do Brasil's outstanding rural credit portfolio represents 52 percent of all directed and subsidized rural credit in Brazil. The CEF, as of January 2005, accounted for 42 percent of total subsidized housing finance operations in Brazil.

The object of interest is a supply effect: has the court decision shifted the supply of payroll loans? We do not, however, pursue the strategy of searching for exogenous variation to estimate the supply directly. As it will become clear in the following, a reduced-form object is estimated for price, risk, and quantity. The strategy consists of using standard personal loans as a control group. This way, one can gauge the effect of the court decision above and beyond unobserved concurrent factors that might have affected both the demand and supply of payroll loans.[26]

Standard personal loans are a reasonable control group for payroll personal loans. The two products are the same, with the exception of the payroll deduction.[27] That is, both products are personal lending operations, consumption oriented, and have no formal collateral or real guarantee attached to them. Finally, because standard loans do not have payroll deduction, they were not directly affected by the June 2004 court ruling.

A fair question is why standard loans exist at all given the presence of an apparently superior very similar credit instrument. As a matter of regulation, payroll loans were confined to special classes of borrowers up until the December 2003 law and the subsequent chartering of banks to provide these loans on a more general basis.[28] In particular, it could be the case that public-sector employees were significantly more present in payroll vis-à-vis standard loans. This, however, does not seem to be the case, especially for our specific sample: payroll lending with the observed average size consists of both private-sector employees (through agreements with private companies or professional associations) and public servants.

While differences in the composition of the pool of borrowers is not a threat to our identification strategy, whether these two pools of borrowers *changed differently over the sample period* is. There are two reasons why this does not seem to be the case. First, the main change in composition of the pool of borrowers occurred during 2005, when banks started getting chartered by the Social Security Agency to lend to private-sector retirees. Therefore, there were no significant changes in the compositions of the pool of borrowers in the two groups. Second, economic conditions could have changed differently for the two groups, holding constant the composition of both pools. This would happen if, for instance, the public sector was downsizing at the time or if the private formal sector was experiencing a particularly turbulent period. Neither was the case.

Table 5.1 presents summary statistics on the variables that are used as regressands in the following analysis. As expected, the average interest rate is

26. We do not have overall demand shifters, that is, exogenous variation to estimate the supply, let alone product specific (to payroll loans, for instance) demand shifters. For example, there is no compelling economic reason why seasonality (a candidate) would affect payroll loans differently than standard loans.

27. As a matter of regulatory taxonomy, standard and payroll loans are two subcategories of personal loans.

28. See section 5.2.

Table 5.1   **Summary statistics**

	Mean		Standard deviation	
	Whole period	Subsample (month >12 and <18)	Whole period	Subsample (month >12 and <18)
Average interest rate (% points)				
Treatment: Payroll	45.07	46.08	12.21	8.80
Control: Standard	56.67	53.93	24.62	26.05
Total amount of loans (R$)				
Treatment: Payroll	6.83E+07	5.93E+07	1.38E+08	1.13E+08
Control: Standard	6.54E+07	5.90E+07	1.43E+08	1.19E+08
Average risk (from categories 1 to 10)				
Treatment: Payroll	2.51	2.63	0.55	0.66
Control: Standard	3.17	3.31	0.99	1.13

Source: Banco Central do Brasil.
Notes: Subsample of forty banks included in the regression analysis. Market averages, weighted by bank size of operations, except for total amount of loans.

lower in payroll than in standard loans: the instruments are very similar, and the former has wages as collateral. Similarly, standard loans are riskier, which is consistent with a higher voluntary—and involuntary—default probability. The amount lent in payroll loans is higher than in standard loans and has increased more pronouncedly over the sample period.[29]

When one compares the summary statistics for the control and treatment groups, a few points emerge. First, for payroll loans, both interest rate and risk were slightly higher than average on the subperiod before the court ruling. For standard loans, the interest rate was below average, and risk was slightly above average. This is important for our purposes as the different types of loans could be, on the months before the ruling, on different parts of a mean-reversing process. This does not appear to be the case, and, if anything, interest rates should tend to increase more (decrease less) for standard loans, vis-à-vis payroll loans, if a mean-reversing force is operative. It is similar for risk.

As for amount lent, one can see, from both table 5.1 and figure 5.4, an increase in both categories over the period, with a more pronounced increase for payroll loans. The two categories are following, over time, different paths, which could lower the value of standard loans as a control group. However, if anything, the pronounced upward trend in payroll loans would make it particularly difficult to document a *decrease* in payroll loans, relative to standard loans.

29. For the thirteen banks of the sample mentioned in section 5.2, granting of payroll loans increased by 66.7 percent during the last twelve months. Outstanding volumes more than doubled during the same period, while total personal loans increased by 50.1 percent (Nota Economica para Imprensa [NEI] and Banco Central do Brasil [BCB] 2005).

5.4.2   The Specifications

The interest rate and the quantity models are quite similar. An observation is a product i, offered by a bank b, at a month t. There are two products, personal credit with and without payroll automatic debit deduction. Let DECISION be a categorical variable that assumes the value 1 for July 2004 and all later months. It denotes the treatment period.[30] PAYROLL is a categorical variable that assumes the value 1 if the product is personal loan *with* payroll deduction. It identifies the treatment group. The estimated model for the interest rate is

$$\Delta \log (\text{INTEREST})_{itb} = \beta_0 + \beta_1 \text{PAYROLL}_{itb} + \beta_2 \text{DECISION}_t$$
$$+ \beta_3 \text{DECISION}_t \times \text{PAYROLL}_{it}$$
$$+ \Omega \text{MONTH}_t + \text{Controls} + \varepsilon_{itb}.$$

INTEREST_{ibtr} is the average interest rate on all loans given by bank b on product i, at month t. The panel unit is a pair bank product. We are interested in the level of log effect, but the data is first-differenced to eliminate fixed effects of the pair bank product. Controls include the log of the average risk on the banks' portfolios, the (lagged) total number of loan operations, and the (lagged) average size of the loan operations. Risk is included for obvious reasons as it should determine interest and is affected by the decision. Total number of loans is included because, as we have seen, payroll and nonpayroll loans have different rates of expansion over the sample period. Because expansion might affect the quality of the loan portfolio, the total number of operations should be controlled for. The average size of operations is included as it is conceivable that banks reacted to the judicial decision by decreasing exposure on operations by decreasing their size.

The main parameter of interest is β_3, the difference-in-differences coefficient. If the judicial decision had an impact on banks' pricing of payroll loans, then β_3 should be positive. We run a ordinary least squares (OLS) procedure on this equation, with the two modifications. First, we weight observations by the size of banks' operations on payroll and standard loans to arrive at an average market response. Second, we correct for between-panel correlation and within-panel autocorrelation.

The model can be viewed as a reduced form in which prices (in this case interest rates) are regressed on exogenous variables. As in any reduced form, there could be supply (which is of interest) and demand effects (not of interest) on the parameters. After controlling for period specific effects, estimates should be clean of most demand effects, and β_3, the main coefficient of interest, should capture a supply response to the ruling. Note that,

---

30. Rigorously, the decision took place in June 2004. It was, however, at the very end of the month (the 28th), so banks only had time to react to it in July. Therefore, all estimated models consider the treatment period to start in July 2004.

precisely to mitigate capturing demand effects, we lag variables such as total operations and average operations.

The quantity model is similar except that we do not control for the total number of operations and the average size of operations. These variables are excluded because the dependent variable, TotalLoans, is the product of average size and number of loans and therefore would unduly capture most of the variation in TotalLoans. With the model in logs, in fact, OLS will make both coefficients equal to one and report an R^2 of 1.

$$\Delta \log(\text{TotalLoans})_{itb} = \beta_0 + \beta_1 \text{PAYROLL}_{itb} + \beta_1 \text{DECISION}_t$$
$$+ \beta_3 \text{DECISION}_t \times \text{PAYROLL}_{it}$$
$$+ \Omega \text{MONTH}_t + \text{Controls} + \varepsilon_{itb}$$

The main control now is the first difference in the log of average risk on the banks' portfolio. Again, the main parameter of interest is β_3, the difference-in-differences coefficient. If banks reacted to the judicial decision by restricting quantity, then β_3 should be negative. We estimate the parameters by an OLS and an instrumental variables (IV) procedure. Different from the interest rate equation, there is empirical reason to believe the lag of the dependent variable belongs to the right-hand side, and there is also reason to believe that there is serial correlation on the error term. In this case, OLS could produce inconsistent estimates (see Arellano and Bond 1991).[31] Similar to the interest model, we weight observations by the size of banks' operations in personal lending, and standard errors are corrected for between correlation and within-panel autocorrelation.

For the risk perception model, an observation is a product i, offered by a bank b, at a month t. In the first specification, the dependent variable, RISK_{ibt}, is a dummy variable, that assumes the value 1 if the average risk on product i loans given by bank b at month t is above the median risk for that bank over the period considered. In the second specification, y_{ibt} is the average risk on product i's loans given the bank b's at month t. The estimated model is

$$\text{RISK}_{itb} = \beta_0 + \beta_1 \text{PAYROLL}_{ibt} + \beta_2 \text{DECISION}_t + \beta_3 \text{DECISION}_t$$
$$+ \text{PAYROLL}_{ibt} + \text{Controls} + \Omega \text{MONTH}_t + \varepsilon_{ibt}.$$

Controls_{bit} are variables that affect risk (such as average size of loans and total number of loans). Because in the case when RISK is a dummy, it is unnatural to first difference the data, so to account for bank-product fixed effects, we include bank dummies in both specifications to maintain homogeneity. With the model in levels, when RISK is the average risk in the

31. Several economic stories could be told to justify the lag of Δ log (Total Loans) to belong, or not, to the right-hand side of both the interest and the quantity equations. Because this is not our variable of interest, we take an agnostic empirical approach and evaluate whether empirically it belongs to the equation and take proper econometric steps to correct (i.e., look for exogenous variation) if it does.

bank portfolio, one has to worry that the lagged dependent variable might belong to the equation, and the lagged average risk is included.[32] When RISK is a dummy, however, including lagged dummies will unduly absorbs most variation: unless the dummy oscillates wildly, it replicates itself most periods, and most variation in the dependent variable is explained by its lag. It is important to notice that this happens not because of the economics of the dynamics of riskiness on these loans but by the way the dependent variable is constructed. Incidentally, this effect is especially pronounced if the hypothesis to be tested is true: the dummy should assume lots of 1 values after the decision and a lot of 0 values before the decision.

Again, the main coefficient of interest is β_3, the difference-in-differences coefficient. If the judicial decision had an impact on banks' risk perception on payroll loans, then β_3 should be positive: risk assessment on payroll loans increased compared to standard loans. We run a logit procedure on this equation, again weighting observations by the size of banks' operations in personal lending.

Notice that in all models, variation among banks is used. This is crucial as the main economic decision unit is a bank. Although the judicial decision hit banks at the same time ($DECISION_t$ does not vary over b), banks potentially differ in their response to the decision, and this provides variation to estimate the coefficient of interest. In the end, the response of an average bank is estimated, with larger banks counting more than smaller ones.

5.5   Results and Discussion

5.5.1   The Risk Equation

We start with the risk equation. In table 5.2, the dependent variable is a dummy for whether bank b's average risk on the product operation (standard and payroll loans) is above the median risk for the whole sample (January 2003 to June 2005). The main hypothesis is tested in column (1). The sample is restricted to five months before the decision and five months after the decision. The coefficient associated with the difference-in-differences regressor (β_3) is 0.357, and it is quite precisely estimated (it is significant at the 1 percent level). This means that, relative to standard loans, the probability that the operation on payroll loans was above the median risk increased. The model is nonlinear, and there is no immediate way to interpret "above the median risk" is an economically meaningful way, so it is difficult to evaluate this coefficient quantitatively. One can, however, state that, qualitatively, risk perception on payroll loans increases in period following

---

32. In reason for this is that banks, by pricing risk, might scare off better borrowers. Hence, higher risk today could cause higher risk tomorrow. One has then to worry about dynamic panel biases (Arellano and Bond 1991). See section on results for more on this.

Table 5.2   **Risk equation: Results 1**

	Subsample			
	Month >Feb/04 and <Dec/04 (1)	Month >Feb/04[a] (2)	Month >Sep/03 and <July/04[a] (3)	Month >July/04[b] (4)
Payroll loan	−0.184	−0.220*	−0.386**	0.153
	(0.137)	(0.120)	(0.176)	(0.116)
Judicial decision	−0.391***	−0.590***		
	(0.172)	(0.154)		
Payroll loan · Judicial decision	0.357***	0.166		
	(0.078)	(0.128)		
Log(number of operations)	−0.154**	−0.017	−0.309*	0.068
	(0.071)	(0.050)	(0.181)	(0.060)
Log(average size operation)	0.071	−0.056**	0.102	−0.020
	(0.061)	(0.026)	(0.157)	(0.026)
Dummy robust			−0.607***	−0.296*
			(0.175)	(−0.184)
Payroll loan · Dummy robust			(0.122)	(0.181)
No. of observations	543	993	626	667

Source: Banco Central do Brasil.

Notes: Dependent variable: dummy for average risk above median. Logit marginal effects estimates. Robust standard errors in parentheses. Control group: Loans without payroll deduction. Weighted by size of banks operation. Bank and month dummies included. Judicial decision taking effect on July/2004 (month 12).

[a]Dummy if month > 13.

[b]Dummy if month > 24.

***Significant at the 1 percent level.

**Significant at the 5 percent level.

*Significant at the 10 percent level.

the court decision. The probability of the average risk on the banks' portfolio being above the median decreases over the subsample period for both loans (coefficient on Judicial Decision, −0.391). However, it decreases much less for payroll deduction loans, only −0.184. Expansion in the number of operations is associated with less risk (a 1 percent increase in the number of operations decreases the probability of being above the median in roughly 15.4 percent), which is likely to indicate that a larger number of operations (and probably a lower average size) provide better diversification, although this result is not robust to different subsamples.

Although month-specific dummies are included, it can always be the case that, for some unaccounted reason, risk perception was decreasing less for payroll deduction loans, relative to plain personal loans, and this had nothing to do with the court ruling. For this reason, we first expand the period under consideration to all months after the law regulating payroll loans passed through congress. If the estimated difference-in-differences had nothing to do with the judicial decision, one would expect that the estimated coefficient on the interaction term to remain somewhat constant. As one can see in column (2), this is not case. Expanding the sample makes the "effect" of the judicial decision decrease by half, and it is no longer statistically significant, although the sample is almost twice the size. Additionally, faux treatment dummies are specified to check whether the same pattern occurs if we consider artificial treatment dates. In column (4), the fake treatment is month twenty-five, and the sample is restricted on purpose to exclude the months before the judicial decision. The estimated fake difference-in-differences coefficient has a reverse sign, and it is well estimated. If anything, the discrepancy between standard and payroll loans was the opposite for this subsample. Finally, the fake treatment period is put in month fourteen, and the sample is restricted to months before the judicial decision (column [3]). Again, the coefficient has the opposite sign, that is, risk increases in *standard* loans relative to payroll loans in this subsample with a fake treatment period at fourteen. Most likely, this captures the effect of the bill regulating payroll loans passing through congress.

Results are similar when risk is measured by the average risk rating on the banks' portfolio (see table 5.3). There are two differences though. First, we difference the log of the data to eliminate for fixed effects.[33] Second, with average risk rating as the dependent variable, one has to account for the possibility that the dependent variable has persistence over time. For this reason, several different specifications are applied. First, an OLS model is used in which the first and second lags of the dependent variable are included as explanatory variables. The standard errors of the estimated coefficients are corrected for between-panel correlation and within-panel autocorrelation. Again, banks' risk perception on payroll loans increased relative to standard loans: the estimated coefficient on the difference-in-differences parameters is 0.014, and it is significant at the 1 percent level (column [1]). Economically, risk perception increased in payroll loans by roughly 1.4 percentage points. In column (2), a model for the dynamics of the errors term is imposed, and the parameters are estimated by a feasible generalized least squares (FGLS) procedure. The results for the parameter of interest (β_3) are exactly the same.

There is, however, the possibility that there is persistence both in the process of the dependent variable and the unobserved factors that affect risk (the error term). Columns (1) and (2) suggest the second lag of the Δ log (Average Risk) does not belong to the equation. Therefore, it arises as a

---

33. This is tantamount to controlling for fixed effects and should be the preferred procedure. When the dummy for risk above median is used as a dependent variable, it is not natural to first-difference the data, and therefore bank dummies are included. See Wooldridge (2002).

Table 5.3 Risk equation: Results 2

	Subsample					
	Month >Feb/04 and <Dec/04[a] (1)	Month >Feb/04 and <Dec/04[d] (2)	Month >Feb/04 and <Dec/04[e] (3)	Month >Feb/04[d] (4)	Month >Sep/03 and <July/04[b,d] (5)	Month >July/04[c,d] (6)
Payroll loan	-0.010** (0.004)	-0.006** (0.003)	-0.012** (0.005)	-0.013* (0.007)	0.002 (0.004)	0.002 (0.006)
Judicial decision	0.009* (0.005)	0.007 (0.005)	-0.001 (0.007)	0.001 (0.009)		
Payroll loan · Judicial decision	0.014*** (0.006)	0.014*** (0.005)	0.009 (0.006)	0.006 (0.008)		
$\Delta\log(\text{average risk})_{t-1}$	0.544*** (0.101)	0.499*** (0.030)	0.497*** (0.030)	0.493*** (0.009)	0.460*** (0.016)	0.505*** (0.012)
$\Delta\log(\text{average risk})_{t-2}$	0.008 (0.101)	0.002 (0.024)				
$\Delta\text{Log(number of operations)}$	0.073 (0.090)	0.065*** (0.010)	0.073*** (0.010)	0.025*** (0.005)	0.037*** (0.006)	0.022*** (0.007)
$\Delta\text{Log(average size operation)}$	0.103** (0.004)	0.008*** (0.002)	0.018*** (0.004)	0.002** (0.001)	-0.000 (0.001)	0.002** (0.001)
Dummy robust					0.002 (0.005)	-0.015* (0.009)
Payroll loan · Dummy robust					-0.006 (0.004)	-0.017** (0.008)
No. of observations	543	543	543	993	626	667

Source: Banco Central do Brasil.

Notes: Dependent variable: Δlog(average risk). Robust standard errors in parentheses. Control group: Loans without payroll deduction. Weighted by size of banks operation. Month dummies included. Judicial decision taking effect on July/2004 (month 12).

[a] OLS estimates, with standard error of estimated coefficients corrected for between panel correlation and within panel autocorrelation using the Prais–Winsten procedure.

[b] Dummy if month > 13.

[c] Dummy if month > 24.

[d] Feasible generalized least squares with AR(1) model for within panel autocorrelation.

[e] IV estimates with Δlog(average risk)t – 2 as instrument for ΔLog(average risk)t – 1.

***Significant at the 1 percent level.

**Significant at the 5 percent level.

*Significant at the 10 percent level.

natural instrument for Δ log (Average Risk)$_{t-1}$ under the identifying assumption the error term has only one period persistence.[34] Now there is not enough independent variation to estimate the parameter of interest: the p-value of estimation is roughly 13 percent. The difference-in-differences coefficient is, nonetheless, still positive, although with a lower magnitude (0.009). Columns (4) to (6) present the same robustness checks as in table 5.3. Results and corresponding interpretations are qualitatively similar.

Results could be driven by two factors unrelated to the STJ ruling but implied by heterogeneity in the dynamics of the treatment and control groups. First, as table 5.1 shows, standard loans are, as expected, riskier than payroll loans. If there are general institutional advances in credit markets during the period and if there are decreasing returns in risk improvement, then one should observe a decrease in riskiness of standard vis-à-vis payroll loans because the former started at a higher level of risk. However, if this was the case, one would expect that the same pattern would emerge for all subsamples of whole period. As columns (3) and (4) in table 5.2 indicate, risk perception on payroll loans *decreases* vis-à-vis standard loans in the periods before and after the STJ ruling. The same is true in table 5.3 (columns [5] and [6]).

Second, as figure 5.4 shows, payroll loans boomed during the period, possibly due to the approval of the December 2003 law. Expansions might be risk-increasing, that is, the marginal borrower may be worse than the inframarginal ones. If this is the case, the pool of borrowers on payroll lending would be changing, compared to standard lending, in such a way that would produce the result regardless of the court ruling. There are, however, at least two reasons why this story cannot rationalize the results. First, the number of operations is controlled for. In table 5.3, for example, changes in the log of average risk are explained by the court ruling with variation above and beyond changes in log of number and average size of operations. Indeed, because the model is in first differences, results are not only controlled for the fact that larger banks might have lower risk borrowers, but also for within-bank expansions of payroll vis-à-vis standard operations. Second, the same argument as in the last paragraph applies. Figure 5.4 shows that payroll operations rose, relative to standard ones, *throughout the period.* Hence, if the changing pool of borrowers argument would apply, one should verify the same increase in riskiness of payroll vis-à-vis standard operations *throughout the period.* As columns (3) and (4) in table

34. Exactly because the second lag does not appear to be a explanatory variable, using further lags as instrument would not be warranted because they do not arise naturally as shifts to the endogenous variable that are not related to the unobserved determinants of risk perception (the error term). As with any identifying assumption, it is impossible to verify it empirically. Because the data is in the first difference of logs, there is no compelling reason why adjustments to unobserved shocks to risk would take more than a month to be incorporated to the banks' credit rating decision.

5.2 and columns (5) and (6) in table 5.3 show, this does not seem to be the case.

5.5.2   The Quantity Equation

The results for the quantity equation are presented in tables 5.4 and 5.5. Column (1) of table 5.4 presents the simplest possible model: OLS omitting $\Delta \log$ (Amount of Loans)$_{t-1}$ as an explanatory variable and no period dummies. As expected, operations of payroll loans are larger (6.5 percent more), and quantities of both standard and payroll loans appear to be increasing over time (coefficient on Judicial Decision, 3.8 percent on average in the subperiod between February 2004 and October 2004), as figure 5.4 suggested. Despite the markedly different slopes of standard and payroll loans, the judicial decision did have a negative effect on payroll loans: relative to standard loans, payroll loans decrease when one compares before and after the court ruling. Indeed, after controlling for average risk, payroll loan quantities decreased 5.8 percent, between the five-month subperiod before the court ruling and the five-month subperiod after the ruling. Inclusion of period dummies hardly changes the results (column [2]). Results are, however, slightly different when the lag of the dependent variable is included: one can see (column [3]) that part of the difference-in-differences coefficient was capturing some variation of the $\Delta \log$ (Amount of Loans)$_{t-1}$. Results, however, remain considerably similar.

The presence of the lag of the dependent variable poses again the challenge of searching for exogenous variation to estimate the coefficient associated with $\Delta \log$ (Amount of Loans)$_{t-1}$ as there could also be persistence on the error term. Again, we follow the strategy of using the second lag ($\Delta \log$ [Amount of Loans]$_{t-1}$) as an instrument. Columns (4) and (5) of table 5.4 present the results. It does appear that part of the estimated coefficient in columns (1) to (3) are unduly capturing variation due to omission of explanatory variables (which are in the dynamics of the error term). The effect, however, still survives: in the most unfavorable specification, there is 3.7 percent difference in the trends of standard and payroll loans when periods before and after the court ruling is considered. This result is not terribly well estimated, but one could reject the null that it is zero at the 5.8 percent level (column [5]).

Table 5.5 presents different specifications. In columns (1) and (3), standard error estimates are corrected for between-panel correlation and within-panel autocorrelation. Notice that the estimates of the difference-in-differences parameters are even more precisely estimated. When a FGLS procedure is used, results are similar (column [2]). These results do not account for the possible omitted variable bias due to the presence of $\Delta \log$ (Amount of Loans)$_{t-2}$ but do suggest that the statistical significance in table 5.4 is not due to underestimation of standard errors. Column (4) of table 5.5 checks the robustness of the results in the same spirit as in tables

Table 5.4   **Quantity equation: Results 1**

			Subsample		
	Month >Feb/04 and <Dec/04 (1)	Month >Feb/04 and <Dec/04 (2)	Month >Feb/04 and <Dec/04 (3)	Month >Feb/04 and <Dec/04: IV estimates[a] (4)	Month >Feb/04 and <Dec/04: IV estimates[a] (5)
ΔLog(amount of loans)$_{t-1}$			0.346***	0.580***	0.586**
			(0.105)	(0.225)	(0.237)
Payroll loan	0.065***	0.065***	0.044***	0.033*	0.032*
	(0.017)	(0.017)	(0.014)	(0.019)	(0.019)
Judicial decision	0.038**	0.026	0.035**	0.034**	0.077*
	(0.016)	(0.018)	(0.015)	(0.016)	(0.041)
Payroll loan ·Judicial decision	−0.058**	−0.058**	−0.045**	−0.038**	−0.037*
	(0.024)	(0.025)	(0.021)	(0.022)	(0.022)
ΔLog(average risk)	0.077	0.026	0.072	0.079	0.029
	(0.468)	(0.446)	(0.437)	(0.420)	(0.404)
ΔLog(average risk)$_{t-1}$	−0.308*	−0.287	−0.289	−0.225	−0.183
	(0.180)	(0.202)	(0.187)	(0.218)	(0.240)
Date dummy?	No	Yes	No	No	Yes
No. of observations	507	507	507	507	507

Source: Banco Central do Brasil.

Notes: Dependent variable: Δlog(amount of loans). OLS estimates. Robust standard errors in parentheses. Control group: Loans without payroll deduction. Weighted by size of banks operation. Bank dummies included. Judicial decision taking effect on July/2004 (month 18).

[a]Instrument: second lag of ΔLog(amount of loans).

***Significant at the 1 percent level.

**Significant at the 5 percent level.

*Significant at the 10 percent level.

Table 5.5   **Quantity equation: Results 2**

	Subsample			
	Month >Feb/04 and <Dec/04[a] (1)	Month >Feb/04 and <Dec/04[b] (2)	Month >Feb/04 and <Dec/04[a] (3)	Month July/04[c] (4)
ΔLog(amount of loans)$t-1$	0.222	0.150***	0.189	
	(0.118)	(0.054)	(0.182)	
Payroll loan	0.052***	0.057***	0.053***	0.036*
	(0.017)	(0.019)	(0.017)	(0.021)
Judicial decision	0.035**	0.057***	0.057***	
	(0.017)	(0.022)	(0.019)	
Payroll loan · Judicial decision	−0.051***	−0.053**	−0.052***	
	(0.018)	(0.024)	(0.018)	
ΔLog(average risk)	0.033	0.067	0.003	−0.082
	(0.144)	(0.093)	(0.151)	(0.103)
ΔLog(average risk)$t-1$	−0.280**	−0.273***	−0.278*	−0.161*
	(0.141)	(0.093)	(0.154)	(0.098)
Dummy robust				0.020
				(0.021)
Payroll loan · Dummy robust				0.015
				(0.034)
Date dummy?	No	Yes	Yes	Yes
No. of observations	507	507	507	665

Source: Banco Central do Brasil.

Notes: Dependent variable: ΔLog(amount of loans). OLS estimates. Robust standard errors in parentheses. Control group: Loans without payroll deduction. Probability-weighted by size and bank operation. Bank dummies included. Judicial decision taking effect on July/2004 (month 18).

[a]Standard error of estimated coefficients corrected for between panel correlation and within panel autocorrelation using the Praiss-Winsten procedure.

[b]Feasible generalized least squares (FGLS) assuming errors within panels follow an AR(1) process.

[c]Dummy robust = 1, if month > 18, most favorable model: FGLS assuming errors within panels follow an AR(1) process.

***Significant at the 1 percent level.

**Significant at the 5 percent level.

*Significant at the 10 percent level.

5.2 and 5.3: it appears that the estimated difference-in-differences coefficient is not due to a long-term pattern over the whole sample period. When the fake treatment period twenty-five is used and the sample is restricted to after the court ruling, the results disappear. Similar robustness results hold for the whole period and for only the period before the court ruling.

5.5.3   The Pricing Equation

The effect of the court ruling on the interest rates of payroll loans can be found in table 5.6. A couple of comments are necessary. Different from the quantity regression, the number of operations and the average size of the

Table 5.6   **Pricing equation: Results**

	Month >Feb/04 and <Dec/04[a] (1)	Month >Feb/04 and <Dec/04[a] (2)	Subsample Month >Feb/04 and <Dec/04 (3)	Month >Feb/04 and <Dec/04[a] (4)	Month >July/04[a,b] (5)
ΔLog(interest rate)$t-1$	0.019 (0.193)	0.008 (0.193)	0.008 (0.039)	0.008 (0.039)	
Payroll loan	-0.063*** (0.020)	-0.061*** (0.020)	-0.061 (0.047)	-0.062*** (0.021)	-0.019 (0.025)
Judicial decision	-0.075*** (0.028)	-0.143*** (0.035)	-0.143*** (0.063)	-0.095*** (0.031)	
Payroll loan · Judicial decision	0.073*** (0.024)	0.071*** (0.024)	0.071 (0.060)	0.071*** (0.026)	
ΔLog(average risk)	-0.464 (0.315)	-0.475 (0.334)	-0.475 (0.273)	-0.480 (-0.325)	0.408 (0.570)
ΔLog(average risk)$t-1$	0.430** (0.221)	0.410* (0.239)	0.410** (0.379)	0.423** (0.179)	0.363 (0.582)
Log(average size of operation)$t-1$	-0.004 (0.098)	-0.016 (0.103)	-0.016 (0.182)	-0.011 (0.101)	-0.134 (0.087)
Log(number of operations)$t-1$	0.049 (0.024)	0.045 (0.052)	0.045 (0.044)	0.045 (0.053)	-0.036*** (0.013)
Dummy robust					0.080* (0.47)
Payroll loan · Dummy robust					0.057 (0.058)
Date dummy?	No	Yes	Yes	Yes	No
No. of observations	507	507	507	507	665

Source: Banco Central do Brasil.

Note: Dependent variable: ΔLog(interest rate). See table 5.4 notes.

[a]Standard error of estimated coefficients corrected for between panel correlation and within panel autocorrelation using the Praiss-Winsten procedure.

[b]Dummy = 1 if month > 24.

***Significant at the 1 percent level.

**Significant at the 5 percent level.

*Significant at the 10 percent level.

operation are included. We do so because there might be (dis)economies of scale involved in granting loans. Both variables are lagged one period to mitigate the possibility of capturing demand side effects. Second, it is important once again to emphasize that the data on prices is problematic, especially for interpretation on levels. Taking the log and first-differencing the data ameliorate somehow the problems with levels but do not solve it. Interpretation on changes, however, is less troublesome, and we proceed by doing so, especially as the results with interest rates are consistent with the results on quantities and risk perception.

Column (1) of table 5.6 shows the OLS results when the lag of the dependent variable is included, but not the period dummies. Consistent with the quantity and risk perception results and with the perception of important market participants, the court ruling appears to have induced an increase in the interest rate charged on payroll loans. After controlling for number of operations, average size of operations and risk, there is a marked difference (7.3 percent) between the trends of interest rates on payroll and standard loans before and after the court ruling. Consistent with the general perception in the market, interest rates on payroll loans are lower than those on standard loans (6.3 percent). Estimates suggest risk perception does indeed affect interest rate as expected: while one cannot reject the null hypothesis that contemporaneous changes in risk perception affect interest rates, one-period lagged increases in risk perception does induce an increase in prices of loans. After standard errors of estimation are corrected for between-panel correlation and within-panel serial correlation, the lag of the dependent variable does not appear to belong to the equation. This renders results less vulnerable to dynamic panel bias.

Columns (2), (3) and (4) of table 5.6 present slightly different specifications. Most noteworthy is column (3), in which the OLS standard errors of estimation are not corrected. Here, one cannot reject the null hypothesis that there are not differences between standard and payroll loans with respect to the court ruling. The estimates suggest that correction on the standard deviation provides better (more precisely) estimates for the difference-in-differences parameter. Column (5) of table 5.6 presents the same robustness check as in all other tables, and it is again consistent with the previous results.

5.6 Conclusion

The results in this paper suggest the conjecture of some market participants that the June 2004 court ruling had an adverse effect on the market performance of payroll loans. Results arise and are consistent among each other for risk perception, quantity of loans, and interest rates, with the data caveat for the latter. Data suggests that the ruling increased risk perception on payroll loans, which in turn led banks to restrict quantity and increase interest rates.

These results are far from obvious. Several key market players anticipated them, but not all. It could have been that lenders had ignored the ruling. As figure 5.4 eloquently suggests, the court ruling did not prevent the boom of payroll loans. It did, however, abate it, and made it such that terms to borrowers were worse.

This paper provides some evidence on the missing link of the institutions-economic performance nexus literature: the micro evidence. Far from contradicting the literature, our results corroborate it with evidence drawn from the unit of decision making: lenders in this case. It reinforces the policy recipes already implied by the literature. Better protection from expropriation most likely increases general welfare, as it improves market performance in informationally and incentive problematic markets, such as the credit market.

References

Acemoglu, Daron, Simon Johnson, and James Robinson. 2001. The colonial origins of comparative development: An empirical investigation. *The American Economic Review* 91 (December): 1369–1401.

Altubas, Yener, Lynne Evans, and Philip Molyneux. 2001. Bank ownership and efficiency. *Journal of Money, Credit, and Banking* 33 (1): 926–54.

Arellano, Manuel, and Stephen Bond. 1991. Some tests of specification for panel data: Monte Carlo evidence and an application to employment equations. *The Review of Economic Studies* 58:277–97.

Djankov, Simeon, Rafael La Porta, Florencio Lopez-de-Silanes, and Andrei Shleifer. 2003. Courts: The Lex Mundi project. *The Quarterly Journal of Economics* 118 (May): 453–507.

Dubey, Martin, John Geanakoplos, and Pradeep Shubik. 2005. Default and punishment in general equilibrium. *Econometrica* 73 (1): 1–37.

King, Robert, and Ross Levine. 1993. Finance and growth: Schumpeter might be right. *The Quarterly Journal of Economics* 108 (August): 717–37.

La Porta, Rafael, Florencio Lopez-de-Silanes, Cristian Pop-Eleches, and Andrei Shleifer. 2004. Judicial checks and balances. *The Journal of Political Economy* 112:445–70.

La Porta, Rafael, Florencio Lopez-de-Silanes, Andrei Shleifer, and Robert Vishny. 1997. Legal determinants of external finance. *The Journal of Finance* 52 (July): 1131–50.

———. 1998a. Corporate ownership around the world. *The Journal of Finance* 54:471–517.

———. 1998b. Law and finance. *The Journal of Political Economy* 106 (December): 1113–55.

Levine, Ross. 1998. The legal environment, banks, and long-run economic growth. *The Journal of Money, Credit, and Banking* 30 (August): 596–613.

Levine, Ross, and Sara Zervos. 1998. Stock markets, banks, and economic growth. *The American Economic Review* 88 (June): 537–58.

North, Douglas. 1994. Economic performance through time. *American Economic Review* 84 (3): 359–68.

Pinheiro, Armando Castelar, and Célia Cabral. 1998. Credit markets in Brazil: The role of judicial enforcement and other institutions. BNDES Working Paper no. 9. Rio de Janeiro, Brazil: BNDES.

Sapienza, Paola. 2002. The effects of government ownership on bank lending. *Journal of Financial Economics* 72 (2): 357–84.

Wooldridge, Jeffrey. 2002. *Econometric Analysis of Cross-Section and Panel Data.* Cambridge, MA: MIT Press.

Comment   Renato G. Flôres Jr.

This paper deals with an interesting problem, relevant both to the theoretical debate and to policy setting, the latter not only in present day Brazil. Though the authors' views on the theoretical impact of their results are somewhat enthusiastic, their effort to resort to microdata is most welcome, as well as the use of recent, program evaluation econometric techniques in a (micro) finance context. My comments will concentrate on this last point as, unfortunately, in spite of its virtues, the paper leaves several unanswered questions as regards methodological and econometric aspects related to their use of the differences-in-differences (DD) estimation technique.

First, however, I'm obliged to come to a minor point. The paper is not very friendly to someone who wants to understand what has actually been done. Different time lengths *seem* to have been used for the computations, labeling the months by ordinals is confusing (to my surprise, July 2004 is 18, not 19 . . .), equations aren't numbered ("controls" are mentioned after each equation), figures have poor labeling, and the technical explanations suffer from a few black holes.

Ideally, as known, the methodology of the DD estimator requires perfect matching between the two populations, but for the treatment, and clearly defined *before* and *after* treatment periods. The matching population to the payroll loans (PLs) one was that of standard loans, and, notwithstanding the reasoning in section 5.4.1, it is not evident that, but for the July 2004 ruling, both populations suffered the same influences. Without entering into the more conceptual issue that the two types of *borrowers*—the ultimate *observational unit*—are probably very different in socioeconomic terms and so don't match, even accepting *loans* as the observational unit, questions arise: Were there not other, specific shocks to standard loans? What is the percentage of movers between the two popu-

Renato G. Flores Jr. is Professor in the Graduate School of Economics, Fundação Geteulio Vargas, Rio de Janeiro, Brazil.

lations, especially given the different stages in PL implementation? Perhaps the answers are on the safe side, but the authors should elaborate more on them. This point is enhanced by the fact that the final sample of banks may easily be biased, and statistics on the structure of the sample are rather incomplete.

Turning to the before and after periods, the impact of the ruling may have had a lag and even an anticipation effect. Combining this with the December 2003 legislation—also a treatment: the powerful Caixa Econômica Federal started to accept individual PLs in May 2004—better support and evaluation is needed for the two periods chosen.

As for the econometrics itself, monthly differences—justified on the grounds of eliminating idiosyncratic effects in the panel at stake—are used for the dependent variable in the interest rate and total loans cases. Then the linear DD model is directly specified for such differences in order to make possible the inclusion of the three classical, required dummies (otherwise, they would vanish when taking the differences). This raises interpretation problems not only in the very specification of the models—which proceeds as if the dependent was in levels—but on the meaning of the ultimate DD expectation itself. The same ambiguous treatment applies to the residuals, though some care is sometimes shown with their correlations. In this particular, the authors seem oblivious of the issues raised in the key contribution by Bertrand, Duflo, and Mullanaitan (2004), and I have some difficulty in explaining a series of values like those in table 5. 6, for instance. In overall terms, the nearly striking results often obtained for the DD coefficients—not supported by the informal analysis of stylized facts and trends—couldn't be an outcome of underestimated standard deviations as, beyond other problems, they might have incurred?

I think questioning along these lines qualify the paper as suggestive, but in order to be trusted certainly demand a more careful and methodologically attentive text.

Reference

Bertrand, M., E. Duflo, and S. Mullanaitan. 2004. How much should we trust differences-in-differences estimates? *Quarterly Journal of Economics* 119:249–75.

Liquidity Insurance in a Financially Dollarized Economy

Eduardo Levy Yeyati

6.1 Introduction

While the foreign currency denomination (dollarization, for short) of external liabilities typical of most financially integrated developing economies has been the subject of a vast body of academic work,[1] the dollarization of domestic financial assets has received comparatively less attention until very recently, when it has been increasingly seen as a key source of real exchange rate exposure and banking (and macroeconomic) fragility.[2] There is, however, an angle of domestic financial dollarization (FD) that, while intuitive, has been somewhat overlooked: the limit it imposes on the central bank as domestic lender of last resort (LLR) and the resulting exposure to dollar liquidity runs à la Diamond and Dyvbig (1983).[3] Thus, the growing literature on balance-sheet effects and dedollarization con-

Eduardo Levy Yeyati is Financial Sector Advisor for Latin America and the Caribbean at The World Bank, and professor of economics (on sabbatical leave) at the Business School of Universidad Torcuato Di Tella and The World Bank, Buenos Aires.

The author wishes to thank Marco Bonomo, Alejandro Werner, and participants at the December 2005 NBER Inter-American Seminar on Economics in Rio de Janeiro for their helpful comments, and Ramiro Blázquez and Luis Casanovas for their outstanding research assistance.

1. Examples include the literature on "original sin" (Eichengreen and Hausmann 2005), "liability dollarization cum sudden stop" (Calvo 2005), and "dollar shortages" (Caballero and Krishnamurthy 2003; Rajan 2004).

2. Domestic FD introduces a hidden short position in the foreign currency (either at the bank or at the debtor level) exposing the economy as a whole to sudden real exchange rate depreciations. See De Nicoló, Honohan, and Ize (2005), and Levy Yeyati (2005) for empirical analyses along these lines. Armas, Ize, and Levy Yeyati (forthcoming) provide a compendium on this relatively new literature.

3. By contrast, this issue has been often highlighted in the *official* dollarization debate (Broda and Levy Yeyati 2003a).

trasts with the less-developed literature on how to manage liquidity in the (potentially long) interim period when FD remains high. This is the subject of the present paper.

The analysis of dollar liquidity runs in FD economies has often centered on the economy as a whole, stressing the need for "insurance" mechanisms and the limitations of the available options.[4] While most of this debate also pertains to the analysis of banking crises, there are some important specificities that the macroeconomic focus has tended to leave in the dark.

In particular, once one considers the banking sector as the object of insurance, a number of questions arise. Are the central bank's (centralized) and the individual banks' (decentralized) hoarding of reserves equivalent? How can the costs of self-insurance be reduced in the absence of an external alternative? Can a suspension of a convertibility clause (often applied ex post, too late, when the bank run is well underway) be used ex ante to supplement self-insurance?

To address these questions, I proceed in four steps. First, I revisit the evidence on the incidence of FD on the propensity to suffer bank runs and document the positive link between FD and reserve accumulation. I show that FD has been a motive for this form of self-insurance—in addition to the capital account reversal often noted in the literature.

Next, I analyze and compare available insurance options and explore the incentive problems associated with centralized holdings of reserves at the central bank, when the latter, among other uses, are expected to provide dollar liquidity insurance to individual banks. In particular, I show that centralized reserves can deepen the moral hazard problem within the banking industry and induce further dollarization.

Then I illustrate the authorities' decision to suspend convertibility in the context of a run with the story of two recent banking crises: Argentina 2001 and Uruguay 2002.

Finally, I argue in favor of a combined scheme of decentralized liquid asset requirement (LAR) to limit moral hazard, and an ex ante suspension-of-convertibility clause or "circuit breaker" (CBR) that mitigates the costs of belated action while limiting the need for costly self-insurance.[5]

The logic behind this combination is simple. Exposure to runs is an inevitable consequence of a banking system that transforms short-run savings into long-run investments. In the absence of an LLR that can produce liquidity on demand, the bank supervisor faces two options to reduce this

4. Thus, Jeanne and Ranciere (2006) discuss the optimal level of self-insurance through reserve accumulation, Aizenman and Lee (2005) show that reserve hoarding provides welfare gains, Caballero and Panageas (2004) propose the use of derivatives to maximize the insurance value of reserves, whereas Cordella and Levy Yeyati (2005a) argue in favor of external insurance, and Cordella and Levy Yeyati (2005b) stress the drawbacks of private external insurance and current International Monetary Fund (IMF)-led packages and point to the convenience of ad hoc multilateral official agreements to reduce the costs of self-insurance.

5. See Ize, Kiguel, and Levy Yeyati (2005), where this scheme was first outlined.

maturity mismatch: (a) liquid reserves, which reduce the average length of bank assets (in the limit, "narrow banking" eliminates both bank runs and bank financing), and (b) CBRs, which increase the average length (reduce the effective liquidity) of bank deposits (in the limit, approaching illiquid corporate debt). If the opportunity cost of reserve hoarding (proportional to the marginal productivity of capital) increases with the volume of reserves, and the liquidity premium (proportional to the marginal utility of consumption) increases as the CBR gets more restrictive, the optimal solution is a combination of LAR and CBR.[6]

6.2   FD, Bank Runs, and Reserves

Deposit dollarization is not only the most amply documented aspect of de facto dollarization but also (and for the same reason) the subject of most of the early FD literature.[7] Despite the recent focus on external (official and unofficial) debt, domestic FD remains a widespread, persistent, and economically significant phenomenon, with distinct prudential implications. A quick look at the map of domestic FD confirms that it is not a localized phenomenon (figure 6.1) and that it has been remarkably stable in recent years (table 6.1). On the other hand, most recent systemic banking crises has taken place in domestically dollarized economies (table 6.2), a link already highlighted in the literature.[8]

Not surprisingly, then, domestically dollarized economies have tended to "insure" themselves through the hoarding of liquid foreign assets, much in the same way as countries experiencing sudden capital account reversals have revealed a preference for a high stock of international reserves. In this particular case, reserves holdings can be centralized at the central bank or decentralized at individual banks (in the form of reserve money or liquid asset requirements). Table 6.3 reports the summary statistics for both types. In addition, it shows that they are highly correlated with the degree of deposit dollarization, and between themselves.

This first impression is confirmed by more rigorous empirical testing.

6. In a sense, this analysis moves a step back from Diamond and Dyvbig's own argument. If dollar deposit insurance cannot be tax- or debt-financed on demand and needs to be funded in advance, the amount of insured deposits (but not insurance coverage) is predetermined, and suspension of convertibility (too rigid relative to a deposit insurance a la Diamond and Dyvbig) looks again as a viable second-best alternative.

7. By contrast, comprehensive data on the currency composition of sovereign debt can be found only for a limited group of middle- to high-income countries (see Cowan et al. 2006).

8. De Nicoló, Honohan, and Ize (2005) report that FD increases banks risk and deposit volatility, and Levy Yeyati (2006) shows that a devaluation raises the banking crisis propensity (only) in the presence of FD. Domestic FD in figure 6.1 is computed as the ratio of on-shore dollar deposits over total onshore dollar deposits. With the exception of FD, all ratios in the paper are normalized by GDP. It is important to note that FD refers to the use of a currency other than the domestic legal tender. Hence, the very low levels of FD in officially dollarized Panama, Ecuador, and El Salvador.

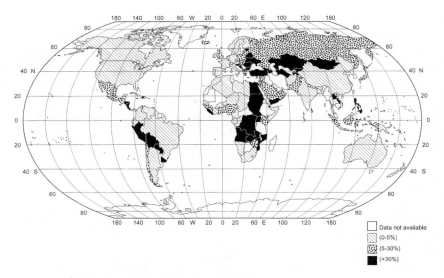

Fig. 6.1   Deposit dollarization around the world
Source: Levy Yeyati (2006).

Table 6.1   **Deposit dollarization over time**

	Latin America	Europe	Asia	Africa and Oceania
1999				
Mean	29.3	41.4	34.7	23.3
Median	20.9	43.7	26.5	16.9
No. of observations	24	25	25	25
Min.	0.1	1.6	2.5	0.0
Max.	92.6	80.0	92.3	81.1
2004				
Mean	30.8	38.4	32.8	26.0
Median	27.3	38.0	29.5	20.1
No. of observations	24	25	25	25
Min.	2.0	8.1	3.3	0
Max.	87.6	79.9	95.7	86.0

Notes: Balanced sample. Deposit dollarization is computed as the stock of dollar deposits over total deposits.

Table 6.4 reports within and between estimates from panel regressions of different types of reserve holdings (including banks' holdings of foreign assets outside the central bank) on deposit dollarization.[9] All within regressions include a time trend to capture the noted trend toward reserve accu-

9. Bank foreign assets are included here for completeness. It should be noted, however, that should not be interpreted as reflection of self-insurance for at least two reasons. First, they are

Table 6.2   **Systemic banking crises and deposit dollarization ratios**

Year	Country	%
1994	Uganda	17.1
1994	Armenia	72.2
1994	Bolivia	78.5
1994	Jamaica	21.0
1994	Mexico	7.1
1995	Guinea-Bissau	50.5
1995	Zambia	20.1
1995	Zimbabwe	13.1
1995	Azerbaijan	49.1
1995	Bulgaria	29.5
1995	Latvia	50.4
1995	Lithuania	40.6
1995	Russia	28.5
1995	Argentina	57.1
1995	Jamaica	18.9
1995	Paraguay	37.9
1996	Yemen	41.4
1996	Croatia	67.6
1996	Ecuador	22.3
1997	Indonesia	28.3
1997	Korea	3.3
1997	Malaysia	1.8
1997	Thailand	1.3
1997	Vietnam	34.1
1997	Ukraine	25.8
1998	Philippines, The	32.6
1998	Russia	44.0
1998	Ecuador	36.9
2000	Turkey	46.8
2001	Argentina	73.6
2002	Uruguay	88.4

Source: Caprio and Klingebiel (2002).

Note: Deposit dollarization is computed as the stock of dollar deposits over total deposits.

mulation due to increased financial integration (irrespective of the degree of FD). All results convey the same message: deposit dollarization is strongly related with the holding of foreign assets, both across countries and dynamically for each country. (In passing, note also that there seems to be indeed a significant upward trend in reserve holdings.)

Table 6.5, in turn, indicates that this association between FD and reserves applies primarily to economies where FD is economically important. Splitting the sample into two groups, according to whether average

---

likely to reflect standard prudential limits on the banks' open foreign currency position. Second, they are likely to be longer, less-liquid assets that offer returns above that paid by liquid reserves and thus may simply be the reflection of the bank's portfolio choice.

Table 6.3   **Deposit dollarization and reserves: Summary statistics**

	CB reserves (i)	Comm. bank reserves in CB (ii)	Total reserves in CB (iii) = (i) + (ii)
Mean	13.6	6.3	19.8
Median	10.7	4.1	15.8
No. of observations	1,781	1,781	1,781
Min.	0	0	0.5
Max.	133.0	94.5	183.5
	Correlations		
Deposit dollarization	0.2945	0.3316	0.3615
	(0.000)	(0.000)	(0.000)
Total reserves in CB	0.9404	0.6497	
	(0.000)	(0.000)	
Comm. bank reserves in CB	0.3524		
	(0.000)		

Notes: Balanced sample. Dollar deposit and reserves ratios are computed over GDP. *P*-values are in parentheses.

dollar deposit-to-gross domestic product (GDP) ratio for the country is below or above the sample mean (roughly 10 percent), shows that link is strong and significant only for the latter. (Interestingly, this appears to be the case also for the time trend.) Figure 6.2 further illustrates this point. The results are robust to the inclusion of a measure of financial depth: broad money over GDP (m2_gdp) to control for the fact that the accumulation of reserves may be simply reflecting financial development. While this prior seems to be right (financial depth does seem to be positively related with the stock of liquid reserves), the results concerning FD remain virtually unchanged. Finally, this specification may be too imprecise should the surge in reserve holding be attributed not to a steady trend but to a response to specific events in the recent past.[10] For this reason, in the last two columns I replace the time trend for individual year dummies. While these time effects seem to exhibit an upward trend in the recent period (coinciding but not necessarily due to the Mexican and Asian episodes, as shown in figure 6.2), their inclusion has no visible effect on the coefficient of interest.

Table 6.6 presents several robustness checks. Columns (1) and (2) replicate the specification of table 6.5, column (5), for the Latin American and nonindustrial subsamples, while columns (3) and (4) add the change in the nominal exchange rate (dler) to control for the mercantilist motivation for reserve hoarding and the external debt ratio (ext_debt_gdp) to capture another source of dollar exposure often highlighted in the literature. With the

10. For example, Aizenman and Lee test the hypothesis of precautionary reserves by regressing reserves holdings on a dummy that is equal to one in the years following the Asian and Mexican crises.

Table 6.4   Deposit dollarization and reserves

	CB reserves		Comm. bank reserves		Total reserves		Comm. bank other foreign assets		Comm. bank total foreign assets		Total foreign assets	
	Within (1)	Between (2)	Within (3)	Between (4)	Within (5)	Between (6)	Within (7)	Between (8)	Within (9)	Between (10)	Within (11)	Between (12)
Dollar	0.172***	0.241**	0.326***	0.141***	0.489***	0.383**	0.203**	0.312**	0.518***	0.453**	0.690***	0.693**
	(0.033)	(0.075)	(0.055)	(0.038)	(0.063)	(0.099)	(0.085)	(0.070)	(0.115)	(0.089)	(0.118)	(0.135)
Year	0.003***		−0.001***		0.0003***	−0.010**	0.003***		0.003***		0.006***	
	(0.000)		(0.000)		(0.000)	(0.004)	(0.001)		(0.001)		(0.001)	
Constant	−6.658***	0.120**	1.310***	0.049**	−5.343***	19.661**	−5.871***	0.079**	−4.894***	0.128**	−11.421***	0.248**
	(0.672)	(0.013)	(0.461)	(0.006)	(0.820)	(7.997)	(1.147)	(0.012)	(1.380)	(0.015)	(1.587)	(0.023)
No. of observations	1,797	1,797	1,822	1,822	1,781	1,781	1,749	1,749	1,730	1,730	1,719	1,719
R^2	0.14	0.07	0.21	0.10	0.021	0.10	0.08	0.14	0.015	0.17	0.22	0.18
No. of countries	131		132		131		125		125		125	

Notes: Dollar deposit and reserves ratios are computed over GDP. All regressions include country-fixed effects. Robust standard errors in parentheses.

***Significant at the 1 percent level.

**Significant at the 5 percent level.

Table 6.5   High and low deposit dollarization and reserves

	CB reserves				Total reserves			
	Low FD (1)	High FD (2)	Low FD (3)	High FD (4)	Low HD (5)	High FD (6)	Low FD (7)	High FD (8)
Dollar	0.112	0.174***	0.219*	0.538***	0.042	0.285***	0.072	0.285***
	(0.115)	(0.041)	(0.132)	(0.086)	(0.152)	(0.096)	(0.133)	(0.088)
Year	0.002***	0.006***	0.002***	0.005***	0.000	0.004***		
	(0.000)	(0.001)	(0.001)	(0.001)	(0.001)	(0.001)		
m2_gdp					0.218***	0.218***	0.184***	0.181***
					(0.049)	(0.055)	(0.042)	(0.047)
Constant	-4.384***	-11.412***	-4.387***	-9.122***	-0.070	-7.912***	0.025	-0.039
	(0.888)	(1.259)	(1.033)	(1.776)	(1.462)	(1.816)	(0.027)	(0.027)
No. of observations	1,211	586	1,199	582	1,184	578	1,184	578
R^2	0.05	0.30	0.05	0.37	0.10	0.41	0.33	0.48
No. of countries	118	130	118	130	115	127	115	127

Notes: Dollar deposit and reserves ratios are computed over GDP. All regressions include country-fixed effects. Low FD denotes observations for which the deposit dollarization ratio of the preceding year is less than 10 percent. Robust standard errors in parentheses.

***Significant at the 1 percent level.

**Significant at the 5 percent level.

*Significant at the 10 percent level.

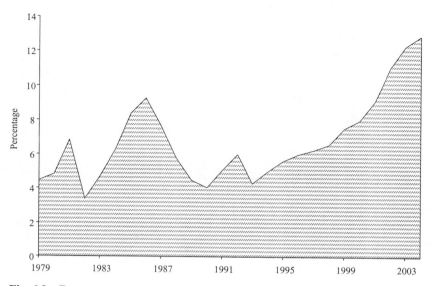

Fig. 6.2   Reserves over time

Note: The figure plots the time dummies estimated from the specification of table 6.5, column [7] when applied to the full sample.

exception of a slightly lower coefficient when debt is included (due to the smaller sample size), the results are unaltered.[11] In turn, columns (5) and (6) revisit the prudential view of high reserves as a response to the vulnerability revealed by recent crisis, by including a systemic banking crisis dummy (crisis), and its first ten lags. While crises do not seem to exert any contemporary influence (indeed, one would expect that reserves go down as a result), the cumulative effect of a crisis is positive and significant, either when estimated as the sum of the lags (column [5]) or by means of an independent dummy (past_crisis_10) that indicates that the country has suffered a crisis in the preceding ten years (column [6]). The same result, stronger, is found when we add banks' foreign assets to the reserve stock.[12]

In sum, there is a strong indication that countries with high FD tend to hold a larger stock of reserves, and tend to adjust it as FD evolves, *besides* the upward trend associated with recent episodes of global financial turmoil and the country's own history of systemic crises.[13] This liquidity

11. Note that the negative correlation with the nominal devaluations is in line with the mercantilist view of reserve accumulation as a buffer against the appreciation of the local currency.

12. An index of exchange rate regime failed to be significant, contradicting the conventional view that pegs induce further reserve accumulation. Results, omitted here, are available upon request.

13. As I will argue in the following, the link between FD and reserves can be bidirectional.

Table 6.6   Deposit dollarization and reserves: Robustness

	Total reserves				Total foreign assets			
	Latin America (1)	Nonindustrial (2)	(3)	(4)	(5)	(6)	(7)	(8)
Dollar	0.335***	0.294***	0.299***	0.157**	0.298***	0.300***	0.270**	0.271**
	(0.091)	(0.067)	(0.067)	(0.070)	(0.063)	(0.063)	(0.0125)	(0.124)
Year	0.002***	0.000	0.000	0.000	0.003***	0.003***	0.006***	0.005***
	(0.001)	(0.000)	(0.000)	(0.001)	(0.001)	(0.001)	(0.001)	(0.001)
m2_gdp	0.160***	0.178***	0.189***	0.201***	0.137***	0.135***	0.320***	0.320***
	(0.044)	(0.034)	(0.035)	(0.043)	(0.028)	(0.028)	(0.042)	(0.042)
dler			-0.019***	-0.014**				
			(0.006)	(0.006)				
ext_debt_gdp				0.004				
				(0.006)				
Crisis					-0.010	-0.009	0.008	0.008
					(0.008)	(0.008)	(0.013)	(0.013)
$\sum_{i=0}^{10}$ crisis_i					0.113*		0.273***	
					(0.059)		(0.077)	
past_crisis_10						0.010*		0.025***
						(0.006)		(0.008)
Constant	-3.649***	-3.298***	-1.845*	-6.998***	-6.101***	-6.190***	-10.822***	-10.802***
	(1.393)	(0.991)	(1.009)	(1.063)	(1.446)	(1.432)	(2.514)	(2.492)
No. of observations	1,202	1,653	1,751	1,271	1,710	1,710	1,651	1,651
R^2	0.21	0.25	0.24	0.33	0.037	0.037	0.35	0.35
No. of countries	98	116	128	100	128	128	122	122

Note: See table 6.4 notes.

***Significant at the 1 percent level.

**Significant at the 5 percent level.

*Significant at the 10 percent level.

buffer, while useful as a natural deterrent against liquidity runs, has proved to be inadequate in practice when a bank runs in FD economies finally materializes, leaving open the door for an undue loss of reserves that may ultimately compromise the payment system.

6.3   Insurance Options

With all its limitations, self-insurance makes perfect sense as the preferred response to the risk of dollar shortages in light of the (lack of) alternative insurance options, namely, *external insurance* through a contract with private providers of dollar liquidity (typically, a consortium of financial institutions).[14]

Privately provided contingent credit lines (or, more generally, the international outsourcing of the LLR function for small open economies) have been advocated in the context of the official dollarization debate,[15] spurring two experiments in Argentina and, partly as a spin off of the latter, in Mexico. In the first case, the Argentine central bank and a consortium of foreign banks subscribed a contingent credit line in the late 1990s, whereby the central bank—as well as participating local banks—had the option to enter a repurchase agreement against Argentine sovereign securities. Despite the fact that the coverage of this contract was relatively limited given the size of the Argentine banking sector, its execution was delayed until August 2001, when the bank run has already eroded the existing liquidity buffer and was executed only up to one fourth of the original limit. The second case also included a contingent credit line between Mexico and international banks, which was withdrawn in its entirety by the Mexican government on September 30, 1998, after a decline in oil prices that reduced Mexican fiscal resources combined with a temporary increase in the country's external borrowing costs. However, as to a lesser degree in Argentina, insuring banks were reluctant to disburse the loan and, after releasing the funds, they refused to renew the agreement.[16]

The numbers of the private external insurance contract looked attractive on paper: the Argentine deal, for example, stipulated an annual commitment fee of 32 basis points for a contingent line at the London Interbank Offered Rate (LIBOR) plus 205 basis points, at a time where the spread over the average return on reserves reported by the central bank (a reasonable proxy for the cost of carry of liquidity) was about 570 basis points. The result, however, was in both cases rather disappointing.

---

14. A third option would be a contract with multilateral financial institutions that may offer the central bank (or individual banks) access to dollar liquidity at a reasonable cost, perhaps the most economically efficient and a constant topic for discussion. The current IMF facilities, contingent and backloaded, are far from being a substitute dollar LLR.

15. See Dornbusch and Giavazzi (1998).

16. See Ize, Kiguel, and Levy Yeyati (2005) for a more detailed analysis of these experiences.

Was it surprising? Are private partners better positioned to provide LLR services at low cost, as the contract seemed to suggest ex ante, or are the convenient terms the reflection of mispricing or unreliable commitment? We can shed some light on this issue by means of a simple analytical example.

Assume that, with probability π, the country faces a systemic liquidity run that leads to an increase in the sovereign spread to the (unsustainably high) ρ_H[17] whereas, with probability $1 - \pi$, the country can access international markets at the low sovereign spread ρ_L. In the absence of liquidity insurance, a liquidity run leads to financial collapse. For the purpose of the example, it suffices to assume that the country has strong incentives to avoid this situation, which carries a substantial real cost K.

Assuming that the country's obligations maturing during the period are equal to R, the authorities have two options to fully insure against the liquidity run (alternatively, against validating unsustainably high rollover costs):

- *Self-insurance:* Hold liquid reserves R, at a cost of carry $\rho = r - r_f$, where r_f is the risk-free rate, and ρ is the expected sovereign spread $\rho = (1 - \pi)\rho_L + \pi\rho_H$, the risk premium on the country's debt demanded in international markets. In this context, the ex ante cost of holding reserves is equal to the precrisis sovereign spread ρ at the corresponding maturity.[18]
- *External (interest rate) insurance:* A fair insurance contract with international financial institutions that allows the country to draw down from a credit line up to a given amount R at a predetermined spread $\overline{\rho}$ at a fair (unit) premium $\gamma = c - \pi\overline{\rho}$, where c is the insurer's own cost of carrying liquid assets.

Setting $\overline{\rho} = \rho - \gamma$ (so that the country pays the same under both insurance options), we obtain

$$\gamma = c - \pi(\rho - \gamma) = \frac{c}{(1 - \pi)} - \frac{\pi}{(1 - \pi)}\rho.$$

Note that, from the insured country's perspective, the cost of carry of self-insurance in good states is replaced by the fair insurance premium. Thus, the cost of self-insurance exceeds that of external insurance due to the lower carrying cost born by the insurer if, and only if $\rho > c$, since *the sole advantage of external insurance relative to self-insurance is precisely the insurer's lower cost of carry.* In other words, they would be equally costly

---

17. Alternatively, we could assume that, beyond a certain level of spreads, the country is simply rationed from international markets (market closure).

18. Note that reserves can take the form of liquid long-term foreign assets (e.g., ten-year U.S. Treasuries) so that no maturity mismatch needs to be incurred.

unless the intermediation of the insurer reduces the credit risk faced by the investor that ultimately finances either alternative.

The relevant question is, then, under what circumstances and to what extent is this the case in practice? The insurer's cost of carry (the difference between the return from the contract and the opportunity cost of hoarding liquidity) may be below that of the country for two reasons. First is enhanced market access: the fact that the insurer can tap international markets on demand so the stock of liquidity that needs to be hoarded is minimal.[19] In addition, the sovereign spread may (and typically does) capture risks not directly associated with the market closure event. Thus, even if the contract increases the exposure of the insurer to the insured country, it does not expose the insurer to all risks affecting sovereign debt (and the country's cost of carry). In particular, an insurance contract aimed at protecting the domestic banking sector from liquidity runs would shield the insurer (at least partially) from debt sustainability problems (whereas the bondholder that helps finance self-insurance will be directly affected by a debt crisis).

The extent to which all these factors combined reduce the costs of carry and whether this reduction justifies external insurance (including the margins charged by the insurer) are difficult to assess. In practice, the two previous experiences with those types of contracts amounted to a rather diluted version of insurance and were subject to serious caveats. Moreover, the low cost of these contracts may have also been reflecting market imperfections that detract from the benefits of external insurance as discussed in the preceding.

The first imperfection relates to what could be called *inverse moral hazard,* or, more generally, the inability of the insurer to commit the resources when the option of borrowing is exercised (a weakness that was at play in the Argentine and Mexican experiments). A second imperfection, perhaps the most determinant, is the capacity of the insurer to dilute its exposure at the expense of the coinsurers by shorting the country's assets.[20]

It has been noted before that these two aspects only enhance the advantages of official agencies to provide international LLR coverage: much in the same way as a domestic central bank, an international financial institution (IFI) may commit the resources without the need to accumulate reserves ex ante, free from the agency problems that undermined the private contract. In the context of the present paper, it is enough to stress that,

19. A consortium of insurer banks exposed to the country through the insurance contract may still be able to borrow at reasonable rates while the country cannot, thanks to a more diversified asset portfolio, a higher creditworthiness, and even the presence of explicit or implicit guarantees from their home countries. Note that this is essentially the main argument for a centralized LLR in the domestic currency, except that in that case the advantage is rooted in the central bank's capacity to print liquidity on demand.

20. See Broda and Levy Yeyati (2003a).

while no official version of the LLR is in sight, it is not surprising that governments in FD economies have chosen to self-insure.

6.3.1 The Problem with Self-Insurance

Self-insurance in its most commonly found form of centralized reserve accumulation may have at least two undesired incentives effects. A stylized example may help illustrate the point.

Consider an economy populated by a continuum of D risk-neutral depositors with one unit of cash savings, where atomistic banks collect short-term deposits at a rate r_D and invest them in long-term investments L (loans, for short) with certain returns r_D and liquid reserves R_B that pay the risk-free rate r_f. Assume for the moment that banks are always solvent (there is no default risk). Let the size of the *systemic* deposit run x be distributed according to cumulative distribution function $F(x)$, monotonically increasing and convex over the range $[0,1]$ and, given its systemic nature, independent from bank-specific characteristics.[21]

In the absence of default, a bank facing a liquidity shortage is forced to liquidate its assets at a constant (unit) discount θ.[22] At the beginning of the period, the bank chooses the liquidity buffer R_B to optimize the tradeoff between the cost of hoarding liquidity and the probability of incurring liquidation costs. For expositional simplicity, all variables are expressed as a share of deposits D.

Replacing $L = 1 - R_B$, bank profits (per unit of deposit) in the absence of centralized reserves can be characterized as[23]

$$\max_{\{R_B\}} \pi^e = (1 + r_L)(1 - R_B) + \int_0^{R_B} (1 + r_f)(R_B - x)dF(x)$$
$$- \int_{R_B}^1 (1 + r_L)(1 + \theta)(x - R_B)dF(x)$$
$$- \int_0^1 (1 + r_D)(1 - x)dF(x)$$

or, alternatively, as

$$\max_{\{R_B\}} \pi^e = r_L - r_D - C_{LAR},$$

where the costs associated with liquidity runs C can be expressed as

---

21. The example focuses on pure liquidity runs and deliberately abstracts from currency mismatches and currency risk; hence, it is independent of the evolution of the exchange rate. Naturally, if—as is often the case—the dollar deposit run is accompanied by a currency run, the resulting real depreciation would only add to the banks' problems via losses on its currency position or—if the dollar deposits are onlent in the same currency—a lower recovery value of dollar loans to nondollar earners.

22. Letting the discount increase with x does not alter the implications of this example.

23. In what follows, under the assumption of no default risk, the deposit rate is equal to the risk-free rate r_f. However, the current notation is kept for expositional purposes.

$$C_{LAR} = [(r_L - r_f)F(R_B)] - [(1 + r_L)(1 + \theta) - r_L][1 - F(R_B)])R_B$$
$$- \int_0^{R_B} (r_D - r_f)xdF(x) + \int_{R_B}^1 [(1 + r_L)(1 + \theta) - r_D]xdF(x)$$

and associated first order condition is given by

$$-\frac{\partial C_{LAR}}{\partial R_B} = -(r_L - r_f)F(R_B) + (1 + r_L)\theta[1 - F(R_B)] = 0.$$

Thus, the optimal liquidity buffer is the one that equals the expected carrying costs (the left-hand-side term) to the expected savings in liquidation costs from holding additional reserves (the right-hand side). In turn, the optimal amount of bank reserves R_B is given by

$$R_B = F^{-1}\left(\frac{1}{[1 + (r_L - r_f)/(1 + r_L)\theta]}\right)$$

from which

$$\frac{\partial R_B}{\partial \theta} > 0; \frac{\partial R_B}{\partial r_L} < 0; \frac{\partial R_B}{\partial r_f} > 0.$$

Consider now the influence of centralized reserves. Assume that the central bank assist banks through a liquidity window that commands a penalty rate r_{LLR} such that $1 + r_L < 1 + r_{LLR} < (1 + r_L)(1 + \theta)$ so that the penalty does not exceed the liquidation cost.[24] Then, if access to the LLR is unlimited, the problem is similar to the previous one with the facility rate substituting the liquidation cost so that the cost of liquidity runs are now

$$C_{LLR} = [(r_L - r_f)F(R_B)] - (r_{LLR} - r_L)[1 - F(R_B)])R_B - \int_0^{R_B} (r_D - r_f)xdF(x)$$
$$+ \int_{R_B}^1 (r_{LLR} - r_D)xdF(x),$$

from which

$$-\frac{\partial C_{LLR}}{\partial R_B} = -(r_L - r_f)F(R_B) + (r_{LLR} - r_L)[1 - F(R_B)] = 0.$$

Or

$$R_{B, LLR} = F^{-1}\left(\frac{1}{\left[1 + \frac{(r_L - r_f)}{(r_{LLR} - r_L)}\right]}\right)$$

So that cheaper centralized reserves substitute for decentralized reserves.

Under the more general (and realistic) assumption that the facility is limited and that this limit is binding ($R_{LLR} < \overline{R_{LLR}} < 1$), the amount available to assist each individual bank would be insufficient in the event of a

24. Note that the latter compounds the liquidation discount and the interest that the bank loses on the liquidated loans.

large enough systemic event, and some liquidation costs should be factored back into the problem:

$$C_{LLR} = \{(r_L - r_f)F(r_B) - (r_{LLR} - r_L)[F(R_B + R_{LLR}) - F(R_B)]$$

$$- [(1 + r_L)(1 + \theta) - (1 + r_L)][1 - F(R_b + R_{LLR})]\} R_B$$

$$- \int_0^{R_B} (r_D - r_f)xdF(x) + \int_{R_B}^{R_B + R_{LLR}} (r_{LLR} - r_D)xdF(x)$$

$$+ \int_{R_B + R_{LLR}}^1 [(1 + r_L)(1 + \theta) - (1 + r_D)]xdF(x)$$

$$- [(1 + r_L)(1 + \theta) - (1 + r_{LLR})][1 - F(R_B + R_{LLR})]R_{LLR}$$

for which the first order condition reads

$$-\frac{\partial C_{LLR}}{\partial R_B} = -(r_L - r_f)F(R_B) + (r_{LLR} - r_L)[F(R_B + R_{LLR}) - F(R_B)]$$

$$+ (1 + r_L)\theta[1 - F(R_B + R_{LLR})] = 0,$$

which tells us, again, that the larger the stock of decentralized reserves R_{LLR} or the lower the interest rate charged by the LLR, the weaker the incentives to hold liquidity at the individual bank level ($\partial R_B/\partial R_{LLR} < 0$, $\partial R_B/\partial r_{LLR} < 0$).[25]

In this light, what is the optimal (centralized-decentralized) composition of reserves? Intuitively, the answer depends on the carrying costs for each of the players involved. To examine that, we need to be more precise about these costs: It is there that the currency of denomination matters.

When the run is on short-term peso liabilities, the central bank can produce the peso liquidity on demand at a limited cost: Absent solvency concerns, it can borrow directly in the local market at the risk-free rate (or, if needed, finance the assistance through the inflation tax). At any rate, when bank deposits are denominated in pesos, the central bank has a clear advantage because, unlike the commercial banks, it does not need to accumulate reserves in advance. In particular, it can offer centralized reserves at the risk-free rate, bringing the optimal level of decentralized reserves to zero (because $r_{LLR} - r_f = 0 \Rightarrow \partial R_B/\partial R_{LLR} = -1$, so that both sources of insurance are perfect substitutes). In turn, a centralized LLR in pesos entails an efficiency gain for the whole system, as it eliminates the costs associated with hoarding liquidity and (because no resource needs to be invested in

25. Also, as before,

$$\frac{\partial R_B}{\partial \theta} > 0; \frac{\partial R_b}{\partial r_L} < 0; \text{ and } \frac{\partial R_B}{\partial r_f} > 0.$$

liquid assets in advance) enhances the maturity transformation role of the financial sector.[26]

By contrast, when bank liabilities are denominated in dollars, and under the assumption that systemic banking and currency runs coincide cutting the country's access to international markets, dollar liquidity has to be ensured in advance. Therefore, centralized reserves merely substitute for decentralized reserves, and any potential efficiency gains hinges only the relative cost of carry that, in principle, should not differ.[27] In this case, to the extent that the penalty rate charged to the bank underprice the effective cost to the LLR (alternatively, to the extent that the bank prefers insurance with the central bank than self-insurance), the latter would introduce a subsidy to dollar intermediation that may foster FD beyond the level that banks would choose individually should they have to pay for the required liquidity. However, this is not the only distortion that centralized reserves may introduce, as I show next.

6.3.2   Default Risk and Moral Hazard

If there is a positive probability of default, limited liability matters.[28] The simplest way to see this is by assuming that, with probability $1 - p$, the investment of the bank goes sour and returns drop to zero. Moral hazard implicitly assumes that the bank has some degree of control over this risk. Here, I simply assume that there is a continuum of investment projects (borrowers) with identical expected returns (pr_L) = $\tilde{r} \geq r_f$ so that $r_L(p) = \tilde{r}/p$. Then, if the probability of a systemic run is uncorrelated with the bank's idiosyncratic credit risk, the bank's problem can be written as

$$\max_{R_B, p} \pi^e_{LLR} = p(r_L - r_D - C_{LLR}),$$

where the first order conditions are

$$\frac{\partial \pi^e_{LLR}}{\partial R_B} = -p \frac{\partial C_{LLR}}{\partial R_B} = 0$$

$$\frac{\partial \pi^e_{LLR}}{\partial p} = r_L - r_D - C_{LLR} + p\left(1 - \frac{\partial C_{LLR}}{\partial r_L}\right)\frac{\partial r_L}{\partial p} = 0.$$

26. In a competitive banking sector, liquidity costs would reflect directly in the intermediation spread and that a LLR at the risk-free rate brings these costs from $C_{LAR}(R_B^*) > 0$ to $C_{LAR+LLR} = 0$. Note that I am deliberately abstracting from diversification gains, as the focus of the paper is on systemic (rather than bank-specific) runs.

27. In equilibrium, the lending rate should equal the marginal return to capital that, in the absence of financial constraints, in turn determines the government's discount rate (and the marginal borrowing cost it is willing to pay).

28. The only exception in which the previous results are not altered is under perfect information and no LLR (assuming further that the costs of liquidation of an insolvent bank do not exceed those associated with the fire sale of assets by the bank itself), as the *expected* return on deposits demanded by depositors (and faced by banks) is independent of the incidence of default. A case along these lines is discussed in Aizenman and Lee (2005).

It follows that

$$\left.\frac{\partial p}{\partial R_B}\right|_{R_B = R_B^*} = \frac{\partial^2 C_{LLR}}{\partial R_B^2} \bigg/ \left[\left(\frac{\partial^2 C_{LLR}}{\partial R_B \partial r_L}\right)\left(\frac{\partial r_L}{\partial p}\right)\right] \geq 0$$

as $\partial r_L/\partial p < 0, -\partial^2 C_{LLR}/\partial R_B^2 \leq 0$, and

$$\frac{\partial^2 C_{LLR}}{\partial R_B \partial r_L} = F(R_B + R_{LLR}) - \theta[1 - F(R_B + R_{LLR})] > 0.$$

Thus, riskier banks choose to hoard a lower level of reserves. The reason is clear: the opportunity cost is higher for a riskier bank that invests in high-return projects (note that both the returns on investment and the costs of hoarding liquidity are relevant only in the event that the bank does not go bankrupt). Moreover,

$$\frac{\partial^2 C_{LLR}}{\partial R_B \partial R_{LLR}} = [(1 + r_L)\theta - (r_{LLR} - r_L)]F'(R_B + R_{LLR}) > 0$$

implies that

$$\left.\frac{\partial p}{\partial R_{LLR}}\right|_{R_B = R_B^*} = -p \frac{\partial^2 C_{LLR}}{\partial R_B \partial R_{LLR}} \bigg/ \left[\left(\frac{\partial^2 C_{LLR}}{\partial R_B \partial r_L}\right)\left(\frac{\partial r_L}{\partial p}\right)\right] \geq 0,$$

which tells us that centralized reserves induce more risk-taking (and, in turn, a lower level of reserves).[29]

In sum, centralized reserves not only partially transfer the cost of the liquidity buffer to the central bank; in addition, it induces more risk-taking overall (relative to the case of no LLR).

6.3.3   Liquid Asset Requirements (LARs)

Naturally, there are ways in which the undesired effects of centralized reserve holdings (or a dollar LLR) described above can be addressed, at least in theory. The central bank can (and usually does) restrict its liquidity assistance to limited temporary shortfalls that, if persistent, may lead to intervention and, ultimately, closure. Moreover, the incentive problem can

---

29. Ize, Kiguel, and Levy Yeyati (2005) present an alternative illustration of the moral hazard implication of centralized reserves, arguing that, in a world with risky and safer types, centralized reserves entail a cross subsidy from the latter to the former. More precisely, they lead risky types to choose a lower R_B than safer types, crowding out the use of the LLR assistance, thereby forcing safer banks to hoard an additional amount of reserves. Similarly, in a bicurrency economy with currency risk, it can be shown that a dollar LLR lead banks to incur more risk fostering financial dollarization (Broda and Levy Yeyati, forthcoming).

be addressed by conditioning the access to and cost of the liquidity facility on the degree of risk much in the same way as a risk-based deposit insurance scheme.[30]

However, as the examples of Argentina and Uruguay discussed in the preceding illustrate, when left to the discretion of the supervisor, limits, and conditions on LLR access in the midst of a systemic run are difficult to enforce. The costs of bank closures (economic contraction, possible domino effects in the banking sector, and even personal costs to the supervisor due to potential litigation) create a serious problem of time inconsistency that, often, results in undue delays or forbearance.

In this context, the most sensible avenue to circumvent the banking sector's free riding on central bank reserves appears to be the requirement of a high liquid asset ratio for banks with dollarized liabilities, as most financially dollarized economies have introduced in the late 90s.

What is the optimal LAR? It is easy to show that, even in the absence of market imperfections, a central planner would not choose the same reserves-to-deposits ratio as the individual bank in the absence of a LLR. Following Aizenman and Lee (2005), assume a Cobb-Douglass technology $y(K) = K^{\alpha}$, where K denotes the stock of capital. A central planner choosing the optimal allocation between investment and the liquidity buffer R in order to optimize returns would solve

$$\max_{\{R\}} W^e_{LLR} = \int_0^R (1 - R)^\alpha \, dF(x) + \int_R^1 [1 - R - (1 + \theta)(x - R)]^\alpha dF(x)$$

$$+ \int_0^R (1 + r_f)(R - x)dF(x) - \int_0^1 (1 + r_f + \rho)(1 - x)dF(x),$$

from which

$$\frac{\partial W^e_{LLR}}{\partial R} = -[\alpha(1 - R)^{\alpha-1} - (1 + r_f)]F(R)$$

$$+ \theta \int_R^1 \alpha[1 - R - (1 + \theta)(x - R)]^{\alpha-1} \, dF(x) = 0.$$

A simple comparison reveals that the optimal level of reserves for the planner exceeds that for the individual bank.[31] In addition, in the presence of externalities (e.g., the social costs of a financial collapse, reflected in a

---

30. See Broda and Levy Yeyati (2003b) for an argument along these lines.
31. Note that, under the assumption of a competitive banking sector, in both cases the first term equals the marginal productivity of capital. However, in the second term, the central planner not only considers the liquidation cost but also the positive impact of the reduced stock of capital on the marginal returns to investment in the event of early liquidation (which a price-taking bank does not internalize) increasing the marginal cost of a run.

larger discount factor θ), the planner would prefer a still higher level of coverage. This is yet another reason to imposing LAR.

Liquid asset requirements, however, represent a suboptimal self-insurance response to systemic runs. Recall that, in equilibrium,

$$\pi^e(R_B) = 0 \Rightarrow r_L - r_D = \alpha(1 - R_B)^{\alpha-1} - r_f = C(R_B) > 0$$

So that borrowing costs (and, in turn, the cost stock of capital and the level of income) depend negatively on the degree of self insurance—irrespective of whether this level is voluntary or mandatory.

In the limit, they approach a narrow banking structure that makes the banking sector safer at the expense of its financing clout. As such, self-insurance is no panacea: there is, indeed, a tradeoff between insurance and intermediation costs, as liquid reserves detract from the level of productive investment and, at the optimum, still leave room for liquidation losses if the run is deep enough.

6.3.4   Circuit Breakers (CBRs)

Can we improve upon this result (that is, reduce R_B and increase total output $[1 - R]^\alpha$ without raising the exposure to a liquidity run; in other words, reducing the optimal amount of self-insurance R_B^*) by limiting the convertibility once the run exceeds certain predetermined threshold? Can we use such a limit to deal with large dollar liquidity runs that exceed the optimal amount of liquid reserves? In this section, I argue that we can.

In the absence of a liquidity premium, a suspension of convertibility clause that works as a CBR for the dollar hemorrhage, is a trivial solution to the problem because it eliminates the need for costly liquidation at no cost. In reality, a CBR would amount to limiting ex ante the liquidity of deposits (and the maturity transformation role of banks) and would be therefore penalized by a liquidity premium $\rho(\bar{x})$, with $\rho' < 0$, $\rho'' > 0$, and $\rho(0) = \rho'(0) = 0$, on the banks' borrowing costs, where $\bar{x}$ is the parameter that characterizes the CBR policy: the threshold beyond which the run is short-circuited by the CBR. The tradeoff between borrowing costs and liquidation costs is what would determine the optimal LAR-CBR mix.

More formally, under a LAR/CBR policy $\bar{x} > R$, (where $\bar{x}$ is the CBR threshold and R the level of LAR), the central planner's problem can be written as

$$\max_{\{\bar{x}, R\}} W^e_{LLR} = \int_0^R [(1 - R)^\alpha + (1 + r_f)R - (1 + r_f + \rho) + \rho x] dF(x)$$

$$+ \int_R^{\bar{x}} \{[1 - R - (1 + \theta)(x - R)]^\alpha - (1 + r_f + \rho)[1 - x]\} dF(x)$$

$$+ \int_{\bar{x}}^1 \{[1 - R - (1 + \theta)(\bar{x} - R)]^\alpha - (1 + r_f + \rho)(1 - \bar{x})\} dF(x)$$

from which the first order conditions are

$$\frac{\partial W_{LLR}^e}{\partial R} = [-\alpha(1 - R)^{\alpha-1} + (1 + r_f)]\int_0^R dF(x)$$
$$+ \int_R^{\overline{x}} \{\alpha\theta[1 - R - (1 + \theta)(x - R)]^{\alpha-1}\} dF(x)$$
$$+ \alpha\theta[1 - R - (1 + \theta)(\overline{x} - R)]^{\alpha-1} [1 - f(\overline{x})]$$

and

$$\frac{\partial W_{LLR}^e}{\partial \overline{x}} = -\{\alpha(1 + \theta)[1 - R - (1 + \theta)(\overline{x} - R)]^{\alpha-1} - (1 + r_f + \rho)\}[1 - F(\overline{x})]$$
$$- \rho'\{\int_0^{\overline{x}}(1 - x)dF(x) + (1 - \overline{x})[1 - F(\overline{x})]\} = 0.$$

As expected, a tighter CBR avoids liquidation costs at the expense of higher borrowing costs.[32] A second thing to note is the fact that LAR and CBR are substitutes (differentiating implicitly, we obtain $\partial R^*/\partial \overline{x} > 0$). Thus, a stricter CBR (a lower threshold $\overline{x}$) is associated with a lower optimal level of reserves. The optimal mix between the two will depend on the liquidity premium charged by depositors.[33]

6.4   Two Banking Crises: Argentina and Uruguay

Two recent systemic banking crises (Argentina 2001 and Uruguay 2002) provide the best illustration of the link between FD and banking fragility and the limits to crisis management faced by the supervisor in the midst of a crisis—the perfect motivation for the use of a CBR as described in the preceding. In both episodes, sudden and devastating runs on dollar deposits crippled banks irrespective of their idiosyncratic fundamentals which, judging from the standard prudential indicators, were a priori in excellent shape.[34] In both cases, the supervisor intervened belatedly and only after losing most of the (at the time, important) stock of liquid foreign assets, contaminating the payments system.[35]

32. It can be shown that, when $\rho'(0)$ is sufficiently high, the solution is interior. Note that a similar tradeoff applies to the analysis of sovereign debt policies (sovereign debt restructuring mechanism, collective action clauses) aimed at lowering the incidence of contractionary adjustments in the event of a capital account reversal, at the expense of a liquidity premium that makes up for the limited liquidity of financial claims.

33. An interesting (albeit lateral) aspect of this discussion relates to the fact that this tradeoff entails a sequence of costs: since the CBR eliminates liquidation costs associated with large runs at the expense of higher borrowing costs in good times, a myopic planner may have a preference for partial self-insurance through LAR.

34. In particular, the average capital-to-asset ratio was approximately 20 percent in Argentina and 14 percent in Uruguay, above the 13 percent in Chile, Peru, and Mexico and the 11 percent in Colombia.

35. For a more detailed account, see Levy Yeyati, de la Torre, and Schmukler (2003) and Levy Yeyati, Martínez Pería, and Schmukler (2005) for Argentina, and de Brun and Licandro (2006) for Uruguay.

By late 1999, due to a combination of external factors (the devaluation of the Brazilian real, a strong dollar, and high international interest rates) and internal vulnerabilities (most notably, the presence of substantial private and public dollar liabilities), the Argentine economy was caught in a currency-growth-debt (CGD) trap, whereby the peso was perceived as overvalued, limiting investment and growth, and raising the costs of debt service that in turn induced a reversal of capital flows feed bank into the perceived overvaluation. Still, even by end-2000, judging from standard prudential indicators, Argentina could have been characterized as having a well-capitalized, liquid, and strongly provisioned banking resilient banking sector (in no small part due to the regulatory reform prompted by a previous banking crisis in 1995).[36]

Doubts about the peg to the U.S. dollar built up with the announcement of a plan to peg of the peso to an equally weighted dollar-euro basket (viewed as a disguised devaluation), the resignation of the governor of the central bank (viewed as a guarantor of the peg), and a reform of the central bank charter that blurred the limits on money issuance that underpinned the currency board. As a result, between January 2001 and December 2001, time deposits fell by almost 50 percent (figure 6.3). The pattern by currency suggests that deposit dollarization within the system—the depositors' first reaction—turn into a run on dollar deposits as depositors gradually realized that, in a context of dwindling dollar liquidity, a devaluation would inevitably result in bank failures or a forcible currency conversion (figure 6.4). By mid-November, with dollar liquidity rapidly running out, the central bank attempted a partial suspension of deposit convertibility with the so-called corralito (or little fence), which imposed limits on cash withdrawals out of the banking system, but did not restrict transfers between bank accounts.[37] Thus, the corralito only spread the virus within the banking system, compromising the payments system by failing to isolate stable transactional peso deposits from free-falling dollar saving deposits and dragging down the real sector by creating a liquidity crush.

Only after civil riots prompted the resignations of two presidents, a sovereign default, the exit of the currency board, a predictable conversion of dollar financial assets into pesos at the below-market 1.4 AR$/US$ exchange rate, and the additional loss of some US$2 billion in dollar reserves (all of which happened between December 2001 and late-January 2002) did the government proceed to suspend convertibility of time and (most of) saving deposits in full, by reprogramming them into longer inflation-

36. In 1998, right before the recession, the World Bank (in 1998) ranked Argentina second among twelve emerging economies based on CAMELOT scores (the World Bank's in-house CAMEL rating).

37. The name "corralito" (little fence) was initially adopted because deposits could be used freely inside the financial system but could not leave the system.

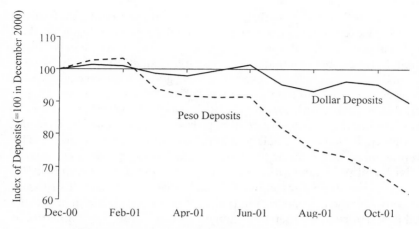

Fig. 6.3   Anatomy of the bank run: Pesos and dollars
Source: Levy Yeyati, de la Torre, and Schmukler (2003).

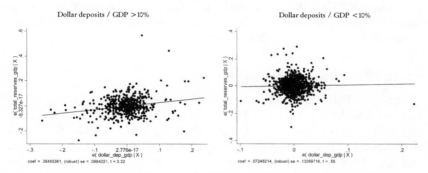

Fig. 6.4   High and low deposit dollarization and reserves: Partial regression plots;
***A,* Dollar deposits/GDP > 10%; *B,* Dollar deposits/GDP < 10%**

indexed deposits (the so-called corralón, or large fence). Ultimately, these new securities were partially exchanged for dollar-denominated sovereign bonds in what amounted to tax-financed exchange rate insurance.

The Uruguayan crisis followed a very similar pattern: Uruguay's economy fell into recession in 1999 due to the same set of international factors (plus two idiosyncratic shocks: a severe drought with strong effects on the agricultural sector and the Argentine recession), public-sector finances deteriorated and concerns about the crawling exchange rate band started to increase (which the authorities validated with a forced adjustment of the prefixed devaluation rate from 0.6 to 1.2 percent per month in June 2001).

However, there is an important difference with the Argentine episode that helps illustrate the nature of liquidity runs in dollarized economies.

Unlike Argentina, Uruguay (helped both by its track record and its advocacy of bank secrecy) has been long considered a regional safe haven. Year 2001 was no exception: despite the recession, total deposits increased by 12 percent, fueled by dollar deposits by nonresidents, primarily Argentineans. It was precisely the reversal of this "good" Argentine contagion, however, that triggered the bank run in 2002. Argentineans trapped in the corralito started to withdraw from their Uruguayan accounts, initially from the country's two largest private banks, Banco Galicia Uruguay (BGU) and Banco Comercial (both affiliated with Argentine banks).[38] The overdue intervention of the latter, and the government's apparent lack of dollar liquidity to cope with a sustained run (and honor the implicit 100 percent deposit guarantee under which the system had historically worked) increased the distrust in the Uruguayan banking system and fueled a generalized run. Between January 2002 and July 2002, dollar time deposits in Uruguay fell by about 50 percent (figure 6.5). The resulting decline in international reserves led to the abandonment of the crawling bank on June 19—and to the resignation of the minister of economy on July 22. Only on July 30 did the government declared a four-day bank holiday, at the end of which the maturity of dollar time deposits in state-owned (or intervened) banks were extended by law.

6.5   LAR + CBR: A Prototype

The LAR/CBR scheme described in the preceding intends to implement in a predictable way the limits that a supervisor typically introduces at a late stage of a crisis once (centralized and decentralized) dollar liquidity is about to run out, in an improvised way that magnify existing uncertainties and pave the way for endless litigation and ultimately fiscally costly settlements.[39]

However, the main advantage of such an explicit scheme is also its main drawback: if correctly publicized, they force to fully internalized the hidden costs of dollar intermediation that are largely socialize during a systemic crisis—which could only result in higher dollar funding costs in noncrisis times.

As usual, there are a number of questions that need to be answered before a LAR/CBR scheme is put in place in practice. What deposits should be affected by the scheme? When and how should the CBR be activated?

38. Levy Yeyati, Martínez Pería, and Schmukler (2004) reports econometric evidence on the "good" and "bad" contagion from the Argentine crisis.

39. The CBRs resemble the suspension-of-convertibility clause included in bank contracts in Scotland and other European countries during the free banking era (in the eighteenth and nineteenth centuries), and in the United States during the national banking period (1863–1914). See Shah (1997) and Calomiris and Gorton (1991) for evidence in favor of using some form of CBR.

Argentina (September 2000 – December 2001)

Uruguay (December 2001 – July 2002)

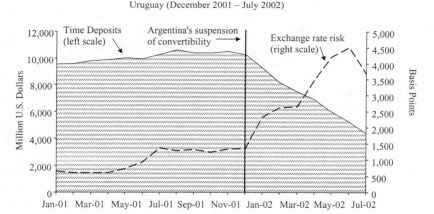

Fig. 6.5   Two banking crises; *A*, Argentina, September 2000–December 2001; *B*, Uruguay, December 2001–July 2002

Note: Exchange rate risk is the devaluation implicit in the twelve-month forward (NDF) for Argentina and the (annualized) peso-dollar interest rate differential on time deposits for Uruguay.

Source: Levy Yeyati, Martínez Pería, and Schmukler (2004).

How should the level of LAR and the CBR threshold be chosen? How should they be applied selectively in a way that prevents arbitrage between deposit types?

While the preferred combination may depend on a number of case-specific aspects, the previous discussion implicitly suggests a standard prototype of the scheme that may serve as a concrete starting point. First, given that the specific liquidity problem in domestically dollarized economies concerns bank dollar deposits, it is on those deposits that the CBR needs to be applied. However, extending the restriction to dollar demand deposits would be at odds with the objective of preserving the payments system that is built precisely on these transactional accounts. Leaving them CBR-free would, in turn, call for a (substantially) higher LAR on these deposits.[40]

If the aim is to fully rule out the need for costly assets fire sales, a natural choice would be to set the CBR threshold as a function of the bank's stock of liquid reserves. More precisely, once the LAR earmarked to meet withdrawals of fully convertible demand deposits is determined, the CBR clause would automatically kick in once the liquidity in excess of those LAR is exhausted. However, even if the CBR is explicitly written in the deposit contract, its recurrent application may create undesired costs for the supervisor and incentives for banks and depositors to misprice liquidity risk in anticipation of a bailout. Thus, the supervisor should require a LAR specific to dollar time deposits so as to reduce the incidence of a CBR application—leaving to the bank the option to hold additional liquidity or to attract new capital in the event of a run, to avoid the reputation costs of resorting to the CBR scheme. In this way, the CBR, by protecting the backing of transactional deposits, is activated automatically while preserving the bank's incentives to seek a less disruptive solution.[41]

Finally, in an uncertain world where liquidity and solvency issues are intimately intertwined, the effectiveness of a CBR in preventing liquidity runs would ultimately depend on depositors' perception of the length of the freeze and the value of the bank (and, in turn, of their claims) once the freeze is lifted. While the final toll of the run on the market value of individual banks will certainly depend on the broader prudential framework and the macroeconomic context in general, a well-designed LBR/CBR should prevent losses associated with early liquidation and, in the limit, help avoid avoidable runs altogether.

References

Aizenman, J., and J. Lee. 2005. International reserves: Precautionary versus mercantilist views, theory and evidence. IMF Working Paper no. WP/05/198. Washington, DC: International Monetary Fund, October.

Armas, A., A. Ize, and E. Levy Yeyati, eds. 2006. *Financial dedollarization: The policy agenda.* New York: Palgrave Macmillan.

40. Whether the LAR should be close to, or exactly equal to, 100 percent of deposits is debatable. What is important is that the level should be significantly higher than encountered in real life cases.

41. There is an interesting parallel between this scheme and the final approach adopted in Uruguay in 2002: banks that could not meet deposit withdrawals were intervened by the central bank, in which case their deposits were reprogrammed.

Broda, C., and E. Levy Yeyati. 2003a. Dollarization and the lender of last resort. In *Dollarization: Debates and policy alternatives,* ed. E. Levy Yeyati and F. Sturzenegger, 101–32. Cambridge, MA: MIT Press.

———. 2003b. Endogenous deposit dollarization. Federal Reserve Bank of New York Staff Report no. 160. New York: Federal Reserve Bank of New York.

Caballero, R., and A. Krishnamurthy. 2003. Excessive dollar debt: Financial development and underinsurance. *Journal of Finance* 58 (2): 867–94.

Caballero, R., and S. Panageas. 2004. Contingent reserves management: An applied framework. NBER Working Paper no. 10786. Cambridge, MA: National Bureau of Economic Research, September.

Calomiris, C., and G. Gorton. 1991. The origin of banking panics: Models, facts, and bank regulation. In *Financial markets and financial crisis,* ed. G. Hubbard, 109–73. Chicago: University of Chicago Press.

Calvo, G. 2005. *Emerging capital markets in turmoil: Bad luck or bad policy?* Cambridge, MA: MIT Press.

Caprio, G., and D. Klingebiel. 2003. Episodes of systemic and borderline financial crises. World Bank Research Data Sets. Washington, DC: World Bank.

Cordella, T., and E. Levy Yeyati. 2005a. Country insurance. *IMF Staff Papers* 52 (September): 85–106. Washington, DC: International Monetary Fund.

———. 2005b. A (new) country insurance facility. *International Finance,* forthcoming.

Cowan, K., E. Levy Yeyati, U. Panizza, and F. Sturzenegger. 2006. Public debt in the Americas: New data and stylized facts. IDB Working Paper no. 577. Washington, DC: Inter-American Development Bank, October.

De Brun, J., and G. Licandro. 2006. Crisis management in a dollarized economy: The case of Uruguay. In *Financial dedollarization: The policy agenda,* ed. A. Armas, A. Ize, and E. Levy Yeyati, 147–76. New York: Palgrave Macmillan.

De Nicoló, G., P. Honohan, and A. Ize. 2005. Dollarization of the banking system: Good or bad? *Journal of Banking and Finance* 29 (7): 1697–1727.

Diamond, D., and P. Dyvbig. 1983. Bank runs, deposit insurance, and liquidity. *Journal of Political Economy* 91 (3): 401–19.

Dornbusch, R., and F. Giavazzi. 1998. Hard currency and sound credit: A financial agenda for Central Europe. http://www.mit.edu/~rudi/papers.html.

Eichengreen, B., and R. Hausmann. 2005. *Other people's money: Debt denomination and financial instability in emerging-market economies.* Chicago: University of Chicago Press.

Ize, A., M. Kiguel, and E. Levy Yeyati. 2005. Managing systemic liquidity risk in financially dollarized economies. IMF Working Paper no. WP/05/188. Washington, DC: International Monetary Fund, September.

Jeanne, O., and R. Ranciere. 2006. The optimal level of international reserves for emerging market countries: Formulas and applications. IMF Working Paper no. WP/06/229. Washington, DC: International Monetary Fund, October.

Levy Yeyati, E. 2006. Financial dollarization: Evaluating the consequences. *Economic Policy* 21 (45): 61–118.

Levy Yeyati, E., A. de la Torre, and S. Schmukler. 2003. Living and dying with hard pegs: The rise and fall of Argentina's currency board. *Economia* 5 (2): 43–99.

Levy Yeyati, E., M. S. Martínez Pería, and S. Schmukler. 2004. Market discipline under systemic risk: Evidence from bank runs in emerging economies. World Bank Working Paper no. 3440. Washington, DC: World Bank.

Rajan, R. 2004. Dollar shortages and crises. NBER Working Paper no. 10845. Cambridge, MA: National Bureau of Economic Research, October.

Shah, P. 1997. The option clause in free-banking, theory and history: A reappraisal. *Review of Austrian Economics* 10 (2): 1–25.

Comment   Marco Bonomo

As the paper documents, deposit dollarization is a widespread phenomenon in the world. Because the central bank has limits in acting as a lender of last resort for foreign currency, a financial dollarized economy would be vulnerable to liquidity runs in foreign currency a la Diamond and Dybvig. With this motivation, Eduardo Levy Yeyati studies alternative mechanisms of liquidity management in a financial dollarized economy.

The analysis, which has a simple and convincing economic intuition, suggests that a combination of liquidity asset requirements and limits to convertibility should be optimal in terms of social welfare. The main point of my comment is that this analysis is limited to dollarization experiences in fixed exchange rate regimes. I start by questioning whether the increase of dollar deposit renders the financial system more fragile, once the possibility of exchange rate fluctuations is taken into account. I first analyze the empirical evidence, then I turn to theoretical arguments. In doing so, we assess whether the mechanisms of liquidity management proposed in the paper are still appropriate in a floating exchange rate regime.

Dollarization is increasing in the world, despite decreasing inflation rates. This fact suggests that deposits in dollars are desired for reasons other than hedging against macroeconomic risk. Therefore, there is no indication that dollarization will disappear or even reduce substantially, despite the widespread view among analysts that it makes the financial and economic system more prone to risk. The increased trade and financial openness of national economies, as measured by trade ratios and foreign exchange deregulation, is possibly the main driver of the recent growth trend of local dollar deposits, which in part replaces the "capital flight" dollars previously held abroad.

The underlying view in the paper that dollarization increases the financial fragility of the system is apparently supported by table 6.2, which shows that systemic banking crises have occurred mostly in countries with relatively high dollarization ratios and also by the more formal evidence provided by De Nicoló, Honohan, and Ize (2005). However, most of the evidence that dollarization of deposits increases the probability or the cost of a banking crisis or a currency crash could be biased because it does not control for the exchange rate disequilibrium (which is correlated with the deposit dollarization ratio). The work of Arteta (2003) indicates that, once a control for the exchange rate disequilibrium is introduced, deposit dollarization has no effect on the probability of a banking crisis or a currency

Marco Bonomo is an associate professor at the Graduate School of Economics, Fundação Getúlio Vargas.

I would like to thank Edmar Bacha and Cristina Terra for very useful suggestions and discussions.

crash. Someone could argue that even if dollarization does not affect the probability of a crisis it does increase its costs. Again, this view is not supported by the empirical evidence in Arteta (2003). On the contrary, deposit dollarization is found to lower the cost of both banking crises and currency crashes.[1]

My reading of this evidence is that it reinforces my earlier impression that one cannot analyze dollarization in isolation. One context is deposit dollarization in a fixed exchange rate regime, which is prone to attacks, and this is, in my opinion, the environment where the paper's analysis applies.[2] However, in the same way as the fixed exchange regime tends to disappear, so does this pattern of dollarization. Dollarization of deposits in an open economy with low inflation and a floating exchange rate regime is a different situation and one that is becoming more common in the world. There is no convincing evidence up to now that in this type of regime countries with higher deposit dollarization ratios are more likely to suffer bank runs.

One can dismiss the empirical evidence as insufficient if forceful theoretical results are available that higher deposit dollarization ratios make the system more prone to bank runs. Despite the substantial progress represented by Chang and Velasco (2000) work on dollarization and financial fragility, one cannot find such answer in the theoretical literature.[3]

Dollarization of demand deposits is usually partial when the exchange rate is floating. In this case, we can separate the problem in two. One is the problem of banks' liquidity, and the other is their balance sheet. The central bank can always act as a lender of last resort in pesos, solving the problem of liquidity in pesos. The depositors in pesos, knowing this, will not make a run on their deposits.[4] Thus, the run should be only in dollar deposits.

Usually economies with a relatively high proportion of dollar deposits have also a relatively high proportion of dollar loans. A bank must deliver the called dollarized deposit in dollars. Then it should buy dollars or

1. This is once one controls for the exchange rate regime. In the case of an exchange rate devaluation, it is possible that the positive income effect due to the dollarization of households or firms assets counteract the negative effect of dollar debts. A higher dollarization ratio may be related to better integration with international financial markets and better management skills. Both of those attributes could result in a better ability from domestic banks to deal with banking crises, lowering their negative impact.

2. Note that, even in this situation, one interpretation of the evidence in Arteta (2003) is that it is not the dollarization that increases the probability of banking crisis, but the fixed exchange rate regime.

3. Although they conclude that dollarization does make a flexible exchange rate regime prone to bank runs, their special setup has some important shortcomings, which could alter their results. One of them is that there are no goods in the home country. Thus, the exchange rate is not a relative price that equilibrates demand and supply for goods but only a mechanism that distributes income among owners of assets and liabilities in pesos and in dollars. Another is that they do not consider a system where part of the deposits are denominated in dollars and part in pesos.

4. Chang and Velasco (2000) argue that the threat of devaluation will deter the run on peso deposits.

liquidate assets in dollars. Assuming that its assets in dollars are illiquid, it should buy dollars. In a systemic run, all banks are doing it at the same time, and the exchange rate should depreciate. Differently from a fixed exchange rate regime, where the excess demand for dollars would persist, the depreciation should make demand and supply of dollars equal. It may also make the liquidity shortage worse, but this can be solved by central bank loans. The crucial issue is whether it will lead to the bank's insolvency. The potential loss of the bank will depend on the ratio between the bank's dollar assets (adjusted by the probability of default that increases with the devaluation) to its dollar liabilities. Then the effect will depend on the bank's balance sheet mismatch of risks and currencies.

The runners could make money with the devaluation, justifying the run. But this is not different than a speculative attack in a flexible exchange rate regime. The equilibrium exchange rate ex ante should reflect the probability of runs (a "peso problem" valuation, reflected in the exchange rate, not only in the local interest rate) and maybe could prevent runs from happening. If the resulting equilibrium exchange rate is higher because of the threat of devaluation represented by dollar deposits, then the flow-supply of dollars from the trade account will also become higher in this economy.

All this should be analyzed in a rigorous model. The bottom line is that the situation is complex, and one cannot guarantee that dollar deposits will make the economy prone to bank runs in a flexible exchange rate system. If there is a run on the dollar deposits, the result should be banks losses if the matching of dollar assets and liabilities is poor. Then the mechanism to prevent bank failures could be the monitoring of the banks' risk positions, as it is currently made.

The analytical framework in the paper is not in any case appropriate to answer those questions. First, bank runs are exogenous. Second, there is no exchange rate in the models, and deposits have all the same denomination (which is in dollars for the authors). When banks' assets enter the analysis, they are always in the same denomination. Thus, there is no explicit exchange rate on the banks' balance sheet problem. There is no definition of exchange rate regime either. The only implicit system consistent with the models is a fixed exchange rate regime, as argued above. In fact, the only assumption made by the authors that renders the dollarized banking system different from a banking system entirely in pesos is that the central bank cannot lend to the banks without limit. This should not cause problems if the exchange rate is free to float and the banks are well covered against devaluation-related risks in their portfolio.

References

Arteta, C. 2003. Are financially dollarized countries more prone to costly crises? Board of Governors of the Federal Reserve System International Finance Discussion Paper no. 763. Washington, DC: Board of Governors of the Federal Reserve System.

Chang, R., and A. Velasco. 2000. Financial fragility and the exchange rate regime. *Journal of Economic Theory* 92:1–34.

De Nicoló, G., P. Honohan, and A. Ize. 2005. Dollarization of the banking system: Good or bad? *Journal of Banking and Finance* 29 (7): 1697–1727.

Comment   Alejandro Werner

The paper's objective is to study the implications for liquidity runs in an economy where domestic financial assets are dollarized. As a result, the paper proposes a scheme to manage liquidity in an "interim period" in which financial dollarization is still high.

According to the paper, this is an important topic given the extent of dollarization (or some type of indexation) around the world as shown in figure 6.1 in the paper and the correlation that exists between this variable and the propensity that an economy has to suffer a bank run. However, as I will argue in these comments, the relative importance of this topic could be put into question with alternative data.

Although the paper stresses that this is a transitional issue and the instrument it proposes to deal with it should be transitory, an important shortcoming is the absence of a discussion on what the long-term structure of banking liabilities should be and how the implementation of the proposed mechanism helps or hinders the transition toward that equilibrium.

In this discussion, the key question is whether it is desirable to have financial intermediation in foreign currency by domestic financial institutions. The alternative could be to leave this business to foreign banks abroad or to allow branching at home. I think that depending on how this question is answered, the mechanisms to handle the transition should be different.

Another key comment is related to the proposal to use clauses for ex-ante suspensions of convertibility clauses to minimize the probability of a liquidity run and to manage one once it happens. I am very skeptical that an instrument such as this could be beneficial for the following reasons:

1. Once this mechanism is announced, there is a very high probability that foreign currencies depositors will take their money out of the country toward a system in which there are "real dollar deposits." Therefore, the announcement, or even the rumors of this measure, could trigger the crisis that is supposed to avoid. Therefore, given the high degree of capital mobility, this scheme could be very difficult to implement.

2. Given that most of the time a banking system liquidity crisis happens

Alejandro Werner is the deputy minister of Finance and Public Credit of Mexico.

together with recessions, devaluations, and so on, domestic depositors have the rest of their portfolio (real estate, human capital, other investments) exhibiting a high correlation with the ex post nonconvertibility of their dollar deposits. Therefore they will be asking for a very high premium, or they will be rushing for the exit. In this case, it seems that the likelihood of finding an external lender of last resort is higher than successfully implementing an ex ante suspension of convertibility.

In the empirical section, a correlation between deposit dollarization and international reserves is established. However, the role that the exchange rate regime plays in explaining both of these phenomena is not explored. Obviously, the presence of a fixed exchange rate regime has promoted the accumulation of international reserves and the dollarization of liabilities in many countries.

Regarding the differences between self-insurance and external insurance, the paper claims that the sole advantage of the latter is that the external insurance has a lower cost than the cost of funding that the government faces when accumulating reserves for self-insurance. This seems to be an odd conclusion because the investors who end up financing both alternatives are foreign (sometimes they are even the same) with similar funding opportunities and portfolio. The only difference is that the investors financing the self-insurance option also face some "country risk" during good times that the external insurer does not face. On the other hand, while paying for this "extra risk," the country guarantees that the money will be there if the liquidity run scenario materializes, while under the external insurance option there is always the risk of noncompliance by the insurer. I think this is the key issue between the two options. The other shortcoming of external insurance is the dynamic hedging through which the insurer unloads his position. Although important, I think that there are two objections to this argument:

1. First, through the external insurance contract and dynamic hedging the borrowing country can accomplish a desirable result to smooth capital flows through different states of nature, reducing them in good times and increasing them during bad times.

2. Dynamic hedging will be imperfect because of a lack of instruments to short the country.

Regarding the widespread nature of dollarization that is shown in figure 6.1, the paper does not provide the definition used to construct the dollarization ratio. This is important to the extent that maybe some of the dollar liabilities that are included are not covered by the domestic lender of last resort, are not held by domestic agents, or not all the dollars liabilities covered by the LLR are included in the measure and, therefore, this indicator might be a misleading indicator of the problem addressed in the paper.

		In checking accounts[a] +
Year	In checking accounts[a]	other deposits[b]
1995	10.1	7.3
1996	10.2	8.1
1997	10.4	5.8
1998	13.4	6.1
1999	12.9	6.0
2000	12.4	7.4
2001	17.0	8.8
2002	15.3	8.2
2003	12.1	6.9
2004	14.6	7.7
2005	12.6	7.7
Mar 2006	15.5	8.5

Table 6C.1   **Deposits: Share of dollar denominated accounts in total (%)**

Source: Banco de México.

[a]The amount per checking account is limited to that insured by the deposit insurance.

[b]"Other Deposits" include savings accounts.

When analyzing dollarization ratios of deposits, it is also important to know the domestic regulation to understand the nature of this deposit. In the case of Mexico, foreign deposits are only available for foreign companies and border residents: therefore, they respond to real transactional factors more than speculative issues. In addition, the regulation oblige the banks to hold liquid dollar denominated assets to hedge these deposits, therefore, eliminating any possible mismatch. Additionally, the presence of a floating exchange rate regime suggests that if depositors want to shift from peso to dollar deposits the banks should buy dollar assets to cover these deposits increasing the price of this transaction and, therefore, reducing the incentive to undertake it.

Finally, I think that the relevant measure should not be the dollarization ratio of deposits but rather the dollarization ratio of foreign currency liabilities of the banking system that are insured by the government. When we do this calculation (table 6C.1) for the case of Mexico, the dollarization ratio falls below 10 percent (table 6C.1).

Sudden Stops and
IMF-Supported Programs

Barry Eichengreen, Poonam Gupta, and Ashoka Mody

7.1 Introduction

The debate over the role of the International Monetary Fund (IMF) in a world of capital mobility shows no signs of dying down. There is broad awareness that the single factor that most distinguishes our current economic and financial environment from that of the preceding period is high capital mobility. There is also a widely held view that while exposure to international capital markets promises benefits, those benefits come packaged with risks. But there is no consensus on what the IMF should do about it. Should the Fund reduce its role as emergency lender on the grounds that countries enjoy increasing access to markets as an alternative source of finance? Or should it expand its role as relations with international financial markets expose countries to abrupt and potentially costly reversals in the direction of capital flows? Are existing IMF facilities adequate for these needs? Or is there a case for a new facility capable of disbursing large amounts of financial assistance quickly, perhaps on the basis of prequalification, to countries experiencing sudden shifts in the direction of capital flows?[1]

Barry Eichengreen is the George C. Pardee and Helen N. Pardee Professor of Economics and Political Science at the University of California, Berkeley, and a research associate of the National Bureau of Economic Research. Poonam Gupta is a professor of economics at the Delhi School of Economics. Ashoka Mody is an assistant director in the European Department of the International Monetary Fund.

We thank Mohammed Dairi, Matthew Fisher, Marianne Schulze-Ghattas, Jeromin Zettelmeyer, and other colleagues at the International Monetary Fund (IMF) for comments and Sudarat Ananchotikul and Anna Unigovskaya for research assistance. The views expressed in this paper are those of the authors and do not necessarily represent those of the IMF or IMF policy.

1. Two recent reviews of the debate that elaborate these points are Ostry and Zettelmeyer (2005) and Truman (2005).

More evidence may help to answer these questions. There exists substantial empirical literature on both shifts in the direction of capital flows (known by the moniker "sudden stops") and the effects of IMF-supported programs (see tables 7.1 and 7.2). Empirical analyses focus on the impact of policies and characteristics like a country's exchange rate regime, financial openness, and dependence on international trade on the incidence, magnitude, and effects of sudden stops. Analyses of IMF-supported programs examine the behavior of inflation, output, fiscal effort, and, most relevant to the questions at hand, the balance of payments, compared to a control group of country-year cases with no program in place. But, to our knowledge, there exists no study focusing on the impact of such programs on the incidence, severity, and effects of sudden stops.

In this paper we take a first stab at developing such evidence. Our results suggest that IMF-supported programs and IMF credits reduce the likelihood of sudden stops. There is some evidence that this stabilizing effect is stronger for countries with strong fundamentals. This can be interpreted in terms of the literature on global capital account shocks and the stabilizing effect of liquidity insurance. Even countries with strong policies may experience a sudden curtailment of capital inflows and a shift to outflows if investors suspect that other investors for whatever reason are primed to take their money out of the country. Emergency financial assistance can then reassure individual investors of the country's continued ability to finance its international transactions and reduce their incentive to liquidate their positions. Emergency lending by the IMF can ensure the continued provision of private finance in much the way that lender-of-last-resort intervention by a central bank can limit the scope for bank runs. But if country fundamentals are weak, IMF financial assistance may only come in the front door and go out the back door with no impact on the incidence of the sudden stop.

There are reasons to treat these results with caution. There is the difficulty of measuring both IMF-supported programs and sudden stops. There is the challenge of identifying the impact of the former on the latter—of addressing potential endogeneity. Our solutions to these problems are imperfect. Our analysis also leaves open a variety of issues such as appropriate modalities for lending to countries in this position, the feasibility of identifying qualifying countries in the relevant time frame, and moral hazard. While these are not our topics in this paper, this does not mean they are unimportant. Still, we believe that our results are the first evidence of the insurance properties of IMF-supported programs.

7.2   Sudden Stops and Multilateral Insurance

The fact that sudden stops cluster in time is taken as suggesting that they have more to do with the behavior of global financial markets than with country policies, which some commentators take to imply that their

Table 7.1   Literature on sudden stops

Reference	Countries/Types/Years	Dependent variable	Main explanatory variable(s)	Main results
Calvo, Izquierdo, and Mejía (2004)	15 emerging market countries and 17 developed countries, 1990–2001	Sudden stop dummy	1) Degree of domestic liability dollarization. 2) 1 – (the degree of trade openness)—to proxy for the sensitivity of the real exchange rate to capital flow reversals. *Control variables*: two measures of exchange rate regime flexibility, ratio of foreign reserves to current account deficit, credit growth, FDI, fiscal balance, terms of trade growth, public sector debt, yearly dummies.	Domestic liability dollarization and trade closedness are positively correlated with the probability of a sudden stop. The effect of openness and liability dollarization on the probability of a sudden stop could be nonlinear. High current account average (i.e., less open) is particularly dangerous for countries with a high degree of dollarization.
Frankel and Cavallo (2004)	141 countries, 1970–2002	Sudden stop dummy	1) Trade openness. 2) Foreign debt to GDP. 3) Current account balance to GDP. *Control variables*: log of reserves in months of imports, log of GDP per capita, FDI/GDP, institutional quality ratio of short-term debt to total debt, and a measure of nominal exchange rate rigidity.	Openness makes countries *less* vulnerable to sudden stop. This negative relationship is even stronger when correcting for the endogeneity of trade using the gravity instrument for trade openness. Sudden stops are more likely when initial current account deficit to GDP is high. Foreign debt to GDP does not appear to have significant impact on the probability of a sudden stop.

(continued)

Table 7.1 (continued)

Reference	Countries/Types/Years	Dependent variable	Main explanatory variable(s)	Main results
Hutchison and Noy (2004)	27 emerging market countries, 1975–1997	GDP growth rate	1) Currency crisis dummy. 2) Current account reversal dummy. 3) Sudden stop crisis dummy (interaction of the two dummy variables above). *Control variables:* (lagged) real GDP growth, change in budget surplus to GDP ratio, credit growth, foreign output growth, real exchange rate overvaluation, openness, country dummies.	Currency crises and current account reversals have significant negative effects on output growth. Sudden stop crises have a large negative, but short-lived, impact on output growth over and above the currency crises.
Edwards (2005)	157 countries, 1970–2000	GDP per capita	1) Sudden stop dummy. 2) Current account reversal dummy. *Control variables:* External terms of trade shocks (change in terms of trade), the growth gap (the difference between the long run rate of real per capita GDP and the current rate).	Reversals and sudden stops each have a significantly negative effect on per capita growth. However, when both reversals and the sudden stop dummies are included in the growth regression, the reversal dummy continues to be significantly negative while the coefficient for the sudden stop dummy does not.

Table 7.2   Literature on IMF-supported programs

Reference	Countries/Types/Years	Dependent variable(s)	Measurement of IMF program effect	Control variable(s)	Findings regarding IMF programs
Goldstein and Montiel (1986)	58 developing countries, 1974–1981	1) Overall balance of payments/GNP 2) Current account/GNP 3) Inflation rate 4) GDP growth	The mean change between the pre- and the post-program periods across the group of program countries for each of the outcome variables. The difference in mean changes of the outcome variables for program and nonprogram countries The sign and statistical significance of the coefficients of the IMF program dummy.	(For GEE method.) *Policy instruments:* 1) The change in domestic credit. 2) The real effective exchange rate. *External exogenous variables:* 3) Time dummy variables. *Others:* 4) Country dummy variables. 5) Lagged outcome variables.	*Before-after analysis:* There is a marked difference in the nature and pattern of estimated program effects from year to year and none of them is significant. This could be because this method does not control for non-program influences on the changes in outcome variables. *With-without analysis:* Program countries appear to have lower BOP, lower current account deficit, lower real growth, and higher inflation rate than nonprogram countries. However, these estimates of program effects could be biased due to nonrandom selection.
Pastor (1987)	18 Latin American countries, 1965–1981	1) Balance of payments measures 2) Inflation rate 3) GDP growth 4) Labor's share of income	The mean change between the pre- and the post-program periods across the group of program countries for each of the outcome variables.	—	Insignificant changes in current account. Significant increases in inflation. Significant improvements in the overall balance of payments. Mixed effects on growth.

Table 7.2 (continued)

Reference	Countries/ Types/Years	Dependent variable(s)	Measurement of IMF program effect	Control variable(s)	Findings regarding IMF programs
Khan (1990)	69 developing countries, 1973–1988	1) Balance of payments to GDP 2) Current account surplus to GDP 3) Inflation rate 4) Real GDP growth rate	The mean change between the pre- and the post-program periods across the group of program countries for each of the outcome variables. The difference in mean changes of the outcome variables for program and nonprogram countries. The sign and statistical significance of the coefficients of the IMF program dummy.	(For GEE method.) *Policy instruments*: 1) The change in domestic credit. 2) The real effective exchange rate. 3) The ratio of fiscal balance to GDP. *External exogenous variables*: 4) Changes in terms of trade. 5) Time dummy variables.	*Before-after analysis*: Programs lead to an improvement only in the current account position. *With-without analysis*: Programs lead to balance of payments improvement, current account improvement, and reduced inflation rate. All of these effects are larger in magnitude relative to the before-after estimators. *GEE method*: The current account improves and the growth rate is significantly reduced in program countries relative to the change in nonprogram countries. Two-year comparisons show that the positive program effects on the BOP, the current account, and inflation become stronger, and the negative effects on growth rate become weaker over time.

| Conway (1994) | 74 developing countries, 1976–1986 | 1) Economic performance—GDP growth, domestic investment to GNP ratio, current account-to-GNP ratio, inflation rate. 2) Policy variables—the ratio of government consumption to GNP, the rate of domestic credit creation, budget surplus/deficit as a share of GNP, real exchange rate. | The sign and statistical significance of the coefficients of: 1) A binary indicator of participation (P_{it}). 2) Percentage of year t that country participated (F_{it}). 3) Percentage of available funds for country i for period t that is disbursed (V_{it}). | 1) Terms of trade. 2) Long- and short-term debt per capita. 3) Real interest rate. 4) Share of total output coming from agricultural sector (proxy for secular stage of economic development). 5) Foreign reserves to imports. 6) Country-specific dummy variables. 7) Dependent variable lagged once and twice. | The current account ratio improves concurrently with participation in an IMF program, while the investment ratio declines. Inflation and real GNP growth fall contemporaneously, but effects are insignificantly different from zero. The lagged effects of IMF programs on real GNP growth and the current account are positive and statistically significant. Both concurrent and lagged evidence1 suggests that IMF program participation is associated with significantly reduced budget deficits. Reduction in government current expenditure and depreciation of the real exchange rate concurrent with the IMF program but are statistically insignificant. |
| Dicks-Mireaux, Mecagni, and Schadler (2000) | 74 low-income countries, 1986–1991 | 1) Real GDP growth rate. 2) Consumer price inflation 3) The ratio of external debt/service to exports (measure of external viability) | The sign and statistical significance of the coefficients of the IMF program dummy. | *Policy instruments:* 1) Lagged fiscal balance to GDP. 2) Lagged net domestic asset growth. 3) Lagged percentage change in the nominal effective exchange rate. *Exogenous external variables:* 4) Changes in terms of trade. 5) Growth of export markets. *Lagged dependent variables:* 6) Lagged real GDP growth rate. 7) Lagged inflation rate. 8) Lagged external debt/service ratio | There are statistically significant beneficial effects of IMF support on output growth and the debt/service ratio, but no effects on inflation. |

(continued)

Table 7.2 (continued)

Reference	Countries/ Types/Years	Dependent variable(s)	Measurement of IMF program effect	Control variable(s)	Findings regarding IMF programs
Przeworski and Vreeland (2000)	79 developing countries, 1971–1990	Output growth	The difference between values of growth expected in the two situations (under and not under IMF programs) independently of selection	—	IMF program participation lowers growth rates for as long as countries remain under a program. Once countries leave the program they grow faster than if they had remained, but not faster than they would have without participation.
Hutchison (2001)	67 developing countries, 1970–1997	Real GDP growth	The sign and statistical significance of the coefficients of: 1) IMF program dummy. 2) Interaction term between the currency crises dummy and the IMF program dummy (measuring additional effects on output growth arising from a currency crisis that is immediately followed by an IMF program)	*Policy instruments:* 1) Lagged change in budget surplus to GDP. 2) Lagged inflation. 3) Lagged credit growth. *External exogenous factors:* 4) Trade-weighted lagged external growth rates of major trading partners. 5) Lagged rate of real exchange rate overvaluation.	Both a currency crisis and an IMF program leads to an output loss. IMF program lowers output growth somewhat on average, but there is no additional effect of the program when associated with a severe currency or balance of payments crisis. The adverse effects from participating in an IMF program are significant in the first year of the IMF program but no significant additional effects in subsequent years.
Barro and Lee (2004)	81 developing countries, 1975–1999	GDP growth rate	The sign and statistical significance of the coefficients of: 1) IMF loan size—the period-average of the ratio of IMF loans to GDP. 2) IMF participation—the fraction of months during each five-year period that a country is under and IMF loan program.	1) Log of initial per capita GDP. 2) Human resources (educational attainment, life expectancy, and fertility). 3) The ratio of investment to GDP. 4) Changes in the terms of trade (export prices relative to import prices). 5) Institutional and policy variables (government consumption, a subjective index of the rule of law, international openness, and inflation.	With simple OLS, and increase in IMF lending is associated with a contemporaneous reduction of economic growth. After controlling for endogeneity with the instrumental variables, there is no statistically significant impact of IMF lending on economic growth in the contemporaneous five-year period, but there is a statistically significant negative effect on growth in subsequent five years.

Study	Sample	Variables	Method		Results
Evrensel (2002)	91 developing countries, 1971–1997	1) Current account 2) Overall balance of payments 3) Reserves 4) Domestic credit 5) Inflation rate 6) Budget deficit 7) Net domestic borrowing 8) Net foreign borrowing 9) Real growth rate	The mean change between the pre- and the post program periods across the group of program countries for each of the outcome variables.	—	The only significant results are: One year after the program, program participating countries appears to have smaller overall BOP deficit, smaller domestic credit, lower inflation rate, smaller net foreign borrowing and smaller foreign debt. However, all of these effects disappear in subsequent years.
Hardoy (2002)	109 developing countries, 1970–1990	The annual rate of growth of real GDP per capita	Matching estimator = average difference in the values of the outcome variable between participant observations and the matched nonparticipant observations. Difference-in-difference matching estimator = difference between the matching estimators in pre-program and post-program periods.	1) Government expenditure to GDP. 2) Investment to GDP. 3) Exchange rate. 4) Level of economic development. 5) Dummy = 1 if period 1979–87, 0 if 1973–78. 6) Regional dummies. 7) Cumulative number of years under IMF program. 8) Past participation index. 9) Legislative election index. 10) Growth of consumption to GDP. 11) Current account balance to GDP. 12) Terms of trade index. 13) Balance of payment to GDP. 14) Total debt service to GNP. 15) Political regime dummy.	No statistically significant effects of IMF program on growth after program participation. Estimated effects are always negative three years after participation. Estimates are sensitive in many respects: the choice of sample, the reduction of the information set, the choice of time period, and the method applied.

(continued)

Table 7.2 (continued)

Reference	Countries/ Types/Years	Dependent variable(s)	Measurement of IMF program effect	Control variable(s)	Findings regarding IMF programs
Hutchison and Noy (2003)	67 developing countries, 1975–1997	Real GDP growth	The sign and statistical significance of the coefficients of: 1) IMF program dummy. 2) Latin American IMF program dummy. 3) IMF program dummy in the 1990s. 4) Latin American IMF program dummy in the 1990s.	*Policy instruments:* 1) Lagged change in budget surplus to GDP. 2) Lagged inflation. 3) Lagged credit growth. *External exogenous factors:* 4) Trade-weighted lagged external growth rates of major trading partners. 5) Lagged rate of real exchange rate overvaluation. *Crisis variables:* 1) Currency crisis dummy. 2) Sudden stop crisis dummy.	The average effect of an IMF program on output is statistically significant and negative. However, once controlled for the difference between IMF programs in Latin America and elsewhere, the average effect of IMF program disappears while the Latin American IMF program appears to lead to a statistically significant reduction of output growth. IMF programs in Latin America are associated with very small positive output effects in the 1990s, but large negative effects during the 1975–1989 period.
Bordo, Mody, and Oomes (2004)	29 emerging market countries, 1980–2002	1) Current account balance to GDP 2) Reserves to imports 3) Short-term debt to reserves	Difference between program participating and nonprogram participating countries (with similar fundamentals) in probabilities of moving to a better state	—	IMF programs are generally associated with improvements in external fundamentals, except when these fundamentals are already in very good shape.

Study	Sample	Dependent variable	Independent variables / method	Results
Atoyan and Conway (2005)	95 developing countries, 1993–2002	1) Changes in real per capita economic growth rate 2) Changes in fiscal surplus to GDP ratio 3) Changes in current account surplus to GDP ratio.	Difference in intercepts from the two subsamples Coefficient of the propensity score (predicted value of probability of participation); intercept coefficient	For the censored-sample and the instrumental variable approaches, the "inverse Mills ratio" (probability of selection) is included to control for selection bias. For the matching approach, the "matching" of participant and nonparticipant observations based on propensity scores readily controls for potential selection bias.
Dreher (2005)	98 developing countries, 1970–2000 (5-year intervals)	Average five-year growth rate of per capita GDP	The sign and statistical significance of the coefficients of 1) IMF programs—continuous variable from 0 to 1, measuring the fraction of each period that a country operates under an IMF program (Barro & Lee 2005). 2) IMF loans to GDP. 3) Compliance with conditionality variables: i) No program suspension dummy (Edwards 2005), ii) Equally phased loan disbursements (Dreher 2005). iii) The share of the agreed money actually disbursed (Killick 1995).	1) Log of per capita GDP at the beginning of each period. 2) Human resources (secondary school enrollment, life expectancy, fertility rate). 3) Lagged values of investment to GDP. 4) Lagged values of government consumption to GDP. 5) Inflation rate. 6) Terms of trade growth. 7) Index of globalization. 8) Country dummies. 9) Time dummies (5-year periods).

(Results — Atoyan and Conway 2005): IMF programs have little impact on real economic growth in immediate year following the program initiation, but have an increasingly positive impact on growth in participating countries as the time horizon grows longer.
Both the fiscal ratio and the current-account ratio improve contemporaneously with IMF participation relative to the counterfactual, with effects in succeeding years differing little from the immediate effects.

(Results — Dreher 2005): There is considerable evidence from both SUR and 3SLS regressions suggesting that participation in IMF programs reduces economic growth. Compliance with conditionality mitigates this negative effect on growth, although the overall impact remains substantially negative. The amount of loans has no significant impact on growth.

incidence would likely decline with the stepped-up provision of multilateral insurance. Calvo (2005) takes the often rapid recovery of growth from sudden stops as evidence that country policies are not at the root of this phenomenon. He concludes that sudden stops in emerging market countries reflect inefficiencies in international financial markets and argues for emergency financial assistance to countries suffering sharp interruptions in capital flows.[2]

A number of questions can be raised about this argument. One is why countries cannot obtain insurance by establishing credit lines on international capital markets or issuing securities with embedded options that have the same insurance properties. If the argument for insurance is strong, then the private sector should be prepared to provide it for a fee. This objection seems especially compelling in light of the recent growth of international financial markets and transactions. It is not clear why contracting for private insurance is not more widespread.[3]

- One possible explanation is that capital requirements and other regulations prevent potential suppliers from providing insurance on the requisite scale. Commercial counterparties may also be worried about concentrated country exposures and demand a prohibitive price for the provision of contingent credit lines. Still, if the case for private insurance is strong, financial markets and institutions adept at diversifying and repackaging risks should find a way around these obstacles.
- Another possibility is adverse selection. If asymmetric information prevents potential insurers from discriminating among borrowers in different risk categories, then only risky countries will wish to contract for such lines. The higher are the fees and interest rates charged, the greater will be the riskiness of willing clients, causing the private market to collapse. The limitation of this argument is that insurers are far from ignorant of variations in country risk. Thus, while information asymmetry is a concern, especially when crisis conditions begin to develop, lenders should still be able to establish ex ante differences in charges for borrowers subject to different levels of country risk.[4]

2. Calvo's preferred variant of the mechanism would have the stabilization fund purchase the bonds of adversely affected economies to prevent their spreads from rising (Calvo 2002).

3. There has, in fact, been some experimentation with private insurance by, inter alia, Argentina in the 1990s. (The experiment in question involved a contingent repurchase contract between the Argentine central bank and a consortium of foreign banks, under which the central bank was allowed to withdraw funds in the event of a crisis via a renewable credit line collateralized by dollar-denominated government bonds.) But the Argentine credit line was small, and execution was delayed until well into the crisis. There is also the recent development of credit derivatives markets, which offer the possibility of purchasing protection against a range of emerging market credit events, although data on these markets are hard to come by. This is especially true of their use—for obvious reasons—by emerging market sovereigns.

4. A related argument is that a public insurance agency may have more ability or stronger incentives to gather information on the financial condition of its clients, in turn enabling it to

- Yet another possibility is that commercial insurance providers have an incentive to take a short position against the country when the latter is likely to draw down its credit line. In turn this will destroy the effectiveness of the insurance (Broda and Levy Yeyati 2003). Presumably this problem does not carry over to public insurance providers.[5]

A second question is whether bunching—that multiple countries tend to experience sudden stops simultaneously—limits the feasibility of multilateral insurance. If a substantial subset of IMF members needs to draw on the resources of the Fund simultaneously because they experience shocks simultaneously, then the financial feasibility of an insurance arrangement may be questionable.

A third question is whether it is, in fact, correct that sudden stops are not really a function of country policies. Empirical analyses from Calvo, Izquierdo, and Mejia (2004) to Edwards (2005) identify roles for both internal and external factors.[6] Insofar as the relevant characteristics include policies under the control of the domestic authorities, this means that the moral hazard problem must be addressed.[7]

Moral hazard does not render insurance infeasible, but it requires that a reasonable insurance scheme be designed to limit its extent. An obvious way of doing so is through surveillance and conditionality. A key question is whether such conditions are better applied ex post or ex ante. Specifically, should the IMF announce in advance what countries are eligible for

better tailor incentive-compatible contracts. The obvious objection here is that private financial institutions with their own performance at stake have at least as strong an incentive to invest in these monitoring functions.

5. This problem would be ameliorated if the insurance liability was securitized and widely distributed as diversification would then provide the insurers with the protection they need (obviating the need to hedge on a large scale). But in turn this begs the question of why emerging market countries find it hard to place innovative securities containing put and call options that kick in, reducing debt service or even calling for reverse payments, when economic conditions deteriorate.

6. To quote Calvo (2005, 26), "Econometric studies do not reject the hypothesis that Sudden Stops are largely prompted by external factors but, at the same time, strongly suggest that the probability of Sudden Stops reflects domestic characteristics." In other words, even analysts emphasizing the importance of global factors acknowledge that domestic characteristics shape the impact and response to external shocks.

7. The extent and economic importance of moral hazard in this context is disputed; for a review of the evidence, see Lane and Phillips (2000). There is also the possibility that, in the presence of other distortions, adding insurance will lead to less risk taking rather than more. Thus, in a model of finite-lived governments, where the probability of government survival declines with the incidence of financial crises, Cordella and Levy Yeyati (2004) show that insurance, by reducing the risk of financial collapse, may in fact encourage the authorities to invest more in policy reform (in the present context, to reduce the riskiness of their policies). Of course, there are actually two effects of insurance here: insurance reduces the pressure on the government to head off a crisis, but it also strengthens the incentive to pursue reforms that pay off in the future. Predictably, the net effect is ambiguous. Cordella and Levy Yeyati show that insurance is more likely to encourage reforms that pay off in good times (because it reduces the risk of falling into a crisis in the first place) than reforms that reduce the risk of a crisis in the event that one occurs.

a credit line and specify the amount of assistance that they can expect to receive? Or should it proceed on a case-by-case basis and decide whether to provide additional credit once the sudden stop and the severity of the output decline have been observed?

Those who argue for insurance against sudden stops generally favor ex ante contracts. First, the problems of illiquidity that arise when capital flows are interrupted can lead to problems of insolvency unless funds are disbursed quickly. Determining eligibility quickly requires that countries be deemed eligible for assistance ex ante. Second, if the terms and amounts of external assistance are specified ex ante, then the government has a stronger incentive to take steps to expedite the economy's recovery from the sudden stop.

Cohen and Portes (2004) describe an insurance contract in which countries prequalify for assistance if their debt ratios remain below a critical ceiling consistent with moderate spreads, say 400 basis points above London Interbank Offered Rate (LIBOR). By assumption, any crisis that the country then experiences is a crisis of liquidity, not a crisis of debt sustainability. Payments are triggered when spreads on the debt rise above the threshold level. The IMF would then lend to the country at the threshold spread. It would thus contain the effects of the sudden stop that caused spreads to rise and prevent the liquidity crisis from degenerating into a solvency crisis. Cordella and Levy Yeyati (2005) propose a country insurance facility that would provide eligible countries with automatic access to a credit line at a predetermined interest rate, where eligibility criteria would again focus on debt sustainability—not just the level of the debt but also its maturity and currency composition. Dervis and Ozer (2005) similarly propose a Stability and Growth Facility that would provide insurance against unforeseen shocks and for which countries would prequalify on the basis of their policies.

Chami, Sharma, and Shim (2004) provide a model laying out the analytics of this approach. They assume that the insurer has two objectives: safeguarding its assets and providing for the borrowing country's welfare, which it can enhance by extending a loan. A governmental counterparty decides in each of two periods how much unobserved effort to exert in order to avoid and, if necessary, recover from a financial crisis, which in turn affects how much will be asked to repay to the insurance pool.

In this model it is preferable for the insurer to specify eligibility and the terms of the credit line—how much assistance will be extended as a function of the severity of the decline in output that occurs in the first period—before the country enters a crisis and the full output consequences are revealed. Knowing that it stands to receive official support, the efforts of the national authorities to avert the crisis are correspondingly less. But the extent of the moral hazard affecting the authorities' efforts to recover from the crisis varies with the form of the contract. Under an ex post contract, the crisis country repays more if it makes a greater effort to recover from the crisis, which works to depress adjustment effort. In contrast, under the ex ante contract, when terms are agreed prior to the government's decision of how much adjustment effort to extend, repayment is independent of effort; hence adjustment will be greater, and outcomes will be superior. In general, an insurer that both has a fiduciary responsibility to safeguard its assets and that cares about the welfare of the crisis country will prefer an ex ante contract in which the operator of the reserve pool specifies who is eligible and the terms and amounts of the assistance that will be forthcoming.

But there may be a problem of time consistency with the ex ante contract. The insurer may want to renege on its fixed commitment if it observes that the recession is unusually severe. Because it values the welfare of the insured, it may then wish to offer more generous terms. Hence ex ante contracts fixing the amount and terms of the credit line will not be credible. And because the insured knows this, moral hazard lending to less adjustment effort will still be a problem, surveillance and conditionality or not.[8]

This suggests that the IMF may wish to deem certain countries eligible for a fixed credit line as this is better than a discretionary, case-by-case approach at preserving its financial solvency, while at the same time supporting the welfare of its members, but that the time-consistency problem may undermine the feasibility of this approach and aggravate moral hazard. And if moral hazard is serious, such an insurance arrangement may turn out to be welfare reducing rather than welfare improving for the membership as a whole.

Two further questions can be raised about these ideas. First, doesn't the unsatisfactory experience of the IMF's contingent credit line (CCL), for which no country applied prior to its expiration in 2003, raise questions about the enthusiasm of countries for ex ante insurance? Insofar as executive directors have a responsibility for the IMF's own solvency, members running risky policies that may prevent them from paying back credits would have to be denied the privilege of borrowing. Such an outcome would send a negative signal to the markets. This seems to have been what deterred governments from applying for a CCL. A further problem was that eligibility could be rescinded at some future date, sending a negative signal that might precipitate a crisis.

The Fund could meet its fiduciary responsibility by announcing unilaterally which members were eligible for financial assistance. But it would then send a negative signal about the financial condition of other countries when it declared them ineligible for insurance. In turn this might render

---

8. Theoretically, this problem could be solved by repeated interaction between the insurer and the country, through which the former develops a reputation for acting consistently.

countries reluctant to participate in the insurance arrangement in the first place. And the exit problem would remain.[9]

Finally, such schemes assume the ability of the agency operating the facility to discriminate between solvent and insolvent countries, where the solvent countries are still susceptible to liquidity crises and should thus be made automatic beneficiaries of the new facility. Cohen and Portes (2004) assume the existence of a well-defined amount of debt that forms the ceiling on what is sustainable and a stable linkage running from debt levels to spreads. Cordella and Levy Yeyati (2005) argue that a ceiling should be defined for the overall debt-gross domestic product (GDP) ratio but also recommend that foreign-currency debt and short-term debt should receive heavier weights in the calculation of this total. They suggest imposing a ceiling on the fiscal deficit in each of the preceding three years.

In the real world, sustainability depends on forecasts of future growth rates and interest rates that are disputable and uncertain. It depends on estimates of the political will of a government and society to mobilize and transfer resources for purposes of debt service. Given this uncertainty, it seems unavoidable that any insurance facility will occasionally lend to countries that find it impossible to repay. Or it will not lend to countries whose problems are liquidity related, leading to complaints and recrimination. Any automatic scheme that depends on the existence of an operational distinction between insolvent and illiquid crisis countries is unlikely to be feasible in practice.[10]

7.3   Capital Flows and Sudden Stops

As our measure of capital flows we use the financial account balance, a summary measure of net capital flows that includes net foreign direct investment, net portfolio investment, and other investments. The advantage of this measure is its comprehensiveness; in principle, it should capture net capital flows of all kinds.[11] One exception is that it does not include official

9. Cordella and Levy Yeyati (2005) suggest "smoothing" the eligibility criteria so that exogenous shocks temporarily pushing a country above the eligibility threshold do not precipitate a sudden jump in interest rates or a crisis. While this might help for small exogenous shocks that the authorities wish to offset, it will not help for large exogenous shocks that cannot be offset in the medium term.

10. This argument is developed and defended at greater length in Eichengreen (2000).

11. Other investigators, presumably with stronger priors about which capital flows are the primary source of instability, have focused on narrower measures (considering only financial flows for example) or on the change in gross rather than net inflows. Some have adjusted their preferred measure of capital flows for identifiable exogenous shocks to the current account (exports, the terms of trade, etc.). Some will argue for the exclusion of foreign direct investment (FDI) from the capital flow measure on the grounds that FDI flows are more stable and less prone to sudden stops. However, this conclusion is not universally accepted (for a flavor of the debate, see, e.g., Sarno and Taylor 1999). If FDI inflows fall dramatically, this is as much a problem for capital-importing countries as if portfolio inflows fall abruptly. This approach is not without implications for our sample of sudden-stop cases; see note 16.

transfers associated with IMF programs, a fact that is important for what follows.

Following Calvo, Izquierdo, and Mejia (2004) and Cavallo and Frankel (2004), we consider both the first and the second moments of the capital flow series in identifying sudden stops. First, we identify the years where the financial account balance exhibited a large decline relative to its long-term average. We require this to be a large discrete drop and not just a correction of a large temporary inflow. Second, we calculate the mean and one-standard-deviation band of the financial account balance using the data up to the years identified in the first stage as potential sudden stops and retain only years that qualify on the basis of this criterion.[12] Other authors have used two-standard-deviation bands, but because we are using annual data, a two-standard-deviation criterion turns out to be very strict.

Our empirical analysis focuses on emerging market countries significantly involved with international capital markets. For the period 1980 to 2003, we identified twenty-four such countries (listed in appendix A), which in turn experienced thirty-five sudden stop episodes.[13] Our dates are very similar to those of Calvo, Izquierdo, and Mejia (2004) and Cavallo and Frankel (2004). However, they differ from those of Edwards (2005), where a sudden stop is said to occur when a country had previously been receiving significant capital inflows (where it ranked in its region's third quartile in terms of capital inflows in the two previous years) and their volume declines by at least 5 percent of GDP in a given year. This is a lenient criterion that tends to capture episodes where the financial account balance declines only from, say, 20 percent to 15 percent of GDP, as well as episodes where there is a correction of a temporary increase in the balance the year before.[14]

For this group of countries we present descriptive statistics for the twenty-four year period 1980 to 2003.[15] In our sample, there a 5.5 percent

12. The moments were calculated using data up to the crisis year and not including the potential crisis year.

13. The "significant contact with international capital markets" criterion means that not all countries feature for the full length of the period. Thus, of the countries that transitioned from central planning, we include only Hungary and Poland and only after 1990, when they had moved significantly toward functioning markets. We include Bangladesh, Bolivia, Ghana, and Pakistan, which were recipients of concessional finance and were not as exposed to large market-based capital inflows. But even if these last four countries are dropped from the regression analysis, our findings remain robust, as we report in the following.

14. We note the omission from this list of a couple of cases—Russia and Brazil in 1999—that feature prominently in qualitative discussions of capital market disruptions. For Russia, the short time series precluded the estimation of a reliable measure of standard deviation of the financial account. Brazil in 1999 is a close call by our measure; in this instance, the decline in portfolio and bank flows was offset by an increase in FDI, cushioning the decline in the financial account. In the section on robustness checks in the following, we show that the key results remain the same when we treat these observations as sudden stop cases.

15. For purposes of regression analysis, however, we concentrate on the period 1990 through 2003, when capital flows to emerging market countries, bond-market intermediated

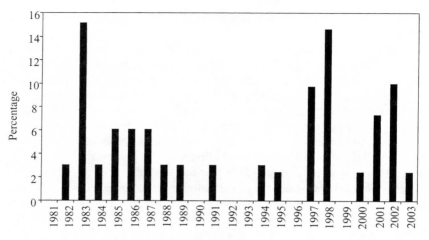

Fig. 7.1   Year-wise probability of a sudden stop
Source: Authors' calculations.

probability of a sudden stop in a given country in a given year. Figure 7.1 shows the time profile of these events. There is a clear bunching of sudden stops, as emphasized by Calvo (2005). Peaks coincide with the 1982 debt crisis, the Asian crisis of 1997, and the aftermath of the Argentine crisis in 2002. Typically, countries experience a net capital outflow on the order of 5 percent of GDP in the first year of a sudden stop episode (figure 7.2). The swing in the net portfolio capital flow is on the order of 2 percent of GDP. In contrast, there is no discernible impact on net FDI flows.[16] By implication, net capital outflows consist mostly of other forms of capital, such as funds channeled through the banking system, commercial credits, and so forth (see also table 7.3).

Typically, countries experiencing a sudden stop also experience an improvement in the current account balance on the order of 4 percent of GDP (figure 7.3). Note that we are not looking here at "current account reversals," where a current account reversal is typically defined as an episode when there is a large reduction in the size of an existing current account

flows in particular, were especially prominent. It is this subperiod that is most relevant for thinking about the future. Calvo, Izquierdo, and Mejia (2004) also consider the period since 1990. They draw a sample of fifteen emerging market economies and also include seventeen developed economies in their sample. By using monthly data, they are able to increase the number of their observations. Note that to ensure that our findings are not dictated by the period considered, in the section on robustness checks we also present regressions covering a longer period.

16. Recall that in the preceding we addressed the question of whether it was appropriate to include changes in net FDI in our measure of sudden stops and argued that the answer is yes on the grounds that one should not prejudge the stability of different forms of imported capital. Figure 7.2 suggests that this procedure does not have strong implications for our findings.

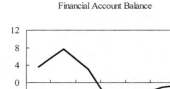

Financial Account Balance

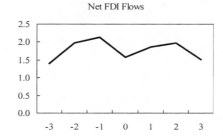

Net FDI Flows

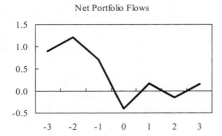

Net Portfolio Flows

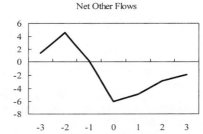

Net Other Flows

**Fig. 7.2   Magnitude and composition of financial flows (in percent of GDP):
A, Financial account balance; *B,* Net FDI flows; *C,* Net portfolio flows; *C,* Net
other flows**

Source: Authors' calculations.

Table 7.3   **Magnitude and composition of capital flows during and prior to sudden
stops (percentage of GDP)**

	Three year average prior to a sudden stop	During the first year of a sudden stop
Total net financial inflows	4.2	−4.6
	(6.8)	(4.8)
Net FDI	1.5	1.2
	(1.9)	(1.6)
Net portfolio flows	.62	−.21
	(1.5)	(1.46)
Net other capital flows of which:	2.1	−5.6
	(6.5)	(4.6)
Net government flows	.52	−1.2
	(2.8)	(3.5)
Net banks flows	.82	−2.0
	(3.6)	(3.0)
Net other flows	.92	−1.9
	(3.1)	(3.6)

Note: Standard deviations are given in parentheses.

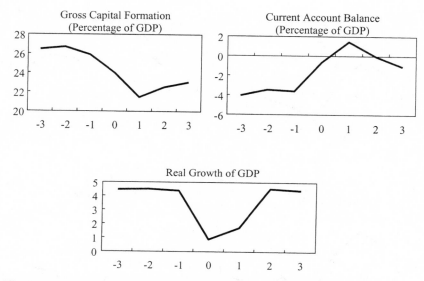

Fig. 7.3   Macroeconomic effects of sudden stops: *A*, Gross capital formation (percentage of GDP); *B*, Current account balance (percentage of GDP); *C*, Real growth of GDP

Source: Authors' calculations.

deficit; rather, we are summarizing the average behavior of the current account balance in our episodes of capital account reversal. The current account being the difference between savings and investment, the consequences are necessarily reflected in these variables. Figure 7.3 shows that the action is mainly on the investment side—that capital formation declines sharply. It follows that GDP growth is close to zero although it rebounds after one year. A statistical summary of these patterns is in table 7.4.

Sudden stops are also not the same as currency crises. For comparison, we use crisis dates from Kaminsky and Reinhart (1999), Berg and Patillo (1999), Frankel and Rose (1996), and Milesi-Ferretti and Razin (1998).[17] Only about one-third of the sudden stops in our sample are associated with contemporaneous currency crises (see the first panel of table 7.5). The picture is the same when we lag the currency crises (as in the second panel of table 7.5). While we have fewer observations for banking crises, a larger share of sudden stops (about a half) appears to coincide with banking crises (see third panel of table 7.5).[18]

17. For recent years we supplement these with the dates from Frankel and Wei (2004). These data are merged following the procedures in Gupta, Mishra, and Sahay (2003).
18. This suggests a complex relationship between sudden stops, currency crises, and banking crises—which we leave for another paper.

Table 7.4   **Real effects of sudden stops**

	Three year average prior to a sudden stop	During the first year of a sudden stop
Current account balance (% of GDP)	−4.2	−0.20
	(5.2)	(6.2)
Real growth	3.7	0.39
	(4.2)	(5.5)
Export growth	1.2	1.2
	(5.4)	(4.1)
Capital formation (% of GDP)	25.3	22.5
	(7.4)	(6.9)
Fixed capital formation (% of GDP)	23.8	20.8
	(6.6)	(6.5)

Note: Standard deviations are given in parentheses.

Table 7.5   **Sudden stops and banking and currency crises**

	No CC	CC	Total
A. Sudden stops and currency crises			
No SS	546	45	591
SS	23	10	33
Total	569	55	624

B. Sudden stops and lagged currency crises			
	No CC (Lag)	CC (Lag)	Total
No SS	544	47	591
SS	25	8	33
Total	569	55	624

C. Sudden stops and banking crises			
	No BC	BC	Total
No SS	430	133	563
SS	13	15	28
Total	443	148	591

D. Sudden stops and lagged banking crises			
	No BC (Lag)	BC (Lag)	Total
No SS	412	135	547
SS	20	8	28
Total	432	143	575

Note: SS = sudden stops; BC = banking crises; CC = currency crises.

7.4   IMF-Supported Programs

Information on IMF programs is drawn from a data base maintained by the Fund's Policy Development and Review Department. We have information on the years in which a program started and ended, whether it was precautionary from the outset or turned precautionary in the course of its operation, the value of the funds approved, and the amount used under the program. (Under precautionary programs, the IMF and the country agree on conditionality and monitoring, but the country declares its intention to not draw on resources from the Fund, though this declaration is not binding.) Slightly more than 12 percent of the Fund programs in our sample were precautionary from the start.[19]

Table 7.6 is a first look at the association of Fund programs and sudden stops. We differentiate between "new" programs initiated in either of the two years prior to the sudden stop, and "existing" programs in place in still earlier years.[20] In approximately a third of sudden stop cases, a new IMF program was negotiated in one of the two years immediately preceding the sudden stop, and in 20 percent of the sudden stop cases a program was already in place in still earlier years. Whereas the unconditional probability of a sudden stop in our sample is 5.5 percent, the probability of a sudden stop is about 1 percentage point lower if an IMF program was in place (whether the program was contracted in the two immediately preceding years or existed previously). This with and without IMF program differential is more pronounced if we limit ourselves to data for the period after 1989.

The raw data are consistent with the idea that whether a Fund program is in place matters for consumption, the trade balance, and the current account. Here the averages (in figure 7.4) refer to all programs, whether initiated in the two years immediately preceding the crisis or prior to that. Program countries indicated by the broken line receive access to credit from the IMF that enables them, not surprisingly, to run larger current account deficits (or smaller surpluses) and to maintain higher levels of consumption. The impact on the other variables is unclear. Program countries appear to enjoy more stable portfolio capital flows following the sudden stop,

19. We use the outstanding amount of the credit disbursed. The alternative is to use the "approved" lending amount, that is, the amount that a country can draw on. The approved amount has the advantage of measuring the prospective envelope of resources. However, the country must go through a review process to access those resources. In practice the results were more robust when we used the outstanding credit variable. The implication is that where programs were precautionary and no amounts were disbursed, IMF credit should take on a value of zero. This is the approach we use to testing separately for the influence of precautionary programs in what follows. Finally, because the outstanding credit also includes funds borrowed by a country under concessional credit programs, we check in our robustness analysis if dropping those countries (Bangladesh, Bolivia, Ghana, and Pakistan) makes a difference to our results (the answer is that it does not).

20. The rationale for this will become clear in the following.

Table 7.6   **IMF-supported programs and sudden stops: Number of sample observations**

	IMF Program		
Sudden Stop	No	Yes	Total
A. New IMF-supported programs and sudden stops (1980–2003)			
No	396	256	652
Yes	26	13	39
Total	422	269	691
B. New or existing IMF-supported programs and sudden stops (1980–2003)			
No	300	373	673
1	21	18	39
Total	321	391	712
C. New IMF-supported programs and sudden stops (1990–2003)			
No	261	148	409
Yes	18	6	24
Total	279	154	433
D. New or existing IMF-supported programs and sudden stops (1990–2003)			
No	185	224	409
Yes	15	9	24
Total	200	233	433

but investment is no stronger, and the recovery of growth is not obviously superior.

7.5 Multivariate Analysis

We now present a regression analysis of the association of IMF programs with sudden stops, conditioning on other determinants of the change in the financial accounts and instrumenting for the endogeneity of the program variable. This section presents the benchmark regressions with just the conditioning variables. The choice of conditioning factors is important as omitting an important country-specific or global determinant of the risk of sudden stops creates the danger that we may incorrectly impute this risk to the presence or absence of an IMF program.

We construct the dependent variable two ways: first, as a simple binary indicator equaling one in the first year of a sudden stop; second, as the financial account balance if and only if a sudden stop occurred as a way of capturing the severity of the event.[21] Regressions using the first dependent variable are estimated by probit (we report the marginal probabilities),

---

21. In addition to the financial account balance, we also look at the change in financial account balance in the year of the sudden stop as compared to the average of presudden stop years. The two measures are highly correlated, and the results are similar across the two measures.

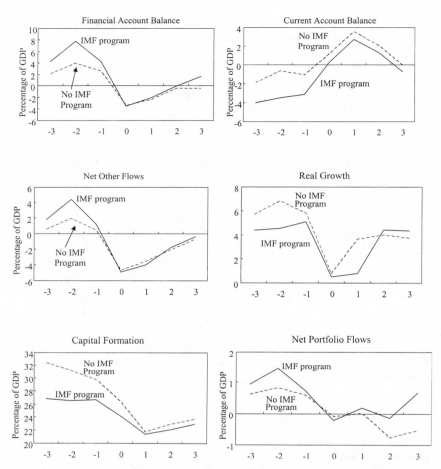

Fig. 7.4   IMF-supported programs and effects of sudden stops: *A,* **Financial account balance (as percentage of GDP);** *B,* **Current account balance (as percentage of GDP);** *C,* **Net other flows (as percentage of GDP);** *D,* **Real growth;** *E,* **Capital formation (as percentage of GDP);** *F,* **Net portfolio flows (as percentage of GDP)**
Source: Authors' calculations.

while regressions using the second dependent variable are estimated by Tobit. In principle, the Tobit regressions should make more complete use of the available information. Country fixed effects are used throughout. But because we also use global time-varying variables, time-period fixed effects are not included in the analysis of sudden stops.

The benchmark regressions for the determinants of sudden stops in table 7.7 suggest that global factors matter, as emphasized by, inter alia, Calvo

Table 7.7   **Determinants of sudden stops**

	Indicator for the first year of sudden stop				
Dependent variable	1990–2003				1984–2003
Treasury bill rate	0.007				
	[0.97]				
High yield spread	0.008	0.006	0.011	0.012*	0.013*
	[1.36]	[1.08]	[1.61]	[1.68]	[1.88]
Change in real oil prices	−0.001***	−0.001***	−0.001***	−0.002***	−0.001***
	[3.29]	[3.08]	[2.98]	[3.10]	[2.91]
GDP growth	0.011***	0.012***	0.008**	0.007**	0.0001
	[3.15]	[3.11]	[2.12]	[1.99]	[0.05]
Trade balance/GDP	−0.006*	−0.006	−0.006	−0.007*	−0.008***
	[1.73]	[1.63]	[1.51]	[1.74]	[2.70]
Debt servicing/Exports	0.001	0.002	0.002*	0.002*	0.001
	[1.64]	[1.64]	[1.81]	[1.89]	[0.99]
Domestic credit/GDP	0.002***	0.002**	0.002**	0.002**	0.002***
	[2.69]	[2.49]	[2.25]	[2.35]	[3.04]
Change in domestic credit/GDP	0.004***	0.004***	0.005**	0.005***	0.003**
	[2.99]	[2.91]	[2.47]	[2.72]	[2.05]
Debt/GDP	0.003***	0.003***			
	[2.87]	[2.83]			
Change in debt/GDP	0.001	0.001	0.001		
	[1.23]	[1.25]	[0.86]		
Country fixed effects	Yes	Yes	Yes	Yes	Yes
Time fixed effects	No	No	No	No	No
Pseudo R^2	0.26	0.26	0.21	0.20	0.17
No. of observations	227	227	227	227	332

Notes: Columns reporting probit results present marginal probabilities, based on the STATA command "dprobit." Robust *z* statistics are presented in brackets.

***Significant at the 1 percent level.
**Significant at the 5 percent level.
*Significant at the 10 percent level.

(2005), although the obvious suspects are not always prominent.[22] The U.S. high-yield spread (the spread over risk-free U.S. government bonds) is generally positive and on the margin of significance. The high-yield spread is often used as a measure of the global risk premium, with the implication that a rise in the risk premium can trigger reversals in capital flows to emerging markets. At its strongest, the coefficient estimate implies that

22. We do not claim that we provide here a definitive analysis of the role of global factors in sudden stops—nor do we attempt to do so, given that the available space is fully occupied by our analysis of the effects of IMF programs. But this deserves to be a high priority for future work on the feasibility of an insurance facility, insofar as the importance of common global factors is directly related to the capacity of the IMF as a financial pool to provide assistance to different countries experiencing sudden stops.

every 100 basis point increase in this spread increases the probability of a sudden stop by between 1 and 1.5 percentage points. In contrast, the U.S. treasury bill rate is not significant.[23] A somewhat surprising result is that an increase in the real price of oil appears to reduce the risk of a sudden stop—surprising because many emerging markets countries are net oil importers. However, not all emerging market economies are oil importers; indeed, some of those that have been historically most susceptible to sudden stops are substantial oil exporters. High oil prices tend to coincide with high commodity prices generally, and it is not surprising that emerging market countries, many of which are commodity exporters, enjoy larger and steadier capital inflows when commodity prices move in their favor. Moreover, a rise in oil prices also improves global liquidity because oil-rich nations run balance of payments surpluses that need to be reinvested, and this may work to the advantage of emerging market countries.

Among the country-specific factors, high and rising ratios of domestic credit to GDP are strongly associated with sudden stops, as emphasized in the credit-boom literature (IMF 2004). There is some suggestion that periods of rapid growth associated with credit expansions are likely to end in sudden stops.[24] Presumably, some of these high credit growth episodes are fuelled by the inflow of foreign capital, which can reverse abruptly. A high ratio of debt to GDP (in levels but not rate-of-change form) also increases is vulnerability. A smaller trade balance and a larger ratio of debt service to exports increase the likelihood of a sudden stop. The message seems to be that the combination of a domestic credit boom and the emergence of external payment risks heightens the risk of a sudden stop.

A variety of sensitivity analyses left these basic results unchanged.

- We dropped the country dummies, thus adding cross-section variation, without significantly altering our findings. However, it remains the case that most of the variation in the dependent variable is still explained by within-country variations rather than by cross-country differences.
- Results for the longer period 1984 to 2003, in the last column of table 7.7, continue to produce qualitatively similar findings.

23. That the usual measures of global financial stress are not prominent in their explanation of the incidence of sudden stops is not necessarily inconsistent with their bunching in time. It is possible that measures of "common vulnerability" may attract the attention of international investors, causing them to retreat from a broad range of countries (see Mody and Taylor 2003). As such, country factors remain important in understanding the frequency of sudden stops. A previous study showing that the correlation between changes in U.S. Treasury yields and capital flows to emerging markets was not always stable (that the correlation depended on the reason behind the change in U.S. Treasury yields) is Eichengreen and Mody (1998).

24. As in Calvo, Izquierdo, and Mejia (2004), we also included a measure of dollarization. Confirming their finding, dollarization is associated with a higher probability of a sudden stop. However, our other findings do not change, and we do not include dollarization in the regressions to preserve the sample size.

- We relaxed our stringent criteria and mechanical procedures for identifying sudden stop episodes, adding additional borderline cases such
as Russia and Brazil at the end of the 1990s. Again, the results carried
over.[25]
- Using the Reinhart-Rogoff classification of exchange rate regimes, we
added dummy variables for pegged rates and regimes of limited flexibility (managed- and freely-floating regimes are the omitted alternative).[26] We find (in table 7.8) that the more rigid the regime, the greater
the likelihood of a sudden stop.[27] This negative association of sudden
stops with exchange rate flexibility is consistent with the literature in
which it is argued that currency flexibility encourages creditors and
debtors to more fully internalize the risks of foreign lending and borrowing (see, e.g., Goldstein 1998). This is also the same result as in Edwards (2005). While the vector of exchange rate regime variables is not
significant here, it turns out to be significant in some of the additional
specifications below.[28]
- Because exchange rate regime and capital account regime choices are
related, we also considered the effects of financial opening. We use a
one-period lag of the Mody and Murshid (2005) measure of financial
integration.[29] The point estimate (again in table 7.8) suggests that
countries that are more deeply integrated with global financial markets are less vulnerable to sudden stops, as if countries better integrated into international financial markets have stronger institutions.
Again, this is the same result as in Edwards (2005). And although this
variable is also not significant here, it turns out to be significant in
some of the further specifications in the following.

7.6 IMF Programs and Sudden Stops

Table 7.9 adds IMF programs. Recall that we distinguish "existing" programs (in place at least two years prior to the occurrence of the sudden stop)
from "new" programs negotiated in the immediately preceding two years.
The coefficient on preexisting programs is arguably less contaminated by
simultaneity (which should in any case bias the coefficient in a positive direction, the opposite of the sign we find). Preexisting programs, as a mea-

---

25. Similarly, all the results reported in the following continue to obtain when we add these
borderline cases to our list of sudden stop episodes.
26. See Reinhart and Rogoff (2004). In principle, it captures the de facto operative regime.
27. Although the effect is not statistically significant, it is found to be significant in the later
tables.
28. Note, however, that the new IMF classification of exchange rates produces more ambiguous results.
29. The financial integration index is based on four measures of the intensity of capital controls that are published in the IMF's annual *Report on Exchange Arrangements and Exchange
Restrictions.*

Table 7.8   **Financial mobility, exchange rate regimes, and sudden stops**

Dependent variable	Indicator for first year of sudden stop			
High yield spread	0.012*	0.013*	0.011	0.012*
	[1.84]	[1.91]	[1.61]	[1.73]
Change in real oil prices	−0.002***	−0.002***	−0.002***	−0.002***
	[3.11]	[3.08]	[3.17]	[3.19]
GDP growth	0.007**	0.007**	0.007*	0.007**
	[2.16]	[2.21]	[1.90]	[2.02]
Trade balance/GDP	−0.006	−0.007*	−0.007*	−0.008**
	[1.47]	[1.66]	[1.76]	[2.08]
Debt servicing/Exports	0.002**	0.002**	0.002**	0.002**
	[2.03]	[2.01]	[2.05]	[2.09]
Domestic credit/GDP	0.003**	0.002**	0.002**	0.002**
	[2.41]	[2.28]	[2.35]	[2.41]
Change in domestic credit/GDP	0.005***	0.005***	0.005***	0.005***
	[2.68]	[2.70]	[2.75]	[2.82]
Exchange rate regime: Pegged	0.028	0.033		
	[0.54]	[0.61]		
Exchange rate regime: Limited flexibility	0.03	0.03		
	[0.69]	[0.53]		
Exchange rate regime: Pegged (IMF)			−0.03	−0.04
			[1.15]	[1.27]
Exchange rate regime: Limited flexibility (IMF)			0.02	0.02
			[0.52]	[0.57]
Financial mobility		−0.01		−0.02
		[0.75]		[1.06]
Country fixed effects	Yes	Yes	Yes	Yes
Time fixed effects	No	No	No	No
Pseudo R^2	0.21	0.21	0.21	0.21
No. of observations	227	227	227	227

Note: See table 7.7 notes.
***Significant at the 1 percent level.
**Significant at the 5 percent level.
*Significant at the 10 percent level.

sure of the IMF's ongoing commitment to the country, may also have a stronger signaling effect. In practice, we find that both preexisting and new programs negatively affect the probability of a sudden stop. In the present specification, the coefficient on new programs is larger in absolute value, although it does not differ significantly from that on existing programs.[30]

The insurance analogy is sometimes taken as an argument for exceptional access—as justifying a credit line sufficiently large to reassure private investors. This suggests distinguishing effects by the size of the program.

30. The size of the coefficients differs more noticeably when we correct for endogeneity, as suggested by the observation that preexisting programs should be less contaminated by this bias (see the following).

Table 7.9   **IMF program and probability of sudden stops (probit estimates)**

Dependent variable	Indicator for first year of sudden stop				
High yield spread	0.011*	0.011**	0.011*	0.012**	0.006
	[1.81]	[1.98]	[1.94]	[2.04]	[1.03]
Change in real oil prices	−0.001***	−0.001***	−0.001***	−0.001***	−0.001***
	[3.15]	[3.19]	[3.18]	[3.10]	[3.69]
GDP growth	0.006*	0.007**	0.007*	0.007**	0.009***
	[1.73]	[2.00]	[1.93]	[2.11]	[2.66]
Trade balance/GDP	−0.005	−0.002	−0.002	−0.003	−0.003
	[1.37]	[0.63]	[0.62]	[0.96]	[0.99]
Debt servicing/Exports	0.002**	0.002***	0.002***	0.002**	0.001
	[2.29]	[2.69]	[2.70]	[2.46]	[1.49]
Domestic credit/GDP	0.002***	0.003***	0.003***	0.003***	0.002***
	[2.66]	[3.08]	[3.06]	[3.02]	[2.95]
Change in domestic credit/GDP	0.004***	0.003**	0.003**	0.004***	0.004***
	[2.63]	[2.53]	[2.49]	[2.59]	[3.18]
Exchange rate regime: Pegged	0.067	0.07	0.071	0.069	0.022
	[1.14]	[1.23]	[1.24]	[1.20]	[0.53]
Exchange rate regime: Limited flexibility	0.007	−0.006	−0.005	−0.006	−0.003
	[0.20]	[0.20]	[0.16]	[0.19]	[0.11]
Financial mobility	−0.018	−0.017	−0.016	−0.017	−0.016
	[1.45]	[1.59]	[1.40]	[1.52]	[1.51]
Existing IMF program	−0.054***	−0.046**	−0.046**	−0.049**	−0.043**
	[2.98]	[2.57]	[2.56]	[2.56]	[2.47]
New IMF program	−0.053***	−0.042*	−0.041	−0.047*	−0.040
	[1.99]	[1.73]	[1.63]	[1.81]	[1.64]
New program · Fundamentals					0.046**
					[2.32]
Precautionary IMF program	−0.014		−0.01		
	[0.51]		[0.38]		
IMF credit/GDP		−0.008*	−0.008*		
		[1.66]	[1.66]		
IMF credit/Short-term debt				−.0001	−.0001
				[0.63]	[0.84]
Country fixed effects	Yes	Yes	Yes	Yes	Yes
Time fixed effects	No	No	No	No	No
Pseudo R^2	0.26	0.28	0.28	0.27	0.30
No. of observations	227	217	217	217	217

Note: See table 7.7 notes.

***Significant at the 1 percent level.

**Significant at the 5 percent level.

*Significant at the 10 percent level.

We do so in two ways, scaling programs by short-term external debt and GDP. Both ratios are lagged by one period. International Monetary Fund credit as a share of GDP is negative and significant at conventional confidence levels, but not so IMF credit scaled by short-term debt.

Next we test for whether IMF programs have a more powerful preemptive effect in countries with strong fundamentals, as suggested by the insurance analogy. We construct the first principal component of the vector of variables capturing country policies and conditions included in table 7.9.[31] We normalize the resulting variable so that it has zero mean and so that a positive value indicates worsening fundamentals. We then interact the resulting index of fundamentals with the new IMF program variable. The positive and significant coefficient on the interaction term in table 7.9 suggests that as the strength of domestic fundamentals declines, the effectiveness of IMF programs in reducing the likelihood of a sudden stop diminishes.[32]

A key question is whether the negative association of programs and sudden stops reflects causality running from the latter to the former. Actually, it is not clear that endogeneity is a serious problem; one can argue that reverse causality should bias the coefficient toward zero because a sudden stop will increase the likelihood of a Fund program and thus produce a positive relationship, whereas we find a negative coefficient.[33] Be that as it may, the appropriate treatment is instrumental variables. These authors argue that decision making in the Fund is influenced by the organization's principal shareholders, above all the United States. They model the likelihood of a program as a function not just of country characteristics but also of its links with the United States.[34] To capture the latter they include U.S. aid as a percentage of total foreign aid received by the country and the share of votes in the United Nations (UN) General Assembly in which the country voted the same way as the United States, both lagged.[35] In our sample, U.S.

31. We use high-yield spreads, oil prices, real GDP growth, the trade balance-GDP ratio, the debt service-export ratio, and the domestic credit measure in calculating principal components. The first principal component captures 21 percent of the variation in the underlying series. In theory it would be possible to interact the IMF program dummy with each of the variables used to represent fundamentals (or to include additional principal components beyond the first), but this creates problems of multicollinearity and complicates interpretation. We could also construct our own linear combination of the variables representing fundamentals, but it seems preferable to let this simple statistical methodology do so for us.

32. This is a congenial finding for those who advance the insurance analogy for IMF programs. In earlier work analyzing the catalytic effect of the IMF on capital flows, we find similar evidence of threshold effects, especially for access to bond markets (Mody and Saravia 2003; Eichengreen, Kletzer, and Mody 2006). In particular, countries in an intermediate state of vulnerability seemed to benefit from improved market access, while others did not.

33. We provide some evidence on this in the following.

34. Dreher and Jensen (2003) take a similar empirical approach but take as their dependent variable the number of conditions attached to a program. Oatley and Yackee (2004) consider instead the political determinants of the size of IMF loans.

35. The authors also use past participation in Fund programs as an instrument. The problem with using lags of the endogenous variable as an instrument is, of course, that they may be picking up omitted country characteristics that are slow to change and durably associated with financial problems; see Mody and Stone (2005). Alternatively, we can follow Celasun and Ramcharan (2005) by using the share of G3 exports going to each subject country as a measure of the importance the principal shareholders may attach to extending assistance through the Fund. However this variable turns out to be a poor instrument for the incidence of the

aid enters the first-stage regression positively, as predicted, and is significantly different from zero.[36] United Nations voting patterns, in contrast, do not exhibit the expected sign.[37] Given the counterintuitive sign on this variable, we rely on the specification in the first column of table 7.10, which excludes UN voting patterns, for purposes of instrumentation.[38]

Table 7.11 shows the second-stage estimates. The presence of a new IMF program continues to negatively influence the probability of a sudden stop. Both the statistical significance and absolute value of the coefficient are greater than before. This is to be expected: if susceptibility to a sudden stop increases the likelihood of an IMF program, then reverse causality will bias the coefficient in a positive direction; correcting for simultaneity thus yields a more significant negative coefficient whose absolute value is larger. Preexisting programs are significant as well. All this is consistent with the hypothesis that IMF programs provide valuable insurance against sudden stops.

Given the strong policy implications of these findings, we considered a number of further robustness checks.

- When we consider the longer period starting in 1984, as in the last column of table 7.11, the strength of preexisting programs remains. In contrast, the coefficient on new programs becomes less significant. It would thus appear that the signaling effect of an ongoing IMF commitment to the country is particularly important in the more recent period. The interaction between new programs and fundamentals remains unchanged even in the longer period, pointing to continued importance of country fundamentals in determining the influence of IMF programs.

IMF program. The coefficient of this variable is consistently negative and significant in the first stage regressions of IMF programs. One interpretation is that it is a proxy for the size of the country, and the larger countries are probably less susceptible to problems necessitating an IMF program.

36. Use of voting in the UN General Assembly has been criticized in the political science literature for being dominated by nonconsequential votes and thus containing relatively little information on political affinity. This is one interpretation of what we find in the first-stage regressions.

37. Note that we include also a number of addition global and country-specific variables that may influence the decision to approach the Fund (and the Fund's decision to extend assistance). While these variables do not provide identification in the second stage (they do not plausibly satisfy the exclusion criterion for an instrumental variable), they reassure us that any significance we impute to the U.S. aid in the first stage is really attributable to these other characteristics.

38. Of interest also in the determinants of IMF programs are the similarities and contrasts with the determinants of sudden stops. External debt and debt service indicators work in the same way (though with differing strengths): more debt and debt service increase the likelihood of both IMF programs and of sudden stops. In contrast, domestic growth based on high and growing levels of credit are associated with a lower likelihood of IMF programs. Thus, countries experiencing such exuberant growth are unlikely to contract with the IMF and remain susceptible to sudden stops.

Table 7.10   **Determinants of IMF programs**

Dependent variable	New IMF program in T-1 or T-2					
U.S. aid	0.058***	0.078***	0.072***	0.079***	0.071***	0.080***
	[3.79]	[3.09]	[3.24]	[3.15]	[3.16]	[3.15]
Real growth	−0.011	−0.027**	−0.018*	−0.027**	−0.018*	−0.028**
	[1.53]	[2.56]	[1.76]	[2.51]	[1.68]	[2.47]
Trade balance/GDP	0.024***	0.047***	0.038***	0.046***	0.042***	0.046***
	[3.49]	[3.95]	[3.15]	[3.69]	[3.52]	[3.69]
Debt servicing/Exports	0.008***	0.009**	0.008**	0.009**	0.009**	0.009**
	[2.95]	[2.36]	[2.11]	[2.37]	[2.06]	[2.23]
Domestic credit/GDP	−0.004*	−0.006*	−0.006	−0.006*	−0.005	−0.006*
	[1.83]	[1.68]	[1.62]	[1.71]	[1.54]	[1.74]
Change in domestic credit/GDP	−0.007*	−0.006	−0.008	−0.007	−0.007	−0.007
	[1.79]	[1.23]	[1.38]	[1.35]	[1.25]	[1.37]
Debt/GDP	0.007***	0.009***	0.01***	0.01***	0.01***	0.01***
	[3.84]	[3.49]	[3.73]	[3.70]	[3.55]	[3.64]
Change in debt	0.002	0.007*	0.009**	0.008*	0.009**	0.008
	[0.57]	[1.76]	[2.29]	[1.88]	[2.14]	[1.89]
Reserves/Imports	0.001	−0.001	0.001	0.001	0.001	0.0003
	[0.63]	[0.10]	[0.53]	[0.19]	[0.21]	[0.13]
Short-term Debt/Reserves	−0.001***	−0.001***	−0.001***	−0.001***	−0.001***	−0.001***
	[2.68]	[2.76]	[2.63]	[2.82]	[2.58]	[2.77]
Exchange rate regime: Pegged	0.28***	0.45**	0.37*	0.46**	0.40**	0.47**
	[2.69]	[2.29]	[1.86]	[2.21]	[2.29]	[2.27]
Exchange rate regime: Limited flexibility	−0.006	−0.035	−0.103	−0.071	−0.052	−0.067
	[0.08]	[0.27]	[0.75]	[0.48]	[0.41]	[0.46]
UN voting		−0.045***		−0.046***		−0.046***
		[2.92]		[3.00]		[2.95]
Exposure of U.S. banks					−0.004	−0.011
					[0.18]	[0.51]
Exports by G3 countries			0.017	0.076		0.067
			[0.14]	[0.60]		[0.53]
Country fixed effects	Yes	Yes	Yes	Yes	Yes	Yes
Time fixed effects	Yes	Yes	Yes	Yes	Yes	Yes
Pseudo R^2	0.27	0.36	0.32	0.37	0.26	0.37
No. of observations	379	284	302	283	303	283

Note: See table 7.7 notes.
***Significant at the 1 percent level.
**Significant at the 5 percent level.
*Significant at the 10 percent level.

- As in the preceding, we analyzed whether our results held up when we relaxed the stringent criteria used to identify sudden stops. First, we added Brazil and Russia in 1999, two cases that many would regard as sudden stops but which are not picked up by our criteria. Second, we dropped Bangladesh, Bolivia, Ghana, and Pakistan, which drew on the Fund's concessional financing facilities, indicating that their

Table 7.11   Determinants of sudden stops: Dealing with the endogeneity of programs

Dependent variable	Indicator for first year of sudden stop					
	1990–2003			1984–2003		
High yield spread	0.001 [0.24]	-0.003 [0.83]	-0.004 [0.95]	-0.0002 [0.28]	-0.001 [0.95]	0.007 [1.47]
Change in real oil prices	-0.001*** [3.17]	-0.001*** [3.90]	-0.001*** [3.98]	-0.0002*** [3.14]	-0.0002*** [3.68]	-0.001*** [3.13]
GDP growth	0.009** [2.40]	0.011*** [3.11]	0.009*** [2.98]	0.002*** [2.84]	0.002*** [3.00]	0.007** [2.20]
Trade balance/GDP	-0.001 [0.37]	-0.002 [0.65]	-0.002 [0.79]	0.0004 [0.81]	0.0002 [0.40]	-0.003 [1.36]
Debt servicing/Exports	0.002** [2.06]	0.001 [1.08]	0.001 [1.18]	0.001*** [3.49]	0.0003*** [2.71]	0.001 [0.70]
Domestic credit/GDP	0.001* [1.78]	0.001 [1.47]	.00005 [1.04]	0.0003** [2.24]	0.0002** [1.99]	0.001** [2.45]
Change in domestic credit/GDP	0.003*** [2.51]	0.003*** [2.90]	0.002*** [2.93]	0.0004** [2.12]	0.0003** [2.26]	0.003** [2.55]
Debt/GDP	0.003*** [2.97]	0.002*** [2.97]	0.002*** [3.24]	0.001*** [4.26]	0.001*** [4.27]	0.001* [1.92]
Change in debt/GDP	0.001 [1.57]	0.001 [1.42]	0.001 [1.61]	0.0002** [2.14]	0.0002** [2.23]	0.001 [1.63]
Exchange rate regime: Pegged	0.118* [1.65]	0.097 [1.52]	0.115* [1.82]	0.112** [2.48]	0.090** [2.37]	0.185** [2.22]
Exchange rate regime: Limited flexibility	0.016 [0.59]	0.007 [0.35]	0.003 [0.16]	0.001 [0.30]	0.001 [0.15]	-0.007 [0.43]
Financial mobility			-0.007 [1.15]	-0.001 [1.30]	-0.001 [1.50]	-0.0002 [0.02]

(continued)

Table 7.11   (continued)

| Dependent variable | Indicator for first year of sudden stop | | | | | |
	1990–2003					1984–2003
Existing IMF program	−0.027** [2.08]	−0.023** [2.10]	−0.021** [2.20]	−0.004* [1.75]	−0.003* [1.83]	−0.025* [1.80]
New IMF program, instrumented	−0.011* [1.81]	−0.092* [1.90]	−0.096*** [1.99]	−0.030*** [3.04]	−0.026*** [3.10]	−0.041 [0.90]
Fundamentals · Program, instrumented		0.051** [2.36]	0.049** [2.31]		0.006* [1.96]	0.048** [2.17]
Precautionary IMF program			−0.014 [1.21]			
IMF credit/GDP				−0.004*** [2.70]	−0.003*** [2.69]	0.001 [0.33]
Country fixed effects	Yes	Yes	Yes	Yes	Yes	Yes
Time fixed effects	No	No	No	No	No	No
Pseudo R^2	0.30	0.33	0.34	0.42	0.43	0.25
No. of observations	227	227	227	217	217	282

Notes: Columns reporting probit results present marginal probabilities, based on the STATA command "dprobit." Robust z statistics are presented in brackets. Probability of IMF program is estimated from the first column of table 7.10. The last column includes 1980s in the sample.

***Significant at the 1 percent level.

**Significant at the 5 percent level.

*Significant at the 10 percent level.

international capital market linkages were qualitatively different from those of the other country samples. The results remained the same.[39]

- We considered alternative instrumentation strategies. For example, following Oatley and Yackee (2004), we constructed a measure of country indebtedness to U.S. banks as a further instrument. Adding it has relatively little impact on the results (perhaps because this variable turns out to be a relatively weak instrument in this context).

7.7   Extensions

We also asked whether IMF programs reduce the intensity (as opposed to the frequency) of sudden stops. For this purpose we constructed our dependent variable as the financial account outflow if and only if a sudden stop occurs. Regressions using this dependent variable are estimated by tobit.

The results, in table 7.12, are similar to the earlier probit estimates, though with some noteworthy differences. There is stronger evidence for an increase in high-yield spreads, reflecting a rise in risk aversion, to be associated with a reduction in capital inflows. As before, a rise in oil prices works in the opposite direction. Among country factors, a high credit-to-GDP ratio and rapid credit growth are associated with larger capital outflows, and a more open capital account regime appears to reduce the intensity of a sudden stop.[40] Compared to new programs, preexisting programs seem to have a clearer effect in reducing the intensity of capital outflows; also while new programs and their interaction with fundamentals work in the same way as before, the statistical significance is weaker. Note that when new programs are instrumented, the size of the coefficient again becomes noticeably, even implausibly, large in absolute-value terms. Finally, when all the relevant IMF variables are included, as in the last two columns of table 7.12, the precision of the estimates declines.

We also considered the impact of IMF programs on growth around the time of sudden stops. The raw data in the second panel of table 7.13 suggest the recessionary impact of sudden stops in countries both with and without Fund programs. Growth is even slower following sudden stops in those cases where IMF programs are present. But the financial balance (in the first panel of table 7.13) is also worse when a Fund program is present—suggesting, plausibly, that programs are put in place in cases where economic circumstances are worse—reminds us that other things are not in fact equal, and the slower growth cannot be attributed to IMF programs without further investigation.

39. In fact, dropping the country with concessional financing strengths the results, pointing especially to the risks to the others of pegging exchange rates and indicating greater value to a more open capital account (see appendix A, 7A.1 and 7A.2).
40. Other conditioning variables are less significant, though virtually always of the same sign as in the probit estimates.

Table 7.12   **IMF programs and intensity of sudden stops**

Dependent variable	Financial account outflow if a sudden stop occurred				
High yield spread	1.38**	1.35**	0.49	1.23*	0.73
	[2.17]	[2.12]	[0.73]	[1.74]	[1.00]
Change in real oil prices	−0.11*	−0.11*	−0.16**	−0.12*	−0.15**
	[1.86]	[1.87]	[2.32]	[1.93]	[2.20]
GDP growth	0.61	0.58	0.97*	0.67	1.04*
	[1.30]	[1.24]	[1.72]	[1.26]	[1.71]
Trade balance/GDP	−0.35	−0.35	−0.32	`0.20	0.17
	[0.89]	[0.88]	[0.74]	[0.41]	[0.34]
Debt servicing/Exports	0.23**	0.23**	0.16	0.38**	0.29*
	[2.16]	[2.19]	[1.21]	[2.50]	[1.80]
Domestic credit/GDP	0.20*	0.19*	0.09	0.21*	0.16
	[1.81]	[1.79]	[0.74]	[1.67]	[1.23]
Change in domestic credit/GDP	0.53***	0.52***	0.59***	0.51***	0.58***
	[3.35]	[3.30]	[3.41]	[3.08]	[3.27]
Exchange rate regime: Pegged	1.94	1.96	3.16	6.28	5.69
	[0.37]	[0.38]	[0.50]	[1.00]	[0.88]
Exchange rate regime: Limited flexibility	2.47	2.56	2.90	3.06	3.34
	[0.54]	[0.56]	[0.63]	[0.59]	[0.67]
Financial mobility	−2.73*	−2.57*	−3.23**	−3.48**	−3.62**
	[1.85]	[1.70]	[1.99]	[2.06]	[2.09]
Existing IMF program	−7.98**	−7.79**	−5.44	−6.48	−5.04
	[2.03]	[1.99]	[1.62]	[1.54]	[1.46]
New IMF program	−4.75	−4.54			
	[1.60]	[1.52]			
New IMF program, instrumented			−16.94	−12.60	−18.18
			[1.56]	[1.16]	[1.58]
Fundamentals · Program, instrumented			7.80*		6.01
			[1.69]		[1.27]
Precautionary IMF program		−2.32			
		[0.37]			
IMF credit/GDP				−1.23	−1.35
				[1.30]	[1.43]
Country fixed effects	Yes	Yes	Yes	Yes	Yes
Time fixed effects	No	No	No	No	No
Pseudo R^2	0.18	0.18	0.19	0.20	0.21
No. of observations	227	227	227	217	217

Note: These estimations are based on the "tobit" procedure, with a cut-off at zero outflows.
***Significant at the 1 percent level.
**Significant at the 5 percent level.
*Significant at the 10 percent level.

It turns out to be difficult to draw firm conclusions about the impact on output of IMF programs in these episodes. As a first cut, we regressed annual growth (again in a country panel covering the period 1990–2003) on a vector of controls, the presence or absence of a sudden stop, a dummy variable for the presence of a Fund program, and the interaction of the sudden

Table 7.13   **Unconditional growth effects**

	Sudden Stop		
Program	No	Yes	Total
Financial account balance (% of GDP)			
No	3.05	−2.73	2.46
Yes	2.23	−6.56	1.61
Total	2.7	−4.01	2.1
Real growth			
No	4.18	0.68	3.82
Yes	2.54	−2.5	2.19
Total	3.48	−0.38	3.14

stop and the presence of a program (table 7.14). In the benchmark regression in the first column, per capita income in the previous year enters negatively and significantly, suggesting some short-term mean reversion. More rapid U.S. growth is conducive to more rapid recovery in emerging market countries. A sudden stop leads to slower growth, as expected. The dummy for the presence of a Fund program is negative and significant, with two alternative interpretations: the strict conditionality generally associated with programs leads to slower growth in the short run or that programs are associated with weak fundamentals not included in the regression.

Importantly for present purposes, the interaction between the IMF programs and sudden stops is not significant. In other words, even if Fund programs reduce the incidence of sudden stops, they do not obviously shape their impact on growth in one direction or the other. We find the same basic results on adding additional financial controls in columns (2) and (3) of table 7.14.

We know from earlier sections that countries with IMF programs are not randomly selected from the larger population. Before drawing conclusions about their impact on growth, we therefore need to control not just for observed differences between program and nonprogram countries but also for unobserved heterogeneity. In columns (4) to (5) we use the two-stage Heckman procedure, adding as an additional regressor the Inverse Mills ratio, denoted Lambda, derived from the first-stage regression of the determinants of IMF programs (in the first column of table 7.10).[41] Sudden stops continue to exert a negative impact on growth (significant in column [4], insignificant in column [5], where the financial balance is introduced directly). IMF programs now have a positive rather than a negative impact

41. Dropping the interaction term allows us to estimate the same relationship using STATA's more efficient Heckman procedure (where the selection and growth equations are estimated simultaneously). In the present instance, results using the two estimation procedures are virtually indistinguishable.

Table 7.14   Growth regressions: Effects of sudden stops and IMF programs

	GDP growth				
Dependent variable	(1)	(2)	(3)	(4)	(5)
GDP growth, lagged	0.003***	0.002**	0.001	0.002**	0.001*
	[4.88]	[2.60]	[1.62]	[2.57]	[1.93]
Per capita income, lagged	−0.064***	−0.066***	−0.057***	−0.062***	−0.050***
	[4.90]	[3.90]	[3.48]	[3.64]	[3.02]
Sudden stop	−0.041***	−0.027***	−0.015	−0.025***	−0.011
	[3.88]	[2.94]	[1.63]	[2.72]	[1.22]
IMF program	−0.013**	−0.009*	−0.010**	0.007	0.016
	[2.31]	[1.88]	[2.10]	[0.55]	[1.24]
Sudden stop · IMF program	0.002	−0.004	0.003	−0.006	0.002
	[0.09]	[0.25]	[0.20]	[0.40]	[0.11]
Debt/GDP		−0.001***	−0.001***	−0.001***	−0.001***
		[4.18]	[2.75]	[4.56]	[3.28]
Change in debt/GDP		−0.001***	−0.001***	−0.002***	−0.001***
		[7.78]	[6.37]	[8.51]	[7.27]
Debt service/Exports		0.0001	−0.0002	−0.0001	−0.0003
		[0.81]	[0.12]	[0.29]	[1.28]
Financial balance/GDP			0.002***		0.003***
			[4.14]		[4.42]
Lambda				−0.01	−0.016**
				[1.28]	[2.11]
Country fixed effects	Yes	Yes	Yes	Yes	Yes
Time fixed effects	Yes	Yes	Yes	Yes	Yes
No. of observations	238	230	230	227	227
No. of countries	17	17	17	17	17
R^2	0.32	0.51	0.55	0.54	0.58

Notes: Robust t-statistics are presented in brackets. Columns (4) and (5) were estimated to allow for the possibility of selection bias on account of countries selecting themselves into IMF programs because they expect slow growth. The two-step "heckman" procedure was used. A first-stage selection equation estimated the probability of an IMF program (using the specification in table 7.10, column 1) and the estimated inverse-Mills ratio was added to the determinants of growth.
***Significant at the 1 percent level.
**Significant at the 5 percent level.
*Significant at the 10 percent level.

on growth (though with weak statistical significance). The change in sign is consistent with the negative coefficient on the Inverse Mills ratio, which implies that unobserved country-specific factors that raise the likelihood of an IMF program also reduce the country's growth rate. But the t-statistics leave us reluctant to push any conclusion about this too far. The key finding remains: the interaction of sudden stops and IMF programs is still indistinguishable from zero. Thus, while the presence of a program may reduce the incidence of sudden stops, there is no evidence that programs affect short-term output losses, one way or the other, when sudden stops do occur.

7.8 Conclusions and Implications

In this paper we have presented a first attempt to identify the impact of IMF programs on sudden stops. The literature on self-fulfilling crises and the insurance motive for IMF lending suggests that Fund programs could reduce the incidence of these episodes characterized by disruptive capital-flow reversals. In contrast, a literature critical of IMF programs suggests that such programs, especially those negotiated in the Asian crisis, have tended to be too small or too late and too laden with burdensome economic and political conditions to restore confidence.[42]

Much of the evidence invoked in this debate is, however, anecdotal. A more systematic analysis such as that we have sought to provide here is clearly needed. Our results are broadly consistent with the notion that IMF programs have some effect in reducing the incidence of sudden stops. The evidence that negotiation of a Fund program in immediately prior years reduces the likelihood of a sudden stop is relatively robust. As economic logic suggests, this finding is, if anything, strengthened when we correct for endogeneity. The results further suggest that this effect operates more powerfully in countries with strong fundamentals, consistent with the insurance argument.

One should be cautious with these findings. The literature on the effects of IMF programs is notorious for its methodological limitations. Countries approaching the Fund differ systematically from other countries, creating problems of endogeneity and selectivity. In this paper we have described some instrumental-variables strategies and statistical adjustments for these problems. However, these approaches have limitations, and many of the same critiques levied against the related literature apply to the results reported here. These are more reasons for regarding the results as a first cut and not a definitive guide to policy.

Even if one accepts that there is evidence that IMF programs reduce the incidence and virulence of sudden stops, this leaves open the question of whether and how the institution's lending practices should be adapted. One view would be that such findings strengthen the case for a generously en-

---

42. Experience during the Asian crisis does not, of course, negate our findings on the insurance value of IMF programs, as when we limit the sample to the 1990s and after we find that preexisting programs were most effective, and in fact programs were not already in place in the countries with the most severe crises. Thus, in the case of Thailand, it can be argued that the problem was the absence of a program prior to the sudden stop—and that by the time an arrangement was negotiated, things had gotten out of hand. In contrast, the Philippines, which did have a program in place, experienced a milder sudden stop.

dowed, quick disbursing, automatic facility for which countries with strong policies would presumably be prequalified. A different view would be that prequalification is impractical and automaticity is infeasible but that the Fund can still streamline and enhance access to its resources for countries with strong fundamentals.[43] The results in this paper will not resolve this debate, but they will be more grist for the mill.

Appendix A
Sudden Stop Dates and Sensitivity of Results to Sudden Stop Sample

As described in the main text, a sudden stop is defined as occurring both when the financial balance is negative, that is there is a capital outflow, and there is a sharp increase in the capital outflow, measured by an increase equal to at least one standard deviation from the country's own history. These criteria lead to the identification of sudden stops listed in table 7A.1.

As also discussed in the text, there remain ambiguities and close calls in identifying a sudden stop. Some, for example, would argue that Brazil experienced a sudden stop in 1999. This would be true if attention was focused only on non-FDI flows. However, FDI inflows partially compensated in that year for non-FDI outflows. Another instance widely viewed as a sudden stop is Russia in 1999, following the events in the final quarter of 1998. Because we have only a short time series on Russia, the measured standard deviation of the financial balance is not very informative. Because these events are plausible candidates for sudden stops, we examined if our results were robust to their being so identified. The first column in table 7A.2 shows that the results remain largely unchanged. The conditioning variables retain their direction of influence and statistical strength. A pegged exchange rate regime is clearly associated with a higher probability of a sudden stop than are more flexible regimes. All the IMF variables are, in this sample, solidly significant.

There is also a concern that sudden stop measured by our procedure may not always reflect the same pressures. Specifically, countries differ in the degree to which they have contact with international financial markets and, hence, in the degree to which they are subject to sharp changes in market sentiment. One criterion for differentiating countries in this dimension is the degree to which they have access to concessional official finance. Pre-

---

43. Thus, the IMF's then managing director suggested in a February 9, 2006, speech (de Rato 2006) "an instrument carrying relatively high access, available in a single purchase if a capital account crisis occurred, subject to a Fund-supported program being in place and on track."

Table 7A.1   **Countries in the sample and sudden stop dates**

Country	Year
Argentina	1989
Bangladesh	1998
Bolivia	1983
Brazil	1983
Chile	1983
Colombia	1991
Costa Rica	1982
Czech Republic	1997
Egypt, Arab Republic of	2002
Ghana	2002
Hungary	1990
Indonesia	1997
Korea, Republic of	1986
Malaysia	1998
Mauritius	1985
Mexico	1983
Pakistan	1998
Peru	1983
The Philippines	1998
Poland	1990
South Africa	1985
Thailand	1997
Turkey	1994
Uruguay	2002

Note: China, El Salvador, Jordan, Jamaica, and India were included in the sample but they did not have a sudden stop.

sumably, countries that can borrow from the IMF on a concessional basis have less sustained interactions with financial markets than countries that do not so borrow. Four instances of sudden stop are associated with countries that borrowed on concessional terms: Bangladesh (1998), Bolivia (1983), Ghana (2002), and Pakistan (1998). Also, it is possible that the Ghana's sudden stop is misidentified to the extent that capital inflows were recorded as an unusual change in errors and omissions. The second column in table 7A.2 reports the results when these four sudden stops are dropped. The results stay robust. Finally, in column (3), we add Brazil and Russia 1999 and drop the four countries with concessional finance. Once again, our results are confirmed.

Table 7A.2 Determinants of sudden stops: Sensitivity to sample composition

	Added Brazil and Russia 1999	Dropped Bangladesh, Bolivia, Ghana, and Pakistan	Added Brazil and Russia 1999 and dropped Bangladesh, Bolivia, Ghana, and Pakistan
High yield spread	−0.002	0.0004	0.0004
	[1.03]	[0.08]	[0.11]
Change in real oil prices	−0.001***	−0.001***	−0.001**
	[3.07]	[3.18]	[2.11]
GDP growth	0.005***	0.002***	0.007***
	[2.82]	[3.35]	[3.11]
Trade balance/GDP	0.001	0.0002	0.0002
	[0.51]	[0.06]	[0.20]
Debt servicing/Exports	0.001**	0.0002**	0.001**
	[2.37]	[2.21]	[2.05]
Domestic credit/GDP	0.001**	0.0002***	0.001**
	[1.97]	[2.76]	[2.39]
Change in domestic credit/GDP	0.001*	0.0002**	0.001**
	[1.71]	[2.03]	[1.98]
Debt/GDP	0.002***	0.001***	0.003***
	[3.80]	[4.34]	[3.65]
Change in Debt/GDP	0.001**	0.0001**	0.001**
	[2.47]	[2.50]	[2.51]
Exchange rate regime: Pegged	0.145**	0.188***	0.238***
	[2.41]	[2.72]	[2.60]
Exchange rate regime: Limited flexibility	0.03	−0.004	0.046
	[1.41]	[0.22]	[1.42]
Financial mobility	−0.004	−0.001*	−0.005
	[1.10]	[1.65]	[1.25]
Existing IMF program	−0.010**	−0.002*	−0.015**
	[1.99]	[1.74]	[2.10]
New IMF program, instrumented	−0.071***	−0.021***	−0.089***
	[2.91]	[3.25]	[2.61]
Fundamentals · Program, instrumented	0.020**	0.005**	0.025*
	[1.97]	[2.09]	[1.82]
IMF credit/GDP	−0.011***	−0.003***	−0.014***
	[2.58]	[4.07]	[2.59]
Country fixed effects	Yes	Yes	Yes
Time fixed effects	No	No	No
Pseudo R^2	0.38	0.48	0.48
No. of observations	217	175	175

Note: Dependent variable = indicator for first year of sudden stop. Columns reporting probit results present marginal probabilities, based on the STATA command "dprobit." Robust z statistics are presented in brackets. Probability of IMF program estimate as in the first column of table 7.8.

***Significant at the 1 percent level.

**Significant at the 5 percent level.

*Significant at the 10 percent level.

Appendix B

Table 7B.1   **Sources of data and construction of variables**

Variable	Data source and construction
Sudden stop	Identified as described in the text using the annual data on financial account balance from the BOP database, IMF
Real growth	Calculated using data from the WEO, IMF
Export growth	Calculated using data from the WEO, IMF
Domestic credit	IMF's IFS database
External debt	World Bank's GDF database
Debt servicing	World Bank's GDF database
IMF program	Data from the Policy Development and Review Department of the IMF
Precautionary program	Data from the Policy Development and Review Department of the IMF
IMF credit	IMF's BOP database
Financial account balance	IMF's BOP database
FDI	IMF's BOP database
Portfolio flows	IMF's BOP database
Other capital flows	IMF's BOP database
Current account balance	IMF's BOP database
Capital formation	IMF's IFS database
Financial integration	From Mody and Murshid (2005), updated using data from the IMF
Exchange rate regime	From Reinhart and Rogoff (2004)
Currency crisis	From Kaminsky and Reinhart (1999), Berg and Patillo (1999), Frankel and Rose (1996), Milesi-Ferretti and Razin (1998) and Frankel and Wei (2004)
Banking crisis	From Demirgüç-Kunt and Detragiache (1998) supplemented with Goldstein, Kaminsky and Reinhart (2000), and Caprio and Klingebiel (1996)
U.S. aid	OECD's DCA database
UN voting pattern	From the web site http://home.gwu.edu/~voeten/UNVoting.htm.
U.S. bank's exposure in emerging market countries	Calculated using data from the BIS web site.
U.S. growth rate	IMF's IFS database
U.S. treasury bill rate	IMF's IFS database

References

Atoyan, Ruben, and Patrick Conway. 2005. Evaluating the impact of IMF programs: A comparison of matching and instrumental-variable estimators. University of North Carolina at Chapel Hill. Unpublished Manuscript.

Barro, Robert, and Jong-Wha Lee. 2004. IMF programs: Who is chosen and what are the effects? Harvard University and Seoul National University. Unpublished Manuscript.

Berg, Andrew, and Catherine Patillo. 1999. Are currency crises predictable? A test. *IMF Staff Papers* 46:107–38. Washington, DC: International Monetary Fund.

Bordo, Michael D., Ashoka Mody, and Nienke Oomes. 2004. Keeping capital flowing: The role of the IMF. NBER Working Paper no. 10834. Cambridge, MA: National Bureau of Economic Research, October.

Broda, Christian, and Eduardo Levy Yeyati. 2003. Dollarization and the lender of last resort. In Dollarization: Debates and policy alternatives, ed. Eduardo Levy Yeyati and Federico Sturzenegger, 101–32. Cambridge, MA: MIT Press.

Calvo, Guillermo A. 2002. Globalization hazard and delayed reform in emerging markets. Economia 2 (Spring): 1–29.

———. 2005. Crises in emerging market economies: A global perspective. NBER Working Paper no. 11305. Cambridge, MA: National Bureau of Economic Research, April.

Calvo, Guillermo, Alejandro Izquierdo, and Luis Mejia. 2004. On the empirics of sudden stops: The relevance of balance-sheet effects. NBER Working Paper no. 10520. Cambridge, MA: National Bureau of Economic Research, May.

Caprio, Gerald J., and Daniela Klingebiel. 1996. Bank insolvencies: Cross-country experience. World Bank Policy Research Working Paper no. 1620. Washington, DC: World Bank.

Cavallo, Eduardo, and Jeffrey A. Frankel. 2004. Does openness to trade make countries more vulnerable to sudden stops, or less? Using gravity to establish causality. KSG Working Paper no. RWP04-038. Cambridge, MA: Kennedy School of Government.

Celasun, Oya, and Rodney Ramcharan. 2005. The design of IMF-supported programs: Does the balance sheet of the IMF matter? International Monetary Fund. Unpublished Manuscript.

Chami, Ralph, Sunil Sharma, and Ilhyock Shim. 2004. A model of the IMF as a coinsurance arrangement. IMF Working Paper no. WP/04/219. Washington, DC: International Monetary Fund, November.

Cohen, Daniel, and Richard Portes. 2004. Towards a lender of first resort. CEPR Discussion Paper no. 4615. London, UK: Center for Economic Policy Research, September.

Conway, Patrick. 1994. IMF lending programs: Participation and impact. Journal of Development Economics 45:365–91.

Cordella, Tito, and Eduardo Levy Yeyati. 2004. Country insurance. IMF Staff Papers 52 (special issue): 85–106.

———. 2005. A (new) country insurance facility. IMF Working Paper no. WP/05/23. Washington, DC: International Monetary Fund, January.

Demirgüç-Kunt, Asli, and Enrica Detragiache. 1998. The determinants of banking crises in developed and developing countries. IMF Staff Papers 45 (1): 81–109. Washington, DC: International Monetary Fund, March.

De Rato, Rodrigo. 2006. The IMF's medium-term strategy: New priorities, new directions. http://www.imf.org.

Dervis, Kemal, and Ceren Ozer. 2005. A better globalization: Legitimacy, government and reform. Washington, DC: Center for Global Development.

Dicks-Mireaux, Louis, Mauro Mecagni, and Susan Schadler. 2000. Evaluating the effect of IMF lending to low-income countries. Journal of Development Economics 61:495–526.

Dreher, Axel. 2005. IMF and economic growth: The effects of programs, loans, and compliance with conditionality. Department of Management, Technology, and Economics ETH Zürich Working Paper. Zürich, Switzerland: Swiss Federal Institute of Technology Zurich, August.

Dreher, Axel, and Nathan Jensen. 2003. Independent actor or agent? An empirical analysis of the impact of U.S. interests on IMF conditions. Yale University Leitner Working Paper no. 2003-4. New Haven, CT: Yale University.

Edwards, Sebastian. 2005. Capital controls, sudden stops and current account reversals. NBER Working Paper no. 11170. Cambridge, MA: National Bureau of Economic Research, March.

Eichengreen, Barry. 2000. Can the moral hazard caused by IMF bailouts be reduced? Geneva Reports on the World Economy Special Report no. 1. London: Center for Economic Policy Research, September.

Eichengreen, Barry, Kenneth M. Kletzer, and Ashoka Mody. 2006. The IMF in a world of private capital markets. *Journal of Banking and Finance* 30 (5): 1335–57.

Eichengreen, Barry, and Ashoka Mody. 1998. Interest rates in the north and capital flows to the south: Is there a missing link? *International Finance* 1:35–58.

Evrensel, Ayse Y. 2002. Effectiveness of IMF-supported stabilization programs in developing countries. *Journal of International Money and Finance* 21:565–87.

Frankel, Jeffrey A., and Andrew Rose. 1996. Currency crashes in emerging markets: An empirical treatment. *Journal of International Economics* 41:351–66.

Frankel, Jeffrey A., and Shang-Jin Wei. 2004. Managing macroeconomic crises. NBER Working Paper no. 10907. Cambridge, MA: National Bureau of Economic Research, November.

Goldstein, Morris. 1998. *The Asian financial crisis.* Washington, DC: Institute for International Economics.

Goldstein, Morris, Graciela Kaminsky, and Carmen M. Reinhart. 2000. *Assessing financial vulnerability: An early warning system for emerging markets.* Washington, DC: Institute for International Economics.

Goldstein, Morris, and Peter Montiel. 1986. Evaluating fund stabilization programs with multicountry data: Some methodological pitfalls. *IMF Staff Papers* 33:304–44. Washington, DC: International Monetary Fund.

Gupta, Poonam, Deepak Mishra, and Ratna Sahay. 2003. Output response to currency crises. IMF Working Paper no. WP/03/230. Washington, DC: International Monetary Fund, November.

Hardoy, Ines. 2002. Effect of IMF programmes on growth: A reappraisal using the method of matching. Institute for Social Research Paper 2003:040. Oslo, Norway: Institute for Social Research.

Hutchison, Michael M. 2001. A cure worse than the disease? Currency crises and the output costs of IMF-supported stabilization programs. NBER Working Paper no. 8305. Cambridge, MA: National Bureau of Economic Research, March.

Hutchison, Michael M., and Ilan Noy. 2003. Macroeconomic effects of IMF-sponsored programs in Latin America: Output costs, program recidivism and the vicious cycle of failed stabilization. *Journal of International Money and Finance* 22:991–1014.

Hutchison, Michael M., and Ilan Noy. 2004. Sudden stops and the Mexican wave: Currency crises, capital flow reversals and output loss in emerging markets. University of California at Santa Cruz, Department of Economics. Paper no. 573.

International Monetary Fund. 2004. Are credit booms in emerging markets a concern? *World economic outlook* (April): 147–66.

Kaminsky, Graciela, and Carmen M. Reinhart. 1999. The twin crises: The causes of banking and balance of payments problems. *American Economic Review* 93:473–500.

Khan, Mohsin S. 1990. The macroeconomic effects of fund-supported adjustment programs. *IMF Staff Papers* 37:195–231. Washington, DC: International Monetary Fund.

Killick, Tony. 1995. *IMF programmes in developing countries: Design and impact.* London, UK: Routledge.

Lane, Timothy, and Steve Phillips. 2000. Does IMF financing result in moral hazard? IMF Working Paper no. WP/00/168. Washington, DC: International Monetary Fund, October.

Milesi-Ferretti, Gian Maria, and Assaf Razin. 1998. Current account reversals and currency crises: Empirical regularities. IMF Working Paper no. WP/98/89. Washington, DC: International Monetary Fund, June.

Mody, Ashoka, and Antu Murshid. 2005. Growing up with capital flows. *Journal of International Economics* 65:249–66.

Mody, Ashoka, and Diego Saravia. 2003. Catalyzing capital flows: Do IMF programs work as commitment devices? IMF Working Paper no. WP/03/100. Washington, DC: International Monetary Fund, May.

Mody, Ashoka, and Randall Stone. 2005. The scope of IMF conditionality: How autonomous is the fund? University of Rochester. Unpublished Manuscript.

Mody, Ashoka, and Mark P. Taylor. 2003. Common vulnerabilities. CEPR Discussion Paper no. 3759. London, UK: Center for Economic Policy Research, February.

Oatley, Thomas, and Jason Yackee. 2004. American interests and IMF lending. *International Politics* 41:415–29.

Ostry, Jonathan D., and Jeromin Zettelmeyer. 2005. Strengthening IMF crisis prevention. IMF Working Paper no. WP/05/206. Washington, DC: International Monetary Fund, November.

Pastor, Manuel. 1987. The effects of IMF programs in the third world: Debate and evidence from Latin America. *World Development* 15:249–62.

Przeworski, Adam, and James Raymond Vreeland. 2000. The effect of IMF programs on economic growth. *Journal of Development Economics* 62:385–421.

Reinhart, Carmen, and Kenneth Rogoff. 2004. The modern history of exchange rate arrangements: A reinterpretation. *Quarterly Journal of Economics* 119:1–48.

Sarno, Lucio, and Mark P. Taylor. 1999. Hot money, accounting labels and the permanence of capital flows to developing countries: An empirical investigation. *Journal of Development Economics* 59 (2): 337–64.

Truman, Edwin. 2005. International Monetary Fund reform: An overview of the issues. Institute for International Economics . Unpublished Manuscript.

Comment   Ilan Goldfajn

This is a very nice and important paper that the authors have written. It asks the relevant question whether the IMF helps reduce the incidence and impact of sudden stops. Sudden stops are abrupt declines in net capital inflows, leading to balance of payment crises and output losses. Given their importance and high incidence, it is quite surprising that this question was not analyzed earlier.

The main results of the paper could be summarized as follows:

I. Economies that have IMF programs in place (existing or recently negotiated) reduce their probability of suffering a sudden stop.

Ilan Goldfajn is a professor of economics at the Pontifical Catholic University of Rio de Janeiro (PUC-Rio) and a director of the Casa das Garças Institute for Economic Policy Studies (IEPE/CdG).

    a. IMF programs work best for countries with stronger fundamentals.

    b. Larger IMF programs reduce the incidence of sudden stops.

II. IMF programs do not attenuate the impact of sudden stops on GDP growth.

Let's concentrate on the first result. Do IMF programs reduce the incidence of sudden stops? The paper provides a clear yes answer to the question with convincing evidence: The results hold notwithstanding that there is a reverse causality (sudden stops generate IMF programs) that tends to bias the coefficients to zero. When using the U.S. "friendship" instrument (proxied by U.S. aid to the country and UN voting with U.S. record, borrowed from Barro and Lee), as expected, the coefficients become stronger.

This result is a very important policy issue since it provides evidence in favor of the insurance role of the IMF. The insurance role is the provision of emergency financial assistance that reassures investors of the country's ability to pay its liabilities and avoid costly defaults. This insurance result gives support to those who would like to strengthen the IMF role in providing facilities with quick disbursements in order to prevent and reduce the incidence of sudden stops.

Since larger IMF programs (and not only the existence of a program) and stronger fundamentals also help reduce the incidence of sudden stops, the results call for facilities with larger disbursements that are conditional on economies that follow strong economic policies. This would mimic the lender-of-last-resort role of central banks: quick, large, automatic facilities for prequalified countries.

The results of the paper cannot distinguish completely the insurance role of IMF programs from other roles of the IMF programs as the signalling effect: the positive signal that an IMF program in place gives investors regarding the willingness of countries to adopt strong measures and also to pay the existing liabilities.

It is important to note that the insurance role of the IMF is broader than what the regressions in the paper can capture. The sheer IMF existence (and potential lender of last resort role) should reduce the incidence of sudden stops, even if there are no programs in place in a specific country. The lender of last resort role affects expectations even before IMF programs are designed and take place. It is clear that the insurance role of the IMF is even stronger than what the results of the paper suggest.

One could even test this broader insurance role using the data in the paper. One could regress the U.S. support proxy on sudden stops. A positive coefficient would provide a first pass evidence for this broader insurance role (provided one believes that U.S. support increases the probability of receiving an IMF program ceteris paribus).

Given the importance of the insurance role, one should take seriously into consideration the moral hazard issue: do countries adopt less stringent policies because of the lender of last resort role of the IMF? The paper does not address this issue, but it is clearly an important topic for discussion.

In this regard, any IMF facility for insurance purposes should target countries with preexisting conditions (good policies, etc.). The recent failed IMF's Credit Contingent Line (CCL) is an important warning for practical obstacles: the facility failed not only because of the exit problem (any IMF expelled country is a crisis-prone one) but also because of its negative signalling (if a country applies, it must believe there is a problem in the making. It is the Groucho Marx paradox).

The second result of the paper is more negative for the role of the IMF. Do IMF programs reduce the impact of sudden stop on growth? Although figure 7.4 in the paper (and my prior—more reserves to intervene and avoid the need for sharp current account reversals) suggests this is the case, the empirical results in the paper do not back this proposition.

In sum, the paper asks very important questions and provides useful preliminary evidence. Further work on the impact of IMF programs on the costs of sudden stops is needed.

8

Mutual Reinforcement
Economic Policy Reform and Financial Market Strength

Anne O. Krueger

In the past decade or two, we have all become acutely aware of the importance of strong financial markets and particularly of their crucial importance for sustained economic growth. As a result of the lessons we have all learned in recent years, considerable progress has been made in strengthening financial markets in emerging economies. But much remains to be done, and the currently benign global environment is exactly the right time to press ahead with further reforms.

The importance of the opportunity afforded by the favorable present conjuncture is not to be underestimated. Reforms introduced in such circumstances have many advantages and a better prospect of long-term success. They can be properly thought through, rather than, as is the case at times of crisis, introduced hastily and with an increased risk that mistakes will be made in either the formulation or the implementation. Reforms introduced in an upturn also have fewer adjustment costs and, in general, face less opposition. Adjustment is more easily absorbed in the context of growth.

In this chapter I want to examine some of the lessons we learned during the financial crises of the 1990s. I want particularly to focus on what we learned about the close relationship between financial markets and the macroeconomic environment that provides the framework for rapid and sustained economic growth—and the rise in living standards and reduction in poverty that growth makes possible. And I want to comment on the way the International Monetary Fund (IMF) is ready to help its member

Anne O. Krueger was First Deputy Managing Director at the International Monetary Fund at the time of the conference, and she is currently a professor of international economics at the School of Advanced International Studies, Johns Hopkins University. She is also a research associate of the National Bureau of Economic Research.

countries to undertake and implement reforms, especially those in the financial sector.

8.1   The Role of the Financial Sector

We have long known about the importance of the financial sector in supporting economic growth. As economies grow more sophisticated, an efficient banking and financial system becomes increasingly important in helping to ensure the allocation of scarce resources in an efficient manner.

When economic activity is at its most basic and is carried out within a confined geographical area, bartering and, in time, the reliance of family finance to provide limited capital for investment might suffice. But as productive activities increase, reliance on family finance soon starts to inhibit growth. More financial intermediation is needed if economic activity is to reach its productive potential because of constraints otherwise imposed on the growth of more profitable activities (especially when small). Banking comes to play a greater role in increasing resources for high-return activities and reducing the amount wasted in lower return ones. As economic activity becomes more sophisticated and complex—a consequence of growth—so the banking and financial system becomes more important. Banks need to grow in order to meet the demand for investment capital. And at the same time they need to develop their ability to assess risk and creditworthiness.

Without banks able to assess risk, creditworthiness, and potential rates of return, resources are allocated inefficiently, and growth is slower than would otherwise be the case. The banking system performs a crucial role in the early stages of economic growth by making credit available to the potentially most productive sectors of the economy. It allocates—or ought to allocate—much of the increment in resources available for investment. And this allocation does a great deal to determine the growth rate of the economy as a whole.

As the economy grows, and also grows more complex, the financial sector needs to keep pace. Banks need to grow and become more sophisticated in their ability to assess prospects for returns; risk; and to allocate resources efficiently; and, in parallel, there needs to be the development of other financial sources of investment capital. Sustained and rapid growth needs to be underpinned by a broadening and deepening of the financial sector, capable of serving the needs of agriculture, industry, and services. The breadth and depth of financial markets becomes ever more important as growth accelerates. High growth rates are only attainable and sustainable if they are supported by a strong and efficient financial sector. The economies that have sustained rapid growth over the long term are those whose financial sectors have become increasingly sophisticated, complex, and adaptable as the economy grows.

This was certainly the history of the industrialized countries. As they grew in the eighteenth, nineteenth, and twentieth centuries, their financial systems grew in depth and breadth. In the nineteenth century, London achieved its status as the world's leading financial center because it had developed rapidly in order to serve the needs of British industry and British exporters. As it grew in order to support Britain's economic growth, it also became a major contributor to that growth—and, for that matter, to growth in other parts of the world as it exported capital and financial skills.

In the twentieth century, New York played a similar role in relation to the American economy. As New York developed as a financial center to serve the needs of the dynamic and rapidly growing American economy, so it developed skills and services that could themselves be exported.

And this process has continued. As the industrial economies have grown ever more complex, so their financial sectors have continued to develop in order the meet the changing needs of the economies that they serve. The growth of hedge funds in recent years is an example of this continuing development in financial markets. And as the financial sector in industrial countries has become more complex, it has posed fresh challenges for those charged with ensuring that the financial sector is sound and well functioning.

Even twenty or thirty years ago, no one would have quarreled with what I have just said. Ronald McKinnon, my Stanford colleague, wrote of "financial repression" and its costs in terms of foregone growth in the 1970s.

But the financial crises of the 1990s brought home to all of us an increased understanding of the importance of the financial system and its smooth functioning. What we had perhaps not fully appreciated was the extent to which the health and effectiveness of the financial sector was bound up with the performance of the economy as a whole. It took a series of crises in emerging market countries to enable us to understand more about the linkages between the financial sector and the rest of the economy and their importance.

I want to illustrate my argument by examining the extent to which failings in the financial sector contributed to the Korean crisis of 1997–1998.

8.2   Korea

By the time the Korean financial crisis broke in late 1997, the crises in Indonesia and Thailand had already occurred. Initially, the Korean crisis manifested itself as a foreign exchange crisis: capital flows out of Korea forced the government both to float the won and to raise interest rates in order to stem the outflows. That, in turn, exposed the degree to which Korean firms and banks had a mismatch between their assets (in won) and liabilities (many of which were denominated in foreign exchange). The principal source of Korea's problems lay in the low and falling rates of return of the Chaebol, the large conglomerates that were so important to the economy and, hence, of the banking system. These low rates of return were a consequence of credit rationing in earlier years that in turn had led to an overreliance on debt financing for business investment.

For most of the three decades following the start of Korea's reform program in the 1960s, this Asian tiger was the example that other developing countries sought to emulate. It is hard to remember that what is today the world's eleventh largest economy and one of the richest economies in Asia was, in the 1950s, one of the poorest in the world and the third poorest in Asia. Many economists and policymakers believed at the time that this was an economy that could never be viable without sustained transfers of foreign aid.

Yet the reforms introduced in the late 1950s and early 1960s had a remarkable—and remarkably swift—impact. Korea's growth record is dazzling even with hindsight. Real gross domestic product (GDP) grew at an average of 10 percent a year in the ten years from 1963. By the mid-1990s, real per capita income was close to nine times what it had been in the early 1960s.

The thrust of the reform program was to turn Korea into an open economy, with a consistent and single-minded focus on exports. In 1960, at the start of the reforms, Korean exports accounted for 3 percent of GDP and imports for 13 percent of GDP. By 1970, the export share of GDP had risen to 14 percent, and by 1980 it stood at 33 percent. Between 1959 and 1969, exports and export earnings grew at an annual average rate of 41 percent.

The Chaebol played a central role in this spectacular export performance. The Chaebol were conglomerates, usually family-owned, that grew rapidly as a result of the reforms introduced from the early 1960s that provided strong incentives for exporters. The Chaebols' success in exporting was aided by government policies that allocated low interest toward successful exporters, gave exporters tax breaks, and provided a realistic exchange rate. As companies grew rapidly and expanded, access to credit was vital: and this was made available on the basis of their export performance.

It is important to remember that the export incentives on offer were uniform, available to any that increased exports: they were not geared specifically toward the Chaebol. Rather, the Chaebol were those firms, or conglomerates, that grew most rapidly and were exporters. For much of the three decades or so of spectacular Korean growth, the Chaebol were national heroes—they were seen as spearheading the remarkably successful growth performance, itself understood to be the result of opening up the economy.

Trade was liberalized at an early stage in the Korean reform process, but in the early years, the banking system was tightly controlled. Credit rationing according to preset criteria—predominantly export performance—continued well beyond the mid-1960s. The real interest charged on these loans was positive but below the market-clearing rate. Deregulation of interest rates only started in the late 1980s.

At the outset of the reforms, rationed credit financed a very large part of investment, and that credit enabled more rapid expansion of exporting companies than would have been possible if companies had relied on reinvested profits. It also ensured very high rates of return: in the first decade, the Chaebol enjoyed rates of return estimated at 35 percent or more—so high that most Chaebol would have borrowed even more, had they been able to. Of course, these high rates of return resulted from the allocation of resources to exportables, earlier seriously underdeveloped.

But over the next three decades, as growth and investment continued, these rates of return fell, as indeed they should have. The real interest rate charged on loans rose, and the gap between the controlled rate and the market-clearing rate narrowed.

By the 1980s, the rates of return were slightly lower for the Chaebol than for Korean manufacturing firms as a whole. By the latter part of that decade, rates of return in Korea were, on average, slightly above 4 percent; they fell to under 2 percent in the early 1990s and were negative by 1997. This is in marked contrast to rates of return in the United States, which were higher and more sustained, and with Japan, where even after falling after the Asian crisis were still 2.3 percent.

The Chaebol continued to increase in importance relative to the economy as a whole, as credit continued to be allocated to them, with dangerous consequences. From the mid-1980s, the largest thirty, and the largest five Chaebol, were growing at around 20 to 30 percent annually. By the time of the crisis in 1997, their assets were many times higher than they had been in 1985 (fourteen times for the largest thirty and nineteen times for the Big five). By 1997, the Big Five Chaebol firms accounted for about 40 percent of manufacturing sector assets. But the close links between firms in a Chaebol included investing in each other and guaranteeing bank debt for each other and, indeed, borrowing from some banks owned by the same Chaebol.

Because of the history of credit rationing and the reliance on debt finance, Korean firms were highly leveraged. Firms in the manufacturing sector had debt equivalent to about three and a half times their equity in the mid-1990s. This figure declined somewhat in the 1990s, but it was still around two or three times higher than in the United States. Chaebol firms were even more highly leveraged than Korean firms as a whole. And they had strong incentives to continue to rely on debt financing, not least because the equity market was so small.

The highly leveraged position of the Chaebol had serious implications for the Korean economy as a whole. Sustaining rapid growth meant providing a continuing flow of credit to the Chaebol. But as rates of return, of manufacturing firms and the banks, declined, so maintaining the credit flow became more difficult.

Although bank assets rose sharply between 1992 and 1997, net income had peaked in 1994, and the rate of return on bank assets was falling continuously, as was the rate of return on equity. Nonperforming loans (NPLs) had not increased prior to the crisis—although NPLs rose sharply after the crisis started—but in hindsight that appears to be, at least in part, the result of "evergreening." This is the practice by which banks extend new loans to enable borrowers to avoid default and service old debts. In other words, the financial health of borrowers was deteriorating before the onset of the crisis.

Conventional wisdom at the time of the crisis attributed the source of the trouble to the foreign currency exposure of the banking system. But this foreign borrowing had been needed to help sustain the rapid credit expansion at home. Foreign borrowing was needed to cover the problem of (mainly disguised) NPLs at home. The real source of Korea's problems was homegrown, as the quality of bank loan portfolios declined.

In a paper I prepared with Jungho Yoo, we described early-1997 Korea as a disaster waiting to happen. Because of the need to sustain lending to the Chaebol, the banking system and, ultimately, the economy had become so vulnerable that any relatively small shock would have been enough to bring the system to breaking point. The trigger was the foreign exchange crisis that resulted in the sharp rises in interest rates needed to stem the outflow of capital. But it was the rise in interest rates that made debt servicing impossible for many firms and so ultimately brought the banking system to its knees. The situation was complicated by the need to restructure the Chaebol as well as tackling the problems of the banks themselves.

Korea's painful experience helped bring home to economists and the policy community the importance of a well-regulated and transparent banking system—and the damage that can be inflicted on the economy as a whole by the absence of a healthy financial sector. Tackling the problem of nonperforming loans is always challenging for policymakers, as we can observe from Japan's long (albeit ultimately successful) efforts to do this. But NPLs must be easily identifiable by bankers and regulators. Lack of transparency in the system, which gives bankers an incentive to ignore deterioration in the quality of their loan portfolios, can mean that NPLs only become apparent at a late, and even more dangerous, stage. And attention to balance sheet soundness, and the degree of open exposures, is crucial.

The events in Korea showed that weaknesses in the financial sector feed through directly into economic performance. A problem for the banking system is a problem for the economy as a whole. But this was greatly compounded in Korea's case by the absence of well-functioning financial markets beyond the banking system—the lack of efficient bond and equity markets made the vulnerability of the banking system all the more dangerous. Crises and chronic weaknesses in the financial sector lead to low growth rates—or, in the worst cases, a contracting economy. Output is lost, and poverty reduction efforts are halted, at least temporarily.

8.3   Lessons from the 1990s

It is difficult with an open trading economy to have other than a fairly open capital account. But in the absence of a strong regulatory framework, there is always a risk that financial deregulation will lead to a lending boom and create vulnerabilities in the banking system. The rapid expansion of domestic credit such as occurred in Korea in the 1980s and 1990s is always dangerous. When credit expands too rapidly, the quality of bank portfolios declines. Credit allocation becomes increasingly indiscriminate. The ability to assess risk is severely impaired, not least because the banks will lack sufficient experienced personnel to judge risk properly in a credit boom.

In such a scenario, even a small shock can be sufficient to turn many loans into nonperforming ones. That damages the banking system. But the too-rapid expansion of credit and the growth of poor quality loans also hamper economic growth.

A healthy banking sector is crucial. But it should not be the only source of finance and credit allocation. I noted at the outset that as an economy grows in size and complexity, the financial sector needs to grow with it. It must become wider and deeper in order to spread risk and fund high-quality investment. The more sources of finance and the more sources of credit—and the greater the competition—the better placed the financial sector is to assess risk and potential rates of return. The more efficient credit allocation is, the more likely it is that credit goes to where it will deliver the best return, so raising the potential growth rate of the economy as a whole. The better risk assessment and management, the better credit is allocated; and the better-regulated the financial sector, the more resilient the economy as a whole will be to external shocks.

Economies need well-developed bond and equity markets. As firms grow in size, diversity, and complexity, they need access to credit on the best terms; they also need access to different kinds of finance according to their needs. The ability to raise longer term finance through equity or securities reduces firms' reliance on short-term bank finance that might make long-term investments vulnerable to shifts in interest rates. And citizens and institutions of different countries need to be able to hold each others' securities. This is a natural part of the process of global economic integration and can also reduce the concentration of risk in each country in any one sector. The problems that Korea experienced underline the dangers of overreliance on bank loan finance for investment.

A final lesson pertains to the importance of assessing balance sheet risks. The severity of the Korean crisis had much to do with the mismatch in currency exposure between bank assets (won) and liabilities (more foreign exchange).

8.4   The Impetus for Reform

So the role of domestic policymakers is clear. A healthy efficient financial sector is a vital component of economic growth. Putting the necessary measures in place to ensure the banking system is sound, that nonbank financial systems are well managed, and that banks have incentives to identify both risk in the system and potential rates of return all contribute significantly to growth, even in the short term. But such measures bring significant rewards in the medium and longer term. And as those involved in the aftermath of the financial crises on the 1990s can attest, financial sector reform is far more difficult when undertaken in a crisis atmosphere.

Hence my earlier emphasis on the need to push ahead with reforms now, when change can be implemented in a relatively benign global environment. It is important for emerging market economies—here in Latin America as elsewhere—to address remaining vulnerabilities while the outlook remains favorable. It is not simply a matter of creating a stable macroeconomic framework, important though that is. Reforms need to go beyond this and lay the foundations for more rapid and sustained growth. The aim should be to raise the potential growth rate of an economy. Macroeconomic stability is a prerequisite for this, of course. But it is not enough. Structural reforms aimed at making economies more flexible and thus capable of achieving more rapid growth are also essential.

And financial sector reforms are a vital element of these structural reforms. The latest issue of *Doing Business,* published annually by the World Bank, underlines the importance of financial sector reforms and the contribution they can make to stability and growth. Each issue of *Doing Business* assesses individual country performance against a wide range of measures that create a business-friendly environment. It makes for interesting—and salutary—reading.

The latest issue has a section entitled "Getting Credit" and illustrates the links between such factors as legal rights for borrowers and lenders and the level of nonperforming loans and between the quality of credit information and the strength of the financial system.

The evidence clearly shows that the more legal rights that borrowers and lenders enjoy, the lower the level of nonperforming loans a country is likely to have. As you might expect, many of the industrial countries score highly on the strength of legal rights index that includes the ability of lenders to enforce collateral, for instance, as well as the time such enforcement takes. Out of a possible score of 10, the United Kingdom gets full marks, Australia 9, Germany 8, and the United States 7. But Botswana and Albania also score 9, whereas Italy only manages 3. Latin American countries also tend to have low scores: Argentina manages 3, while Brazil and Mexico only score 2. Many countries elsewhere in the world score 1 or 0.

Strengthening the legal rights of borrowers and lenders is crucial if productive investment is not to be stifled. Lenders are understandably reluctant to lend to any but the lowest-risk borrower if they cannot enforce collateral contracts or if such enforcement takes an unreasonable length of time. Businesses with investment possibilities offering potentially good returns find it hard to obtain credit in such an environment. And credit allocation in an economy with weak legal protection for financial transactions is likely to be suboptimal at best, with the inevitable consequence that growth is below potential.

Doing Business also notes a correlation between ratings of financial system strength and the presence of private credit bureaus that are seen as improving the provision of credit information. The provision of good credit information—including negative as well as positive information on would-be borrowers—makes it easier for business to obtain credit because lenders are more accurately able to assess creditworthiness and risk. Making it hard for lenders to obtain information simply penalizes all would-be borrowers, including those whose creditworthiness is sound and whose borrowing would bring good returns.

Again, the industrial countries score well on credit bureau coverage. The United States, Sweden, Ireland, and Canada are among those countries where credit bureaus cover the entire adult population. Argentina also scores highly on this measure, with 95 percent coverage. But Brazil and Paraguay have coverage of barely half the population, while Mexico doesn't quite have 50 percent. Chile has 22 percent coverage and Costa Rica less than 5 percent. More than half the 155 countries surveyed have no private credit bureau coverage at all.

Reforms are under way in some areas. Brazil, for example, was one of ten countries in 2004 that made it easier to create and then enforce collateral agreements, which make access to credit easier for borrowers and provide better incentives for lenders. Among the others introducing similar reforms were India, Japan, Finland, and Croatia—a mixed group that demonstrates that reform is, and ought to be, an ongoing process for all countries, be they low income, emerging market, or industrial.

8.5   The Role of the IMF

The IMF has an important role to play here. Our central task, according to our mandate, is the promotion of international financial stability. That is not meant to be an end in itself, of course. Our Articles of Agreement make clear that a stable international financial system is a vital ingredient in promoting the sustained rapid economic growth that brings rising living standards and poverty reduction. And, as our Articles also emphasize, international financial stability is essential for the expansion of trade that enables rapid growth.

But international financial stability needs sound national financial systems. So the Fund, in the context of our Article IV and surveillance work, as well as in our work with program countries, focuses much of its work on the health of the financial sector. We have introduced new tools, including the Financial Sector Assessment Program, about which I will say more in a moment, to help us in this work.

We try to assess financial sector robustness in a variety of ways. We pay close attention to banks' balance sheets and the extent of NPLs. We also examine the extent to which risk is clearly defined in the financial system as a whole. And we look at the degree of competition within both the banking system and the financial sector as a whole: competition improves the efficiency of credit allocation, and it also helps diversify financial risk and cut borrowing costs. We examine issues such as the rate of credit expansion; and we look for mismatched exposures as these are a potential source of instability.

I noted earlier that the breadth of financial instruments is important, as is the transparency of the system that enables more accurate assessments to be made of the asset and risk position of individual institutions. And a strong, effective regulatory regime, following international best practice, is vital.

I mentioned the Financial Sector Assessment Program (FSAP). Introduced in 1999, this is part of the attempt to enhance the Fund's work in this area. It is a voluntary program—member countries request an FSAP, which involves bringing in a team of experts to undertake a detailed examination of the financial system of the country in question. The work carried out under an FSAP program involves a broad range of financial experts, many of them from outside the Fund. Some come with substantial experience in regulating the financial sector of individual member countries; others are involved with international regulatory bodies. Still others have specific qualifications needed for the tasks involved.

The FSAP program—which the Fund runs jointly with the World Bank when low-income countries are involved—aims to help member governments strengthen their financial systems by detecting vulnerabilities in financial supervision at an early stage, to identify key areas which need further work, to set policy priorities and to provide technical assistance when this is needed to strengthen supervisory and reporting frameworks. The end result is intended to ensure that the right processes are in place for countries to make their own substantive assessments.

Financial sector assessment programs don't examine the balance sheets of individual banks, or even the banking sector as a whole. Their purpose is to help our member countries ensure that an appropriate framework is in place so that domestic regulators and supervisors are able to make accurate judgments about the health of the banks and other financial institutions under their jurisdiction.

A large number and a wide range of our member countries have now had an FSAP program. The feedback we get is overwhelmingly positive, from both industrial countries with highly developed financial sectors as well as others.

The FSAP also forms the basis for Financial Stability Assessments (FSAs) in which IMF staff address issues related to the Fund's surveillance work. These include risks to macroeconomic stability that might come from the financial sector and the capacity of the sector to absorb shocks. Is the level of NPLs a cause for concern? Are the banks well regulated and sound? How would the financial sector be affected by sharp rises in interest rates—would this lead to a rise in NPLs? Again, these FSAs cut across the full breadth of our membership.

We have also worked with the World Bank to develop a system of Standards and Codes—using internationally recognized standards—that result in Reports on Standards and Codes (ROSCs). These cover twelve areas, including banking supervision, securities regulation, and insurance supervision. The financial sector ROSCs are an integral part of the FSAP and are published by agreement with the member country. They are used to sharpen discussions between the Fund—and, where appropriate, the World Bank—and national authorities and, in the private sector, including rating agencies, for risk assessment purposes.

It is perhaps worth noting that some Fund research done a couple of years ago suggests that there is a tangible payoff—in the form of lower spreads—for member countries where the Fund has undertaken ROSCs *and* where the reports have been published in full. The markets take a favorable view of this transparency which can translate into lower borrowing costs.

8.6   Conclusion

For economists and policymakers, the experience of the 1990s taught us a great deal. Of course, we learned that reliance on fixed exchange rates can make economies vulnerable in the event of crisis (and most emerging market economies have, as a consequence, adjusted their exchange rate regime). We learned that in an increasingly integrated world economy a strong macroeconomic framework is essential *both* to make possible more rapid and sustained growth *and* to reduce vulnerability to shocks.

But we learned perhaps above all that financial sector soundness is vital—for its own sake, yes, but also for the health of the economy as a whole. Weaknesses in the financial sector result in lower growth than would otherwise be possible and make the economy more vulnerable to crises.

Financial sector health depends on a sound regulatory framework, relying on incentives, sound banking procedures that permit the proper assessment of risk, and the progressive widening and deepening of the financial sector to ensure that it continues to meet the needs of the economy. Like economic policy reform in general, financial sector reform cannot be a one-off. It has to be a continuous process, partly to reflect our growing understanding of the issues and partly to reflect the need for constant adaptation and refinement in the financial sector and in the economy as a whole.

Let me emphasize once again that policy made on the hoof in a crisis situation is always difficult to get right. Reforms forced on the authorities as they respond to a crisis stand less chance of long-term success because they are less likely to be well-thought out. But planned reforms implemented in the context of an expanding national and global economy have lower adjustment costs and present fewer political difficulties.

Financial market strength is vital in a successful and growing national economy. It is also vital for the smooth functioning and long-term growth prospects of the global economy. It is a central part of the economic policy reform process and, as such, is an important priority for the Fund in its role of promoting international financial stability and growth.

Contributors

Marcelo Abreu
Department of Economics
Pontifical Catholic University
Rua Marquês de São Vicente, 225
Gávea, Rio de Janeiro-RJ, Brazil
22453-900

Joshua Aizenman
Department of Economics; E2
University of California
1156 High Street
Santa Cruz, CA 95064

Edmar L. Bacha
Casa das Garças Institute for
   Economic Policy Study
Avenida Padre Leonel Franca, 135
Gávea, Rio de Janeiro-RJ, Brazil
22451-000

Marco Bonomo
Graduate School of Economics
Fundação Getúlio Vargas
Praia de Botafogo, 190 Sala 1100
Rio de Janeiro-RJ, Brazil 22250-900

Bernardo S. de M. Carvalho
Gávea Investments
R. Dias Ferreira, 190, 7º Andar, Leblon
Rio de Janeiro-RJ, Brazil 22431-050

Ana Carla A. Costa
Tendências, Consultoria Integrada
Rua Estados Unidos, 498
São Paulo-SP, Brazil 01427-000

Augusto de la Torre
The World Bank
1818 H Street, NW
Washington, DC 20433

João M. P. De Mello
Department of Economics
Pontifical Catholic University
Rua Marquês de São Vicente, 225
Gávea, Rio de Janeiro-RJ, Brazil
22453-900

Sebastian Edwards
Anderson Graduate School of Business
University of California, Los Angeles
110 Westward Plaza, Suite C508
Box 951481
Los Angeles, CA 90095-1481

Barry Eichengreen
Department of Economics
549 Evans Hall 3880
University of California
Berkeley, CA 94720-3880

Renato G. Flôres Jr.
Graduate School of Economics
Fundação Getúlio Vargas
Praia de Botafogo, 190 Sala 1100
Rio de Janeiro-RJ, Brazil 22250-900

Gustavo H. B. Franco
Department of Economics
Pontifical Catholic University
Rua Marquês de São Vicente, 225
Gávea, Rio de Janeiro-RJ, Brazil
    22453-900

Márcio G. P. Garcia
Department of Economics
Pontifical Catholic University
Rua Marquês de São Vicente, 225
Gávea, Rio de Janeiro-RJ, Brazil
    22453-900

Ilan Goldfajn
Department of Economics
Pontifical Catholic University
Rua Marquês de São Vicente, 225
Gávea, Rio de Janeiro-RJ, Brazil
    22453-900

Juan Carlos Gozzi
Department of Economics
Box B
Brown University
Providence, RI 02912

Poonam Gupta
Department of Economics
Delhi School of Economics
University of Delhi
Delhi, India 110007

Marcelo Kfoury Muinhos
Citigropu
Avenida Paulista 1111, 14º andar, Sala 4
São Paulo-SP, Brazil 01311-920

Anne O. Krueger
Department of International
    Economics
School of Advanced International
    Studies
Johns Hopkins University
1740 Massachusetts Avenue NW
Washington, DC 20036

Ashoka Mody
International Monetary Fund
700 19th Street, NW
Washington, DC 20431

Ilan Noy
Department of Economics
University of Hawaii
Saunders 542
2424 Maile Way
Honolulu, HI 96822

Ugo Panizza
Debt and Development Finance
    Branch, DGDS
UNCTAD
Palais des Nations
8-14, Avenue de la Paix
1211 Geneva 10, Switzerland

Sergio L. Schmukler
The World Bank
1818 H Street, NW
Washington, DC 20433

Maria Cristina Terra
Graduate School of Economics
Fundação Getúlio Vargas
Praia de Botagofo, 190 Sala 1100
Rio de Janeiro-RJ, Brazil 22250-900

Thierry Verdier
Paris-Jourdan Sciences Economiques
    (PSE)
Ecole Normale Supérieure
48 Boulevard Jourdan
75014 Paris, France

Alejandro Werner
Ministry of Finance and Public Credit
Palacio Nacional S/N 1er.
Patio Mariano, 4to Piso.
Col. CENTRO, C.P. 6000
Cuauhtémoc, México, D.F.

Eduardo Levy Yeyati
Business School
Universidad Torcuato Di Tella
The World Bank
Saenz Valiente 1010
C1428BIJ, Buenos Aires, Argentina

Author Index

Acemoglu, Daron, 156, 157, 157n2
Aizenman, Joshua, 2, 9, 10, 11, 13, 16,
    16n5, 17, 19, 100n7, 113n20, 186n4,
    201n28, 203
Altubas, Yener, 166
Arellano, Manuel, 171n32
Areta, C., 212, 213n2
Arida, P., 33, 35
Armas, A., 185n2
Atoyan, Ruben, 229

Bacha, E., 35
Barcinski, A., 32, 33, 52, 66
Barro, Robert J., 109n18, 226
Bartolini, L., 71
Bates, Robert, 6
Batten, J., 128n14
Beck, T., 138
Bekaert, G., 11, 131, 131n20, 132n22
Bencivenga, V. R., 131
Berg, Andrew, 138
Bertrand, M., 183
Bhagwati, J., 124n7
Blanchard, O., 30
Blonigen, B. A., 10n1, 12
Bond, Stephen, 171n32
Bordo, Michael D., 228
Borensztein, E., 148
Boyd, J. H., 122n2, 131, 136n31
Broda, C., 185n3, 197n20, 202n29, 203n30
Broda, Christian, 231
Bushman, R. M., 138

Caballero, R., 185n1, 186n4
Cabral, Célia, 156
Calomirs, C., 208n39
Calvo, Guillermo A., 2, 78, 78n1, 98, 99,
    185n1, 221, 230, 230n2, 231, 231n6,
    235, 236, 236n15, 244n24
Cardoso, Eliana, 32, 33, 36, 37, 38, 39, 41,
    42, 42n15, 48, 49, 66, 88n8, 94, 95
Carvalho, Bernardo, 3
Cavallo, Eduardo, 113n20, 221, 235
Celasun, Oya, 248n34
Cespedes, Luis F., 98
Chami, Ralph, 232
Chan, N., 31
Chang, Roberto, 98, 213, 213n4
Chatusripitak, N., 128n14
Chinn, Menzie, 100n5, 131
Claessens, S., 130
Cohen, Daniel, 232, 234
Conway, Patrick, 225, 229
Corbo, Victorio, 78
Cordella, Tito, 186n4, 231n7, 232, 234,
    234n9
Costa, Ana Carla A., 4
Cowan, K., 31n4, 32, 186n7, 187n7

Daude, C., 11
De Brun, J., 205n35
De Gregorio, J., 31n4, 32, 38, 39, 42n15,
    52, 60
De la Torre, A., 122, 122n5, 124n8, 128n12,
    139, 139n35, 141, 142, 205n35

Subject Index